HOW YOU CAN BUILD A FORTUNE INVESTING IN RESIDENTIAL REAL ESTATE

Gil Armen

Prentice-Hall, Inc., Englewood Cliffs, New Jersey 07632

Library of Congress Cataloging in Publication Data

Armen, Gil.
    How you can build a fortune investing in residential real estate.

    Includes index.
    1. Real estate investment.   2. House buying.
3. House selling.   4. Rental housing.   I. Title.
HD1382.5.A75   1983   332.63'24   83-554
ISBN 0-13-444125-7
ISBN 0-13-444117-6 (A Reward book: pbk.)

This book is available at a special discount when ordered in bulk quantities. Contact Prentice-Hall, Inc., General Publishing Division, Special Sales, Englewood Cliffs, N.J. 07632.

© 1983 by Gil Armen.

All rights reserved. No part of this book may be reproduced in any form or by any means without permission in writing from the publisher.

Printed in the United States of America.

10 9 8 7 6 5 4 3 2 1

ISBN 0-13-444125-7

ISBN 0-13-444117-6 {PBK.}

"This publication is designed to provide accurate and authoritative information in regards to the subject matter covered. It is sold with the understanding that the author and publisher are not engaged in rendering legal, accounting, or other professional service. If legal advice or other expert assistance is required, the services of a competent professional should be sought." (From a declaration of principles jointly adopted by a committee of the American Bar Association and a committee of the Publishers' Association.)

Editorial/production supervision by Chris McMorrow
Cover design © 1983 by Jeannette Jacobs
Manufacturing buyer: Pat Mahoney

Gil Armen, a real estate investment advisor and lecturer, is founder and president of Aaron-Armen, Inc., a professional educational corporation. He is an electrical engineer by degree and owns more than one million dollars worth of residential real estate.

Prentice-Hall International, Inc., *London*
Prentice-Hall of Australia Pty. Limited, *Sydney*
Prentice-Hall Canada Inc., *Toronto*
Prentice-Hall of India Private Limited, *New Delhi*
Prentice-Hall of Japan, Inc., *Tokyo*
Prentice-Hall of Southeast Asia Pte. Ltd., *Singapore*
Whitehall Books Limited, *Wellington, New Zealand*
Editora Prentice-Hall do Brasil Ltda., *Rio de Janeiro*

This book is dedicated to my most precious investments: my wife, Darlene, and my lovely children, Amelia, Ava, and Aaron, for without their love and understanding this book would not have been possible.

To my Mom and Dad, for it was their values that have provided the cornerstone to my life.

Contents

Preface ix

Acknowledgments xi

Phase 0

The Summary 1

Phase 1

Overcoming Inertia 45

Phase 2

Critical Decision 72

Phase 3

The Hunt 89

Phase 4

The Buy   175

Phase 5

Your Investment Property   212

Phase 6

Sell/Profits   234

Glossary of Terms Frequently Used in Real Estate Investment   285

Index   299

Preface

This book is written with a dual purpose: (1) to serve as a textbook completely on its own and (2) to be used to complement national-level seminars on the subject of investing in residential real estate. The book contains considerable details in all areas of the investment process. It has been written with the first-time or small-money investor in mind. Professionals requiring tax shelters can also greatly benefit by reading and applying the techniques described in this book. Renters need to understand that owning their homes provides much greater benefits in the long run. Lawyers and bankers can greatly benefit from this book because the investment process is discussed from the layperson's point of view. Realtors can also be greatly helped by this book, for it provides graphics that can tremendously assist the realtor in explaining the financial side of real estate. I have made it a policy to use graphics in the form of tables, graphs, figures, curves, and plots, because it is my belief that a picture is indeed worth a thousand words.

This book was organized and written in what I call a decision-flow format. Over the past several years, I have dedicated my time and energy to the broad field of investments (stocks, bonds, commodities, and real estate), and I have found that, in general, books, manuals, and pamphlets are written by subject matter. This book, however, is not written by subject matter. It is written in the same order as an individual who is interested in investing in real estate would approach the investment: first, the decision that the potential of investing in real estate is worth pursuing; second, entering the potential field in controlled stages by investigating to a certain depth; and third, if the opportunity continues to present itself as favorable, by harnessing all one's energies (and one's husband's and wife's or partner's) and by committing oneself to the investment process.

The book is written to provide a thorough understanding of the residential real estate investment process. It is vitally important that all readers clearly understand the objectives of the book from the beginning; we must have predefined objectives before we start. In this case, we start with the last stage first—profits and benefits of residential real estate investments. After the reader clearly understands the value of residential real estate investments, we return to the initial stages and provide a summary overview of the investment process. Through the summary, the reader obtains a good working knowledge of the investment decision process. Having this all-important knowledge, we then return to the beginning and dedicate the main text of the book to a controlled, detailed chronological decision-flow process.

The chronological decision-flow process is divided into six major phases: (1) Overcoming Inertia, (2) Critical Decision, (3) The Hunt, (4) The Buy, (5) Your Investment Property, and (6) Sell/Profits. I have purposely selected common, ordinary words, such as *sell, buy,* and so forth, to describe my process, as it is my belief that these words carry more meaning and impact. All phases are divided into sections and subsections. Each phase is preceded by a list of objectives. The objectives emphasize the important points to be discussed within each phase. At the end of the last phase, there is a summary in the form of major conclusions. The intent of this format is twofold: it provides continuous positive reinforcement, and should the reader have the opportunity to complete the seminar, the objectives can be used as quick reference during the investment process.

As stated previously, I have made it a policy to make extensive use of graphics to describe such complex subjects as assumptions, discounted second trusts, moving the mortgage, wraparounds, all-inclusive trusts, land contracts, equity participation mortgages, renegotiable mortgages, flip mortgages, silent seconds, exchanges, tax shelters, and other investment subjects. I have also made it a policy not to use the lawyer-banker-bureaucrat–type sentences that leave the reader wondering, "Just exactly what did I read?" I am sure that those of you who have tackled the income tax forms know what I am referring to.

I wish to extend my congratulations to you for having purchased this book. The process I have outlined has been rich and rewarding to myself and my family. Remember the key word *leverage,* and the following quotes from two famous Americans:

> Invest in inflation; it's the only thing going up.
>
> WILL ROGERS

> Real estate cannot be lost or stolen, nor can it be carried away; managed with reasonable care, it is the safest investment in the world.
>
> FRANKLIN DELANO ROOSEVELT

Acknowledgments

Special recognition must be given to my brother, Jay, for selected contributions, and to my dear friend Worth Sauls, who never doubted that this book would be published.

Many thanks to Jeanie Sauls for her long hours in typing the manuscript, Sherry Hume and Bess Sauls for their positive contributions, and Gene Wugofski for his constructive criticism.

Finally, I would like to thank all the librarians across America not only for their assistance in my manuscript research, but also for the valuable information they provided me during the building of my investment portfolio.

How You Can Build a Fortune Investing in Residential Real Estate

Phase 0

The Summary

WHY REAL ESTATE?

As stated in the preface, we shall pursue the subject of the value of investing in real estate in controlled stages. Phase 0 establishes why investing in residential real estate offers such a lucrative investment area, and it offers the reader an overview of the entire investment process. A glossary is provided at the end of the book to provide the reader with a quick reference to the most frequently used terms in real estate. You must learn that when you invest in real estate, *you* are the single most important element in the investment process. You must also learn and understand the subject in sufficient detail to form your own opinions based on volumes upon volumes of information available to the investor. Frequently you shall read in newspapers and magazines that real estate, when compared to the traditional investments of the 1980s, is a money loser. The point is made that treasury bills, bonds, gold, money market funds and other more traditional investments will return the investor greater than 10% of his money throughout the 1980s. Real estate, because of the high appreciation rates of the 1970s and the high interest rates of the 1980s, has started a deflationary cycle that will continue through the 1980s. However, one has to ask himself, "Has all real estate decreased in value?" The answer is no! Medium priced income producing real estate in expanding population areas has continued to increase in price and will continue through the year 2000. For example, in the Washington, D.C. area of northern Virginia, property that was selling for $51,000 in the fall of 1980 was selling for $69,500 in the summer of 1982. This property appreciated by a factor of 36% in under two years with interest rates averaging above 15%. Why? Because the demand has shifted from the more expensive homes to lower priced affordable housing. This brings me to the second issue concerning the traditional investments that return greater than 10%. The argument is often made that the median price of a 1968 used family home increased from $20,000 to the 1982 price of $68,000. To match the gain of $48,000 in 14 years you would require an investment to pay only 9.2% compounded annually. Frankly, there is nothing wrong with the above numbers. Ten years ago I read this type of information as if it were the gospel. The inference is why bother with real estate when you can do better in other fields? However, what the majority of investment advice for the 1980s fails to point out is that only in real estate can you buy a $20,000 or a $68,000 asset with only 5% or 10% of its value. In many cases properties can be bought using creative financing techniques that use 100% of other people's money (OPM). The return is not the percentage in appreciation, but rather the appreciation over the initial amount invested, divided by the investment period. In the above example concerning the 1968 home of $20,000 that returned 9.2% when compounded annually, one must understand that this is only true if the home was originally purchased all cash. In 1968 you could buy the average home with a $2,000 down payment. The return in 14 years would be $48,000 or 2,400%! From 1968 to 1982 the Standard and Poor's 400 Index went from 102 to less than 165, for a percentage increase of 162%, or your $2,000 in 1968 would be $3,235 in 1982, less than 4.5% per year.

You must thoroughly understand the value of investing in real estate, because you will continuously run across so-called experts who completely distort information or provide you with false data. Do not be discouraged; learn all you can and form your own opinions.

I cite an additional example of totally misinformed people in so-called positions of responsibility. Recently I was reading the sports section of the *Washington Post*. A nationally syndicated sports writer was discussing the poor performance of the Washington Redskins professional football team prior to the championship season of 1982–83. The writer was defending the former head coach's philosophy of trading away young players and draft choices for veteran players of proven quality. The reporter wrote that the acquisition of a veteran player over a young draft choice was comparable to an individual obtaining a mortgage on his or her own home. The writer reasoned that in both cases you would risk or mortgage your future away for proven performance or shelter. What the nationally syndicated writer (in a position of high visibility) fails to realize is that veteran players *decrease* in value (true depreciation) because of old age, whereas real estate property *increases* in value. Because we continuously read stories such as the one mentioned above, people are hesitant to invest in real estate. Remember you are your own adviser and should be able to weed out the trash stories and false information from the true value of investing in America.

The Value of Investing in Residential Real Estate

More money will be made in real estate in America in the 1980s than in the entire history of this nation. Four major reasons will ensure that this prediction will come true: (1) inflation will continue, (2) housing will reach peak demand in 1985 and continue unabated through the year 2000, (3) the high interest rates of the late 1970s and early 1980s have caused a decrease in the supply, and (4) the tax laws enacted in 1981 favor the investor.

First, let us turn our attention to inflation. *Inflation will continue!* Regardless of what the federal government does, inflation will continue. The only question is at what rate. Even if the federal government should balance the budget, inflation will still continue in the housing market. The reasons are simple: We now live in an international marketplace, and the supply cannot keep up with the demand. Raw materials required to produce the basic building blocks of the housing industry will continue to increase in price. A case in point is oil. We have little control over this vital resource. Oil is used either directly or indirectly in over 75% of all items required to build a home, including shingles for the roof, vinyl for the floors, synthetic rugs, insulation materials, asphalt roads, plastic inserts, rubber moldings, appliances, and bathroom fixtures. Also, all the lumber, bricks, stones, shrubbery, and so on must be transported in gasoline-powered trucks. Indeed, even the workers must be paid more because of additional expenses caused by expensive oil! As of this writing, the United States gets over 40% of its required oil supply from foreign sources. The great majority of that oil comes from the tremendously unstable Middle East. Any shift in policy of the Saudi Arabians will cause major perturbations throughout the United States. For example, through 1980 and 1981 the Saudi Arabians flooded the market with excess oil, causing a small oil glut. This policy cannot continue. The religious fundamentalists and the technocrats within Saudi Arabia will simply not allow the country to waste its natural resources. The Saudi Arabians can and will control the price of oil to the benefit of their national policy. It is predicted that the United States will continue to depend on foreign oil sources through the year 2000. Only the recession of the early 1980s has caused a lessening in the demand for oil. Once the recession is but a memory, the economies of the Western nations and the emerging Third World countries will increase their demand for energy ... oil. Over the long run (5, 10, or 15 years), the cost of oil will continue to rise, and housing costs will follow!

The federal government is tackling the inflation problem head-on, proposing cutbacks in government spending while providing inducements to encourage business investments, in order to spur productivity. Unfortunately, the problem is tremendously more complex than simply reducing deficit spending! Do not wages contribute to inflation when they rise rapidly? Does not the decontrol of natural gas contribute to inflation? Do you think for one minute that the much-publicized and highly paid professional athletes will not continue to push for sky-high bonuses and salaries? What about food costs? Will not the world population explosion continue to increase the demand for food? The Reagan proposal to reduce federal spending is solid and has tremendous merit. However, the root causes of inflation are caused by issues more deeply involved than just government spending. The post–World War II business and economics corollary that consumer demand is the cornerstone of the economic machine will prevail. The main cause of inflation can be found in the push caused by oil prices, farm prices, cost of raw materials, and wage demands. I agree that reducing the deficit of the federal budget will decrease the rate of inflation simply because the federal government will not have to borrow money. Investors must understand that there are only three methods available to the government to raise money: (1) by taxing the people, (2) by printing more money, and (3) by borrowing. It is highly unlikely that the politicians in Washington will increase the taxes paid by the people any time in the mid-1980s. The country is simply not in the mood to pay more taxes. Should the policies of the Federal Reserve allow the U.S. Treasury to print more money, the result would be increased inflation. Should the government decrease the federal deficit by spending less, the result would be a decreased requirement to borrow money. When the government decreases its demand to borrow money, the interest rates will fall and *real estate will skyrocket in value!* Adding to the falling interest rates will be the continued world population explosion that will ensure the continued demand for *all the necessities of life.*

The following is from the *United States Budget, Fiscal Year 1981,* executive office of the President, Office of Management and Budget, page 4, concerning the economy:

> During the last decade we withstood a series of economic shocks unprecedented in peacetime. The most dramatic of these were the explosive increases of OPEC oil prices. But we have also faced world commodity shortages, natural disasters, agriculture shortages, and major challenges to world peace and security. Our ability to deal with these shocks has been impaired by slower productivity growth and persistent underlying inflationary forces built up over the past 14 years.

All these factors will continue through the 1980s and will result in continued inflation. Again the question: Inflation, at what rate? The Reagan team chose not to discuss these points early in the administration, simply because they did not wish to get pushed into a complex international cash-flow analysis policy. The single item that is most directly controllable by the government is the federal budget. Certainly, reducing the deficit spending to zero is an admirable and noble goal. We wish the president the best of luck and Godspeed. However, we must not be fooled. The laws of the land and the U.S. budget are written by Congress. For example, the majority of the "pork barrel" projects that benefit only the Congressperson's home district were left virtually untouched in the 1982 federal budget. Entitlement programs such as social security and government retirement pay are difficult to cut because they affect large concentrated blocks of voters. A congressperson knows that any unfavorable treatment of any large block of voters could prove fatal to that congressperson's political career. All legislators are basically in favor of reducing the federal deficit, as long as it does not affect his or her individual subsidy. Reducing the deficit to zero will be almost an impossible task. If you think inflation will be less than 4% by the mid- to late 1980s, then you probably also believe that gasoline will return to the 1960 price of $0.28 per gallon. If inflation can be controlled to slightly less than 10%, it will be a totally workable inflationary rate. Even with 8% to 10%, analysts predict that the median price of a home will rise from the 1980 level of $66,000 to over $400,000 by 1990! Difficult to believe? Why should it be? From 1960 to 1981, the median price increased from $14,000 to $66,000, an increase of over 500% in a fairly low inflationary period. Remember, inflation was well below 5% throughout the 1960s and early 1970s. In Phase 1 of this book, I discuss my experiences in Europe in the early 1970s. West Berliners were paying for homes three to four times the price of houses in southern California. Why? Because there was not any more land in West Berlin. The city is fenced in by a ten-foot wall bordered by a mine field.

Second, housing will reach its peak demand in 1985 and continue unabated through the year 2000. From 1975 to 1985 the total number of Americans in the age bracket of 18 to 34 shall increase from 50.1 million to 67.7 million. These figures were taken from a study conducted by the U.S. Department of Commerce for the U.S. Office of Management and Budget. (*Housing Affordability in an Inflationary Environment*, PB-297-432, June 1979). The majority of Americans believe that the steep increases seen in the housing industry in the 1970s are over and that prices will stabilize. They will not. What we saw in the 1970s is only the beginning. Only the tight money policy of the federal reserve in the early 1980s has dampened the increase in the price of housing. Even with the high interest rates, the sale prices continued to increase. The principal reason for the increase in housing prices is still here—*demand*. The situation is similar to a boiling pot of water. You can contain the steam only so long by applying pressure on the lid. As long as the fire (demand) continues, it is only a question of time before the lid will explode off the pot, releasing the pressure created by the steam.

Third, the tight money policies of the federal reserve will have the opposite effect of the desired condition in the area of housing costs. High interest rates have caused the number of housing starts to decrease. The number of private housing permits in America peaked in 1978 at 2.02 million. In 1979 it was approximately 1.6 million, and in 1980 it was less than 1.4 million. Due to high interest rates, a considerable number of builders have gone out of business. The supply has actually decreased, whereas the demand has increased. Surely it does not take a mathematician to predict the results. Available housing will simply skyrocket in price.

Fourth, the new tax laws enacted in 1981 have favored the investor. Investment properties can now be depreciated in 15 years at 175% accelerated depreciation. The old law was 30 to 40. The net result is that an investor can now purchase a property with the tax savings offseting three to four times the negative cash flow. Additionally the new tax laws enacted in 1982 have provided the savings and loan institutions the ability to compete favorably with the money market funds. This new supply of money will create a competitive spirit among the savings and loans that will drive the interest rates down. As interest rates go down, the price of housing goes up.

An investor who understands all the foregoing and applies the techniques described in this book will greatly benefit from investing in America. Because I believe that residential real estate offers the best possible buy for the small-money investor, I have concentrated on the subject of residential properties only. As you will learn in the pages to follow, they offer the best of all worlds. Good luck and remember to pursue your dreams with vigor!

Leverage

We need to establish early in this book the all-important advantage of purchasing income-producing (rentals) properties using leverage. *Leverage* means that a property may be purchased with a down payment that represents a small percentage of the total value. For example, a $100,000 home may be purchased with a down payment of $10,000. The ratio of down payment to total value is one to ten (1/10), thus you can purchase a property worth $100,000 with a $10,000 down payment. The property that is purchased increases in value (appreciation) at the inflation rate. Your investment return is based on the total value of the property ($100,000), not just the $10,000 down payment! Your investment property increases in value at a rate that is equal to at least the area's economic growth plus any inflation! Your return is based on the appreciation (added value) of the total value of the investment. Assuming you purchase a $100,000 investment with $10,000 down payment, your return after two years of 10% increase in property appreciation is 200%, since the property is now valued at $120,000. If you purchased the property with only $5,000 down, your return after two years would be 400%! No other investment provides such lucrative returns.

The reason you can purchase a $100,000 investment with $5,000 down is *leverage*. A lending institution will lend you $95,000 of other people's money to finance the purchase. In order to pay the mortgage, you can rent the investment property. The combination of the rent and tax savings on depreciation allowances results in approximately zero cash flow (no money out of your pocket) to sustain the property during the investment period. Obtaining a zero cash flow during the investment period is a completely doable proposition. The key is knowledge. Purchase properties that have existing loans that can be legally assumed by the buyer. Since these properties have old loans, this technique is often referred to as the purchase of properties using old money. Creative financing methods, such as assumptions, second trusts, wrap financing, wraparounds, land contracts and other creative financing methods are available to the knowledgeable investor to purchase income producing properties. Anyone can do it. (I discuss all these methods in Phase 3, The Hunt.) The appreciation of the property is a total profit and is taxed as a long-term capital gain; 60% of a capital gain is tax free! The tax laws are structured to favor the investor. In 1981 Congress enacted tax laws that provide strong incentives to investors with rental properties. The Economic Recovery Tax Law of 1981 allows for residential rental properties to be depreciated in 15 years, at 175% declining balance. For example, a $75,000 investment property with the building structure valued at $60,000 will produce a total of $7,000 tax deductions ($60,000 ÷ 15 × 1.75). The 15-year, 175% accelerated depreciation is discussed later in this phase and in Phase 6. Also the Tax Reform Act (TRA) of 1976 instituted major penalties against capital investments, with one exception—real estate. Because of the 1976 TRA, investors in fields that were negatively affected transferred their holdings to the real estate field. This increased demand for real estate added to the appreciation rates of the 1970s and will continue through the 1980s.

Before I continue with the tremendous benefits enjoyed by investing in real estate, I should mention that there are three exceptions to the trend of real estate *always* outpacing the economy in terms of growth value. The first and second will result in the value of real estate depreciating in value. The third is an artificially created lessening in demand, which will cause a temporary deceleration to the appreciation rate. The three exceptions are:

1. Due to a man-made or natural disaster, the population of America decreases; for example, as a result of a nuclear holocaust or a medical epidemic, the ratio of land to people increases. The demand for real estate would decrease, driving the price of real estate downward. Such a worldwide calamity would affect the value of all commodities, including gold, diamonds, food, oil, stocks, and so forth. Needless to say, the population of America and of this earth continues to increase in geometrical proportions. The demand will continue to increase and the value of real estate will in-

crease accordingly. The old saying "God stopped making land long, long ago" still applies.

2. When a property is located in a section of the city or county that has deteriorating buildings due to the neglect of the property owners. This is the reason why the location of your investment property is so important. Locating the ideal investment property that fits your conditions and terms will be discussed in Phases 3 and 4.

3. The Federal Reserve charges the U.S. banking system high interest rates and restricts the growth of money (tight money policy). The high cost of money causes high interest rates. The resultant high interest rates will cause high monthly payments when amortizing a loan, thus a lower percentage of individuals can qualify for loans. The short-term result is a lessening of demand. The appreciation rate is dampened but not reversed. However, high interest rates affect every phase of the American industrial machine. Interest rates that exceed the inflationary rate over long periods of time would be disastrous to the American economy. In time the interest rates will come down. The true demand (increasing population) continues, driving residential real estate prices skyward.

Comparing Residential Real Estate with Other Investments

If you are convinced that you would like to invest in real estate, you may now advance directly to the second section of this summary. If you are still undecided and prefer the conventional investments, such as savings accounts, bonds, stocks, or gold, continue reading this section.

Let us take an unbiased view. Consider that we would like to invest a fixed sum of money in the investment field that returns the maximum profit. We shall establish that the return is required in five years. The investment period is not important, but it does simplify the process when explaining percentage of profits for a specified period of time. The conditions that we apply to our investment are:

1. *Maximum leverage.* Invest as little of your own money as possible and use borrowed money for the remainder of the purchase. Down payment should be no more than 10% of the purchase price of the investment.

2. *Maximum return.* Interested in a return of greater that 500% over the specified period of time, greater if possible. Later we shall see that down payment, leverage, and return are all directly related.

3. *Minimum risk.* Assurance that our investment will not go bankrupt or depreciate in value. For example, if you invest in an automobile, the

chances are reasonably good that it will be worth less in five years than it did on the day it was purchased.

4. *Little or no maintenance.* Buy our investment and forget about it during the investment period. Stocks and bonds require no maintenance, since you merely hold a certificate indicating the amount of investment.

5. *Maximum liquidity.* Be able to convert the investment to ready cash at a moment's notice. For example, checking accounts offer maximum liquidity.

6. *Income producing.* The ability of the investment to produce an income. For example, dividends, interest, and rents are in this category.

7. *Tax-sheltered profits.* The ability of the investment to reduce the taxable income earned by the investor during the investment period. Simply stated, the profits produced by the investment are either not taxed or are taxed at some percentage that is less than the ordinary rate. For example, if your total profit on the investment is $25,000, and the profit is not tax sheltered, you would pay taxes on the entire $25,000. If the profit is tax sheltered at 60%, $15,000 (60% of $25,000) is tax free. Taxes are thus paid on $10,000 (40% of $25,000). Your taxable income is reduced from $25,000 to $10,000.

8. *Hedge against inflation.* The investment must produce a profit that will result in positive dollars when compared with inflation. For example, if inflation is 12% and the interest on your checking account is 5%, the value of your monies in your checking account is reduced by more than 7% because the inflation rate is greater than the interest earned. Also all interest over a certain value is taxed as ordinary income. Remember that the percentage of interest paid on certificates of deposit (CDs), treasury bills (TBs), and bonds is generally less than the inflation rate. As a general rule, these types of investments actually produce little or no profits when compared with inflation. Thus, if profit *with inflation taken into consideration* is our objective, CDs, TBs, and bonds clearly do not provide this capability. They merely allow the investor to stay slightly behind the inflation rate.

Let us summarize the eight conditions that we wish our investment to provide. They are:

- Maximum leverage
- Maximum return
- Minimum risk
- Little or no maintenance
- Maximum liquidity
- Income producing

10   THE SUMMARY

- Tax-sheltered profits
- Hedge against inflation

Table 0-1 compares four fields of investments: (1) stock market, (2) gold, (3) treasury bills/certificates of deposit, and (4) residential real estate. The grade scale is from 0 to 10, with 0 providing no benefit in the desired condition and 10 providing maximum benefit. There are differing opinions concerning what a particular field should be graded against a possible condition. For the sake of brevity, I shall make no argument for the grades that the fields of stock market, gold, TBs, or CDs received against a particular condition. For example, it should be obvious to the reader that, in order to purchase common stock or gold, the entire purchase price has to be committed for the investment. Stock brokers can arrange for stock to be purchased on margin, and it is true that margin accounts do exist. However, if you wish to purchase $10,000 of a blue-chip stock with $500, good luck—legally, it cannot be done. Now you could pay $500 and borrow the $9,500 against the purchase price and use the stock as collateral against the loan. I recommend you attempt this approach and see if any lending institution will advance you the required 95% financing. Yet in residential real estate, it is a common, everyday occurrence that home buyers put down 5% to 10% of the purchase price and finance the remainder. Lending and mortgage institutions allow the purchase to be used as collateral because they know that the investment *will not decrease in value.*

TABLE 0-1. Potential Investments

CONDITION	FIELD			
	Stock Market	Gold	Treasury Bills/ Certificates of Deposit	Real Estate
Maximum leverage	4	0	0	10[b]
Maximum return	5	7	0	10[b]
Minimum risk	3	8	10	8
Little or no maintenance	10	10	10	5[a]
Maximum liquidity	8	7	10	6[a]
Income producing	7	0	5	8
Tax sheltered profits	5	5	3	10[b]
Hedge against inflation	4	8	0	10[b]
Totals	45	45	38	67

[a] I have purposely graded real estate low in these two areas, as they are traditionally what have kept potential investors away from the real estate field. Actually if the techniques applied in this book are used, both of these conditions can receive scores comparable to those of the stock market and gold.

[b] These areas are the subject of continued discussion. Maximum leverage, maximum return, tax sheltered profits, and hedge against inflation at minimum risk is what makes *residential* real estate so attractive.

Property Appreciation Rates

We shall now proceed with our analysis concerning why residential real estate offers maximum return, tax-sheltered profits, and is the best hedge against inflation.

Table 0-2 shows the appreciation rate of a residential home with inflation at 10% over a period of five years. Bear with me while some very important points are explained. If the down payment on the property is $5,000 (10% of purchase price), the return on the initial investment is as follows:

TABLE 0-2. Property Appreciation Rate

INITIAL COST	FIRST YEAR	SECOND YEAR	THIRD YEAR	FOURTH YEAR	FIFTH YEAR
$50,000	$55,000	$60,500	$66,500	$73,200	$80,500
Net increase = $30,500					

$$\text{Return} = \frac{\text{Net increase (profit)}}{\text{Down payment (investment)}} \times 100$$

$$\text{Return} = \frac{30,500}{5,000} \times 100 = 610\%$$

However, if the investor also lived in the property he or she bought, there would be a mortgage of $462 per month in order to amortize the loan over 30 years at 12% interest. Remember you paid $5,000 down, thus we need to finance $45,000 to purchase the property. Total payments over five years would be $462 × 12 × 5 (12 payments per year, five years in the investment period), for a total of approximately $28,000. Total investment would be $5,000 + $28,000 = $33,000. Remember, the appreciation on the property was from $50,000 to $80,500, or a gain of $30,500. Thus with a total investment of $33,000, the gain was $30,500. The end result is a negative return. The following list summarizes the data given above.

Residential Real Estate Investment
- Buyer (investor) lives in house he or she bought at 12% interest
- Principal & Interest = $462 per month × 12 × 5 = $28,000
- Net gain (profit).

$$\text{Return on investment} = \frac{30,500}{5,000 + 28,000} \times 100 = 92\%[1]$$

- Loss of 8% on the investment[1]

---

[1] Thus only 92% of investment is return; loss is 8% or negative 8% return.

12 THE SUMMARY

Actually, in a real life situation, you would come out slightly ahead because of the benefits in tax shelters. Assuming that the investor has a taxable income of $25,000, the following list describes what happens when the interest paid on the loan is tax deductible.

Effects of Tax Shelter Benefits
- Buyer lives in house he or she bought without tax break and $25,000 taxable income. Tax paid = $3,504 (from 1980 tax tables).
- With tax shelter and $25,000 taxable income,[2] tax is $2,144.
- Savings due to tax break equals ($3,504 − $2,144) $1,360 per year.
- Return = $\dfrac{30.5 + 1.36(5)}{28 + 5} \times 100 = 113\%$
- Gain = 13% on investment.

Thus, 13% of the original investment is returned to the investor. Now comes the really interesting part; let us assume that the investor had bought not one home but two homes. This is a reasonable assumption since a large percentage of Americans currently own their home of residence. First, two terms need to be defined: positive and negative cash flow. *Positive cash flow* simply means money coming in, for example, pay from your present place of employment is positive cash flow. *Negative cash flow* is money going out, for example, payments to the bank for a car loan would be a negative cash flow. We now summarize the results in another list. Let us assume that both properties were purchased at $50,000 with $5,000 down and financed at 12% interest.

Tax Deductions with Two Properties
- Buyer (investor) buys two properties—one his or her home, the other rental

Home	Positive Cash	Negative Cash[3]
A	None (lives here)	$5,544
B	$350 per month, $4,200 per year rent	$5,544

- Negative cash − positive cash = tax deduction

$$\$5{,}544 + \$5{,}544 - \$4{,}200 = \$8{,}666$$

- Home B can also be depreciated[4] = $5,250
  Total deductions are $8,666 + $5,250 = $13,916.

How do the allowable deductions of $13,916 affect the taxes the investor must pay? Assuming he or she had no deductions and thus had to pay tax on the entire $25,000, the tax bite would be $3,504 (taken from the 1980

---

[2] Interest paid on $45,000 loan = $5,374. Thus taxable income is reduced from $25,000 to $19,626.

[3] Principal and interest at 12% on $45,000.

[4] We shall discuss depreciation allowance in detail later in this book.

tax tables with four exemptions—husband, wife, and two children). If total deductions amounted to $13,916, the investor simply subtracts $13,916 from $25,000 and obtains $11,084. The investor was required to pay only $546 for taxes. *The savings is $3,504 − $546 = $2,958.*

The allowable deductions are a very important point. The majority of Americans will not invest in residential real estate because it is generally accepted that the rent money does not pay for the mortgage. Notice that the rent money equals $4,200 per year and the mortgage payment equals $5,544. Indeed the investor has to finance the rental property with $1,344 (approximately $100 per month) of his or her money. But is this really the case? Of course not! He or she saves $2,958 because less tax is paid. However, proper analysis must be performed for each investor, as the taxable income varies depending on one's salary, number of exemptions, and, most important, the terms of the purchase. However, the more taxable income earned, the more that can be saved. When I started on my investment program, I bought three properties and reduced my taxes from approximately $9,000 to $2,000 per year. For example, an individual with a taxable income of $40,000 will pay $9,355 in taxes. Reducing the taxable income to $26,084 ($40,000 − $13,916) reduces the tax bite to $4,078. The savings in taxes is $5,277 per year ($429 per month).

The following list shows the profits of an investor having two properties.

Real Estate Profits with Two Properties
- Net gain (profit) with properties A and B
- Property A—no return (investor's home)[5]
- Property B—at 10% inflation

INITIAL COST	FIRST YEAR	SECOND YEAR	THIRD YEAR	FOURTH YEAR	FIFTH YEAR
50,000	$55,000	$60,500	$66,500	$73,200	$80,500

- True return = $\frac{\$30,500}{\$5,000} \times 100 = 610\%$

- *Message:—You have to own two properties or more* (one income producing) *to come out ahead!*

The two principal reasons that the above can be accomplished with real estate are: (1) *leverage* and (2) rental monies plus tax-sheltered benefits used to pay the mortgage on the investment property. Remember, Uncle Sam is on your side!

---

[5] *Actual* return was 13% per year and the equity buildup can later be used to purchase additional properties.

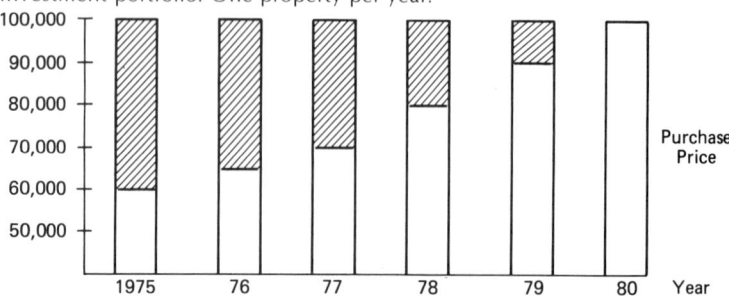

FIGURE 0-1
Investment portfolio. One property per year.

Potential Real Estate Profits

Only real estate gives you the profits indicated above at *minimum risk.* The investment fields of stocks, gold, TBs, CDs, and so forth do not provide these benefits. I have taken the time to explain the value of investing in real estate because it is important that you *clearly* understand the residential real estate process and its inherent positive effect on automatically generating profits. Keep this in mind as we continue with the summary and outline the real estate investment process. For example, review the investment program shown in Figure 0-1. If an investor had purchased one property every year starting in 1975, this investment portfolio would result. In five years, total equity would be over $130,000. The property purchased in 1975 would be ready to return $40,000. In 1975 the property could have been purchased with $6,000 down. Return on the original investment could be 667%. The property appreciation schedule was obtained from information available at any public library and reflects actual appreciation. The property bought in 1977 was purchased for $72,000; by 1981 it was appraised at $110,000.

In Phase 3, The Hunt, I shall discuss methods of buying. Using imagination, innovation, and knowledge, you will see that properties can easily be purchased with down payments of less than 5%, especially if you currently own a home with equity! The key is to get started. Once having purchased your own home and at least one investment property, the equity generated by inflation will automatically allow the properties to be refinanced (or the equity can be used as collateral for a second trust loan), and a third investment can be purchased. Within three to five short years, the investor can begin to harvest his or her crops.

THE DECISION-FLOW PROCESS

I shall now provide an overview summary of what I consider to be the heart of this book—The Decision-Flow Process. There is a tremendous amount of material on real estate investments. I have read more than my share of leaflets, pamphlets, workbooks, and books. In general, I have found these books lacking, since none of them provided a clear, easily understood road map outlining the investment process. The Decision-Flow Diagram described in this section provides the investor with such a road map. Generally, real estate investment books are written by subject matter, and the material in them usually covers all fields of real estate investments. This book, however, is not written by subject matter; it is written in the chronological steps that would be followed by the investor in purchasing residential real estate, that is, one-, two-, three-, or four-unit housing. It is written specifically with the first-time or small-dollar investor in mind. One of the many reasons for writing this book was that, when I started on my investment program, I asked questions on wrap financing, tax laws, assumptions, collateral, discounted seconds, and other investment subjects. The books that I read would refer me to my tax lawyer or some other expert. The majority of small-dollar investors, however, do not have a ready supply of lawyers and other experts. This book provides information on the required subjects related to the investment process. Also, the majority of books that I have read concentrate on large rental (multifamily) units. The "beginner" interested in investing in real estate is interested in properties he or she understands. Residential real estate is understandable and in actuality offers the best return with a minimum risk. This book is thorough, complete, detailed, and written on a level understandable to the average American with a high-school education. I have prepared this book with the knowledge that it will be used in my seminars. Taking the seminar will add great value to the investor's bank of knowledge, and I strongly recommend that all readers attend my seminar when it is presented in your area of the country. In the seminar, I present 35mm slides and overhead transparencies that clearly present the methods of buying, tax depreciation laws, and creative financing techniques that are discussed. The few dollars that I charge for the seminars are well worth the knowledge you will gain.

To allow the reader to follow the investment process in an organized manner, I have developed the Vector Bracketed Decision-Flow Diagram. (See Figure 0-2.) A few words on the title. I selected the word *vector* because the word means force and magnitude that result in direction. It is important that you, the investor, gather force through yourself and your spouse, create momentum through knowledge, commit yourself to the process, and follow through with the program for two or three years. I can assure you that within the three years' time frame, your investments will begin to pay off rather handsomely. Just think, if you had bought one house every year over the last five years, you would be receiving approximately $35,000 to $40,000 per year on your investments based on a purchase price of $60,000 and 10% inflation. Actually it would be greater than $40,000, since rent increases with inflation, but the mortgage payments remain fixed. Later in this book we shall describe the process in its entirety.

The second word in the title of the decision-flow process is *bracketed*. I

FIGURE 0-2
Vector Bracketed Decision-Flow Diagram.

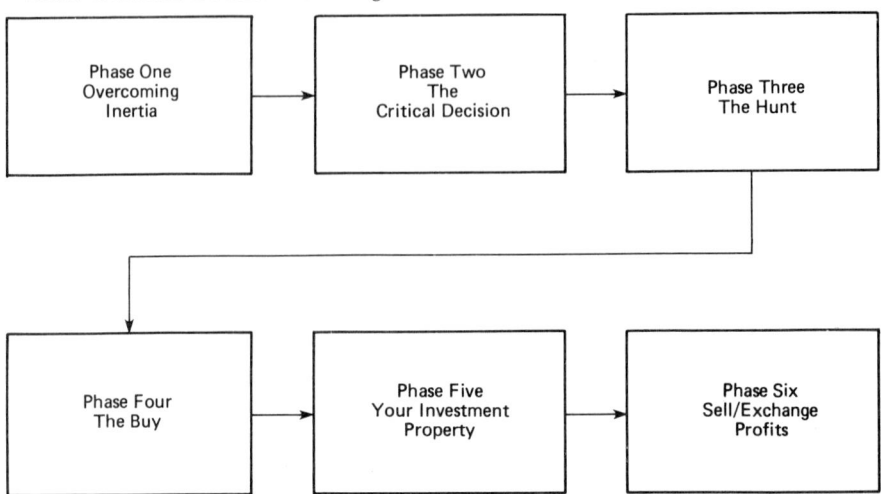

have used this word because the decision-flow process allows the investor the ability to bracket his or her financial position. Only after determining what he or she can afford can the investor proceed with any number of possibilities. For example, the amount of negative cash flow that the investor can afford is directly related to his or her income tax bracket, thus current taxable income determines which investment property can be purchased.

The words *decision-flow diagram* were chosen because they outline the actual decision process that should be used by an investor in purchasing residential real estate. The investor should always be conscious of all phases of the investment process, but should complete each phase before proceeding to the next. I continually refer to this as "presence of mind."

The Vector Bracketed Decision-Flow Diagram is divided into six phases as follows:

Vector Bracketed Decision-Flow Phases
1. Overcoming inertia
2. Critical decision
3. The hunt
4. The buy
5. Your investment property
6. Sell/profits

Phase 1: Overcoming Inertia

Phase 1 is called Overcoming Inertia. You will generally find that most Americans will not invest in residential real estate due to fear of the unknown. The reasons for having this fear are complex, but let us briefly outline the root of the problem.

Other investment fields (stock market, gold, money market funds) are organized by big investment firms. For example, the stock market is represented by Wall Street, gold is minted and sold by various nations, and the money market funds are now organized by international money brokers. You will not find commercials on television outlining the benefits of residential real estate as an investment field, since *you* are your *own* investment consultant. All profits are made by *you* and not by the board of directors of an investment house.

Investing in real estate is disorganized, and no central location exists where information is readily available. The closest thing to organization is a real estate brokerage house. However, real estate agents work as independent salespeople operating largely on a commission basis. It is in their best interest that the sale be as simple and as fast as possible. In my travels throughout America, I make it a point to randomly walk into real estate agencies and discuss investment opportunities. You should not be surprised that any two real estate agents outline two divergent views. For example, I had one agent in Palmdale, California, tell me that assumable loans were just absolutely not found anywhere within a 20-mile radius. Fifteen minutes later (just down the road), the next real estate agent had 20 assumptions with approximately one-third of those willing to finance a portion of the equity (owner willing to carry). In Phase 3, The Hunt, I will explain the different types of buys in detail. Remember the intent of this section is simply to give you a good working knowledge of the investment process.

The terminology is difficult and at times carries a very negative meaning. For example, the word *mortgage* actually comes from the French word *mort*, which means "death." We obtain the word mortgage from the Norman invasion of England; it was used to mean a "death pledge." (Recall the story of the banker dressed in black coming to foreclose on the farmer, and throwing the farmer, his wife, and his beautiful daughter out into the cold Minnesota night.) In the 1930s, foreclosures were common, since the mortgages were short-term and payable in full at the end of the loan period. As a result of the Depression, amortizing a loan was born and the federal government started guaranteeing loans.

In order to overcome the psychological barrier caused by the Depression, the investor must enter an intense study period. I recommend that the following areas be investigated in order to overcome inertia:

- Determine your worth
- Set goals
- Action plan
- Work as a team (husband-wife)
- Use libraries

18 THE SUMMARY

- Analyze locations
- Group discussions
- Money market analysis
- Find good real estate agent(s)

I will briefly discuss each of these areas.

Determine Your Worth Complete an asset-debt data sheet. Table 1–5 in Phase 1 shows a sample of a recommended data sheet. Make a list of all your property (possible collateral), list your positive (incoming) cash, and counter that against your debts and negative (outgoing) cash. List on the chart last year's taxable income and the amount of taxes. Also list savings, CDs, TBs, and the cash value of life insurance. You may be surprised to find that most people are not aware of what type of insurance they have, let alone its cash value. Once you determine what you are worth, use this net worth as a guide as you think through your investment possibilities.

Set Goals Goals are extremely important. Study Figure 0–3. It is a graphic representation of what happens to those individuals who set goals (top line) and those who allow external forces to control them (bottom line). The center line represents time. Time can be days, weeks, months, or years. All in-

FIGURE 0-3
Setting goals.

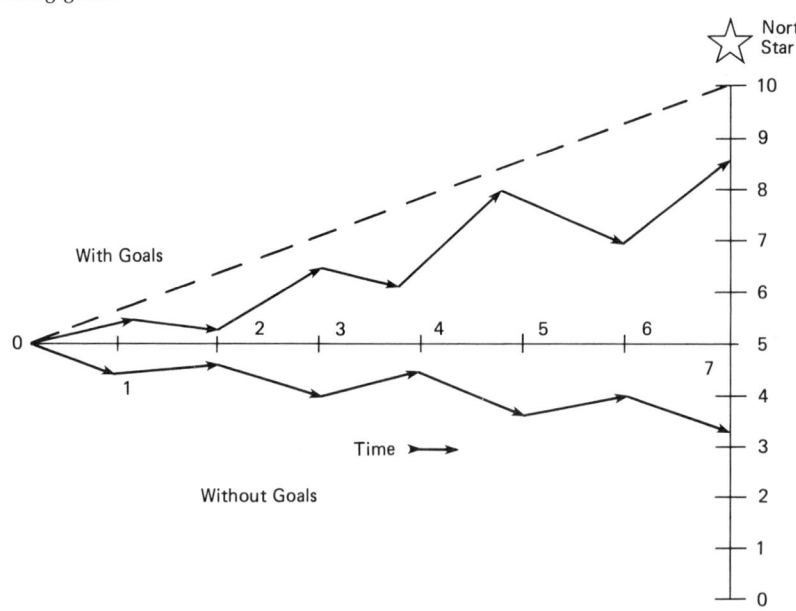

dividuals set goals for a given day or week and sometimes for months. For example, you get up in the morning and you plan your day—drive to work, return from work, go out for dinner, and so forth. You also plan for vacations months in advance.

We as humans, however, do not plan our lives years in advance. Do you have a plan concerning what you expect to be doing five years from now? I seriously doubt if over 10% of the population has a definite plan or goal. They will simply allow unknown external elements (inflation, OPEC, government laws and regulations, or a death in the family) to control their destiny. All individuals should plan their lives in time increments greater than months. I recommend, as a minimum, planning three years into the future. Remember, the future is where you shall spend the rest of your life. We can see that an individual with his or her goal being the "North Star" may not reach the goal after seven years, but an 8.5 on a a scale of 10 is not bad. He or she is 3.5 units higher than when the journey was started seven years earlier. The individual *without goals,* however, has allowed external forces to chart his or her course. Seven years from the start, this individual is 1.5 units worse off than at the start.

Phase 1 provides a description of how to set your goals. In my seminars, I have found that my students either fully understand the "reaching for the 'North Star' " or they are completely perplexed. As an example of setting goals, I will relate how setting one's "North Star" once pertained to me. In 1962, after one semester at the University of Texas, I found myself on probation because of poor grades. In January of 1962 I set my goal to graduate from college. To do this I sacrificed pool and ping pong, cut back drastically on my social life, and dedicated myself to the school library. Actually after I got into a routine it wasn't bad at all because all of us "bookworms" got to know each other. Five years later I graduated with a Bachelor of Science in electrical engineering, and I do not regret it. My only problem was that I didn't set my goals high enough. Nevertheless, I did set my goals and I did reach my "North Star." Several years ago, I basically did the same thing in my real estate investments, but in a much more sophisticated and refined manner. The Vector Bracketed Decision-Flow Diagram was actually the result of my defined path in reaching my goal.

Work as a Team (Husband-Wife)   This is a touchy area. Since I have been involved in real estate investments I have on more than one occasion acted as a family consultant for a number of my friends. It averages about 50-50 between the husband and wife as to who is the investor and who is the "reluctant one." Without both agreeing on a course, one, in essence, cancels the other out, and nothing is accomplished. In Phase 1, Overcoming Inertia, I dedicate considerable time to the all-important issue of the husband-wife partnership. This actually is why I use the word *vector* in the title of the decision flow. Force with magnitude and direction are required throughout the decision process.

Use Libraries   There is a wealth of information at any of the central libraries within your city or county. Information exists that gives all the details of all real estate transactions. For example, real estate guides contain the following information on residential real estate transactions conducted within the city or county: parties selling and buying, interest rate on loans, mortgage company, total amount of the loan, asking price, selling price, assumptions, second trust holders, and length of the second and first trust loan. Property appreciation rates can easily be determined. Using information from the library or the county courthouse you can easily determine if VA or FHA assumable loans are available in a particular area. Information also exists on properties that are delinquent on taxes, which are thus candidates for foreclosure.

Analyze Locations   Using the information obtained from the libraries, real estate agents, owners, newspapers, and all other sources, analyze locations in general. Determine what is a good rental property with a good appreciation rate. Do not buy properties that are too expensive because you may not be able to rent at a level close to the mortgage payment. On the other hand, inexpensive properties bring lower income renters, thus you increase the possibility of problems developing with the rent money. The location is important, since it is directly related to the ability to rent, the ability to sell, and the appreciation rate. All are important. Learn to balance all of your alternatives. To perform a proper balance, however, you must understand the *entire* investment process.

Group Discussions   I have found it to be of immense value to discuss property evaluations, possibilities, and the different ways of buying properties with other investors, especially successful investors. The discussion tends to provide a positive reinforcement, thus adding to the momentum process. Multiple husband and wife teams are dynamite! Each team can research a given area and discussions can be held to transfer information. The effects of positive feedback will act as a positive force to overcome any psychological barriers.

Money Market Analysis   Perform a money market analysis on lending institutions. Determine what type of money is available from which sources. Using information available from real estate agencies and libraries, find out what the comparable purchase price has been for any investment property and who financed the property. You will find that the interest rates and the packages different mortgage institutions offer vary by two or three percentage points, and the conditions vary for renegotiable-rate mortgages (RRMs), fixed-rate mortgages, and equity participation mortgages (EPMs). As an investor interested in the best terms possible, your energy should be used in finding the lending institution with the best commercial loan. Since the first trust will be assumed (i.e. you will take over the payments), and the owner will finance all or a portion of the equity, there may be a requirement to find new money. Visit any mortgage institution that appears to have potential, get to know the loan officers on a first name basis. Phase 3, The Buy, covers this subject in great detail. I believe that high interest rates (10 to 15%) are here to stay; thus, knowing where to obtain the best rates for new money is vital.

Once having completed the money market analysis, the investor will be in an advantageous position to negotiate his or her price and terms on the investment property. When you enter Phases 3 and 4, you will soon find that properties with excellent terms will go fast. When you find the property that fits your terms be prepared to act fast and do not hesitate. Knowing where you can obtain second trust loans (individuals or institutions), wrap financing, or signature loans is important. Considerable time is dedicated to the all-important issue of finding and using other people's money in the main text.

Find Good Real Estate Agent(s)   I strongly recommend the use of a real estate agent when buying and consider not using a real estate agent when selling. The commission earned by the real estate agent comes from the sale price, and I find that having or not having agents involved in the purchase of the property does not usually affect the final price. People that are selling their own properties do not reduce the price of the home by the commission that they would pay the agent since they are not "must sellers." Must sellers are individuals who *must* sell their property because of conditions other than the property itself. Individuals selling because of problems with the property (poor location, bad renter, and so forth) are not must sellers; they are "unloaders." After you have purchased your investment and have held the property for the desired length of time, plan your sell so that you, in turn, do not fall into the must seller category. The ideal situation is to maneuver yourself into a most favorable position, sell the property without the use of a realtor, and realize the maximum profits possible.

When purchasing your investment property, however, do not hesitate to use a realtor. The commission that the agent earns when purchasing the property is well-earned if you use him or her properly. Use as many real estate agents as you can handle. The use of multiple real estate agents (I have used as many as 12 when searching) increases the probability of finding the ideal investment. Always increase your search sensors to the maximum you can handle. Actually it happens quite naturally, since most properties are listed through real estate companies. Thus, when you see a piece of property being advertised, you call the agent and ask the questions that fit your terms. If that particular property does not fit your terms, generally the agent will know of several that do. The key is to define your boundaries, for example, location, asking price, assumption, first trust greater than two-thirds of asking price, townhouse, condo, and so forth. The fact that you apply specific terms actually makes the search much easier for the knowledgeable real estate agent since he or she uses a computer to provide the data for review. Also when you do find good knowledgeable real estate agents, treat them well and they will come to you in the future when the investments with ideal terms and conditions surface.

Phase 2: Critical Decision

Once having completed your initial analysis and having decided to pursue residential real estate investments, you enter a new phase of investigation. Start your investigation to determine *what* you can afford. Do not go out blindly and invest in what you *think* is a good residential real estate investment. You must *know* that it is a good investment. The investment property has to fit your particular set of psychological, physical, and, most importantly, financial circumstances. After you have made the decision to start looking for investment properties, take some time to complete a debt-asset data sheet on yourself; you may also call it a financial analysis profile. Complete the profile on yourself, your spouse, and your family. A blank debt-asset data sheet is provided at the end of Phase 1. It can be used to make the computation. Add the positive numbers on the left, the negative numbers on the right, do the subtraction as indicated, and your net worth is calculated at the bottom of the table. If you have CDs, bonds, or whole life insurance, I recommend that you consider cashing in the certificates and that you consider cashing in your whole life insurance and purchasing term, not whole life, insurance. Insurance should never be considered as part of your investment portfolio. Insurance should only be to provide financial protection in the event of the breadwinner's death. The return on a whole life policy (cash value) is very low. But, by all means, insure the life of the breadwinner. Recently, the tragic and sudden death of an acquaintance of mine drove the point home! He was in his mid-forties, married, the father of four—three young teenagers and one preteen. His total pay was approximately $45,000 per year. He had *no* insurance. He did not believe in having any. He had no will. Why? He believed he would live to be an old man! Also, he had no home, but rented. His wife and children must now search for a cheaper rental home. She must find a job after years of no employment. I leave you with this thought concerning whole life insurance policies. Next time you visit Omaha, Dallas, Milwaukee, New York, or any other city where insurance companies are headquartered, look around—you will find that they have the biggest and most modern of all buildings.

The reason should be obvious, they are investing other people's money (yours) in such things as real estate. Why not do the same thing yourself without having to pay the high overhead rates?

Having once determined your net worth, a thorough analysis must be completed to determine the effects of inflation, rent, interest, and property depreciation on your taxable income as it pertains to any potential investment property. This is extremely important, since it will determine what, if any, negative cash flow you can afford to sustain. To determine your allowable negative cash flow we use the Vector Cash-Flow Analysis outlined in Phase 2, The Critical Decision.

The cash-flow analysis makes basic assumptions on such terms as purchase price, interest on first trust, owner to take back a second trust, and so forth, and we perform the arithmetic to calculate the investor's cash-flow position. You will be pleasantly surprised to learn how quickly you can master the technique. When you actually start looking at properties and asking for the details, your mind will automatically calculate the numbers and provide the result in a relative short period of time. I might add that an inexpensive calculator will help to verify the numbers. The key here is to obtain experience and an understanding of the analysis process and calculating for your terms.

Phase 3: The Hunt

Up to this point, Phases 1 and 2 have been primarily a study on paper. As a potential investor having made the decision to pursue investing in residential real estate, you now enter what I refer to as the "hands-on" phases. However, do not forget that all through the process you must maintain your analyzing and investigatory attitude, coupled with your innovative imagination. I have found that it is at times easy to be swept away by the emotional issues (beautiful home . . . but terms are not right; fast-talking real estate agents . . . and you just can't say *no*). Keep a cool head and always look for the right terms. Phase 3, The Hunt, begins when you actually start looking for your investment properties. During Phase 1 you may have looked at properties but it was merely to conduct your analysis (comparison of prices) and to get a better feel for all the potential areas. Because of your analysis of locations and the money market analysis of Phase 1, by Phase 3 you should have a good idea concerning where, what, and how you wish to purchase. However, remain flexible in regard to general location; terms are the most important. Write down your terms (conditions of purchase). As a minimum, write down the following conditions and the terms that fit your situation.

Terms of Purchase
1. Down payment not to exceed _____. Always strive for minimum cash. Nothing down if possible, remember you want maximum leverage.

2. Location or locations where you will purchase _____. I recommend within one hour's drive time of where you live.
3. Assumptions only, VA or FHA, some conventional loans are assumable at negotiated rates. Consider wraparounds.
4. Owner to take back (OTTB) second trust. If possible have the owner take back the entire equity as a second trust. (I will discuss this in greater detail later.)
5. Buy properties in move-in condition only. (Unless you get a super deal, stay away from "specials" requiring many repairs.)
6. Range of sell prices _____. For example, from $50,000 to $75,000. The terms and the expected rent (positive cash), are most important.
7. Maximum amount of negative cash flow you *can* sustain.
8. Avoid any negative cash flow which you *cannot* sustain.

After having read this book, you will find that there are no bounds to the terms and conditions you can apply; your imagination is your only limit! For example, I tell my realtors; "I am looking for properties three to five years old with the first trust approximately two-thirds or greater of the asking price." Properties that were bought three to five years ago have good interest rates on the loans (less than 10%) and the fact that the equity on the property is only one-third of the asking price puts you as the investor in a good negotiating position. Wraparounds may offer a greater range of the ratio of the assumable first trust to the equity. (I will explain this in Phase 3.) For instance, I purchased a townhouse that had an existing assumable mortgage as low as one-third of the asking price and had the owner carry back the entire equity as a second trust at 12%. If you work out the arithmetic, the PITI (principal, interest, taxes, and insurance) is $485 per month, and I rent the townhouse for $425 per month. The $60 negative cash flow is more than made up in the payment of less income tax. The point that I am making is this—do all of your analyses in Phases 1 and 2, so that when you actually look at the properties and calculate the numbers, you will be able to identify a good buy immediately. Remember, good buys do not last on the market; but be sure, if you purchase on the spot, that it is because you have made the decision and not because someone else is applying pressure.

Now the question you may be asking is: All of the above is fine, but how do I get started in Phase 3? First, you do an extensive search for properties right from your own home. Use the telephone. I found that I was wasting too much valuable time by randomly searching and asking for terms as I inspected the potential investment property. Simply pick up the paper and search for what may be a good investment. If the terms on the advertised property do not fit, ask the realtor to search for properties that do fit your terms and have him or her call back. Do this a number of times, say six to ten times and you will find that approximately half the realtors will call back providing you with a list of possible investments. Another way of getting started is to go down to the local homeowners association and review the list of homes being sold by the owners. However, I have found that the best source of homes being sold by the owners is newspaper advertisements. Learn to use the newspaper extensively. Another method is to take time one afternoon and visit five or six real estate offices. Pick real estate agents at random and describe your terms. Do not be surprised to have four out of five realtors tell you that it is impossible to find a property of your description. Once in Dallas, Texas, I found a realtor who absolutely insisted that I was "nuts." I went to the realtor next door and found properties close to the terms I was describing. The key is to keep searching to find a potential investment that fits your terms. Only after you have reduced the properties to some manageable number do you actually inspect the property. Talk to the owner of the property, if possible, and ask the simple question, "Why are you selling?" If you ask the question with sincerity and honesty you will in most cases get an honest answer. What you are looking for is an owner who is in the position of having to sell fast. I classify this group of sellers as "must sellers," as previously described. Once you establish a good working relationship with knowledgeable realtors, they will be your most important source to finding properties in the "must sellers" category.

During Phase 3 be prepared to do a quick cash-flow analysis on any property that looks like it has potential. The more properties you look at and the more calculations you complete, the faster and easier the analysis becomes. I use a $4.95 paperback listing monthly payments to amortize a loan at any interest rate over any desired length of time, an inexpensive calculator, and all of my data from Phases 1 and 2. In the beginning it took me approximately one hour to complete the cash-flow analysis, but within a few days, after learning the technique, I completed the calculations in five to ten minutes. Actually you get to the point where you can do everything in your head, with the five or ten minutes required only to verify your numbers.

The 1981 Economic Recovery Tax Act allows for 15-year straight-line depreciation with 175% declining balance. This is absolutely outstanding for any investor, as he or she can expect tax savings to increase by 40% to 50% of the former depreciation allowances! The bottom line is that you can absorb a higher negative cash flow.

Also discussed in Phase 3 are the types of buys, for example, asking the sellers or owners to take back a second trust, assuming an existing loan, wraparound mortgages, moving the collateral, and land contracts. Notice that I did not mention new financing. Generally you should stay away from new financing, except on some rare occasions. For example, you may run into a new property that is being built by a custom builder who is having financial problems because high interest rates are keeping potential buyers away from the property. It is possible that you may assume the construction loan at a favorable rate. Remember, the bank carrying the construction loan does not wish to foreclose and go through bankruptcy proceedings. The condition of having builders provide favorable sale terms has existed twice in the last two years, first in the winter of 1979–80 and then beginning in the winter of 1980 through 1981. Both situations occurred because of high interest rates. I am sure you remember hearing someone say that the building industry has been drastically affected by the high interest rates. The larger than normal supply of "must sellers" made the early 1980s an investor's paradise. The reason is simple—high interest rates keep buyers away; thus sellers are willing to accept imaginative, creative financing packages in order to sell their homes.

An area that is coming into being in the 1980s is the equity participation mortgage (EPM) and the renegotiable (variable-rate) mortgage. I will devote considerable time to this area in the main text, since anyone who is serious about investing in real estate must thoroughly understand these types of mortgages. The EPM is money that a financial institution lends at some percentage below the prevailing rate. The agreement between the lending institution and the borrower (the investor) is that profits generated from the future sale of the property are to be split between the lending institution and the borrower.

In the winter of 1980–81, the Advanced Mortgage Corporation was lending money at two-thirds the prime rate with the agreement that at the time of sale the mortgage company would receive one-third of the profits. For example, if the prime lending rate was 15%, the mortgage company would lend the purchase money at 10%. If the profit was $30,000 at the time of sale, the lending institution would receive $10,000. What makes this type of money so attractive to both the lending institution and the investor is that the property must be sold or refinanced (new money) within a specified period of time, for instance, ten years. An individual who is interested in buying his or her home finds this type of arrangement difficult to accept because he or she knows that the mortgage rates are subject to change sometime in the future. Buyers tend to think of themselves as living for long periods of time (over ten years) in the property that they are buying, thus the thought of having to sell or refinance is not considered favorably. However, you as an investor have the conditions and terms in your favor. You will want to sell within the specified period of time, and the interest rate is rather attractive. The one obstacle to overcome is convincing the lending institution that you are a good risk and, more importantly, that you as the landlord will ensure that the renter will take care of the property. In essence, you are forming a partnership with the mortgage company. The advantage is to both parties, as they both make a profit on the sale. You, as the investor, however can depreciate the full value of the property as an income tax deduction. The partnership that you form with the mortgage company is a principal–silent partner relationship. The investor is the principal partner, and the mortgage company is the silent partner.

As this book goes to print, EPMs, also known as Shared Appreciation Mortgages (SAMs), have been "put on ice." The Reagan administration believes that they are counterproductive to the inflationary psychology. However, if interest rates remain high, and they most likely will, I predict that the EPMs or SAMs will reappear as an alternate form of financing. You as an investor and homeowner should be fully aware of the advantages and drawbacks of the investor–lending institution partnerships.

Principal–silent partnerships can also be structured between two or more investors. One becomes the principal, manages the property, and receives the full tax write-offs. The silent partners do not worry about the management of the property but share in the percentage of the profit. This arrangement is even better when the principal becomes the silent and the silent the principal in a second property. That is, reverse the positions, and the arrangement provides you with an investment in multiple properties and automatic collateral between the partners.

The second area that requires our attention is the renegotiable (variable-rate) mortgage. This type of mortgage plan is now common in most states. Simply stated, a financial institution lends money below the prime rate (usually two or three percentage points), with the understanding that the loan will be renegotiated at some time in the future (for example, three years). Conditions and terms that are common to this arrangement are: (1) No prepayment penalty, thus you are at liberty to refinance if the interest rate falls below the negotiated rate. (2) If at the specified time of refinance the interest rate is lower than the agreed rate, the loan will automatically be financed at the lower rate. (3) If the interest rate is higher at the time of renegotiation, the loan will be financed at the higher rate not to exceed one or one and one-half points above the interest rate originally agreed upon. Be sure that the agreement specifies that the rate will not exceed a certain limit. As I mentioned earlier, I dedicate considerable time to both types of mortgages in the main text. It is my belief that these mortgages are the way of the future.

We now leave Phase 3, The Hunt, with the investment property that fits all of our conditions and terms. We should know exactly where we stand concerning our cash flow, which includes the expected rent and the return from our reduced tax payments. The anticipated appreciation (profits) of the selected property should have been calculated. Although the projected figure requires certain assumptions to have been already made (inflation, maintenance, taxes, and so forth), these assumptions can be made with a fair amount of assurance. Actually, we will figure rather conservatively, thus profits will probably be higher than the projected gains.

After we have found our investment property we begin negotiations for the purchase of the property.

Phase 4: The Buy

Negotiations for the purchase of property should be on a plane of complete honesty and respect for the owner-seller. Since we are interested in buying properties in move-in condition, we should not have a problem with terms in the contract that would concern a house in the "fix-it" category. Certainly there should be no holes in the walls or doors that have been splintered because of poor maintenance or family arguments. (I have seen both and, in general, the neighborhood usually fits the state of repair of the property.) Because you have selected a move-in, clean, fairly new home (townhouse, condo, multiplex, and so forth), in a good neighborhood, you should not have to be bothered by any "special" clauses that always prove embarrassing to both parties. Your total energy should be concentrated on the *terms* of the financial arrangements. Since you have selected the property because it involves no new money (except possibly foreclosures or bankruptcies), the negotiations should be centered around the equity in the property. Whether you attempt to have the owner take back a second trust, a wraparound (also known as an all-inclusive trust), or offer another property as collateral, it all basically comes down to the seller trusting you as a good risk. Remember, you do not wish to give a large down payment, nothing down if possible.

I strongly recommend two things during negotiations: (1) Although you may be an excellent negotiator, allow the knowledgeable real estate agent to be your negotiator. Fix the absolute terms that you will agree to, and allow him or her to negotiate for you. The advantage is that he or she is empowered to go only so far and no more. And, even after the realtor has come to an agreement with the seller, he or she still has to come to you, so that you can then have some time on your own to think up a better offer. All of these negotiations should take place over a matter of hours. Remember you have done all your analysis and know exactly where you stand, and have already determined that the property is a good buy. (2) Always be negotiating for more than one property; perform a parallel negotiation on several investments simultaneously, since in the process of completing Phase 3 you will probably find several good properties, all basically equal in the areas of conditions and terms. The best course to follow at this point is to write a contract on potential investments, offering no money down with the equity to be financed by a second trust. Always maximize your options. The more properties, the better. Remember you are only looking for one property, but if all say yes—great, purchase all of the properties since your analysis indicates that the cash flow should be zero or positive in nature. In all probability only one will accept or all will reject. However, some percentage will make a counter proposal. You then analyze all proposals, select the two or three that appear to offer the best potential, and see what happens. Since you are now entering negotiations that require some minimum down payment, you will have to be prepared to reject some of the first counter proposals or even second counter proposals. Let us assume that three of the five offer fairly attractive counter proposals after your offer of no money down. You then make a second proposal, which will be a little less cash than their counter proposal, and all three accept. Remember you are dealing through an intermediary (your negotiator, the real estate agent) and if purchasing all three would leave you with an unacceptable cash flow situation, you can abort the negotiation process at any time on any one of the properties. Pick up the property that offers the best terms, and continue the negotiation process until you are satisfied with the purchase terms. Remember do not waste time with inflexible sellers, continue searching; your time is too valuable.

Other factors affecting Phase 4 are shopping for lawyers (or legal secretaries), escrow companies, and insurance. Contrary to popular belief, the fees charged by lawyers do vary by 200% to 300%, so shopping around for a lawyer can prove to be a money saver.

The date of the contract can also be important, since you shall be required to pay interest for the remainder of the month. I generally try to make all settlement dates late in the month so I have little or no initial interest money. I always have the property rented by the beginning of the next month, thus I see the deposit as well as the first month's rent and I do not have to pay the first mortgage payment until approximately 30 days later (the seller had the property the last date the monthly payment was due). Settling at the end of the month also increases your chances of renting the property since, in general, prospective renters are renting elsewhere and rents run from month to month. We will discuss a list of small but important items that add up to a nice little "windfall" later in this text.

Phase 5: Your Investment Property

The management of the investment property, although the longest phase—from three to five years—should be the least intense and the most trouble-free. If Phases 1 through 4 were properly conducted, you should have a clean property in move-in condition at an affordable negative cash flow. Remember your tax benefits can cancel a $100 to $300 per month negative cash flow on the PITI to rent differential.

Following are tips to help you best manage the property. I emphasize the importance of good records, including all initial cash outlays (settlements, costs, and so forth), rents received, mortgage payments, maintenance, and closing costs. With your investment properties, your allowable number of tax exemptions will double or perhaps triple, thus the probability of the IRS computer tagging your income tax return for audit increases significantly. Having good and accurate records will provide more than sufficient information for any tax review. I will discuss the issue of tax shelters in Phase 6, Sell/Profits.

I also recommend that the rental money be paid utilizing direct bank-to-bank transfers. An interest-bearing checking account (where allowed) should be opened for every property that is being rented. The monthly statements (and canceled checks) provide a beautiful record-keeping system for all financial transactions relative to the particular properties. Another idea for maintenance records includes using different credit cards from one of the many lumber-homeowner discount stores. This will also help in keeping your records in order. During the holding of the investment property, you should strive for good, accurate records reflecting all transactions.

On the issue of a contract between yourself and the renter, I recommend a contract be written for a minimum of one year with an option to extend. After one year, you will have long-term capital gain income from the property, placing you in the position of being able to sell at any time. You may wish to rent with an option to buy. With the option to buy, advance the renter some percentage of the total rent paid against the down payment. For example, you could agree to advance the renter 30% of the rent paid over three years against the purchase of the property. The property was originally purchased for $75,000 and is appraised at $99,825 three years later (10% inflation). Assuming rent was $500 per month, the total rent money over the three-year period is $18,000. Thirty percent of $18,000 is $5,400; hence, $5,400 is deducted from the market value of $99,825 for a price of $94,425. Your profit on the investment property would be $19,425 ($94,425 − $75,000) in three years. Realize that you are giving up $5,400 of your potential profits. However, if you list and sell through a realtor, the commission would be 6% or more of the sell price. If your tenant decides to buy, there will be no need for a realtor. When advertising your investment property for rent, the option to buy will generate a high level of interest. In the main text I discuss numerous methods and techniques to allow your property to stand out when advertising for rent. Learn to write creative and attention-getting advertisements. Additional tips such as doing a credit report, obtaining references, etc. will be discussed in the main text.

Phase 6: Sell/Profits

Phase 5, Your Investment Property, should have been relatively maintenance- and trouble-free; the selling of your property should likewise encounter no difficulties. Let us review the conditions that apply to your property.

- Assumable first trust
- Good location
- Clean property
- Priced at competitive price
- Possible second trust financing

Let us briefly review the items listed above.

1. Assumable first trust: If you assumed the first trust from the original seller, the current buyer can assume the balance of the remaining first trust. Since you only had the property three to five years, you will find that the balance of the first trust will have changed very little. What has changed is your equity in the property which is exactly why you purchased the investment in the first place. The equity is your profit.

2. Good location: Since the good location attracted you, it will also attract other buyers. Generally, I like to buy properties that appeal to middle-class young professionals with children. This group is on the move and hungry to purchase their own homes. The good location should be near schools, parks, public transportation, and the main job centers.

3. Clean property: Remember the property was three to five years old when you bought it. At the time of your sale, it will be six to nine years old. With average to little major maintenance costs, the property should continue to be in excellent condition for at least 15 years. You may want to arrange to have the renter do some painting, with you supplying the paint and possibly providing assistance. My brother, who has assisted with the writing of this book, has numerous properties on the West Coast. He arranges for a gardener to go by every one or two weeks to cut the grass and trim the hedges. This tends to set the tone of maintenance and helps to keep the property in excellent condition.

4. Priced at competitive price: As an investor, if you want a quick sell, place an advertisement in the paper with the sell price slightly below the market value. Without having to pay the sales commission you have a substantial bargaining edge. However, I should warn you that most buyers are not very sophisticated, so proceed with caution when explaining to them such items as assumable loans and financing the equity with a second trust. Quite frankly, you are better off just stating the selling price and allowing the prospective buyer to finance the purchase with new money. Since you will probably have a good understanding of the current mortgage rates, it is possible that you could direct the buyer to a lending institution. I have found that behind the sometimes stoic, expressionless, and conservative personality, bankers are also human. If you, as an investor, develop personal relationships with bankers (remember those checking accounts to

manage your properties), they will expedite the application of the loan based purely on you being a preferred customer.

5. Possible second trust financing: Upon selling the investment property, the first trust will be assumed by the buyer, and the second trust will be paid at settlement. Consider taking back a second trust yourself. For example, assume the first trust was $60,000 (assumed by your buyer); the second trust you had the original owner take back was $12,000, and the current equity equals $25,000, for a total purchase price of $97,000 ($60,000 + $12,000 + $25,000). You could ask for $12,000 down, pay off the second trust and carry back a second trust of $25,000. $25,000 financed at 12% over ten years returns $358.68 per month. Better yet, finance over a short period, for example five years, or balloon the mortgage at three years. The second trust can also be structured as a graduated interest payment. The information above may sound complex, but actually it is quite straightforward; remember we are in the summary portion of this book and the idea is to provide you with a general overview of the process.

The possible ways of financing the sale of your property as described above touch on the outer fringes of the all-inclusive trust or wraparound mortgage, discussed in Phase 3. In the main text we will investigate and study numerous methods of creative financing. All explanations are accompanied by descriptive art work, graphs, curves, plots, and figures. Before we continue with the subject of .depreciation and tax shelters, however, I would like to emphasize the best way of selling your property—new financing with as much cash over the table as possible. This will allow you to pyramid your assets and reach your goal at an accelerated pace. The method used to sell is quite different from the method used to buy; however, do be prepared to be as imaginative with your sells as you are with your buys.

Long-Term Capital Gains   As Phase 1, Overcoming Inertia, was a period of study and setting a course for your financial independence, so Phase 6, Sell/Profits, concerns an all-important subject—tax laws. It is appropriate that I mention one thing about taxes. In real estate there is no such thing as tax-free investment income. However, there are different types of income taxed at different rates. Basically there are two types of taxable income, ordinary and capital gain. Ordinary is the income you are most familiar with, for example, the pay check you bring home every two weeks is classified as ordinary income and is taxed using the tax tables found in IRS Forms 1040 and 1040A. I am sure that all of you are familiar with these tables whether you use the short or long forms for reporting your income and determining your taxes for the year in question. The second type of taxable income is income earned through an investment, such as stocks or real estate. The gain or profit is classified as short-term gain if the investment period was one year or less. Income (profits) from a short-term gain is simply added to your ordinary income and taxed accordingly. The gain or profit is classified as long-term gain if the investment period was longer than one year. Long-term capital gains are taxed differently than ordinary income. To compute the tax on a long-term gain (profit), simply add 40% of your gain to your ordinary income and find your tax using the tax tables. Sixty percent of your capital gain is referred to as *capital gain deduction* and is not taxed. Thus your effective tax for the year in question varies with your taxable income. Allow me to illustrate using the bar graphs in Figures 0–4 and 0–5, for an ordinary income of $25,000 and a profit of $15,000.

It is absolutely vital that the bar graphs be clearly understood *before* embarking on your investment program. I dedicate considerable time to cal-

FIGURE 0-4
Take-home pay. Total income taxed as ordinary income.

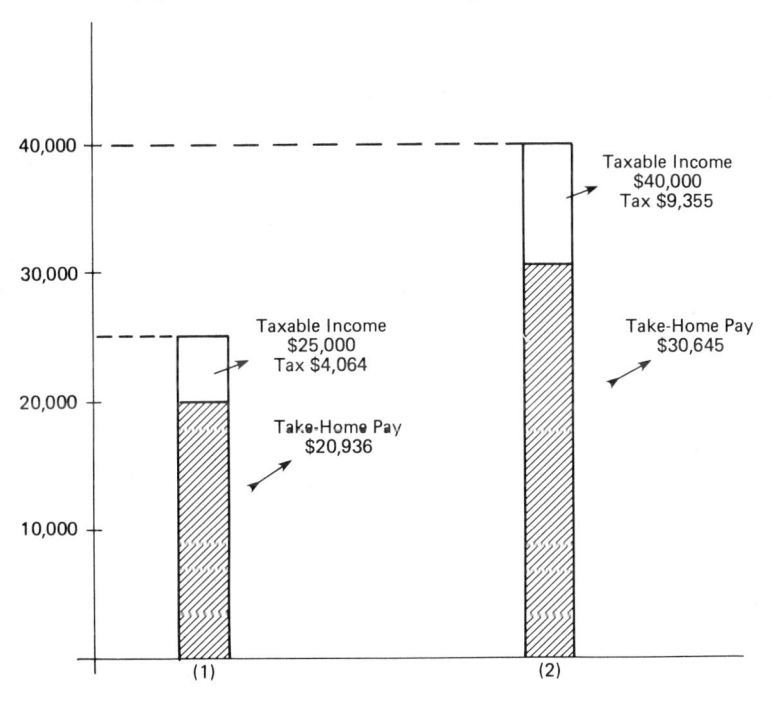

TOTAL TAKE-HOME PAY $30,645

Bar graph (1) represents $25,000 of ordinary income, tax on $25,000 with two exemptions filing jointly equals $4,064. Take-home pay equals $20,936.

Bar graph (2) represents $40,000 of ordinary income, tax on $40,000 with two exemptions filing jointly equals $9,355. Take-home pay equals $30,645.

FIGURE 0-5
Take-home pay. Investment income taxed as long-term capital gain.

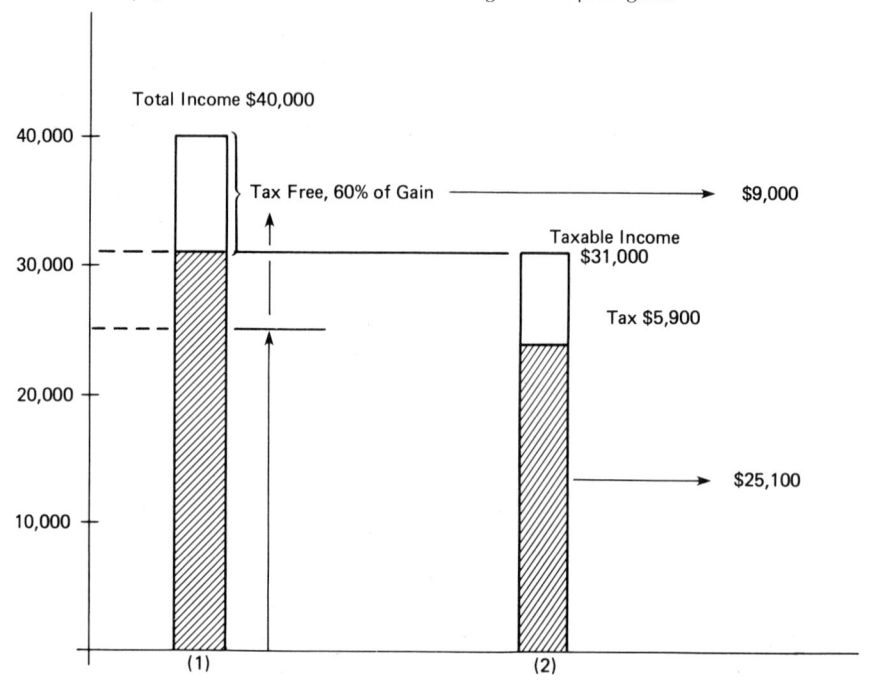

TOTAL TAKE HOME PAY $34,100

Bar graph (1) represents $40,000 of income, $25,000 ordinary and $15,000 long-term capital gain. Sixty percent of the $15,000 long-term gain is tax free. The tax-free gain equals $9,000

Bar graph (2) represents the amount of the $40,000 that will be taxed ($31,000). With a taxable income of $31,000 (ordinary income), the tax equals $5,900. Take-home pay from the $31,000 ordinary income equals $25,100. Total take-home pay equals $34,100.

culating long-term capital gains in the main text. This area will give you a true appreciation for the profits that can be expected from your real estate investments.

Depreciation of Your Investment Property The second area that must be clearly understood when you embark on your investment program is the area of property depreciation and tax-deductible maintenance expenses. In August 1981, Congress enacted the Economic Recovery Tax Act. The new tax law allows for 15-year depreciation and for 175% declining balance, whereas the old tax laws allowed for a straight line depreciation over 30 to 40 years. Allow me to compare the old tax laws with the new laws. With the old laws, a $75,000 investment would depreciate at approximately $2,000 per year (13/16 × $75,000 ÷ 30). With the new laws, first-year depreciation on the same property is $7,000 (13/16 × $75,000 ÷ 15 × 1.75). To an individual with a taxable income of $35,000, the resultant tax savings are simply tremendous. With $35,000 taxable income, tax equals $7,357. With the new depreciation allowance taken into account, the resulting new taxable income equals $28,000 ($35,000 − $7,000). Tax on $28,000 equals $4,961. Thus, the net savings in taxes equals $2,396. The change is significant since the differential between mortgage payments and rent can be greater, thus more properties are available to the investor.

As an investor you must understand depreciation. It is important because it allows you to have a negative cash flow when subtracting the mortgage, taxes, and insurance (PITI) from the rent. For example, if the PITI is $600 per month and the rent $400 per month, you have a $200 monthly negative cash flow. However, since you can depreciate your property and subtract the depreciated amount from your taxable income, the amount saved by simply not paying as much tax will offset the resulting negative cash flow. Thus the amount of tax you are required to pay decreases. The key is to know this at the start of the year, claim additional exemptions on the W–4 form, and not pay the taxes as the year progresses. This is perfectly allowable, and I devote considerable time to the details of performing what is called *front-end analysis* relative to depreciation methods. There are three methods of depreciation: (1) straight-line, (2) declining balance, and (3) sum of years' digits. As an investor, you will want to use the second method, since the declining balance method is nothing more than 175% of the amount that you would depreciate using the straight-line method. However, the law reads that the investor may select any method desired; thus, it is important that all three methods be understood.

Straight-line depreciation is depreciating the value of your investment property in equal increments over the expected life span of the property. The value of the land where your investment property is built cannot be depreciated, since land does not depreciate in value. To use the straight-line method, take the cost of the property (whatever you paid for it), subtract the value of the land, and divide by the expected life span of the property. If you have no records indicating the value of the land (you usually find this in your city or county tax statement), the IRS gives guidance to calculate the value of the land as 3/16 of the total property value. All properties purchased after December 31, 1980 may be depreciated in 15 years. Properties purchased prior to January 1, 1981 continue under the old tax law (30 to 40 years). Assuming the cost of the investment property is $100,000, the allowable depreciation per year using the straight-line method would be

$$\frac{100,000 - 100,000 \,(3/16)}{15 \text{ years}} = \frac{100,000 - 18,750}{15} = \frac{\$81,250}{15} = \$5,416.67$$

Thus the amount of income you could deduct from your taxable income for the year in question is $5,416.67 using the straight-line method of depreciation.

The *declining balance method* allows for an accelerated form of depreciation. Basically, the theory is that properties depreciate faster in their early years. This is true for automobiles. I am sure you have either experienced or have heard of the fact that a new car decreases in value $2,000 or $3,000 when you drive it off the lot. Residential real estate, however, *increases* in value, with the biggest increase occurring in the first year. Generally, with inflation at 8% to 10%, you can expect the value of a new home to increase 15% after the first year. Nevertheless, the income tax laws in the United States allow for depreciation of investments that are quite favorable to the investor, so let us continue with our declining balance method. The 1981 tax law allows for 175% of the straight-line depreciation. The amount that is depreciated in a given year is subtracted from the basis of the property (cost of property the first year), and the new depreciated property value is used to calculate depreciation for the given year.

Let us illustrate the declining balance method with an example. Assume the cost of the property is $100,000. After subtracting the value of the land (3/16 of cost), the value of the building itself is $81,250. We are using the same property that was depreciated using the straight-line depreciation method above. Using the straight-line method, we calculated allowable depreciation as $5,416.67. Using the 175% declining balance, our allowable depreciation the first year would be $5,416.67 × 1.75 = $9,479.17 (175% of the straight-line depreciation). The second year must be recalculated. Subtracting the depreciated amount from the original cost, calculate the straight-line amount. For example,

$$\frac{\$81{,}250 - 9{,}479.17}{15} = \frac{\$71{,}770.83}{15} = \$4{,}784.72$$

Now multiply $4,784.72 by 1.75 (175% of the straight-line amount). The allowable depreciation is $8,373.26 for the second year. To calculate for the remaining years you simply continue the process. Table 0–3 summarizes the straight-line and declining balance methods. It should be obvious to any investor that the declining balance method of depreciation is preferable to the straight-line method.

Another method that can be used for accelerated depreciation is the *sum-of years'-digits method*. Under the sum-of-years'-digits method, you add the digits of the number of years in the useful life of the investment property and use this as the base in your calculations. If the useful life is five years, for example, the digits 1 through 5 total 15 (1 + 2 + 3 + 4 + 5 = 15). Each year the allowable deduction from depreciation is calculated by dividing the useful life minus the investment year by the sum of the digits. Sounds complex, doesn't it? Actually it is rather simple. An illustration can

TABLE 0-3. Depreciation of Property[a]

	STRAIGHT-LINE DEPRECIATION		DECLINING BALANCE METHOD		
Year	Basis of Calculation	Allowable Deduction	Basis of Calculation	Straight-Line Depreciation	Allowable Deduction
					175%
1	$81,250/15	$5,416.67	$81,250.00	$5,416.67	$9,479.17
2	81,250/15	5,416.67	71,770.83	4,784.72	8,373.26
3	81,250/15	5,416.67	63,397.59	4,226.51	7,396.39
4	81,250/15	5,416.67	56,001.20	3,733.41	6,533.47
5	81,250/15	5,416.67	49,467.73	3,297.85	5,771.24

[a] Based on 15 years useful life.

best explain. Assume useful life (later we will get back to our 30-year useful life investment) of 5 years. The first year's deduction is calculated as follows (0 indicates the first year you have held the investment property):

$$\frac{5 \text{ (useful life)} - 0 \text{ (investment year)}}{1 + 2 + 3 + 4 + 5} = \frac{5}{15} = 0.333$$

Thus we can deduct 33% of the value of the investment for the first year's tax return. The second year's deduction is calculated as follows:

$$\frac{5 - 1}{15} = 0.27 \text{ or } 27\%$$

The third year's deduction is calculated as follows:

$$\frac{5 - 2}{15} = 3/15 = 0.20 \text{ or } 20\%$$

Since the new tax law allows only the declining balance method, I shall use the old life span of 30 years to explain the sum-of-years'-digits method. First, calculate for sum of years

$$1 + 2 + 3 + 4 + 5 + 6 + 7 + 8 + 9 + 10 + 11 + 12 + 13 + 14 + 15 + 16 + 17 + 18 + 19 + 20 + 21 + 22 + 23 + 24 + 25 + 26 + 27 + 28 + 29 + 30 = 465$$

An alternate method of calculating the sum of years' digits is to use the following formula (for a 30-year life span):

$$\frac{N^2 + N}{2} \text{ where } N = \text{useful life.}$$

$$\frac{(30)^2 + 30}{2} = \frac{930}{2} = 465$$

Continuing with our calculations, the first year's depreciation will be

$$\text{percentage of deduction} = \frac{\text{useful life span} - \text{year of investment tax return}}{\text{sum of year digits}}$$

Year	Calculations		Percentage
First year	$\frac{30-0}{465}$	=	6.452%
Second year	$\frac{30-1}{465}$	=	6.237%
Third year	$\frac{30-2}{465}$	=	6.022%
Fourth year	$\frac{30-3}{465}$	=	5.806%
Fifth year	$\frac{30-4}{465}$	=	5.590%

Unlike the declining balance method, we need not calculate the basis of the value of the property every year. We simply multiply the original value by the percentage of deduction formula in the year in question. Thus, proceeding with our calculations, we find the following allowable depreciations. Value of the investment is $100,000, and that of the building structure is $81,250. First-year depreciation is $81,250 × 0.06452 = $5,242.25; second-year depreciation is $81,250 × 0.06237 = $5,067.56. Table 0-4 summarizes the three methods of depreciating the $100,000 investment property. Note that the sum of years' digits method uses 30 years as the depreciation period. It should be obvious to the investor that the 175% declining balance method is the best of the three.

The objective of the exercise above is to give the reader an appreciation of the different methods of depreciating investment property. I have found that the majority of real estate agents and tax consultants who I have come in contact with need to brush up on the tax laws. Whenever I am looking for an investment property, I make it a point to ask the realtor basic questions of depreciation schedules and general questions on taxes. Invariably I find that no one individual understands completely how or when to depreciate properties. I have even asked my lawyers about tax laws and, without exception, they refer me to someone else. The point is that you, as the investor and as the one who stands to profit, should have a basic working knowledge of the tax laws and, in particular, depreciation methods. Believe me, it yields good profits. The key is *knowledge*. Take time to learn the tax laws as they pertain to investment properties.

Let's continue with the logical extension of the depreciation methods and investigate the savings that can be obtained by an investor with a taxable income of $35,000. Assuming the investor is married and filing jointly, he or she will pay taxes as indicated in Table 0-5 using one of the three methods of depreciation. Remember depreciation is deductible from your ordinary income. We are assuming that the tax tables remain the same as

TABLE 0-4. Three Methods of Property Depreciation

YEAR	STRAIGHT-LINE		DECLINING BALANCE METHOD (175%)				SUM OF YEARS' DIGITS		
	Basis of Calculation	Allowable Deduction	Basis of Calculation	Straight-Line Depreciation		Allowable Deduction	Basis of Calculation	Percent of Deduction	Allowable Deduction
1	$\frac{\$81,250}{15}$	$5,416.67	$81,250	$5,416		$9,479	$81,250	0.0645	$5,240
2	$\frac{\$81,250}{15}$		71,770	4,784		8,373		0.0623	5,061
3	$\frac{\$81,250}{15}$		63,397	4,226		7,396		0.0602	4,891
4	$\frac{\$81,250}{15}$		56,001	3,733		6,533		0.05806	4,717
5	$\frac{\$81,250}{15}$	5,416.67	49,467	3,297		5,771		0.0559	4,541

TABLE 0-5. Influence of Property Depreciation on Taxable Income

YEAR	ORDINARY INCOME	TAX WITHOUT INVESTMENT	STRAIGHT-LINE Taxable Income	STRAIGHT-LINE Tax with Investment	DECLINING BALANCE Taxable Income[a]	DECLINING BALANCE Tax with Investment	SUM OF YEARS' DIGITS Taxable Income[b]	SUM OF YEARS' DIGITS Tax with Investment
1	$35,000	$7,357	($35,000 − $5,416)	$5,457	$25,521	$4,484	$29,758	$5,521
2		7,357			26,627	4,513	29,933	5,569
3		7,357			27,604	4,833	30,107	5,633
4		7,357	$29,584		28,467	5,105	30,282	5,681
5		7,357			29,229	5,345	30,458	5,745
First-year tax savings				$1,900		$2,873		$1,836

[a] Taxable income = $35,000 − allowable deduction (175%). Note all taxes from Schedule 1040A, 1980 tax tables.
[b] Taxable income equals $35,000 minus allowable deductions from Table 0-4.

they were in 1980. The table uses 15-year depreciation periods for straight-line and declining balance. A 30-year depreciation period is used for sum of years'-digits method. Allowable deductions for all methods are taken from Table 0-4.

Using the figures in Table 0-5, we can see the influence of property depreciation on our cash-flow position. The following can be deducted: If a couple makes a joint taxable income of $35,000 per year, they are paying $7,357 per year on federal taxes. With an investment property purchased after December 31, 1980, the depreciation will reduce their taxable income to $25,521 using the 15-year, 175% declining balance method. The net result is an increase of $2,873 in the take-home pay per year, or $237 per month. Thus, the mortgage payments can be $237 more than the rent.

Before we conclude with the summary of Phase 6, I should mention several items: (1) the above tables in this section show only the paper depreciation of an investment property. All interest paid on the loan or loans is also deductible. (2) Improvements (for example, a new washing machine) qualify for either declining balance or sum-of-years'-digits depreciation methods. These items qualify for accelerated depreciation in three to five years. (3) The rent must be considered as positive cash.

We have now concluded our initial phase of the controlled analysis of the investment process. Recall that I initially stated that the reason I wanted to walk you through the process is so that you would have a clear understanding of where you are headed. It should be clear that Phase 6, Sell/Profits, is directly tied to Phase 1, Overcoming Inertia, and that all phases are directly interrelated. If you do your homework, know where you stand, analyze properties and locations, do your cash-flow analysis, and so forth, the entire process should be enjoyable, free of maintenance headaches, with smooth property management, and with sizable profits and rewards. It is my sincere and honest desire that you enjoy your property investments as much as I have. I also hope that you have enjoyed reading this summary and the text that follows as much as I have enjoyed writing about the investment process. Good luck and Godspeed throughout your journey of "investing in America," where eagles soar.

Overview of the Entire Investment Process

The following pages provide an overview of the entire investment process. Figure 0-6, the Bracketed Decision-Flow Diagram, may appear extremely involved and complex. However, the investor must understand each part of the whole in order to have a sound investment program. Each part is simple to understand, and breaking down the investment process into small understandable steps is one of the first items that must be accomplished.

The problem we humans have is that we communicate in a serial

FIGURE 0-6
Bracketed Decision-Flow Diagram.

PHASE THREE
THE HUNT

- Methods of Buying
  - Assumptions
  - 2nd Trust
  - Land Contracts
  - Wraps
  - OTTB/OWC

- Hunting
  - Newspapers
  - Realtors
  - Owners
  - Friends
  - Foreclosures

- Cash Analysis
  - PITI
  - Down Payment
  - Rent
  - Tax Savings

- Alone/Partners
  - Partnership
  - Corporations

PHASE ONE
OVERCOMING INERTIA

- Set Goals
- Action Plan
- Determine Worth
- Husband Wife
- Use Libraries
- Market Analysis
- Analyze Locations
- Group Talks

PHASE TWO
THE CRITICAL DECISION

Cash Flow Analysis

fashion. That is, our speech and reading is conducted in a serial process. In actuality, the human brain can absorb data at rates much faster than human speech or than words from a book. Our problem is that the input and output communication channels (ears and mouth) can only input and output data at extremely slow information rates. An exception to these slow data rates is the human eye. The human eye can quickly scan the horizon and input masses of information in a parallel fashion. For example, the eye can view a farm scene, and in a matter of 30 seconds the entire condition of the farm could be input into the brain. The brain would receive

FIGURE 0-6 (*Cont.*)
Bracketed Decision-Flow Diagram.

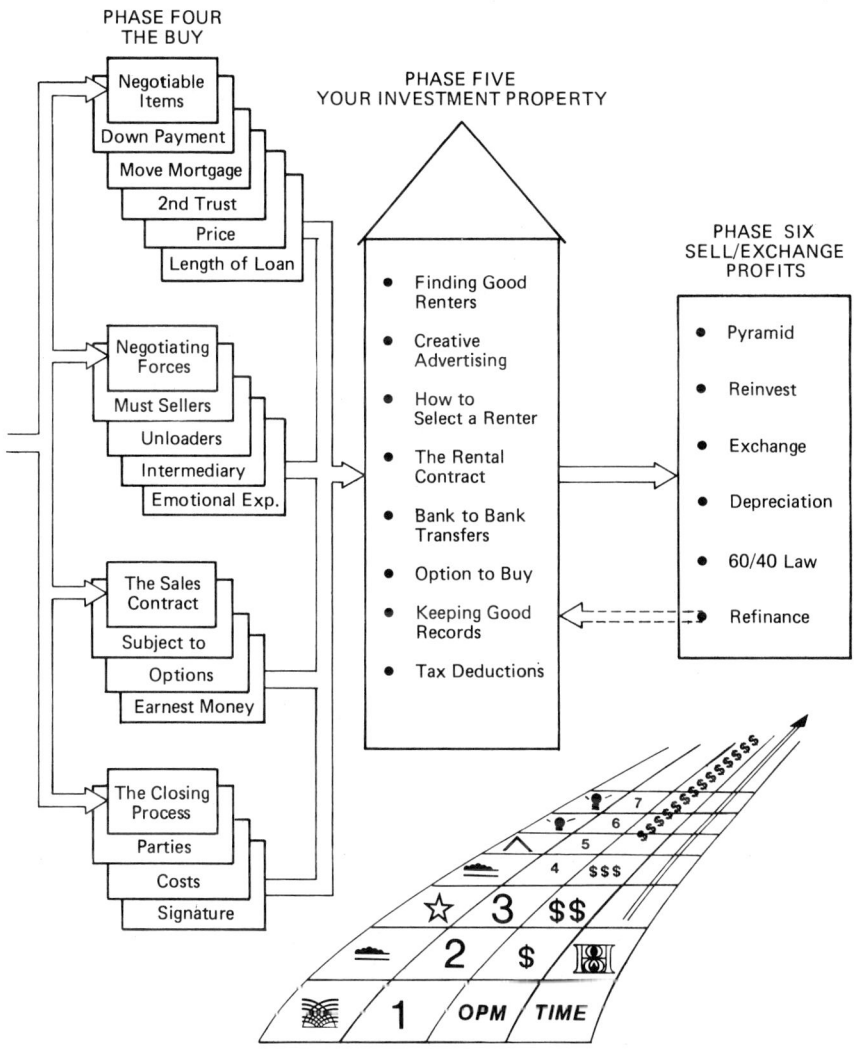

data on the cows, horses, fields, farmhouse, weather, colors, time of day, and so on. Our problem with this mode of communication is one of retainability. That is, in one week we remember little of what we saw on the farm. The Bracketed Decision-Flow Diagram is similar to the farm scene. We can quickly glance at the graphical representation; however, it is highly probable that one week from this date little will be retained of the investment process.

My purpose for having the summary followed by the actual decision-flow diagram is an attempt to defeat the problem of nonretainability. You

43

have now read about the investment process to a certain depth. You should have a good feel for the many items that must be understood before seriously embarking with your investment program. The remaining portion of this book is dedicated to serially inputting all the data that describes the decision-flow process. However, I emphasize that when reading Phases 1 and 2, be aware that Phases 3, 4, 5, and 6 are all interrelated to them. Thus, not understanding one phase of the investment program could jeopardize the success of the entire investment process. For example, not understanding the cash-flow analysis of Phase 2 could certainly prove disastrous. Certainly, the methods of buying (creative use of money) need to be understood. The reader is encouraged to continuously refer back to the graphical representation of the cash-flow analysis and reorient himself or herself relative to the entire investment process.

Phase 1

Overcoming Inertia

PHASE 1 OBJECTIVES

- Establish why residential real estate will continue to appreciate in value.
- Learn that the housing surge in the 1970s was only the beginning of the post–World War II baby boom housing demand.
- Learn to overcome negative terminology used in real estate. Overcome the banker-lurking-behind-the-barnyard syndrome.
- Recognize that Uncle Sam through the IRS is a most supportive financial partner.
- Overcome the "bad renter" syndrome.
- Learn to use realtors; increase the total number of sensors to as many as you can handle.
- Learn to use the library.
- Recognize the positive reinforcement value of group discussions.
- Recognize that your most treasured partner is your spouse. Husband and wife teams are dynamite.
- Establish why setting goals is so important.

Inertia is a word used in physics. It is used to describe Newton's laws of dynamics. One of these laws states that a body at rest tends to stay at rest, or a body in motion tends to maintain that motion unless it is acted upon to change that state by external forces. If a body is at rest, a certain force over and above what is required to maintain motion is required to overcome inertia. For example, consider a wheelbarrow. When you fill the wheelbarrow with sand or firewood and first push on the wheelbarrow to initiate forward motion, a force must be applied that is greater than the force needed to maintain motion. Once motion is initiated, however, the weight of the wheelbarrow acts as momentum to continue the forward motion.

46　OVERCOMING INERTIA

Our investment process is similar to the motion of the wheelbarrow. Think of the many times you have heard people say, "If only I had invested in gold in 1974" or "If only I had bought five houses in southern California in 1969." Since we are investigating investments in real estate, let us concentrate on that subject. The majority of people readily agree that investing in real estate is the correct thing to do. Take your own sample poll—your immediate family, uncles and aunts, your best friends—and ask them what they think about investing in real estate. The majority will agree that real estate is a good investment. However, some might say, "Real estate—yes, it is a good investment, but you should have bought years ago, because people will not continue to pay sky-high prices." (I will return to the issue of sky-high prices later in this book.) In general, then, the reason that the majority of people do not invest in real estate is that they simply do not understand the process of investing. I will be the first to admit that investing in real estate is not a simple matter. However, in the same breath I will add that the knowledge required to give you a good start can easily be obtained.

The primary reason you are reading this book is to gain knowledge in order to overcome inertia. Let's examine some of the hurdles that must be overcome.

Hurdles to Overcome When Investing in Real Estate
- The coming real estate crash
- Negative real estate terminology, for example, mortgage means death pledge
- Bad renters
- High interest rates
- Property maintenance
- Tax laws too complex
- More property, more debt
- Negative cash flow

The list could go on indefinitely, but you get the general trend of the types of hurdles needed to be overcome. Actually, your chances are favorable that just about any property that produces income (rent) will be a good investment. How good of an investment depends on how maintenance-free the property will be. However, let us return to the real issue at hand—how to overcome inertia *through knowledge.*

THE COMING REAL ESTATE CRASH

Let us address the first item—the "coming real estate crash." There is a theory being advocated today (as there has always been) that the real estate market will crash and property values will deflate simply because people will no longer pay the exorbitant prices. Let us examine the issues. In the past 15 years, I have traveled extensively, not only throughout America but throughout the world. I have traveled in Asia, the Middle East, Europe, the Pacific; I lived in the Middle East for four years, and in Germany for six. For three of those years I lived in West Berlin. I paid nearly $1,000 per month for a house rental in 1973. A good friend of mine and now a business partner also lived in West Berlin. At the time, his family included children in their teens and he required a large home. His rental payments were $1,500 per month, utilities not included. Now some of you no doubt will be saying—so you lived like two kings and rented the Charlottenburg Castle. I can assure you that our basic accommodations were no more than two- and four-bedroom homes with 1,250 to 2,000 square feet of space. In 1973, comparable homes in Dallas, Texas, would have sold for $30,000 to $50,000, depending on age and neighborhood. I use Dallas as an example because I was working for a company in Dallas when I left for the overseas job. In 1976, I returned to West Berlin and I made it a point to look up my former landlords, Herr and Frau Preuss-Sokolowski. In 1975 they had sold the two-bedroom home for $275,000. Yes, for over a quarter of a million dollars.

Now one may ask, "How can a German family afford to pay $275,000 for a home?" The truth is they cannot. What happens in Germany and especially in West Berlin is that two or three families buy one home, and the residence becomes a home for the two families. This is quite common. The homes are modified to allow privacy between the families, with such areas as the living room and dining room being shared. The bedrooms and perhaps side and back entrances are private.

When I lived in Germany, I made it a point to learn the German language. I recall my German instructor's home. I drove over to her home and we would read and discuss the latest news from the *Berliner Bild Zeitung*. My lessons would occur in the dining–living room area. For the first few weeks I thought she belonged to a huge family, because a steady stream of young people would troop through the living room. After a few months, I finally realized that three families lived in the same house. My instructor was perplexed that I found it strange and unconventional that two or more families would share one home. After I explained to her that in America the great majority of families own their homes, her initial impression that all Americans are rich was simply reinforced. Also, the fact that I drove a new Porsche (bought with profits from an investment) doubly reinforced her thinking that all Americans are rich. If by this time you haven't grasped the theme of the story, I will leave you with this thought—it is generally accepted that California is five to ten years ahead of the rest of the country. Of course, everyone knows that the price of homes in California (and Hawaii) went sky-high in the 1970s. Based on my firsthand experience in Europe (Germany, England, Austria, and Belgium), California is about ten years behind Europe.

One key factor that will continue to force real estate prices in America up is only in America do people believe that it is their inalienable right to own their home. It is not only their dream, it is, they believe, their heritage. Nowhere else in the world, not in Europe, Asia, Latin America, Africa, or any other place on this earth do people grow up thinking that they will some day own their own home. They have been conditioned to exorbitant prices, and they are destined to rent or participate in ownership partnerships.

Other factors that will push real estate to ever increasing heights are the post–World War II baby boom, coupled together with less building starts over the last two to three years. The average number of new households formed during the 1970s was 1,300,000. The U.S. census department estimates that between 1,600,000 and 2,000,000 new households per year will be formed between 1980 and 1990. This increase in new households should be of no surprise, as one can readily see the tidal wave of the effects of the post–World War II baby boom. In the 1950s the elementary schools were "busting" at the seams. In the 1960s and through the 1970s, the majority of the impact was on the colleges and universities. Now in the early 1980s, we can see universities having financial problems. The problem, of course, is directly related to the crest of the student tidal wave having left the universities.

What has happened to all of these babies born between 1945 and 1960? The answer is simple—they are all educated, productive Americans establishing households. Thus, demand will continue to push residential real estate to ever increasing prices!

Other important sociological events have also taken place:

- Young people are now getting married later in life.
- The population is definitely more mobile.
- Both husband and wife are working.

All three of the factors above are and will contribute to an increase in the demand for housing in the 1980s. Because young Americans are generally waiting until their late twenties to early thirties before establishing a household, the crest of the residential housing demand will be seen in the mid-1980s. The fact that the population is more mobile generates more sales of residential real estate, because each sale tends to increase the value of the property. The third factor (both husband and wife working) gives the family a much broader financial base, thus there is a greater demand for more expensive residential properties.

Let us now return to the issue at hand. Will there be a crash of real estate in the 1980s? The answer is definitely *no*! I can remember when I was growing up in El Paso, Texas, in the 1950s and hearing about homes selling from $5,000 to $10,000. At the time a $10,000 home was 1,000 to 1,400 square feet of space with two or three bedrooms. I recall my aunt and uncle discussing a $5,000 purchase, the price of which, at the time, was considered to be ridiculous. Perhaps the best thing to do was wait until the prices came down, for $5,000 was just too much money. Fortunately, my aunt and uncle did buy in the 1950s. They still have the same house, and it is the best investment they ever made. Had they continued to rent and deposited the $500 down payment in a savings account, the $500 would now be worth about $2,000. The purchasing power of the $2,000 in 1980 would be less than the $500 in 1955. However, the home they purchased in the mid-1950s is now worth over $45,000. Back to the coming real estate crash—in 1955, it was to occur in 1956; in 1965 in 1966; and in 1981, in 1982. Again I say, the coming real estate crash will *always* be in the future, *never* in the present.

Remember my story about my actual experience in West Berlin. People will pay whatever is required to obtain shelter, which, next to food, is the most essential commodity of life. The fact that a $5,000 home was out of the question in the 1950s emphasizes that prices are only relative to salaries and the prevailing conditions of the day. What seems unreasonable today will appear ridiculously affordable five or ten years from now. Another point to remember is that between 1955 and 1978 inflation averaged no more than 4% to 5%.

Even if the federal government is able to corral inflation by balancing the federal budget, residential real estate will continue to appreciate at a rate of 10% simply because its demand will continue to increase. By balancing the federal budget and by removing its policy on tight money, the federal government would cause interest rates to come down. As the interest rates come down, the price of homes goes skyward. Adjustable mortgage rates, graduated mortgages, variable-rate mortgages, and other innovative loan packages simply qualify more buyers. The more buyers, the higher the prices. There is nothing difficult to understand or complex about the supply and demand theory. Because of leverage, even with a reduced inflation rate of 7% to 8%, the percentage return on a $5,000 or $10,000 initial investment will be greater than 500% over a period of five years if your investment property is located in a good neighborhood. If you purchase your investment property with less than $5,000—and it *can* be done—your return is almost astronomical. Remember, only two things can cause your investment to depreciate in value: (1) decreased demand and (2) deterioration of the area where your investment is located. The second cause can be very easily controlled. Simply do not invest in a poor location.

Let us turn our attention to the first point cited above—demand. There are areas or cities that have decreasing demand in which property values *decrease in value.* Anaconda, Montana is one example of this. The value of real estate in Anaconda, Montana, is completely depressed. The reason is that there is no demand. Due to tight anti-pollution standards, the Anaconda Copper Corporation decided to close the copper refinery in Anaconda, Montana. Thus, people have deserted the city by the hundreds. There are simply no jobs. This is an isolated incident in which a city is entirely dependent on one industry. However, the same thing would happen to Odessa, Texas, if the oil wells went dry. It is, therefore, important that, when investing in any area of the country that is dependent on one industry, the industry in question is stable. However, for every area that has decreasing real estate values there are a hundred areas that have increasing real estate values. For example, the downtown areas of Anaheim and Santa Ana, California, are being rebuilt. All surrounding residential real estate is increasing in value. These pockets of upgraded areas exist throughout America. People in general tend to think that all of the big money in real estate has been made and that the boom is over. They are wrong! The boom is just beginning. Real estate will continue to increase in value as long as the population of America continues to expand and grow.

Table 1–1 shows the total number and percentage of adult Americans by age group. The data were taken from a study entitled "Housing Affordability in an Inflationary Environment" (PB-297-432, June 1979), con-

TABLE 1-1. Actual and Projected Estimates of the Adult U.S. Population by Age Groups, 1970–2000

AGE GROUP	1970	1975	1980	1985	1990	1995	2000
18–24	17.2[a]	19.2	29.4	27.8	25.2	23.2	24.6
	(13.5)	(13.8)	(18.4)	(16.4)	(14.2)	(12.7)	(13.0)
25–29	17.3	16.9	18.9	20.6	20.2	17.7	16.4
	(10.7)	(12.1)	(11.6)	(12.2)	(11.4)	(9.7)	(8.7)
30–34	11.6	14.0	17.2	19.3[b]	20.9	20.5	18.0
	(9.1)	(10.1)	(10.2)	(11.4)	(11.8)	(11.2)	(9.5)
35–44	23.1	22.8	25.7	31.3	36.6	40.1	41.3
	(18.1)	(16.4)	(16.1)	(18.5)	(20.6)	(21.9)	(21.8)
45–54	23.3	23.8	22.6	22.4	25.2	30.7	35.7
	(18.2)	(17.1)	(14.2)	(13.2)	(14.2)	(16.8)	(18.8)
55–64	18.7	19.8	21.1	21.5	20.5	20.3	22.9
	(14.6)	(14.3)	(13.2)	(12.7)	(11.6)	(11.1)	(12.1)
65 +	20.1	22.4	24.5	26.7	28.9	30.3	30.6
	(15.7)	(16.1)	(15.4)	(15.8)	(16.3)	(16.6)	(16.2)
Total adult population	127.7	138.9	159.4	169.5	177.4	182.8	189.5

[a] Numbers are in millions; the percentages of population are given in parentheses. Projections are based on an assumed continuation of present mortality trends, a fertility rate of 1.9 children per woman, a 2.7% annual increase in the gross national product, and an annual immigration of 400,000.
[b] Circled area indicates peak demand.

Source: Anthony J. Sulvetta, "Impact of Changing Demographic Patterns on Future Housing Needs: 1980—2000" (policy paper), June 1979.

ducted by the U.S. Department of Commerce for the U.S. Office of Management and Budget.

Note the total increase in both numbers and percentages of adult Americans in the age groups from 18 to 44 between 1980 and 1990. The increase in the number of people flooding into the 18 to 24 age group from 1975 to 1980 is astronomical—an increase of 10.2 million Americans. The number of Americans in the 18 to 24 age group peaks at 29.4 million in 1980 and holds steady until 1990. Even in the years 1995 and 2000 the total number of new adult Americans holds steady at approximately 25 million. The age groups of 25 to 29, 30 to 34, and 35 to 44 reflect a similar pattern. Remember all these increases reflect a staircase-like ascension through the 1980s and 1990s, even though we all tended to think of real estate demand reaching peak levels in the 1970s. The demand will be even greater in the 1980s and 1990s. In essence what we have is a continuous shock wave of Americans reaching adulthood in the 1975 to 1980 time period. Americans having reached adulthood (18 to 20 years of age) in the 1975 to 1980 time frame continue through their most productive years through the year 2000. A steady number of Americans continue to reach adulthood through the year 2000. Also due to the tremendous changes in the moral and social values of young Americans (separated couples, numerous marriages, unwed couples, single parents, and so forth), the need for housing will additionally increase.

The housing supply throughout the late 1970s and early 1980s decreased due to the tight money policies of the Federal Reserve. Because of high interest rates, the number of new housing starts fell dramatically from 1977 to 1980. This trend continues through 1981, and there is no relief in sight for at least one or two years. The bar graphs in Figure 1-1 were constructed utilizing data available from the news magazine *U.S. Housing Markets* published by the Advance Mortgage Corporation and from the *Washington Post*. The bar graphs are a reflection of the total number of building permits for single and dual (duplex) dwellings in the United States for the years 1977, 1978, 1979, 1980, 1981, and 1982.

The bar graph reflects what we all know has been happening to the building industry. Due to tight money and high interest rates, the number of new homes being built in America in the years 1979, 1980, 1981, and 1982 has fallen drastically. In the first half of 1982, the total number of new building starts was less than 452,000. The lessening of demand for new housing is being created artificially by the federal government by its control of the availability of money designed to curb inflation. It is only a question of time before the lid will explode and the value of homes will skyrocket to higher and higher prices. The two ingredients are present—increased demand and less building starts. Thus, new and existing homes will appreciate in value at ever increasing prices!

The underlying fundamental demand for homeownership will be the

FIGURE 1-1
Private housing permits.

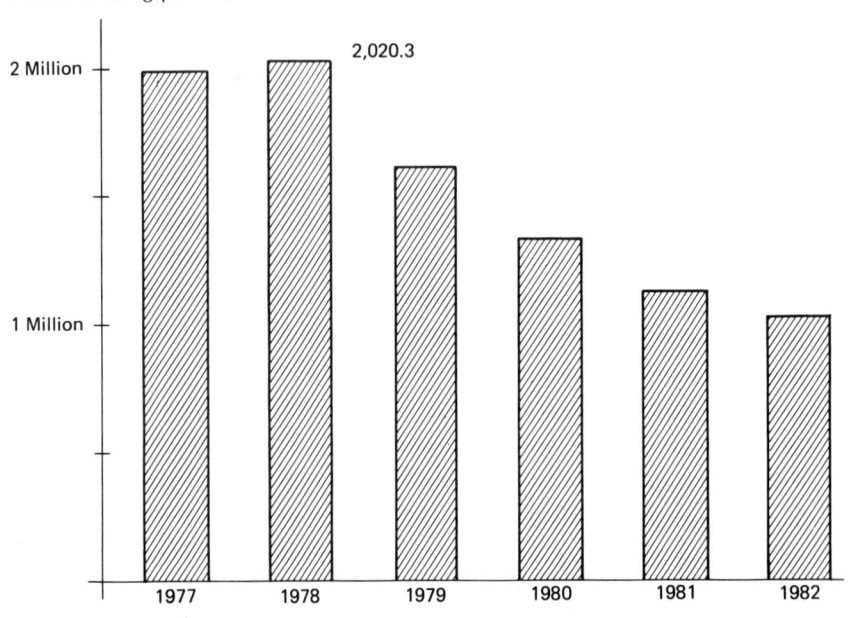

```
2 Million ┤     2,020.3
          │ ▓  ▓
          │ ▓  ▓
          │ ▓  ▓  ▓
          │ ▓  ▓  ▓
          │ ▓  ▓  ▓  ▓
          │ ▓  ▓  ▓  ▓  ▓  ▓
1 Million ┤ ▓  ▓  ▓  ▓  ▓  ▓
          │ ▓  ▓  ▓  ▓  ▓  ▓
          │ ▓  ▓  ▓  ▓  ▓  ▓
          │ ▓  ▓  ▓  ▓  ▓  ▓
          └─1977─1978─1979─1980─1981─1982─
```

continual increase in young people getting married and their establishing a household. All Americans believe that it is their inalienable right to have their own home. This has been hammered into all American minds from the time that they were children—it is part of the "American dream." The population growth attributable to the baby boom as shown so clearly in Table 1-1 and the continuing trend of higher divorce rates will additionally contribute to demand pressures in the housing market, particularly for single-family units.

I paraphrase from the U.S. Department of Commerce publication *Housing Affordability in an Inflationary Environment*: "Household formation for all age groups has been increasing at historically high rates and are projected to increase into the future as illustrated in Table VII. [See Table 1-1 in this text.] In 1960, 47.5 percent of the adult population were heads of households. By 1975 heads of households had increased to 51.2 percent and is projected to increase to 52.1 percent by 1980." Although the study fails to explain why the percentage of adults being the heads of households increases, the reason is the high divorce rate. Families split up and create a double demand for a home.

I have devoted extensive coverage to the subject of the so-called coming real estate crash. This is probably one of the main negative reasons why people hesitate to invest in real estate. I repeat: The "coming real estate crash" will *always* be in the future, never in the present.

Appropriate with my theme, "Invest in America, Where Eagles Soar," I close this section by quoting three famous Americans:

> Real Estate can't be lost or stolen, nor can it be carried away; managed with reasonable care, it is the *safest* investment in the world.
> FRANKLIN DELANO ROOSEVELT

> Invest in *inflation*, it is the only thing going up.
> WILL ROGERS

> Failure is more frequently from want of energy than from want of capital.
> DANIEL WEBSTER

TERMINOLOGY

An additional item that must be overcome when investing in residential real estate is the negative terminology used by lending institutions, for example, the key word—mortgage. *Mortgage* and *mortuary* come from the same French word *mort*, which means "death." *Mortgage* originally meant that a person had made a death pledge and if the conditions of the agreement were not met, the person who carried the loan would pay with his or her life. In actuality, the person would pay off the loan with bondage or become a slave of the holder (owner) of the note. Needless to say, we have come a long way from those days. However, one only has to look back within our lifetime to see that mortgage conditions have improved most favorably. For example, in the 1930s there was a high number of farms that were foreclosed by bankers. During the Great Depression, loans were not amortized, that is, they were not paid off in a specified period of time. Nor were loans guaranteed by the government. In general, if one wanted to buy a house, he or she would borrow money from the bank and the note would become due in five to ten years. Note the word *amortize*. I can only speculate that this meant at one time to reduce or remove the death pledge. I am sure you have at one time or another read a story about a villain dressed in black with a top hat, tails, and moustache, lurking behind the barnyard ready to foreclose on the farm and throw the farmer and his beautiful daughters out into the cold winter night.

I recommend that you do the following: Talk to someone who owns a home and who grew up in the 1930s, and casually discuss with him or her the possibility of taking out a second trust on the equity in the property, or refinancing it. Believe me, the majority of them will adamantly refuse. To borrow money from the equity in their own home is simply ridiculous and to use their own property as collateral on an investment property is simply unthinkable. The reason people will simply not use their property as collateral or will not refinance is highly complex, but I can assure you one of the reasons is that they have been conditioned to high security, and the very thought of possibly losing their home to the banker does indeed play a part in the decision-making process.

The way to overcome the deep and highly complex psychological barriers in people's minds concerning their own property is through knowledge. For example, merely taking out a second trust for the sake of having the money is certainly not recommended. Rather you need to have a certain plan regarding how the money is to be used, for instance, to borrow the money at a specified interest rate and buy high-yield savings certificates or bonds. The return would be the difference between the two interest yields. For example, in the period from 1979 to 1980 and again from 1980 to 1981, when the interest rates were 20% and higher, you could find second trust money for 12% and buy certificates of deposit that were returning 18% interest. The effective return was 6% less the loan origination fees. Another factor that should be taken into account is that the interest paid on the loan is tax deductible; however, the interest earned on certain bonds may be tax free. If the individual, for example, our hypothetical person who grew up in the 1930s with the banker-in-the-barnyard syndrome, was to understand that the second trust money could be used as a down payment on two or three rental properties, and the interest paid on the second trust loan plus the depreciation of the rental properties could be used to decrease his or her taxable dollars, he or she would see that it would be an excellent plan for the use of the equity dollars.

Over the last several years I have noted that a significant number of people suffer from the banker-in-the-barnyard syndrome. Some have mortgage payments of $200 per month with properties valued over $100,000. Their equity is over 80% of the value of the home! The equity sits there doing absolutely nothing. Lending institutions will gladly refinance up to 80% of the appraised value of such a home. With knowledge on how the refinancing of homes is determined, for example, the effective interest rate, and with knowledge of the tax laws, an individual in this position could obtain a $20,000 or $30,000 loan at absolutely no cost. You think it can't be done? Read on—I shall illustrate these figures in Phase 3, The Buy, when discussing methods of buying.

Another area that has people's money tied up is whole life insurance. I am not against insurance, as a matter of fact, I recommend that everyone have insurance. What I do not recommend is that a person carry *whole* life insurance. If you presently have a whole life policy, cash it in and buy term insurance. The reason is simple. Because of inflation, a $50,000 whole life policy purchased today will be worth less than $6,500 in today's market 20 years from now at 10% inflation. Life insurance works exactly the opposite of the equity increase on a home. That is, a $100,000 policy will be worth approximately $12,000 20 years from today because inflation will erode the purchasing power of the dollar. I can easily remember when my father believed that a $10,000 policy would provide him retirement money. Need I say more? When you do decide to cash in your whole life policy, your insurance agent will kick and fuss and fume. He or she will tell you that it is absolutely the worse thing you can do. Do not believe it. Hold steady on course, withdraw your money, and start an investment program. When I "saw the light" and decided to cash in my insurance policies, it took me more than six months to receive my money. My wife, my mother, and I all had to sign forms and more forms to receive the money. Indeed, one insurance company required a certified death certificate of my father, who died in 1978. I had purchased the policy in college, and he was one of the original beneficiaries. It is odd that when I was paying the monthly premiums I did not have any problems. Be patient and insist on your money—in time you will receive what is rightfully yours. Upon receiving the cash value of the policy, invest it in America!

I close this section with the following question: What do the life insurance companies do with the money from the policyholders of whole life? I will give you a clue. They, the life insurance companies, have been investing in America for the last two centuries with other people's money! If you ever go to Omaha, Dallas, New York, or any other insurance capital, scan the building horizon and see if you can guess who has been most successful.

BAD RENTERS

The problem of bad renters is one of the most feared and one of the easiest to correct. In reducing your chances of a bad renter, it is vitally important to buy the correct property at the proper location. Buying property in move-in condition at something better than junkyard, bargain basement prices automatically provides you a safeguard against potentially destructive renters. During Phase 3 of my experience (Hunting for Properties), it was my experience that bad renters come with the terrain. It is unusual to find a property that is in a bad state of repair in a good neighborhood. However, properties that are selling below average—that initially appear to have attractive terms—are generally in decaying, run-down, low-rent districts. You absolutely want to stay clear of low-rent, decaying neighborhoods.

Some books recommend buying run-down properties, and at times it may have some merit. For example, a home that has been unoccupied because of a settlement of a will, for instance, and that happens to be in a good neighborhood may be a good buy. A little paint, a trim of the bushes, and so forth may bring you a nice return in one year or may even turn the property around in a few months.

It is important to stay involved in the process of selecting a renter. There are numerous factors to consider when selecting the family or individual who will rent your investment. I devote considerable detail to this process in Phase 5, Your Investment Property. Always interview any prospective renter. Of paramount importance in the selection is to inspect the home that he or she presently occupies. If the present home of residence is not being maintained, chances are your investment property will not be maintained either. Calling his or her landlord and the previous landlord is also a good idea. In Phase 5 I discuss this subject in detail.

I do recommend you purchase properties in move-in condition. However, be sure you know enough about the entire investment process to deviate from this rule if conditions dictate. Knowledge is your most important tool.

Other items I listed at the outset of Phase 1—high interest rates; property maintenance; tax laws too complex; more property, more debt; and negative cash flow are all interconnected and directly relate to your particular cash-flow situation. I shall discuss interest, taxes, and cash flow in considerable detail in Phase 2, Critical Decision. I call these items my financial vectors because they have force, direction, and magnitude. For the time being I will summarize on a positive note. Being in debt does not necessarily mean that one has less money. What is desired is positive cash (money from renters and tax savings) to offset any negative cash (debts owed). A side effect, but a very important one—being in debt and able to pay your bills—is that you generate good credit. Having good credit is vital for anyone who wishes to seriously pursue investing in real estate. The financial vectors properly handled can become quite manageable. In my treatise on the financial vectors, I reduce the calculations to a five-minute exercise. With a little practice you can do the computations in three seconds. Now you may be asking that if it is so simple, why not tell me now? Good question. The actual computations are not simple. However, if you understand the process, you can make some assumptions (based on the property to be purchased), and the results will be within $\pm$ 5% of the actual cash flow. Remember through knowledge you remove the serious doubt of debt, high interest rates, tax laws and negative cash flow. You must know where you stand financially and be able to determine a good buy within minutes of receiving the conditions and terms of sale.

Now, let us continue with Phase 1. The required knowledge for investing in residential real estate can be obtained. I recommend that you go out for a drive on a Sunday afternoon and get a good feel for the type of property that is for sale. Look at everything—single-family detached, condominiums, townhouses, duplexes, triplexes, and quadplexes. Initially concentrate on the asking price. Take careful notes about the neighborhood: access to major roads, commercial buildings, parks, schools, shopping areas, and so forth. Later in Phase 3, this information becomes very important. Even if you have a good memory, you should take notes, since you will find that after several neighborhoods and 20 or 30 homes, the facts and figures tend to get lost in the mountain of information.

After obtaining a good initial feel for the areas that offer good location possibilities, start looking for properties that fit your terms. At this time you may be asking, *what terms?* The terms that you apply at this stage are general in nature. For example, after you have reduced your area of potential investments to specific locations, choose another Sunday and go look at those investment properties that have assumable loans, for example, those that are owner financed, those that allow for a wraparound loan, those whose owners have stated that they are willing to carry back a second trust, or any combination of the above. In Phase 1, you are in a kind of "spring training." You are merely getting ready for the real season in the fall. Learn from this trial period. Ask questions and broaden your knowledge.

After you have obtained a good understanding of the different areas by inspection, change to a different media to find your potential properties. Start by scanning the advertisements in your local newspapers, and then use your telephone. Circle all potential properties. If the property does not fit your terms, ask the realtor if he or she has any properties that do fit your terms and conditions. Be sure to emphasize your terms and conditions. Do this just one afternoon, and I can assure you that the telephone will not stop ringing for the next two weeks. Through the use of the simple instrument, the phone, you have increased the total number of scanning sensors that are detecting, recognizing, and informing you of any potential investment properties. In essence the realtors are working *for* you, since they understand that finding the right property will generate a sell. This technique can be used very effectively once you have done your basic research. Through the use of verbal descriptors, you can form an opinion of potential investment properties. Only after you have been given the terms and conditions and after you have reduced the number of potential investments to a manageable number do you inspect the properties. I refer to this technique as *telephone leverage.*

The fact that you have given the realtors specific terms will do one of two things:

1. The realtor will be completely turned off, as he or she will quickly determine that you are fairly knowledgeable in real estate and will purchase only what fits your terms. Some will immediately tell you it is impossible, that with an assumable loan you need at least $30,000 down. *Don't believe it,* keep on searching.

2. The realtor will attack your request with the vigor of a hungry tiger. This is the type of vigor and gusto you want. The knowledgeable realtor

58 OVERCOMING INERTIA

understands that if he or she finds the property with your terms, there will be a sale.

Available in all real estate agencies are computerized listings of properties in any given area. All real estate agents can obtain straight listings as a function of geographical areas, type of homes, price, and so forth. You are interested in listings that have assumable loans with the owner carrying back a second trust. I am continuously surprised to find how few realtors can actually do this. Once in Palmdale, California, I talked to one realtor who literally threw me out, saying, "Impossible, it just simply cannot be done!" Next door, his competition had a list of 20 or more properties in the Palmdale-Lancaster area, all with assumable loans and with owners willing to a carry a second trust. Figure 1–2 is a graphical representation of how the system actually functions. In one afternoon you can call about 20 properties that have potential and automatically have 20 realtors working for you. In Phase 3, when you are actually hunting for your property, I shall discuss other means of searching. For example, find a cluster of potential properties. Then, for a few dollars or less make 100 leaflets stating that you are interested in buying real estate, and that the owner should call you *before* listing with a realtor. Take one hour and distribute the leaflets in a

FIGURE 1-2
Shotgun approach for using realtors.

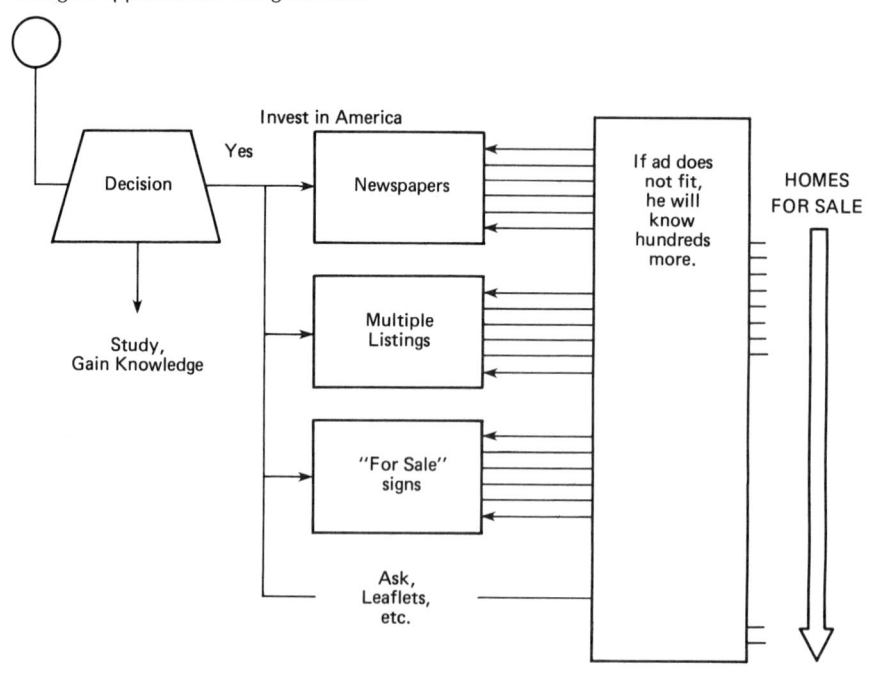

good neighborhood. I discuss in detail other means of advertising in Phase 3. Again, recall that you are now in the phase during which you are gaining knowledge.

USE YOUR LIBRARY

I strongly recommend that you tour every library in your city, county, or district and take some time to chat with the librarian in the reference department. I would like to emphasize one very important point. Throughout your involvement in purchasing investment properties, all individuals who you come in contact with have an interest that is directly opposite to your desire of lowest purchase price with minimum down payment. Reflect upon this. Certainly the seller is not on your side. The bankers, lawyers, and real estate agents are unlikely to be, since they are working off percentage points and it is in their interest to have high prices with plenty of cash on the table. However, one individual *is* in your corner. This is true whether you live in Seattle, El Paso, Cedar Rapids, or Richmond. A librarian will go to great lengths to provide any assistance that you desire. Give it a try. Take a long lunch hour and visit your nearest library. Ask the librarian at the reference department for information on real estate transactions. Next week take another long lunch hour and pick at random a lending institution, walk in, and ask them hard questions on wrap loans, commercial loans, or equity participation mortgages. At first, they probably won't understand what you are talking about, and if they do, obtaining the information will be like pulling teeth. Remember, the loan officers do not write those fancy TV jingles. When you finally do have information, it will probably leave you more confused than when you walked in. Then take a few hours and go to the library. Ask the reference librarian the same questions. Even though the librarian may not understand wrap loans, he or she will certainly assist you in any way possible in finding information. It just so happens that the majority of my information used in Phase 3 concerning equity participation mortgages comes from recent articles in newspapers from all across the country, primarily from the *Washington Post, New York Times,* and *Los Angeles Times.* The librarians in several libraries within a 30-mile radius of my home were most helpful in obtaining this information. Following is an outline of some basic material that can be found in any public library. It is best if you use a main library.

> *Publications Available at Public Libraries*
> - Financial transactions of all real estate sales
> - Newspaper indexes by subject
> - Zoning publications
> - Five-year road plans

60 OVERCOMING INERTIA

- Future development plans (published by city or county)
- Board of Supervisors' minutes
- Planning bulletins
- Rent handbooks
- Population growth trends
- Magazine indexes by subject
- City or county fiscal plans
- Annual reports—have predictions come true?

For the sake of brevity I will not discuss all of the listings given above. However, two areas are of such great importance that it would be a disservice not to mention them. Main libraries carry publications that provide detailed information on all real estate transactions within their boundaries. You usually have to ask more than one librarian and explain more than once what you are looking for, since these publications are not on the best seller lists. These publications contain all of the details of purchased properties. They list the sell price, all trusts (first, second, and so forth), the terms (amount and interest) of the promissory notes, and which lending institutions hold the trusts. Additionally, the publications name the seller and buyer, the address of the property, and the page number of the deed book located at the city or county courthouse. The sales made in the past year are listed in reverse chronological order, alphabetically by subdivision. Sales made approximately one or two years back are recompiled and available *by street!* This type of information is helpful to obtain accurate and detailed appreciation rates.

You can extract mountains of data from the publications. For example, since the guides are in chronological order by subdivision and since very recent transactions are listed in reverse chronological order, you can easily obtain the most current sell prices in a given area. The terms of the sale indicate whether the purchase involved new financing or an assumption. Based on the sell price and the amount of money borrowed (first and second trusts), you can determine the down payment. You can also determine if VA or FHA loans are approved in a given area. Since the guides go back many years and are available at all main libraries, you can do an exact market analysis on a given neighborhood. This type of information can also be used to appraise your investment property when you are ready to sell.

For example, Tables 1–2 and 1–3 show the appreciation of residential real estate in the two subdivisions of Springfield, Virginia. I presently have investment properties on the streets selected, all figures are accurate representations of the overall picture. Note the following points of interest in Table 1–2:

- Properties show steady appreciation, approximately 5% between September 1975 to September 1978.

Overcoming Inertia   61

- Appreciation from September 1978 to November 1980 was 9%.
- Note that properties numbered 9, 10, and 11 have VA loans. VA is approved in this subdivision.
- Property number 2 is interesting. The seller carried the *entire* value of the property. He had no need for cash. (Unfortunately, I wasn't the one who bought the property.)

TABLE 1-2. Property Appreciation
Subdivision: Kings Park, Springfield, Virginia
Street: Morningside Drive

Address	Sell Date	Sell Price	Mortgage	Remarks
1. 5605	9-75	$ 64,500	$64,500	30-year VA
2. 5612	10-75	67,500	50,000	Seller carried back all
3. 5420	6-76	67,000	59,000	30-year conventional
4. 5518	8-76	64,300	55,000	30-year conventional
5. 5535	3-77	71,950	59,000	30-year conventional
6. 5528[a]	2-78	75,950	70,000	30-year conventional
			4,000	5-year seller
7. 5504	5-78	71,750	34,094	Assumption
8. 5501	7-78	77,000	61,600	30-year conventional
9. 5504	8-78	73,000	69,300	30-year VA
10. 5611	9-78	74,000	71,000	30-year VA
11. 5615[b]	8-79	84,950	80,000	30-year VA
12. 5615	4-80	90,900	66,950	30-year conventional
13. 5428	10-80	98,500	90,000	30-year conventional
14. 5517	11-80	102,500	92,500	30-year conventional

[a] My investment property. Note that I paid an above average price; however, the terms were excellent.
[b] Property turned around in six months; profit—$6,000!

Note the following points of interest in Table 1-3:

- Steady appreciation
- VA-approved neighborhood
- Property number 5 was purchased with $7,000 down, assumption, and the owner carrying the remaining equity as a second trust.
- Property number 14 could have probably been purchased with nothing down by finding a buyer for a portion of the second trust.

Other areas that require examination are the five-year development plans of the city or county. Of particular importance is the direction of expansion and any major developments scheduled for the future. For example, major arteries for access and egress, planned shopping centers, and industrial complexes that are scheduled for development within the next two or three years is important information. Purchasing an investment property next to a planned new residential development area is most beneficial. The value of the new homes will pull the market price of your investment property upward.

It may take a little time (two or three hours) to comb through such

TABLE 1-3. Subdivision: North Springfield, Springfield, Virginia
Street: West Road

	Address	Sell Date	Sell Price	Mortgage	Remarks[b]
1.	5414	6–75	$62,750	$40,751	30-year conventional
2.	5215	9–75	58,000	58,000	30-year VA
3.	5600	10–75	46,000	31,636	Assumption
4.	5318[a]	3–76	65,500	47,517	Assumption
				10,000	10-year seller financing
5.	5203	9–76	64,000	57,000	10-year seller financing
6.	5210	6–77	71,200	71,125	30-year VA
7.	5206	8–77	73,950	70,250	30-year VA
8.	5413	8–77	73,950	70,250	30-year VA
9.	5201	10–78	79,900	77,400	30-year VA
10.	5506	10–78	73,500	66,000	30-year conventional
11.	5500	2–80	87,000	87,000	30-year VA
12.	5601	4–80	85,000	55,000	30-year conventional
13.	5413	6–80	95,000	62,500	Assumption
14.	5515	8–80	90,000	16,504	Assumption
				53,300	10-year seller financing

[a] My investment property.
[b] Conventional and VA equals new loans; Assumption equals loan assumed.

items as the minutes of last year's board of supervisor meetings, but doing so will give you a good idea of future development programs. Information contained in the real estate reports will also indicate which lending institutions are lending money and at what rate. Since the sell price and the amount of the mortgage are listed, you can easily determine what percentage of the sell price is being financed. Remember your ultimate goal is to put down as little of your own money as possible.

Using the library, I have been successful in determining which lending institutions have wraparound programs. The wraparound method of purchasing an investment property (also referred to as an all-inclusive deed of trust) literally wraps around an existing mortgage. They offer great benefits, especially if the investor has a second property with collateral. The seller of the property is asked to take back a second trust with the second property acting as collateral. The property being purchased is now free over the top 10% or 20% (size of the second trust), thus allowing the new wraparound loan for the remaining 80% or 90%. The section on methods of buying in Phase 3 uses graphics and bar graphs to explain this method. The point is that you first need to find which lending institutions have wraparound programs. Moving the mortgage off the property can also work using money available from commercial second trust lenders. Newspapers, telephone directories, and libraries provide excellent source information. Your knowledge of the entire investment process shall later prove to be indispensable, especially when discussing possible loans with banking institutions. I have been so successful using this "deal from a position of strength" technique, that on several occasions I have had loan officers suggest that *they* would be interested in a partnership arrangement using *their* money, not the banks.

GROUP DISCUSSIONS

Discuss your ideas, information found in libraries, neighborhood evaluations, financial position, and so forth with a friend or relative who is also interested in investing in residential real estate. Discussions among friends who have a common interest encourage the support of new, innovative, creative, and imaginative thinking. Group decisions carry more weight and thus tend to more strongly motivate all members of the group to carry them out. Be sure to encourage ideas from all members. Give equal time to each one. Listen with as much concentration as when you table your own ideas. Once the group makes a corporate decision to investigate a given area of the real estate investment process, a person who participated in the group will feel that he or she shared in the decision. Thus, the individual will be more interested in carrying out the decision task. One of the great benefits of group commitment is that the corporate body will generally be willing to explore new ideas. Group ideas also tend to be more imaginative. For example, one person or couple acting alone may not be willing to borrow $5,000 at 15% on a signature loan and buy a discounted second trust that pays 23% or more. The $5,000 would be used to buy the second trust from the seller of the property that the other member or couple of the group purchased. The couples would then reverse positions, and the couple that purchased the property would borrow $5,000 on a signature loan and use that to buy a discounted second trust from the seller of the property that the first couple purchased. It is not important at this time that you understand the financial transaction of the exchanged discounted second trust. This particular method is entitled the second trust exchange method (Method 5). I will discuss this method and many more in Phase 3. What *is* important is that you recognize that there is strength in numbers and that there is positive reinforcement gained from groups sharing your common real estate interest.

The value of group discussions is mainly their inherent ability to create a "brainstorming" atmosphere. For example, divide your responsibilities when gathering information. You and your spouse might investigate townhouses/condominiums in the northern section of the city, and your associates (another couple) would investigate properties in the northwestern part of the city. After each couple has completed its investigation, get together and review the findings. This technique is especially worthwhile when doing research at the library. Using real estate guides that provide details of completed sales, four people can do four parallel market analyses of selected subdivisions. You will invariably find that some subdivisions appreciate faster than others. Find out why one particular subdivision is prime for investment. Use the important information you gain to evaluate other locations as well.

Group discussions also provide an intangible positive vector that educators and psychologists call *positive reinforcement*. The group members discuss their findings, and each individual will provide a push to the others to generate the forward motion that overcomes inertia. Be careful that you include in your group only individuals (couples) that are serious about real estate investments. You do not need to carry dead weight, nor do you need an anchor around your neck. Try to divide your tasks equally and commit them to paper. For example:

Items for Frank and Beverly
1. Call five ads from newspapers advertising, "I buy discounted second trusts." Obtain details.
2. Talk to at least three lending institutions about variable-rate mortgages.

Items for Dave and Bess
1. Find and inspect three properties with assumptions and owner will finance part of the equity.
2. Using information from realtors and your own independent analysis (information from library), determine if the properties (assumptions) are good buys.

Set a deadline and reassemble for a discussion of what has been learned. Once having collected the assigned data, the group should encourage brainstorming through creative thinking. Use the method referred to by educators as *deferred judgment*, which encourages off-the-wall, innovative ideas and thoughts. Ideas, thoughts, and dreams are recorded as they surface and evaluated for soundness and practicality at a later session. The purpose of the deferred judgment method is to encourage bold, unique, creative thinking. For example: (1) Can we actually buy an investment property and end up with more cash than we started with? (The answer is *yes*. See Method 8 in Phase 3.) (2) Wraparound loans will only be offered to 85% of the appraised value. How do we obtain 100% financing? (It *can* be done. See Method 10 in Phase 3.) (3) How do we create good credit? (4) How do we find good renters? All of these subjects and many more can be discussed. You will be pleasantly surprised that once you find eager, energetic members within the group, that it is fun to talk about making money.

Remember that you need commitment coupled with determination, persistence, vigor, and gusto! In actuality, once you understand the investment process, you will wonder why it took you so long to find the golden rainbow.

HUSBAND AND WIFE TEAMS

Throughout Phase 0 and Phase 1, I have often referred to the team of the husband and wife. It is generally the single most important hurdle that must be overcome when investing in real estate. Both must understand what is being done. The ideal situation is to have each share equally in the investment experience. However, because of job and household responsibilities to the children, it will not be a 50-50 proposition. Regardless of who pulls most of the workload, it is vitally important that both understand the investment goals. The main reason I use the word *vector* in Vector Bracketed Decision-Flow Diagram and Vector Cash-Flow Analysis is because of my own experiences with husband and wife teams. Since I have been fairly successful with my own investments in residential real estate, I invariably give considerable advice to friends and relatives. Within my own family and friends I encounter the spectrum of all psychological fears and even some advocates of the real estate crash. I have frequently found that one member of the husband and wife team is committed to investing and the other is not. When this condition occurs, there is one force canceling out the other, and the end result is zero. For example, an acquaintance of mine in Texas earns a taxable income of $1,800 per month and has a present mortgage of $192 per month. His equity is 90% of the value of his house, which has two bedrooms. He has three children—two girls and a boy. His wife has been complaining that the children are growing up and that the boy should no longer share a room with the girls. I sat down with both of them and went through a complete financial analysis of their situation. We discovered that, providing they purchase a home with proper terms and they cash in their whole life insurance policies, they could easily buy a $62,000, five-bedroom home. I took two hours the same day and found a property that required a $550 per month mortgage payment. Since the payment on the new property would have a high percentage of interest money, it would be completely tax deductible. If they choose to rent their present home, the property would produce an immediate positive cash flow of $150 per month. Canceling their whole life insurance would net them another $95 per month. They would actually improve their cash-flow situation by assuming a mortgage on a new home, renting their present home, and cashing in their whole life insurance policies. (Recall that earlier in the book I recommended term insurance.) As of this writing, however, the couple has not improved their position. The reason is that she says yes and he says no, we can't afford it. The husband's problem

66 OVERCOMING INERTIA

is fear of the unknown—tax laws, depreciation schedules, W-4 forms, VA or FHA assumptions, discounted second trusts, and so forth. To make matters even worse, he, the "negative force," is a *real estate agent!*

Let me stress again the importance of both the husband and wife acting as one totally integrated team. Acting as one, they can be dynamite. One can search and hunt; the other can handle the financial transactions. One can research the library; the other can comb through newspaper advertisements. One can walk into various real estate agencies and discuss potential investments; the other can take on the bankers. Use your imagination, be innovative, and do not be concerned if your idea initially receives mixed reviews. Keep on with your basic research and learn as much as possible as the investment process unfolds. Be sure that both you and your spouse are in touch with each other's thoughts and ideas. Remember as a total integrated team dedicated to achieving the same purpose, you can be *dynamite!*

SET GOALS

Take a quick look at Figure 1-3. The horizontal line represents time—it can be seconds, minutes, hours, days, months, or years. The vertical line represents your understanding or interpretation of success. Numbers on the

FIGURE 1-3
Setting goals.

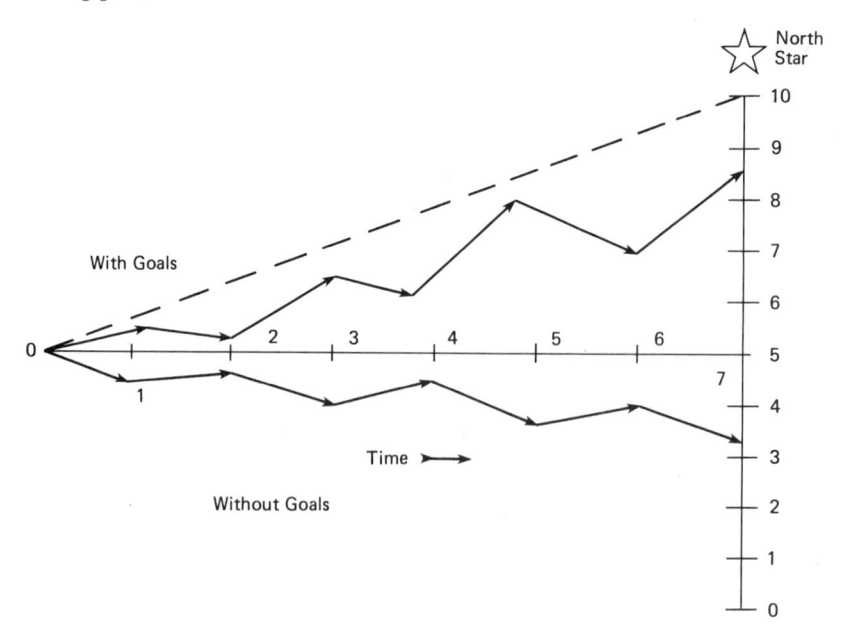

success scale from one to ten represent an average American with a warm, happy, and financially secure life. A zero represents the lowest rung of the success ladder, and a ten represents the highest. The majority of people live their lives setting goals for the near future. For example, when you get up in the morning you know that you are going to work and that you will return home around five or six that afternoon. Perhaps you also have dinner planned for that night, followed by a sporting event. In fact, you plan your day and set out to accomplish your goals. People in general also have goals for the months and perhaps years ahead. A high-school or college student lives for the day he or she graduates. Professionals may have more sophisticated business plans. These business plans set sales quotas and expected profits. These are definite business goals. Without these goals a business or company would wander aimlessly through the business year. Most probably, the company would end in bankruptcy. As individuals, each of us also needs to set far-reaching goals. However, the majority of Americans do not! We set our day-to-day and perhaps month-to-month goals, but we do not set long-term goals, for example, five-year plans. Have you really considered what you will be doing five years from now? Probably not.

Let us return to Figure 1-3. At the top of the success ladder is a star. Let us call this your ultimate goal, your "North Star," your height of success. Your goal is represented by the star, which "guides" you through time as you travel to reach your ultimate goal. Time is represented in years. The figure shows seven years. At the start of your journey, you are at a five on the success ladder. At time equals zero (start of journey), you determine what your goal will be seven years from now. Never lose sight of the ultimate goal as you travel through years one, two, three, and so on. Be prepared to have your setbacks during your travels, but correct your course to reach your ultimate goal. The setbacks are represented by the arrows going downward. Prepare yourself to have setbacks in both your preplanned and unplanned journeys. When setting your goals, the probability of reaching your ultimate goal in seven years is definitely improved. With goals you correct your course at each setback and always reach for the ultimate.

Without goals, you drift aimlessly and may not even recognize that you are losing ground. Think about it. If you have ever said, "the faster I run the further I fall behind," it is because you have no frame of reference. Your frame of reference should be your far-reaching goal. In fact, you may not reach the ultimate goal, but in seven years you could be at the 8.5 rung of the ladder of success, which is 3.5 points above your position at the start of the journey. In general, the majority of Americans travel the journey of life with no far-reaching goals. (Try asking someone what he or she will be doing five years from now.) Without planning, external factors (vector forces) will rule your life, for example, high prices for energy, high interest rates, inflation, and personal success and tragedy. Without planning, you may find that in seven years you are at some point in the success ladder below the start of the journey. You can easily see this happening to people (retirees, for example) who are on fixed incomes or who have not improved their financial positions since inflation began eroding the purchasing power of their dollars.

I am sure that by now you have correctly interpreted the intent of Figure 1-3. Set your goals! Discuss them with your spouse, friends, relatives, boyfriend, or girlfriend. Commit yourself to that designated path. Commit your goals to writing and review them on a frequent basis, especially when you first get started.

COMMITMENT TO A GOAL

Having determined to make your commitment to purchase income-producing real estate, write a contract with yourself and your spouse to purchase a given number of investments over a given period of time. I particularly like this type of commitment because it provides for growth as your investment portfolio pyramids and because it gives your investment program a solid foundation from the initial beginning. The information contained in the following outline, Commitment to a Goal, is a sample contract with solid projected returns (profits) on your investment properties. The commitment should be reviewed on a periodic basis. Feel free to add, subtract and/or modify according to your particular financial position.

Commitment to a Goal
 I. *Purpose*
   A. _____ and _____ is (are) hereby committed _____ to a long-term goal to invest in America. The specific plan shall be to invest in income-producing real estate, preferably residential real estate, for the express purpose of producing a profit _____ years from the date of this commitment.
   B. General rules to be followed are:
     1. Use minimum cash, highest possible leverage.
     2. Buy only in good locations.
     3. Own my own home plus at least one rental.
     4. Seller financing, either a second or a third trust.
     5. Sell, exchange, or refinance after three to five years. Flexible, I (we) can use equity in the investment property to pyramid.
     6. Assumptions or other creative financing techniques.
     7. Avoid low-rent, run-down areas.
     8. Look for properties in move-in condition first, but be aware of possible buys of the worst house in a good location.
     9. Avoid negative cash flow that I (we) cannot sustain.
     10. Use the Vector Bracketed Decision-Flow Diagram and Vector Cash-Flow Analysis.

II. *Specifics*
   A. The commitment will be to purchase _____ property(ies) every _____ year(s) for the next _____ years. Purchase of above properties shall be based on the cash-flow analysis and at no time does the commitment bind me (us) to only the number of properties shown above.
   B. It is my (our) goal to retire within _____ years and devote all my (our) time to the management of my (our) investment properties. I (we) expect to have _____ in assets by the year _____.

III. *Initial Expenses and an Estimate of Projected Profits*
   A. Investment property A
      Address: _____
      _____
      _____
   B. Estimate of profits (_____% inflation).
Down Payment	Initial Cost	0	1	2	3	4	5
____	____	__	__	__	__	__	__
   C. Profit at 1, 2, 3, 4, and 5 years.
      Estimate of sell price at _____ year minus initial cost. (Obtain appreciation rate from library or county courthouse records.)
   D. Tax information
      (Maintain a copy of all tax deductions and depreciation of property.)

DETERMINE YOUR WORTH

Following are instructions to determine your financial worth. See Table 1-4 for a sample chart.

1. List all salaries less taxes.
2. List all accounts, revolving and personal.
3. Subtract total monthly payments for all accounts from total salaries. Continue subtotals for all items.
4. List all cash in checking and savings accounts.
5. List all federal and state taxes currently being paid. Note: Include property taxes in real estate payments below.
6. Market value of all real estate.
7. List holders of all trusts, monthly payments, and the total amount of the lien.
8. List all securities—CDs, stocks, TBs, bonds, and so forth.
9. If securities are purchased on margin, include payments and amount of debt.
10. List all insurance plus cash value.
11. Payments to insurance companies.
12. Other: autos, furniture, jewelry, boats, rugs—anything that has collateral value.

70 OVERCOMING INERTIA

13. Total all columns. The sum total of the center column is the amount that is being used to live on. This amount is used to buy groceries, gasoline, clothes, vacation, and entertainment. You will be surprised just how high this figure is in most individual analyses. If necessary, save some money (if none is listed in items 4 or 8). Start with a small nest egg, buy real estate and build your investment portfolio.
14. Collateral properties: Borrow against your total value and start your investment program!

TABLE 1-4. Asset/Debt Information Table

ASSETS	INCOME/VALUE	DEBTS	
1. salary		2. accounts	payments
sub total	→3.[a]	← sub total	
4. cash—checking-saving	interest	5. taxes	
6. real estate[b]	rent	7. mortgage liens	
sub total	→	← sub total	
8. securities	value	9. margin accts.	
10. insurance	cash value	11. payments	
12. others—auto, jewelry, furniture	value		

13. GRAND TOTALS

14. The difference between the total value of assets and debts is your total worth. The difference between income (salaries, interest, and rent) and payments on debts is a reflection of your cash-flow position.

[a] Difference ±.
[b] Market value, consider refinancing or borrowing money as a second trust.

We now leave this phase with the following thought: Over 90% of the present American population over 65 years of age relies on income other than their own investments for the vital task of sustaining life. I ask you a simple question. Are you preparing for the day when you are 65? Or will you also rely on deflated retirement funds, friends, relatives, social security, medicare, or charity?

Phase 2

Critical Decision

Phase 2 Objectives
- Learn the positive effects of mortgage interest payments and property depreciation on your cash-flow position.
- Realize that cash flow determines whether you buy or do not buy.
- Determine what amount of negative cash flow you can sustain after tax savings are taken into account.
- Understand the five-year effect on cash position due to inflation, tax savings, and property depreciation allowances.
- Understand the new 15-year property depreciation allowance—great for investors!
- Learn to use the abbreviated cash-flow analysis—the vector cash-flow analysis.
- Make your decision, cross the Rubicon, *invest in America!*
- Complete an asset-debt information table on your financial position; find your hidden treasures.

THE VECTOR CASH-FLOW ANALYSIS

Having performed a thorough analysis of the values of investing in residential real estate, you now set your goal and determine what you can afford. It will be necessary to complete this analysis prior to starting your search for potential properties. Review the flow chart in Figure 2-1. On first impressions it may look complex; however, once you grasp the theory, an abbreviated method will be explained that simplifies the actual cash-flow analysis. The abbreviated cash-flow analysis is presented later in this phase.

FIGURE 2-1
The Vector Cash-Flow Analysis.

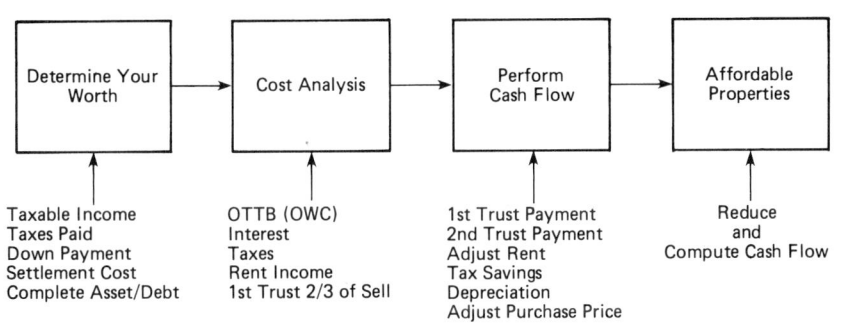

```
┌──────────────┐     ┌──────────────┐     ┌──────────────┐     ┌──────────────┐
│ Determine Your│ ──→ │ Cost Analysis │ ──→ │   Perform    │ ──→ │  Affordable  │
│    Worth     │     │              │     │  Cash Flow   │     │  Properties  │
└──────┬───────┘     └──────┬───────┘     └──────┬───────┘     └──────┬───────┘
       ↑                    ↑                    ↑                    ↑
```

Taxable Income   OTTB (OWC)   1st Trust Payment   Reduce
Taxes Paid   Interest   2nd Trust Payment   and
Down Payment   Taxes   Adjust Rent   Compute Cash Flow
Settlement Cost   Rent Income   Tax Savings
Complete Asset/Debt   1st Trust 2/3 of Sell   Depreciation
                                                  Adjust Purchase Price

CASH-FLOW DETERMINES WHETHER TO BUY OR NOT TO BUY

The reasons for completing the cash-flow analysis are (1) to buy the best available property at the most favorable price and (2) to avoid any negative cash flow you cannot sustain. Unfortunately, the issue of determining your exact financial position relative to purchasing investment properties becomes rather complex because of inflation, mortgage amortization periods (time allowed to pay a loan), taxable income, taxes paid, property depreciation allowance, long-term capital gain, recaptured depreciation, and other factors that are a specific function of the individual investor. However, consistent with the overall philosophy of this book, it is important that we understand the investment process as early as possible in our program. Certainly the financial position relative to any prospective property must be known prior to any commitment to purchase. The single item that adds the greatest degree of complexity to your cash-flow position is taxes. It has been my experience that no one person knows enough about the tax laws of this country, including tax lawyers, tax consultants, and the IRS itself. I recommend that you, the investor, have a good working knowledge of the tax laws relative to investment properties. I also recommend that you, the investor, prepare your own tax returns and seek expert advice on complex issues and special circumstances. Additional questions can be answered by various publications that are currently on the market, for example, *J. K. Lasser's Income Tax* manual.[1]

I developed the Vector Cash-Flow Analysis after having requested investment data from real estate agencies. I found the analyses to be lacking in substance and not detailed enough to answer my basic question: Can I afford this property given these monthly payments, expected rent, and

[1]*J. K. Lasser's Your Income Tax*, Copyright 1980, Simon and Schuster, New York.

this amount of dollars saved on my taxes? In order to answer these questions, I developed a straightforward method that allowed me to plug in the numbers and calculate my financial position.

The Vector Cash-Flow Analysis works as follows: Based on your knowledge of medium priced homes in your area, pick a reasonable selling price: first trust is a given percentage of the sell price, for example, ⅔ or ¾ at an interest rate of 9% or 10%. Owner carries the entire equity as second trust at a negotiable interest rate, for example 12%. Use the information from Phase 1 to assume rent income (for example, $700 per month for a $100,000 property; $400 per month for a $65,000 property). Calculate your tax savings and your cash-flow position for any prospective property. The following example best illustrates that what appears complex is actually an easily learned analysis.

Initially we calculate for only the first year, and then we shall carry our analysis through for the entire five-year investment period. First I will outline and discuss the cash-flow analysis in detail. After we understand the details, I present the abbreviated method to calculate your cash-flow position. Initially, when starting to write this book it was not my intent to outline the cash-flow process in detail. However, after the first revision of the script, it became apparent that the detailed mathematics would require development in order to give credibility to the vastly simplified cash-flow analysis. It is not necessary to fully understand the nuts and bolts of the detailed cash-flow analysis. What is important is that you understand the effects that depreciation and mortgage interest have on your cash-flow position. I recommend that as a minimum you scan the detailed development of the cash-flow analysis. Review Tables 2-1 through 2-4 later in this phase. The tables are summaries of tax savings and the cash-flow position, with tax shelters taken into account. Table 2-5 outlines the abbreviated Vector Cash-Flow Analysis.

CASH-FLOW POSITION WITH A $75,000 INVESTMENT

To compute a cash-flow position, let us assume the following investment data:

1. Original cost: $100,000
2. Address: Anywhere, USA
3. Purchase price = $100,000
4. Assumable first trust = $75,000 at 9%
5. Second trust = $20,000 at 14%
6. Rent $650 per month = $7,800 per year
7. Down payment = $5,000

Payments on the assumable first trust would be $629 per month. This figure is obtained readily from the seller or from the multiple listings. To compute the monthly payments to amortize a loan at any desired interest rate for a specified period, it is best to use any of the various paperbacks that are available at any bookstore. These paperbacks provide information about amortization, such as principal, interest, monthly payments, and so forth, on any loan for any period. I strongly recommend that, as an investor, you purchase one of these handy paperbacks; they sell for $3.95 to $5.95 and are tax deductible.

Payments on the second trust would be $233 per month. Since the second trust is interest only, the monthly payment would be $20,000 × 0.14 ÷ 12. The $20,000 × 0.14 = $2,800 is the yearly interest rate. The division by 12 allows for computation to the month ($233).

Now let us stop and reflect on our financial position. Negative cash per month is $629 + $233 = $862. Positive cash (rental) per month equals $650, which is consistent with a $100,000 property. First indications are that this is not a good purchase, since the negative cash flow is $212 per month. It may in fact be a poor choice for some investors. However, we must continue our analysis because every person is in a different tax bracket, which is based on the amount of tax paid directly related to income.

First let us calculate for allowable deductions due to depreciation of property. Property was purchased for $100,000. Value of structure is 13/16 × $100,000 = $81,250. Remember the IRS does not allow value of land to be depreciated. We touched upon this in the Summary. We are now allowed to depreciate 1/15 of the investment property (less land) per year using straight-line depreciation. Multiply by 1.75 (the 175% declining balance method). Depreciation on the investment property equals $9,479 [($81,250 ÷ 15) × 1.75]. Thus the investor is allowed to deduct $9,479 from his or her taxable earnings before computing taxes. Additionally all interest is deductible, interest on first trust equals $6,648 per year and interest on second trust equals $2,800 per year. Total deductions are $6,648 + $2,800 + $9,479 (depreciation) − $7,800 (rent is considered as ordinary income) = $11,127. Thus, $11,127 is tax deductible. Let us now see what $11,127 as a tax deduction translates into as an actual cost savings. Using the 1980 tax tables we generate the data shown in Table 2-1. Now go back to our negative cash flow of $212 per month. Table 2-2 lists the calculations for the cash flow as a function of earned taxable income.

Tables 2-1 and 2-2 are snapshots of the situation during the first year of holding the investment property. The second year will see less negative cash flow as the mortgage payments remain fixed and two very important parameters change in your favor. One is inflation, which causes the rent to go up. The other is that you will likely receive a pay raise, which will result in a greater percentage of a tax return. For example, using Table 2-1, one

TABLE 2-1. Tax Savings with $11,127 as Tax Deduction[a]

Taxable income	$20,000	$25,000	$30,000	$35,000	$40,000
Taxable income	8,873	13,873	18,873	23,873	28,873
Tax without deductions	2,751	4,064	5,601	7,357	9,355
New tax with deductions	514	1,400	2,475	3,742	5,233
Savings per year	2,237	2,664	3,126	3,615	4,122
Savings per month	186	222	260	301	343

Subtract $11,127

Difference is tax savings

[a] Married filing jointly, two exemptions.

TABLE 2-2. Cash Flow (Monthly) with Tax Deduction of $11,127 (per Year)

Taxable income	$20,000	$25,000	$30,000	$35,000	$40,000
Cash flow before tax savings	−212	−212	−212	−212	−212
Tax savings (from Table 2-1)	186	222	260	301	343
True cash flow (per month)	−26	+10	+48	+89	+131

can see that with the same amount of deductions ($11,127) the person with the taxable income of $20,000 has a savings of $186 per month and the person with the taxable income of $25,000 has a savings of $222 per month. Thus, the more taxable income one has, the larger the tax savings due to deductions. Let us do some quick calculations for the second year. The rent will increase from $650 to $715 per month and all taxable income figures will increase by 10% (remember, 10% inflation). $715 (rent) × 12 = $8,580 per year. Thus, our thumbnail analysis indicates an additional $65 per month (rent increase) of positive cash being used to offset the negative cash flow. Thus, the figures for the second year are

Taxable income[2]	$22,000	$27,500	$33,000	$38,500	$44,000
Cash flow	+$39	+$75	+$113	+$154	+$196

[2] Income increases due to 10% raise.

Actually the true computations are slightly more involved, since the allowable tax deduction changes due to the rent total increase and this must be considered as ordinary income. Also the raise in pay will result in a slightly different tax bracket making the numbers change in your favor. However, without going into detail, the important thing to remember is that merely adding mortgage payments and monthly rent is not sufficient. You must take into account your tax savings in doing any cash-flow analysis. The other important subject that we must not forget is the expected appreciation of the property. With a $100,000 property at 10% inflation, the appreciation is as follows:

PROPERTY APPRECIATION

Year	0	1	2	3	4	5
Appreciation schedule (in thousands of dollars)	100	110	121	133	146	161

At the end of five years, the profit to be realized would be $61,000. Thus an important question needs to be asked by the investor with a $20,000 taxable income (joint income if married). Is it worth $26 per month the first year and a positive cash flow of $10 per month the second year to realize $61,000 five years from now? From $25,000 on up our investors have essentially a zero cash flow after the first year. To be completely fair, I should mention that real estate taxes and insurance must also be taken into account. They are directly deductible but they do add to the expenses. Thus on an average, $50 per month should be added to the negative cash flow.

In doing the cash-flow analysis above, I purposefully selected a property that is slightly higher in purchase price than would be commonly purchased by an investor. The point I wish to make is that a person (or couple) with a yearly income of $20,000 can afford a $100,000 investment property! Remember, the higher the initial price, the greater your percentage return. Ten percent of $100,000 is better than 10% of $10,000. If you currently have an income in the $15,000 to $20,000 range, you must ask yourself, Can I afford out-of-pocket expenses of $50 to $100 a month to realize $60,000 in five years? Remember your cash-flow situation will stabilize after the first or second year. For anyone in the $25,000 to $30,000 income bracket, *go to it!*

The second point I wish to emphasize concerning the $100,000 investment is that what is important are the *terms* surrounding the purchase and the *expected positive cash* generated by the rental. In order to explain the calculation of the cash-flow process I selected an assumption with a second trust. There are an infinite number of financing techniques that can be utilized to purchase your investment property. Phase 3, The Buy, discusses these methods. If you cannot afford the negative cash flow, use your imagination. Find another method or keep searching for the property that fits your terms.

FIVE-YEAR CASH-FLOW ANALYSIS

We will now prepare a detailed cash-flow analysis of what I believe to be an ideal investment. It is ideal because it has a reasonable initial cost and thus produces a solid base for appreciation. (Remember 10% of $100,000 is more than 10% of $10,000.) The property is ideal for renters in the middle- to upper-income classes and thus will attract good renters. Of course, the terms are ideal. Follow along with me as I explain the figures in Tables 2-3 and 2-4. After an explanation of the tables, I will follow with an abbreviated format. The important item to grasp is that you must take into account the influence of your depreciation allowance and interest on loans (first and second trusts) on your taxable income. In all cases, you will pay less tax, thus have more positive cash. The amount of your positive cash is dependent on your taxable income.

Study Tables 2-3 and 2-4 (see pages 80-83) and scan down to row 5 of Table 2-3. This is the amount of cash flow before taxes are taken into account. Now look at row 4 of Table 2-4. This is the amount of cash flow after taxes have been taken into account. Note that the tables reflect a taxable income of $25,000. If your total income is greater than $25,000, your cash-flow position is favorably increased. For example, if your joint income is $35,000, then the first year would see a tax savings of $3,132 ($261 per month), resulting in $100 positive cash flow from the time of the initial buy. However, note that an investor with a taxable income of $25,000 could well afford to purchase this particular property. The first year would show approximately zero cash flow, and the remaining years of the investment would show a positive cash flow. Note that taxes and insurance have not been taken into account. These two items will vary depending on the city, county, state, and other regional factors. Assuming a reasonable figure of $75 per month for other expenses, the investor with a taxable income of $25,000 needs only to ask, "Am I willing to finance the investment with $75 out-of-pocket expenses the first year in order to realize a profit of $46,000 ($121,000 − $75,000)?"

USE THE VECTOR CASH-FLOW ANALYSIS WITH ANY INTEREST RATE

Tables 2-3 and 2-4 use interest rates of 8½% and 14% for the first and second trusts. Even with assumable first trusts between 8½% to 10% and a second trust of 14% to 16%, the numbers still indicate that the majority of investors can well afford the property. For example, a 10% loan amortized over 30 years will carry a monthly payment of $465, and a second trust at 15% with interest only payments will result in monthly payments of $250 per month. Total increase in monthly payments is $75 per month.

Loan Costs per Month		*Loan Costs per Month*	
8½% first trust	$407	10% first trust	$465
14% second trust	$233	15% second trust	$250
Totals:	$640		$715
Difference:	$75		

An additional negative cash flow of $75 per month gives different results. The rental does not completely offset the negative cash flow, thus all expenses will be deductible from your taxable income. With an investor in the 33% bracket, the tax savings will be ⅓ of $75 per month, resulting in an additional $50 in out-of-the-pocket expenses per month.

Again, the question needs to be asked, is it worth an additional $50 per month the first year (remember, it should balance out the second year) in order to realize $40,000 to $60,000 five years from the date of purchase? *Of course it is!*

TAX LAWS

In February 1981, President Reagan recommended to Congress that all residential real estate held for business purposes (rentals) should be allowed to depreciate in 18 years. Congress went beyond Reagan's request and approved a 15-year depreciation period in August 1981. As mentioned earlier in this book, the Economic Tax Recovery Act of 1981 also allows for 175% declining balance. The accelerated depreciation schedule applies only to investment properties purchased after December 31, 1980. All investment properties purchased in calendar year 1980 or previous to that year will continue under the laws existing at the day of purchase. This point is important for it may be in the best interest of some investors to sell their properties and purchase new ones that fall under the accelerated depreciation schedules.

Table 2-5 (see page 84) is a summary of the major features of the 1981 tax law compared with the pre-1981 tax laws.

ABBREVIATED CASH-FLOW ANALYSIS

Now that we have a good working knowledge of the vector cash-flow analysis, we can abbreviate the process and obtain a reasonable calculation reflecting our cash-flow position.

TABLE 2-3. Cash Flow Without Tax Deductions

Prepared for: Mr. Average Joe America
Address: Anywhere, USA
Cost of Property: $75,000

First Trust Information

Assumable First Trust:	$50,000
Original Loan:	$53,022 at 8½% interest, 30 years
Age of Original Loan:	5 years
Monthly Payments:	$407 month, $4,884 per year

Second Trust Information

Second Trust Loan:	$20,000
Interest:	14%
Payments:	$233 per month, $2,800 per year

Rent Income (Positive) $475 per month

ITEM					*YEAR*					
	1	2	3	4	5	6	7	8	9	10
1.	Year of Original Loan	5	6	7	8	9	10				
Year of investment	0	1	2	3	4	5				
Appreciation Schedule 10% Inflation	$75,000	$82,500	$90,750	$99,800	$109,800	$121,000				
2.	Original loan = $52,356 balance	$50,000	$49,371	$48,743	$48,010	$47,225	$46,387				
First trust payments: interest 8½% per year										
Principal		4,824	4,824	4,824	4,824	4,824	4,824			
Interest		625	628	733	785	838				
		4,199	4,196	4,091	4,039	3,986				
3.	Second trust balance (Balloon 5 years) interest paid	$20,000	$20,000	$20,000	$20,000	$20,000	$20,000				
	($233 per month)	2,800	2,800	2,800	2,800	2,800				
4.	Rent income $475 per month 10% inflation		$5,700	$6,270	$6,897	$7,586	$8,344				
5.	Cash-flow analysis 1: difference between payments and rent		−$1,924	−$1,354	−$727	−$38	+$720				

81

TABLE 2-4. Tax Influence on Cash Flow

Prepared for:
Address:
Cost of Property: $75,000
Investor's Taxable Income: $25,000

ITEM		YEAR					
			(6)	(7)	(8)	(9)	(10)
		2	1	2	3	4	5
1.	Year of original loan		($60,937)[a]	($53,829)	($47,550)	($42,002)	($37,102)
	Year of investment						
	Depreciation						
	$13/16 \times \$75{,}000 = \$60{,}937$		4,062	3,588	3,170	2,800	2,437
	Straight-line (15 years)		×1.75	×1.75	×1.75	×1.75	×1.75
	175% declining balance						
	Total depreciation		7,108	6,279	5,547	4,900	4,327
	Recaptured depreciation[b]		3,046	2,691	2,377	2,100	1,854
	Total recaptured depreciation			5,737	8,114	10,214	12,068
2.	Allowable tax deductions						
	Interest first trust		+4,199	+4,196	+4,091	+4,039	+3,986
	Interest second trust		+2,800	+2,800	+2,800	+2,800	+2,800
	Depreciation		+7,108	+6,279	+5,547	+4,900	+4,327
	Rent		−5,700	−6,270	−6,897	−7,586	−8,344
	Interest + Depreciation − Rent		+8,007	+7,005	+5,541	+4,153	+2,769

3.	Taxable Income (10% inflation)	$25,000	$27,500	$30,250	$33,280	$36,800
	Tax	4,064	4,801	5,681	6,691	7,949
	Adjusted taxable income	(16,993)	(20,495)	(24,709)	(29,127)	(34,031)
	Tax with deduction	2,039	2,859	3,980	5,313	6,987
	Tax saving	+2,025	+1,942	+1,701	+1,378	+962
	Cash-flow analysis 1 (from Table 2-3)	−1,924	−1,354	−727	−38	+720
4.	Vector cash flow (per year)	+$101	+$588	+$974	+$1,340	+$1,682
	Vector cash flow (per month)	$8	$49	$81	$111	$140

a Parentheses here indicate the adjusted value of the investment used for tax purposes only.
b Recaptured depreciation is depreciation claimed above straight line.

83

TABLE 2-5. Comparison of Major Tax Law Features

ITEM	PRE-1981 LAW DEPRECIATION	THE 1981 ACCELERATED COST RECOVERY
General applicability	Guidelines vary, depends on many factors and is subject to interpretation by the IRS.	Mandatory.
Recovery periods: tangible personal property	Guidelines allow 2½ to 50 years, depending on asset type or activity, with optional 20% variance for each.	3 years (autos, light trucks, machinery, and equipment used for research and development), 5 years (most machinery and equipment), or 10 years (long-lived public utility property).
Real estate	Determined by facts and circumstances or by guidelines ranging from 25 to 60 years depending on the type of building.	10 years for owner-occupied factories, stores, and warehouses; 15 years for other nonresidential and for low-income housing; 18 years[a] for other residential.
Recovery method: tangible personal property	Straight-line; or for new property, taxpayer may elect declining balance up to 200%, or sum-of-years' digits.	Accelerated write-off into tables.
Real estate	**Same for new residential; up to 150% declining balance for new, nonresidential; up to 125% declining balance for used residential; straight-line for used nonresidential.**	Same for 10-year property. Straight-line. 15-year depreciation. All income-producing real estate (new and old) allowed 175% declining balance.
Recapture provisions: tangible personal property	Ordinary income recapture up to prior allowances (Section 1245).	Ordinary income recapture prior allowances (Section 1245).
Real estate	Ordinary income recapture up to excess over straight-line (Section 1250).	Same for 10-year real property. No recapture for others.

84

TABLE 2-5. Continued

ITEM	PRE-1981 LAW DEPRECIATION	THE 1981 ACCELERATED COST RECOVERY
Asset accounting: general	Vintage accounting.	Vintage accounting.
Investment tax credit	3⅓% for machinery and equipment written off or held for 3 to 5 years, 6⅔% for 5 to 7 years, 10% if longer.	6% for 3-year class and 10% for 5-year and 10-year eligible property.
Carryovers	Choice of 20% shorter or longer lives; straight-line or accelerate methods, where allowed. Deductions may add to net operating loss, which can be carried over 7 years.	Extends net operating loss and investment credit carryover period from 7 to 10 years.
Timing of eligibility	When placed in service.	When placed in service, or for property with at least 2-year construction period, as acquired.

[a] Congress modified the depreciation period to 15 years

Abbreviated Cash-Flow Analysis

1. Compute cash flow without tax savings: Rental income − payment on loans = cash flow.
2. Compute tax deduction: Payment on loans + (13/16 of purchase price × 1/15 × 1.75) − rental income.[3]
3. Obtain taxable income from last year's income tax return.
4. Using the graphs in Figure 2–2 (Tax Bracket Family Curves) in the next section, compute tax. Find your taxable income on bottom line; go straight to curve, find your tax from the line on the left side. *Note:* The Tax Bracket Family Curves use 1980 as the base; because taxes change on a yearly basis it is best to use the IRS tables. However, the curves will provide a reasonable approximation.
5. Subtract tax deduction (step 2) from last year's taxable income.
6. Using adjusted taxable income (step 5), use Figure 2–2 to figure new tax.
7. Subtract taxes without deductions and with deductions. This is your tax savings.
8. Add positive cash of step 7 to cash flow calculation of step 1. This is your net cash-flow position.

[3]Step 2 becomes: payment on loans + (13/16 × 1/15 of purchase price) − (rental income).

The effect of the 15-year depreciation allowance on the cash-flow situation will be most favorable to the investor. For example, let us recalculate the net cash flow of Table 2-4 (row 4). With the 15-year depreciation, the allowable straight-line depreciation allowance is $4,062 ($60,937 ÷ 15). Multiplying $4,062 by 1.75 (175% declining balance), we obtain $7,108. Allowable tax deductions thus amount to $8,007 ($4,199 + $2,800 + $7,108 − $5,700). (See row 2, Table 2-4). Adjusted taxable income is $25,000 − $8,007 = $16,993. Tax with 15-year depreciation deductions equals $2,039. Tax with no deductions equals $4,064. Tax savings are thus $4,064 − $2,751 = $2,025. Net cash flow (row 4, Table 2-4) − $1,924 + $2,025 = $101 per year or approximately $8 per month.

Recall that Table 2-4 is for an investor with a taxable income of $25,000. Obviously, if the investor has a taxable income of $30,000 or higher, his or her savings are significantly improved.

The main purpose of the detailed exercise of calculating for the investor's exact cash-flow position is to gain an appreciation for the process itself. There is a much faster and more straightforward method, which is outlined under the title Abbreviated Vector Cash-Flow Analysis. I developed this method out of necessity. Obviously, I could not perform these detailed calculations as I inspected the property. However, I have on occasion calculated my cash-flow position under a street light in order to give a realtor my decision about a property. With this abbreviated process, you can obtain a reasonably accurate calculation reflecting your cash-flow position.

Let us return to our previous example in Table 2-3 and compute our investor's cash-flow position using the abbreviated cash-flow method. Remember the property costs $75,000, and all conditions remain as stated in the example.

ABBREVIATED VECTOR CASH-FLOW ANALYSIS

The following is an example of the Abbreviated Cash-Flow Analysis for a property having a 15-year property depreciation:

1. Cash flow without tax savings
   $5,700 − $7,684 = −$1,984 per year
2. Tax deduction
   $7,684 + $7,108 ($4,062 × 1.75) − $5,700 = $9,092
3. Taxable income = $25,000
4. Tax = $4,064
5. Adjusted taxable income
   $25,000 − $9,092 = $15,908

6. Tax with deduction = $1,829
7. Tax savings
   $4,064 − $1,829 = $2,235
8. Net cash flow
   $2,235 − $1,984 = $251 per year or $20 per month

Note the following comparisons with the unabbreviated method:

- Cash flow using abbreviated method equals positive $251 per year or $20 per month.
- Using the actual method we calculated $101 per year or $8 per month.

DECISION TIME

After having completed the analysis of your cash-flow position relative to an investment property, you should truly understand the tremendous value of investing in income-producing real estate. The combination of the rental income plus the tax savings allows you to purchase an investment property with little or no need for out-of-the-pocket cash to sustain the property. The return on the investment is the appreciation on the property. Even with an inflation of 8%, your return in five years on a $75,000 property would be $35,000. Your percentage return would be based on the amount of down payment. In the next phase, we see that purchasing an investment property of $75,000 with no money down *is* possible! Even if you purchased a piece of property with $5,000 down, your return in five years would be 600%! No other investment provides such a high return with such a minimum of risk.

TAX BRACKET FAMILY CURVES

The curves in Figure 2-2 are provided in order to give the investor a *quick analysis* capability concerning his or her cash-flow position. To *accurately* determine dollar savings from interest and property depreciation deductions, the investor should use the IRS tax tables. Follow these instructions in using the curves:

1. Find your taxable income on the bottom line.
2. From your taxable income, move straight up to the total number of exemptions (curved lines).
3. Stop at your allowable exemptions and find your tax on the line at the left.
4. To calculate your tax savings, simply add your negative cash (mortgage − rent) to the depreciation of the property for one year (1/15 of the structure value × 1.75).

FIGURE 2-2
The 1981 Tax Law. From *Invest in America Where Eagles Soar*, 1981, Gil Armen.

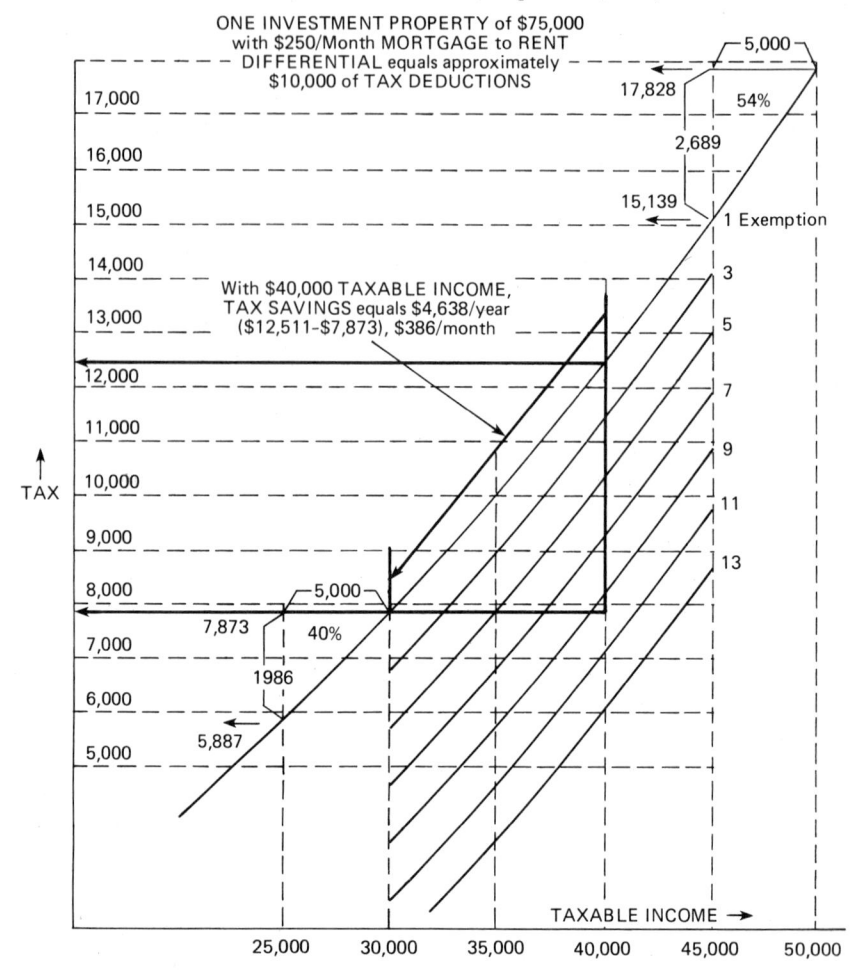

5. Subtract sum of negative cash and depreciation from taxable income. This is your new taxable income.
6. Slide down the family curve until you come to the new taxable income.
7. Find the new tax on the line at left.

For example, using a taxable income of $40,000 and total deductions of $10,000, new taxable income becomes $30,000. Tax savings due to deductions equal $4,638 per year. The investor is allowed $386 per month negative cash flow to break even.

Phase 3

The Hunt

Phase 3 Objectives
- Understand that "The Hunt" is done in a parallel process of (1) methods of buying, (2) affordability/profits, and (3) finding your investment property.
- Maintain presence of mind; be knowledgeable about the complete investment process.
- Know the meaning of *maximum leverage* and *other people's money* (OPM).
- Study and learn the 25 basic methods of financing your investment property with maximum leverage by the use of OPM.
- Use your imagination; the number of possibilities is infinite.
- Always strive for "no money down."
- Learn that no money down does not mean no cash on the settlement table; it means that the cash is not yours.
- Learn how to shop for second trust buyers; there are more than you might think.
- Buy properties from "must sellers"; avoid "unloaders."
- Use the cornerstone of the American system—competition among realtors.
- Learn how to use the newspaper—the "bellringer" of investment opportunities.
- Utilize homeowner associations (owner for sell properties).
- Learn to identify heavy concentrations of VA and FHA mortgage properties.
- Always be aware of foreclosures and bankruptcies. If you look for the "big play" at the outset, it seldom happens. Keep playing, and it comes naturally with time.
- Study and make an educated prediction of future trends.

MAINTAIN PRESENCE OF MIND

During Phases 1 and 2 it was possible to remove yourself from the world around you and concentrate on the problem at hand—gaining knowledge. Overcoming the psychological barrier requires that you discuss prospective properties with realtors and sellers in order to gain knowledge. During the initial phases you discussed the subject of borrowing money from lending institutions. You have also discussed the possibility of purchasing discounted second trusts from individual buyers. In your contact with the outside world, your thrust up to now has been to prepare yourself for the actual hunt and buy. In Phase 3, you will actually seek, search, and find your ideal investment. You will come in contact with sellers, brokers, real estate agents, bankers, lawyers, librarians, court clerks, and others. Do not lose your presence of mind, but seek to maintain an even keel and to keep your balance and true perspective. Always be aware of the overall picture. In Phase 3 it is extremely easy to lose sight of your goal and go off on a tangent.

All parties involved in the investment process have interests that are related to a specific part of the purchase of the property. Generally, their interests are directly opposite to yours. You are the only individual that has a direct interest in the investment process as a whole. Your interest concerns today, tomorrow, next month, and indeed five years from the day of purchase. The realtor is interested in the near time frame—in the sales commission. The lawyer is interested in the settlement fees. The savings and loan officer is interested in making as much money as possible. The seller, of course, is interested in the highest price. You are interested in *all* of the above. However, your interest is in the lowest price possible, at the most reasonable terms possible, and using as little of your money as possible. Other subjects of concern are rent, the amount of maintenance, and property depreciation allowances. Other questions of concern are: When I get ready to sell, can I expect to have problems? What about refinancing? These concerns and questions are legitimate. Your realtor can help you, but be aware that he or she will bias the advice with information that will be favorable to the sale of the property. By keeping your presence of mind, you plan so that you bring the future into the present. Learn to focus your thoughts and ideas through the use of other people's knowledge. The data are overwhelming. However, through knowledge, it is easily translated into your favor. The reason is that you will be the only individual that has taken the time to understand the investment process *as a whole*. Review Figure 3-1. It describes the process of hunting for properties. When involved in the process of hunting for your property, learn to enjoy "the hunt." Hunting for that ideal investment can and should be fun. Think of it as a real live Monopoly game. Through commitment to purpose, pursuing with vigor, and keeping your presence of mind, you translate your dreams into reality.

Be Creative

The process of hunting for your investment property involves three major areas: (1) method of buying, (2) cash-flow analyses, and (3) finding your investment property. The three areas should be covered in a parallel fashion. Obtain listings, find properties, perform cash-flow analyses, and be knowledgeable about the methods of buying *before* you purchase your investment property. You must also know the three previously described areas in detail before you purchase. As you compile your list of potential properties, you need to discard those that do not fit your terms. When you reduce your list to the potential investment opportunities, be prepared to negotiate. (Phase 4 discusses the negotiation process in detail.) Do not waste time with inflexible sellers. There are too many properties that will fit your terms, so why waste time and energy? Time is your most precious commodity; once lost, it can never be regained. Continuously be aware of how to purchase the property; be thinking of your creative financing package as you review and inspect the potential properties. Discuss the terms of the property with the seller and real estate agent. However, when in the search mode, consider all discussions to be of a preliminary nature. Your objective should be to structure a basis for future negotiations. Try to bracket the seller's position (how much cash does he or she *really* need?).

Consistent with the overall philosophy of knowing where you stand at all times in the investment process, we shall first discuss the different ways of buying a property using creative financing techniques. The methods are not limited to the techniques to be discussed, you shall see that methods are limited only by your imagination. Using your imagination, you can find a thousand ways to solve the financing of your investment property. The smart investor (and realtor) needs a better education in creative financing. The traditional method of buying a home (new money) will be used less in the 1980s than it was in the 1960s and 1970s. The reason is simple—high interest rates and high real estate prices. More and more sellers will be directly involved in the sales transaction. For example, the National Association of Realtors reported that no more than 5% of all homes sold in 1979 involved some form of seller financing. By the summer of 1981, over 50% of all sales involved owner financing, and in southern California, seven out of ten sales involved owner financing. Creativity, innovation, and imagination are completely legal. The knowledgeable person is catapulted immediately into a position of strength. Owner financing (second trusts), wrap financing, wraparounds, assumptions, land installment contracts, discounted seconds, balloon mortgages, contracts for deed, options, and other forms of creative financing all circumvent the high interest rate on new money. Should the interest rates come down, purchase your investment property with a combination of new and old money. Be fully aware that when the interest rates come down, prices will go up. Recall the discussion in Phase 1 about the demand for housing, which will peak in 1985 and continue through the year 2000.

When purchasing your investment property, use your imagination. Learn to appreciate the fact that your imagination is uniquely yours. No one else thinks or has the same thought processes as you do. Through imagination and determination, be in charge, learn to control the events surrounding your investment program.

The following story involving the refinancing of one of my investment properties that I had purchased in 1978 best describes how imagination coupled with determination can produce immediate cash. I had originally purchased the property for $75,000 with $5,000 down. The balance on the loan was $68,500, the property had been appraised for $110,000, and the equity was $41,500. I called the savings and loan that was the holder of the first trust and asked for information concerning refinancing. The loan officer explained that they could refinance up to 80% of the appraised value, or $88,000. This would produce $18,000, which I wanted to use to purchase additional investment properties and to provide me with some extra spending money. Everything went well at the refinance interview, until the loan officer asked to see the rental lease. The property was rented for $695 per month, and the monthly payment on the refinance was $837 per month. The loan officer said, "Mr. Armen, we have got a problem. It is the policy of this savings and loan not to lend money for investment properties when the rent money does not cover the mortgage. You have a $142 per month negative cash flow." I explained to her that $142 per month would not be a problem since the $142 was a tax write-off and the depreciation on the property actually produced a *positive* cash flow! She would not listen to any nonsense about taxes or depreciation allowances. She simply stated, "It is a company policy."

I regained my composure and offered a solution: "I am willing to establish an escrow account with a full two years of negative cash flow. At the end of two years, I will establish a new escrow account or present a new rental contract showing that the negative cash flow no longer exists." She thought about the proposal, said it sounded good, and ran off to obtain the approval of the head of the loan department. She came back shaking her head. "Mr. Armen, I am truly sorry, but we just cannot do it, it is company policy."

I asked to see the head of the loan department. I walked into the office, sat in a low chair in front of a big oak desk, and started to plead my case. After approximately 15 seconds, the loan officer cut me off, and in a biting, sarcastic tone overrode my explanation of the escrow account. "The property is an investment, we absolutely will not advance any monies for any refinance and besides, if we did, we would charge two points above prime."

Several years ago, I probably would have quit and simply concluded,

"Just can't be done, guess I'm stuck with the investment until I sell." However, being determined and using my imagination, I continued searching. Next, I talked to a credit union. I explained that I desired approximately $15,000 with an investment property as collateral. They were very polite but explained that if I wanted $15,000, it would require the use of my current home of residence as collateral. Sounded good, however, I wanted to leave the equity on my house of residence untouched, since I was working on another purchase for which I planned to move the mortgage to my own home (see Method 22 later in this phase).

Having struck out at the credit union, I next went to a local bank that had a $2,000 second trust on the investment property that I desired to refinance. They said they appreciated my business, however, they currently had no money to lend as second trust loans.

That evening I picked up the telephone book and made a table listing all mortgage companies with second trust loans. The next day I called 15 mortgage companies and asked questions concerning their loan packages. The rates varied from 16% to 21%. The amount that they would lend varied from 75% to 85% of the appraised value to the value of the outstanding loans. I finally settled on a mortgage company that advanced me $15,000 at 16.5%, interest only, five-year balloon. The monthly payment was $206 per month. Had I refinanced with the original savings and loan, my increased monthly payment would have been $179 per month. Thus, the increased cost was only $27 per month. With the $15,000, I paid off the $2,000 second trust, which had a monthly payment of $86 per month. My total increase in new monthly payments was $120 per month ($206 − $86). The $120 was all interest, thus tax deductible. The investment property is a tax write-off. In actuality I have $13,000 and a net positive cash flow!

Does it sound unbelievable? It is not. The number of possibilities is infinite—you are limited only by time and energy. When I first started on my investment program, I purchased $260,000 worth of residential real estate with only $2,000 of my own money. I quote Daniel Webster: "Failure is more frequently from want of energy than from want of capital."

Real estate as an investment is attractive because only two ingredients are required to purchase the commodity—time and energy. Money helps, but it is not necessary. Recently I was conducting a seminar and I asked Joe, one of my students, "If you had one thing to do over in the last ten years, what would you do differently?" After thinking about the question for a few seconds, Joe answered, "I would work smarter." In other words, use your time smartly and be sure that all energy that is being expended on your investment program is being translated to useful work. For example, you could randomly walk into any real estate agency and make offers on the first ten properties from any real estate listing. You could continue your search randomly in Baltimore, Virginia Beach, Dallas, Kansas

City or Bakersfield. It is certainly a method of using your time and energy. A better method would be to concentrate on two areas. Number one, decide where you wish to invest and number two, find a good knowledgeable real estate agent who understands investors. After having made those two decisions, give your realtor the following task: Provide me a listing of properties selling in a specific area of the city and at a medium price (relative to your particular area)—for example, in the price ranges of $40,000 to $55,000, or $60,000 to $75,000. The properties will all have VA or FHA assumptions and the loans will be under 10% interest. The combination of the assumable first trust and the cash requirements of the seller will be no greater than 80% of the asking price. Have the real estate agent write a contract on properties that fit this description. The contract would be written as follows: You will assume the first trust, the cash requirements of the seller will be in the form of a commercial second trust and the remaining equity (20%) will be in the form of an owner to carry back third trust. I have done the above and the last time I asked my realtor to find me properties with under 10% interest in an area of approximately 25 square miles, he stopped searching after 175 properties. Within one hour, I had reduced the number from 175 to 27 properties that were selling in a particular area of the city. In approximately 4 hours, we had inspected all 27 properties. My realtor wrote and presented contracts on 10 of the 27 as explained above. Three of the 10 accepted. (In all three purchases the owner carried back third trust loans that had payments that were deferred either one or two years from settlement.) All of the above was completed in one day. What I continue to learn since beginning my investment program is exactly what Joe was referring to in my seminar class—learn to work smart.

When determining how to find your investment properties, how to finance, purchase, manage, and sell your property, learn to cultivate and maintain a creative and imaginative mind. Remember the stories about my refinance and the purchase of the three properties in one afternoon. There are an unlimited number of methods you can use to purchase your investment properties. Methods 21 and 22 to be discussed in detail later in this phase are excellent examples of ways of using one's imagination. In one case (Method 21), I had a divorced couple who would sell only to an investor. The down payment was free rent for one year and a third trust on a second investment property. This arrangement completely satisfied the sellers (husband and wife), as it split their equity shares equally. Moving the mortgage was ideal, since the divorcing husband did not want the collateral to be the property where his wife was to reside. Method 22 involved four properties: (1) the property to be purchased, (2) the property where the seller lived, (3) a second investment of mine (realtor's commission was a third trust), and (4) my home of residence. The purchase of these two investment properties required knowledge, determination, persistence, and, above all, imagination! Find the property and terms that fit your condition. Always use as little cash as possible and borrow the remainder. Remember the key words—leverage and other people's money (OPM)—and pursue your quest with vigor and gusto!

OTHER PEOPLE'S MONEY (OPM)

In the world of real estate investments, there are three letters that are used frequently to describe leverage—OPM. OPM stands for *other people's money*. Throughout this book I shall be discussing the purchase of your investment property using the abbreviation OPM. You should always strive for putting down none or very little of your own money! No money down does not mean that the seller walks away without any cash in hand. It simply means that the money he or she carries away is not yours. I know, you may be saying it is impossible, that it cannot be done. Let me give you an excellent example of how to buy a property not using any of your own money. After the purchase of your investment, the seller and all other parties financing the transaction will make money. All will be perfectly happy.

Let's assume you learn all the techniques that are described in this book and you are able to *clearly* show your next door neighbor, Mr. X, how he can make money on the purchase of a discounted second trust. (The purchase of a second trust for anything less than the value of the note is referred to as "purchasing a discounted second.") The discounted second trust is then purchased from the seller of a property that you are purchasing. You will be paying your neighbor the monthly payments. Remember, your renter will in actuality be paying the mortgage. Your neighbor says that it sounds great, but that he does not have the money to buy the discounted second trust. Mr. X has owned his home for five years and has $25,000 in equity. Show him where he can borrow $5,000 on a second trust loan with his home as collateral at 12%, amortized over five years. He then takes the $5,000 and buys a second trust note worth $7,500 with the $5,000. The discounted second is paying your neighbor 14% on $7,500 not the $5,000. The note returns $1,050 per year ($7,500 × 0.14). His return is $87.50 per month. The return on the amount invested is not 12%, but is 21%. The monthly payment that he receives from you, the investor, from paying off the discounted second is used to pay the loan from the lending institution. The monthly installments to amortize the $5,000 borrowed from the lending institution will be $111. However, at the end of five years, the $5,000 loan from the bank is paid off (amortized over five years). The discounted second was interest only and your neighbor receives not $5,000 but $7,500! Positive cash flow in five years is $5,250 ($87.50 × 12 × 5) + $7,500, which equals $12,750. His monthly payments to amortize the $5,000 loan equal $6,600 ($111 × 12 × 5). The profit equals $6,090 ($12,750 − $6,660). Percentage of profit is infinite since all money involved is OPM.

96   THE HUNT

Remember, you as the investor are the person paying off the discounted second. When you find your investment property, you ask the seller to take back all of the equity as a second trust with the offer to find a buyer for $7,500 of the second discounted 33% ($2,500). If he takes back all of the second, fine—you have a property at *no money down!* If he chooses to sell $7,500—great—your neighbor buys the discounted second and makes money off the transaction! Incidentally, the $5,000 borrowed from the lending institution can also be a signature loan. If you presently have good credit, a $5,000 loan from a credit union will not be a problem.

Now to complete the circle, you can exchange places with your neighbor. You borrow $5,000 and buy a discounted second trust from the seller of the investment property your neighbor buys! Super arrangement; everybody is happy. Even the members of the credit union or savers at the bank are happy because they are receiving 7% or 5¾% return. I refer to this method as the *second trust exchange*. The technique and the hard numbers are fully explained in Method 5.

Remember the two properties mentioned above were purchased using OPM. Always attempt to use money other than your own to achieve *infinite leverage*. Your initial investment equals *zero*.

$$\text{Percentage of return with no down payment} = \frac{\text{Gain} - \text{Investment}}{\text{Investment}}$$

$$\text{Percentage of return} = \frac{\text{Gain} - 0}{0} = \text{Infinite Gain}$$

It is important that you learn the basis of OPM. First, finance the purchase of your investment property using as much borrowed money as possible. Sources of financing are Savings and Loan institutions, banks, pension funds, life insurance companies, mortgage brokers, individual investors, credit unions, commercial lenders, and the seller of the property. Second, use the rental income to pay the creditors. Third, through tax shelters (interest and depreciation), offset any negative cash flow (resulting from the mortgage to rent differential) that you cannot sustain.

We shall now turn our full attention to the methods of buying investment property. I consider the following sections, which graphically explain creativity, innovation, and imagination, to be the heart of this book. Read all of the examples and return to the methods that best describe your particular situation.

BASIC METHODS OF FINANCE

The following list outlines the four basic methods of financing the purchase of an investment property. Regardless of all the fancy jingles you may hear on the radio, there are four basic methods: (1) All cash, (2) Owner financed, (3) New promissory notes, and (4) existing promissory notes.

Basic Methods of Finance
- All Cash
- Owner Financed
- New Promissory Notes
- Existing Promissory Notes

All Cash   *All cash* is defined as being your money over the settlement table during purchase. The all cash technique can and should be used very effectively to buy properties at sizable discounts. However, since this book is written for the small-money investor, I shall devote little time to this technique. Once the investor has an established portfolio and the harvest generates the $30,000 to $40,000 profit on a yearly basis, buying properties at discount prices has considerable merit.

Owner-Financed Loans   Owner-financed loans are a form of a new promissory note. However, they are definitely negotiable, and extremely favorable interest rates may be obtained. People nearing retirement offer excellent opportunities for owner financing. The loan will provide steady income with the investment property as collateral.

New Promissory Notes   Generally speaking, the investor should stay clear of conventional new loans. These loans carry interest rates that are at the prevailing rates for residential property, and as an investor you will probably be charged a percentage point or two higher than an owner-occupied property. However, the two methods of financing that come under the category of new promissory notes offering the investor real possibilities are (1) a third party who buys all or a portion of a large second trust at a discount rate and (2) variable-rate or equity participation mortgages. The purchase of a property with a large second trust and new financing is a good method to provide cash to the seller and still allow the investor to purchase with no money down. Variable-rate and equity participation mortgages offer great promise in the future. I predict that they will come into general usage in the 1980s. It is in your best interest to understand these methods of new money financing. Methods 14 and 15 graphically describe the processes.

Existing Promissory Notes   Existing promissory notes offer the most lucrative technique for the creative investor. In this area you have loans that are in existence and can be assumed by the buyer. The existing loan is merely transferred from the seller to the buyer. Having assumed the loan you concentrate all of your energies on financing the equity (difference between purchase price and value of assumable loan). Generally the creative investor will use a combination of owner-financed and existing promissory notes. The following is a list of creative financing methods that can be used with existing promissory notes:

- Assumptions
- Wraparounds
- Owner-financed loans
- Moving the mortgage
- Second trusts
- Discounted second trusts
- Buying second trusts
- Refinance

TWENTY-FIVE METHODS OF BUYS

A total of 25 different methods in purchasing your investment property with maximum leverage are discussed in this book. Any combination of these methods could be used to make a purchase. In the majority of the methods to be discussed, I use assumptions carrying 8½% interest loans. Assumptions with interest rates below 10½% are excellent and can easily be found. Additionally, I use 12% interest to explain second trust financing. Rates for second trusts between 12% and 15% are excellent. You will find that as new money interest rates go up, less people will qualify for new homes. People have to live *somewhere*. Thus, the trend with high interest rates is to rent until the storm blows over. With increased demand for rental units, rent per month increases. This point is tremendously important, since the higher interest rates (owner carry backs and commercial seconds) result in higher mortgage payments. However, rent will also go up, thus offsetting higher purchase costs. For example, in the fall of 1980, I rented a home for $575 per month. My renter was abruptly transferred out of state. I placed a three-day advertisement in the newspaper, listing it for $750 per month. By the end of the first day, the property was rented! The reason for the high demand was that potential buyers are renting, thus driving the rental prices upward.

All of the methods to be discussed and analyzed are in example format. You, as the investor, must use the real numbers when calculating for your own investment property. Methods 21 and 22 use commercial loans at 19% interest; however, the total mortgage payment is still offset by rent and depreciation. There is nothing wrong with using small quantities ($5,000 to $10,000) of high-interest new money, as long as the overall mortgage payment is within the individual's ability to absorb the negative cash flow. Remember that complete accuracy requires adjustments of both the positive and negative numbers.

Real estate taxes vary greatly from city to county to state. For example, my properties in Texas carry taxes of less than $500 per year. Properties in the Springfield and Annandale areas of northern Virginia carry taxes of over $1,500 per year. Insurance for the investment properties ranges from $150 to $250, depending on the value of the property. As a general rule, approximately $100 per month can be added to the total mortgage figure to account for the cost of carrying the property per month. However, I reemphasize the fact that investors must know their cash-flow position as it relates to their taxable income.

Note that all of the examples that are detailed in this section carry a negative cash flow prior to calculating for your tax savings. It should be obvious to the reader that the smaller the negative cash flow, the more properties the investor will be able to buy. Thus, the investor should always attempt to purchase a property with as small a negative cash flow as possible before taking the tax savings into account. Review Table 3–1 and understand that differential between the cost to carry the property and the rent of $200, $300, or $400 per month means little until you perform your cash-flow analysis! If necessary, the reader should return to Phase 2, Critical Decision, to better understand the cash-flow analysis process. The column on the right indicates your tax savings per month on a property purchased for $75,000 with a $250 per month cost-to-carry to rent differential. Tax deduction equals $250 × 12 plus 13/16 × $75,000 ÷ 15 × 1.75. Total tax deduction equals $10,109.

All the numbers used in Table 3–1 are the real numbers that would result from the purchase of the investment property, for I believe that my readers are interested in the methods as well as in the bottom line: (1) how much does it cost, and (2) how do I purchase? Mathematically, I could have proceeded to outline millions of different methods to purchase an investment property, since the 25 methods can be used in any combination. Total number of combinations is the number two raised to the twenty-fifth power, that is, 2 × 2 × 2 × 2 ... a total of 25 times. Your imagination is your only limit.

TABLE 3-1. Tax Savings

Your Taxable Income	Tax Without Investment	Depreciation 15 year, 175 D.B.[a]	New Taxable Income	Tax With Investment	Tax Savings Per Year	Tax Savings Per Month
$20,000	$ 4,133	$10,109	$ 9,891	$ 1,136	$2,997	$250
25,000	5,887	10,109	14,891	2,540	3,347	279
30,000	7,873	10,109	19,891	4,083	3,790	315
35,000	10,092	10,109	24,891	5,829	4,263	355
40,000	12,511	10,109	29,891	7,808	4,703	391
45,000	15,139	10,109	34,891	10,019	5,120	426
50,000	17,828	10,109	39,891	12,438	5,390	449

[a] Declining Balance

100   THE HUNT

The reader is encouraged to refer to the Glossary of Terms Frequently Used in Real Estate Investment at the end of the book when a term or word is used that requires further clarification and understanding.

25 Methods to Purchase Your Investment Property
1. Assumption with owner to take back second trust (OTTB)
2. Assumption with OTTB and small down payment
3. Assumption with OTTB and discounted second trust
4. Assumption, OTTB, discounted second trust, down payment, advantages of purchasing discounted second trust
5. Second trust exchange
6. New mortgage with large second trust
7. New mortgage, use second property as collateral
8. Borrow down payment from seller
9. All-inclusive deed of trust (wraparound)
10. All-inclusive deed of trust with no down payment
11. Refinance, a form of wraparound
12. Individual partner to help finance (split profits at sell)
13. Buy off mortgages at discounted prices
14. Variable-rate mortgage (renegotiable-rate mortgage)
15. Equity participation mortgage (EPM)
16. Short- to long-term rollover
17. Buy below market value and refinance to maximum allowable
18. Undervalued property in good location
19. Owner-financed small first trust
20. Your imagination is your only limit
21. Use the rent as a down payment
22. Moving mortgages
23. A partnership
24. The lease option
25. Land installment contract

METHOD 1—ASSUMPTION WITH OWNER TO TAKE BACK SECOND TRUST

- Property has an assumable VA, FHA, or negotiable first trust.
- Owner takes back the equity as a second trust.
- Try to negotiate the second trust over as long a period as possible.

If a balloon mortgage is used, only interest is paid until the note is due. For example, a five-year balloon mortgage having interest at 12% requires payments of $250 per month. Remember $25,000 is due five years from date of purchase. With little or no cash offered as down payment, structure the balloon mortgage to be paid three to five years from purchase.

FIGURE 3-1
Method 1: Assumption with owner to take back 2nd trust.

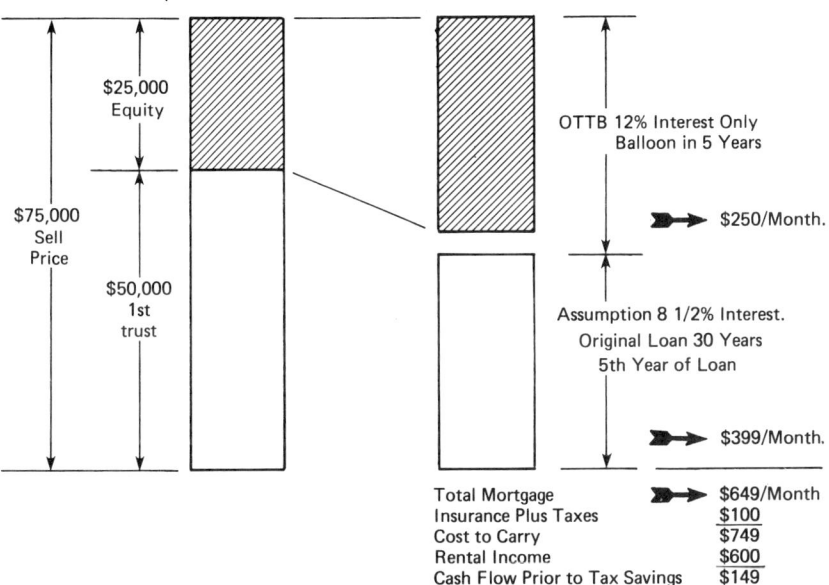

```
$75,000          $25,000
Sell             Equity            OTTB 12% Interest Only
Price                              Balloon in 5 Years

                                   ▶ $250/Month.

                 $50,000
                 1st              Assumption 8 1/2% Interest.
                 trust            Original Loan 30 Years
                                  5th Year of Loan

                                   ▶ $399/Month.
```

Total Mortgage	▶ $649/Month
Insurance Plus Taxes	$100
Cost to Carry	$749
Rental Income	$600
Cash Flow Prior to Tax Savings	$149

Remember, the seller wants his or her money. When the balloon becomes due, refinance using wrap financing. Refinancing will present no problem, as lending institutions will eagerly assume the first trust. This type of method works best with a seller who requires a steady income or is in a "must sell" situation. Usually the seller thinks he or she requires cash; however, if properly explained, this method is perfect for sellers who do not have an immediate requirement to purchase another home. For example, military personnel to be stationed overseas will be out of circulation for three years. It works to their benefit to receive 12% to 14% or better on their equity and be guaranteed full payment in three to five years. I have successfully used this technique. Even when a seller is to purchase a new home, the payment on the second trust can be used to offset the new mortgage.

Figure 3-1 illustrates a $75,000 property that rents for approximately $600 (spring 1983). An investor with a taxable income of $25,000 saves approximately $250 per month in taxes due to interest and depreciation advantages. The depreciation of the property (15 years, 175% declining balance) will easily offset the additional $149 negative cash flow. In fact, the investor would in actuality have more pocket money than before he or she purchased the investment!

Summary of Method 1
- The down payment is 0.
- First trust is assumed.
- There is a second trust (owner carries all of the equity as a second trust).

Additional points to remember are: (1) The second trust is completely negotiable. It could be structured at 10% or 15%. Additionally you could agree to pay off a percentage of the balloon mortgage in two or three years; for example, $10,000 in three years. Refinancing will allow the investor to easily pull $10,000 out of the property. (2) If you structure the second trust as a five-year balloon, refinance in two or three years, and ask the owner of the second trust to allow you to use a portion of the $25,000 as money to buy a discounted second trust in a third investment property. Believe me, it will work the majority of the time.

METHOD 2—ASSUMPTION WITH OTTB AND SMALL DOWN PAYMENT

- Property has an assumable VA, FHA, or negotiable first trust.
- Owner takes back part of the equity as a second trust.
- Small down payment.

As with Method 1, negotiate the second trust at interest only and balloon in three to five years. A small down payment is usually required in order to pay closing costs. However, be aware that closing costs are small compared with new loans, since the assumable loan will not carry loan initiation fees and mortgage insurance costs. It is usually best to concentrate on sellers who have already stated in their advertisement or multiple listing that they are willing to consider a second trust. A solid technique I strongly recommend is to have your negotiator carry your credit report to all negotiations. The seller's main concern will be your ability to pay the loan. Your good credit will prove invaluable.

Remember that even with $5,000 cash (down payment) appearing at the settlement table, it does not mean that the $5,000 is out of your pocket. Borrow the down payment as an equity loan from a second property or a signature loan. Use your imagination! The total number of possible sources for the down payment are infinite.

Note in Figure 3-2 that the total mortgage payment would be $599. Rental income would be approximately $600. Negative cash flow prior to tax savings is $99. As with Method 1, interest on loans and property depreciation will more than offset the $99. All investors with taxable income over $15,000 per year will have a positive cash flow!

Summary of Method 2
- Down payment = $5,000 (This does not mean that the $5,000 is out of your pocket, you can borrow the down payment.)
- First trust is assumed.
- Owner carries $20,000 of the $25,000 as a second trust.

FIGURE 3-2
Method 2: Assumption with OTTB and down payment.

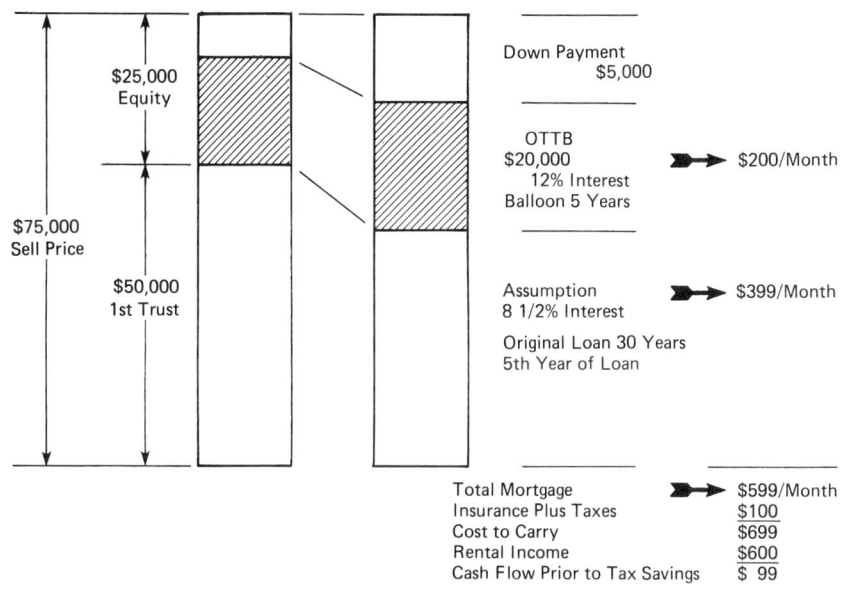

```
$75,000 Sell Price
  $25,000 Equity
  $50,000 1st Trust

Down Payment         $5,000

OTTB
$20,000
12% Interest
Balloon 5 Years      ▶ $200/Month

Assumption
8 1/2% Interest      ▶ $399/Month
Original Loan 30 Years
5th Year of Loan

Total Mortgage              ▶ $599/Month
Insurance Plus Taxes          $100
Cost to Carry                 $699
Rental Income                 $600
Cash Flow Prior to Tax Savings $ 99
```

METHOD 3—ASSUMPTION WITH OTTB AND DISCOUNTED SECOND TRUST

- Property has an assumable VA, FHA, or negotiable first trust.
- Owner takes back the equity as second trust.
- Arrange for institution or individual to purchase second trust at discounted rate (25% total, 5% per year). The discounted rate is negotiable.

I personally prefer Method 3 along with Methods 2 and 10. They are straightforward and not difficult to arrange. It is important that the investor clearly understand the benefits of buying discounted second trusts. (You need this information in order to find second trust buyers.) Assuming the second trust is to be paid at 12% interest only (not amortized) and balloon at five years with 25% discount, the individual who purchases the discounted second trust will have a return greater than 22% per year for five years, and the original investment funds are returned. Because the discounted second trust is so important, I have included a graph in Method 4 that explains the benefits of the discounted second trust.

Not all the equity needs to be discounted. For example, in the example in Figure 3-3, the seller could be asked to take back two subordinate notes (second trusts) of $10,000 and $15,000. You will then offer to find a

FIGURE 3-3
Method 3: Assumption, OTTB, discounted 2nd.

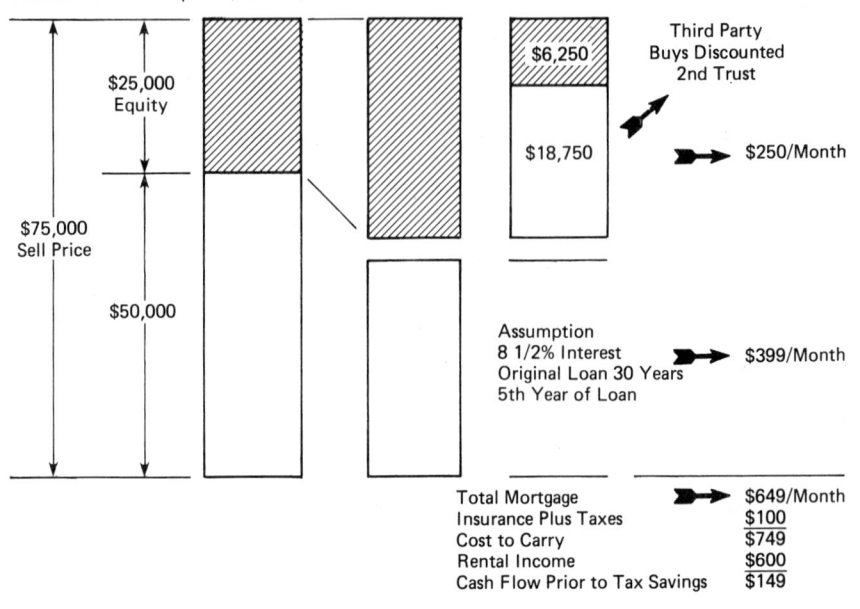

```
                                    Third Party
                        $6,250      Buys Discounted
        $25,000                     2nd Trust
        Equity
                        $18,750     ▶ $250/Month

$75,000
Sell Price

        $50,000
                        Assumption
                        8 1/2% Interest    ▶ $399/Month
                        Original Loan 30 Years
                        5th Year of Loan


                        Total Mortgage         ▶ $649/Month
                        Insurance Plus Taxes     $100
                        Cost to Carry            $749
                        Rental Income            $600
                        Cash Flow Prior to Tax Savings  $149
```

third party to purchase the $10,000 note at a discount price of $7,500. Your key here is to know the seller's *true* cash requirements.

Purchasing an investment property using a third party to purchase the equity in the form of a discounted second trust is an extremely powerful tool. One of the major tasks will be to explain to the buyer of the discounted second his or her high rate of return. I recommend that the investor first try using relatives or friends who have money in savings accounts. The savings accounts are providing 5¼% interest, the discounted second will pay more than 22% interest!

Summary of Method 3
- Down payment is 0.
- First trust is 50,000, assumable.
- Second trust is 25,000, 12%, balloon.
- Third party buys discounted second trust (25%).
- Seller receives $18,750.

METHOD 4—ASSUMPTION, OTTB, DISCOUNTED SECOND TRUST, DOWN PAYMENT

- Property has an assumable VA, FHA, or negotiable first trust.
- Owner takes back part of the equity as second trust at discounted rate (25% total, 5% per year). Discounted rate is negotiable.
- Down payment needed to reduce the required sum to find buyer of discounted second trust.

You may need a small down payment to reduce the amount of cash required to purchase the discounted second trust. If a down payment is required, consider borrowing the $5,000 on a signature loan or use your home of residence (or other investment) as collateral for a loan to generate the down payment. Shop around; signature loans and second trust loans vary by five percentage points or more!

In Methods 1 through 4, I have used assumptions at 8½% interest. Even with an assumption at 9½% interest, the monthly payment to amortize in 30 years would be approximately $425. Assuming the second trust was financed at 14%, compared with 12%, the monthly payment on the second trust would increase from $200 to $233 per month. (See Figure 3-4 for details.) Total mortgage payments per month would increase from $599 to $658. The $59 per month of increased negative cash flow can easily be off-

FIGURE 3-4
Method 4: Assumption, OTTB, discounted 2nd trust, down payment.

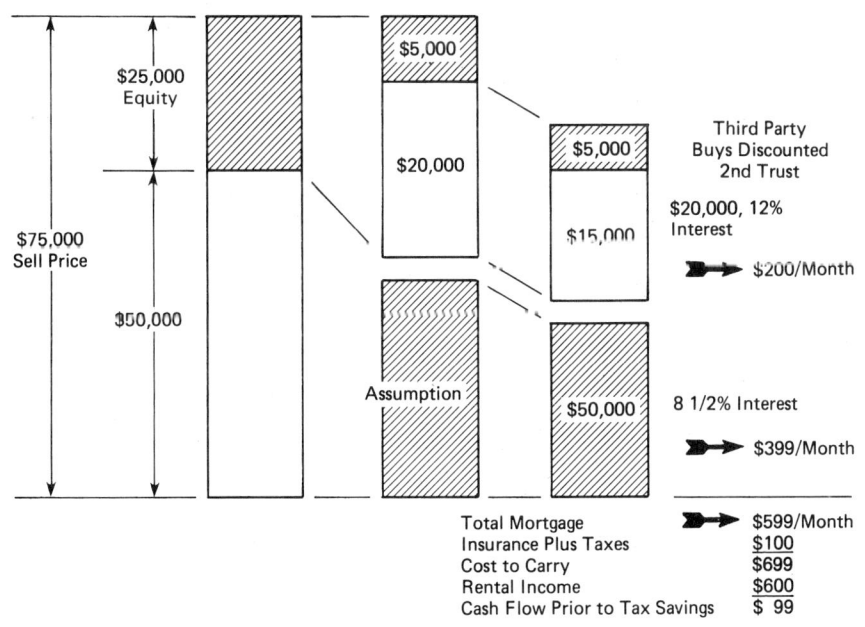

set by tax savings. Additionally, when interest rates increase, buyers will find it more difficult to qualify for new loans. As previously stated, reducing the number of qualified buyers increases the number of renters. Rents go up, further helping to offset increased negative cash flow.

Summary of Method 4
- Down payment is $5,000.
- First trust is $50,000, assumable.
- Second trust is $20,000, 12%, balloon.
- Third party buys discounted second trust (25%).
- Seller receives $5,000 + $15,000, or $20,000.

Advantages of Purchasing Discounted Second Trust
- Second trust note is $25,000.
- Purchased at 25% discount rate. Purchase price is $18,750.
- Payments are 12% per year. Interest only, not amortized.
- Due in five years.

Return Per Year

Original investment	1	2	3	4	5
$18,750	$3,000	$3,000 / 3,000	$3,000 / 6,000	$3,000 / 9,000	$3,000 / 12,000 +25,000 (Orig. note)
Total in dollars	3,000	6,000	9,000	12,000	40,000 (Total return)
Percent return	16%	16%	16%	16%	49.3%

Percentage of return after balloon paid off:

$$\frac{\text{Total return} - \text{Original investment}}{\text{Original investment}}$$

$$\frac{40,000 - 18,750}{18,750} = \frac{21,250}{18,750} = 113\%$$

Percentage return per year = 113/5 = 22.6%

Note that if balloon is paid off before five years, the rate of return *increases*. For example, for a balloon paid off in three years the return is as follows

$$\text{Return} = \$9,000 + \$2,500 = \$34,000$$

$$\% \text{ of return} = \frac{34,000 - 18,750}{18,750} = \frac{15,250}{18,750} = 81.3\%$$

$$\% \text{ per year} = \frac{81.3\%}{3} = 27.1\%$$

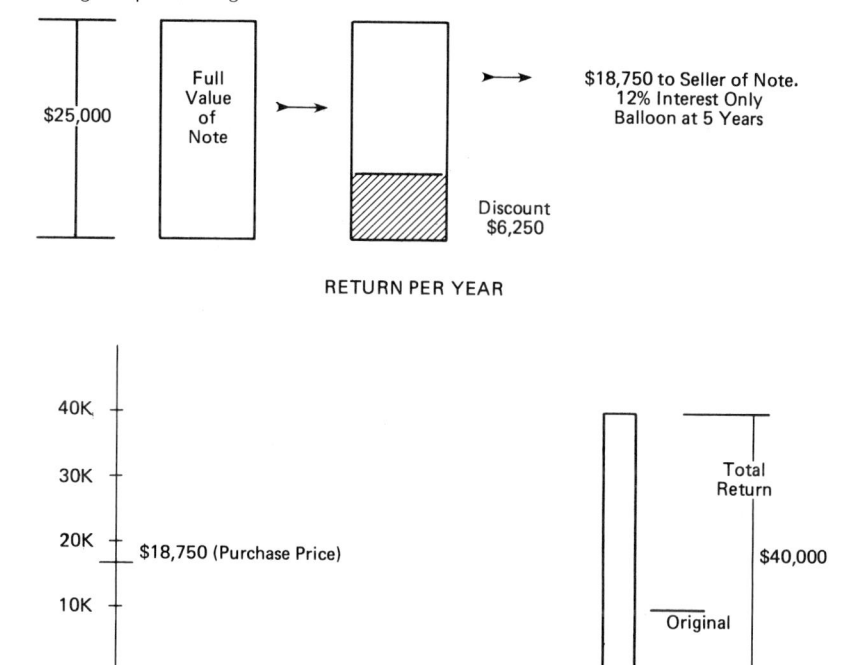

FIGURE 3-5
Advantage of purchasing the discounted 2nd trust.

```
$25,000   Full Value
          of Note     →    [bar with Discount $6,250]    →   $18,750 to Seller of Note.
                                                              12% Interest Only
                                                              Balloon at 5 Years
```

RETURN PER YEAR

```
40K
30K                                                        Total Return
20K  ─┬─ $18,750 (Purchase Price)                          $40,000
10K                                                        Original
      ├────┼────┼────┼────┼────┤
      1    2    3    4    5
RETURN ON NOTE  3,000   3,000   3,000   3,000   3,000
                        3,000                    +
                        ─────                   25,000
                        6,000 →
                                9,000 →
                                       12,000 →
                                              40,000 Total Return
```

Advantages

- Buying discounted second trusts are excellent for retired persons on fixed income!
- Buyer of discounted second trust receives payments of $250 per month ($3,000 per year). At the end of five years (or sooner) receives the full $25,000.
- Note that if the yearly payments are reinvested at 10% return, additional yield is $3,850. Return per year would increase to 23.6%.

The section immediately following Method 25 discusses how to shop for second trust buyers. Because this part of the investment process is extremely important, I suggest that the reader become familiar with the methods of finding second trust buyers at this point.

FIGURE 3-6
Method 5: The 2nd trust exchange.

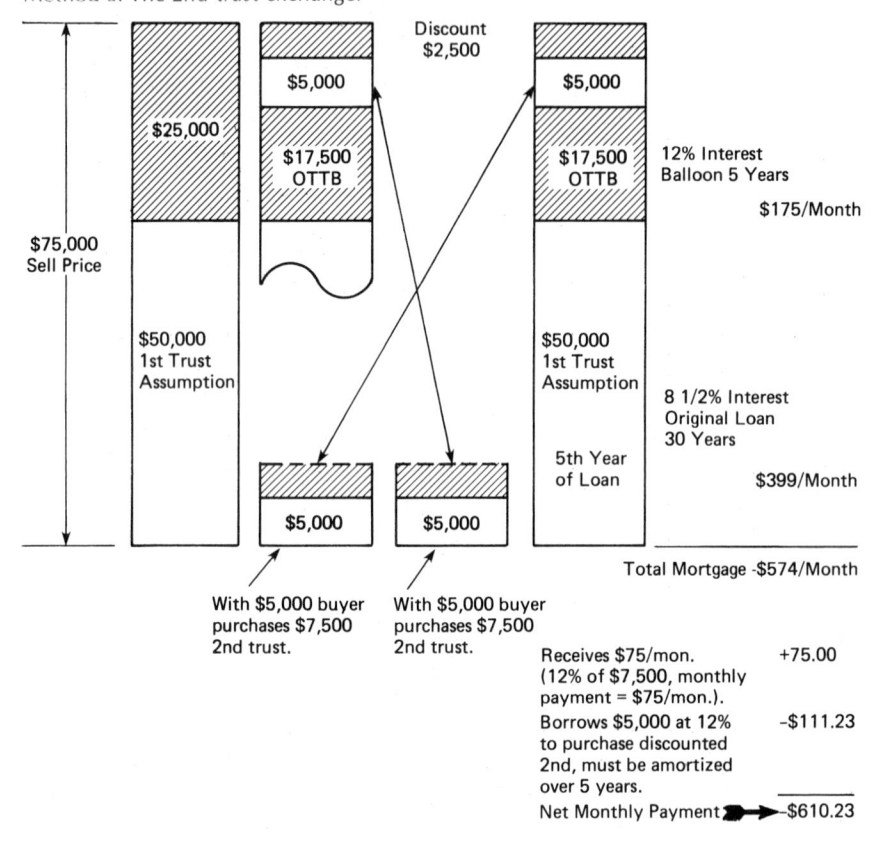

METHOD 5—SECOND TRUST EXCHANGE

- Property has an assumable VA, FHA, or negotiable first trust.
- Owner takes back part of the equity as a second trust.
- Third party, with whom you will exchange discounted second trust, purchases a portion of the equity as discounted second trust.
- Both discounted second trusts are financed from borrowed money. Credit unions will provide $5,000 signature loans with the investor having good credit.

The discounted second trust is a powerful tool. (See Figure 3-6.) Borrowing $5,000 at 12% and using the $5,000 as a down payment (no second trust exchange) would result in the following:

Borrowed amount—$5,000 at 12%, amortized over five years	$111.23
Second trust—$17,500 at 12%	$175.00
Assumption of first trust	$399.00
Total Negative Cash Flow	$685.23

The monthly payment utilizing the second trust exchange results in a monthly payment of $610.23. The reason for this is that you are making money on the purchased second trust. One additional point: If the investor borrows $5,000 of OPM to purchase a discounted second trust on a property to be purchased by the third party who purchased the discounted second on your investment, you in essence exchange discounted second trusts. Both of the discounted seconds will be worth their full value at the end of the balloon.

Summary of Method 5
- Rent will be approximately $500 per month.
- After five years the borrowed $5,000 is paid off. The purchased second trust becomes due—$7,500.
- Taxes and insurance not included. Assuming PITI of $710.22 and rental income of $600.00, the cash flow prior to tax savings is a negative $110.23.

METHOD 6—NEW MORTGAGE WITH LARGE SECOND TRUST

- Used when property has large equity.
- New mortgage used to pay off existing conventional mortgage.
- New mortgage approximately 60% or less of the sell price.
- Second trust has an interest rate less than the first trust.
- You may be required to advance a down payment. Lending institutions will generally not approve the new mortgage if the equity is fully financed using a second trust.

In general it is best to stay clear of new financing. However, if the owner carries a large second trust at favorable rates, it is possible that new financing could be obtained that will result in a total monthly mortgage payment that is acceptable. (See Figure 3-7.) Remember, always calculate your cash-flow position. If new money is required, try to obtain a wraparound loan (Method 8) or a renegotiable-rate mortgage (Method 13). They carry smaller interest rates with no prepayment penalties. Generally the lending institution will require 20% of the appraised value of the property to be free and clear. Consider moving all or part of the second trust (OTTB) to another property; for example, your present home of residence. This will allow for purchase of the property with no money down! Another tech-

FIGURE 3-7
Method 6: New mortgage with large 2nd trust.

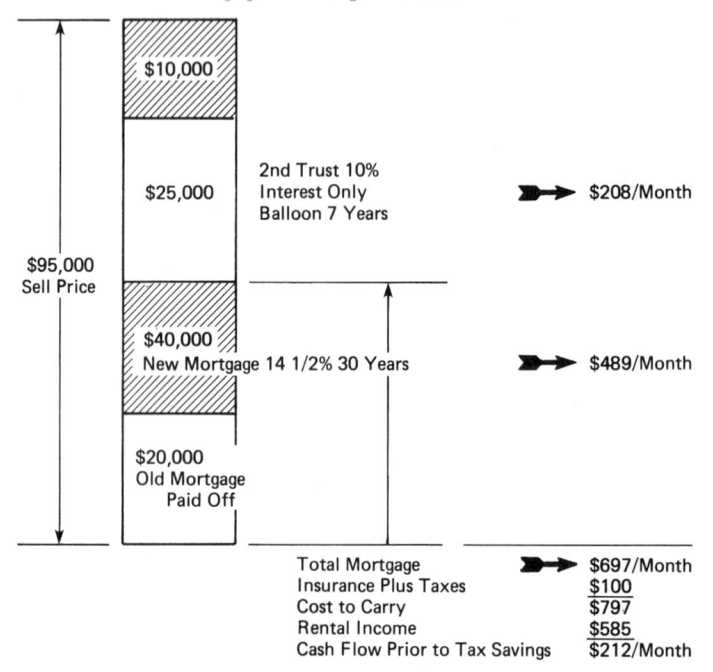

```
                    ┌─────────┐
                    │ $10,000 │
                    ├─────────┤
                    │         │    2nd Trust 10%
                    │ $25,000 │    Interest Only         ──▶  $208/Month
                    │         │    Balloon 7 Years
    $95,000         ├─────────┤
    Sell Price      │ $40,000 │
                    │         │    New Mortgage 14 1/2% 30 Years  ──▶  $489/Month
                    ├─────────┤
                    │ $20,000 │
                    │ Old Mortgage │
                    │ Paid Off│
                    └─────────┘
```

Total Mortgage	▶ $697/Month
Insurance Plus Taxes	$100
Cost to Carry	$797
Rental Income	$585
Cash Flow Prior to Tax Savings	$212/Month

nique that could be used here is to have the seller refinance the property and the refinance assumable by the buyer. Write a contract for the purchase of the property contingent on the refinance assumable by you, the buyer.

Summary of Method 6
- Ballooning the second trust at five years and paying 12% interest results in monthly payments of $250 (second trust, 12% interest only).
- New mortgage payment is $489 per month, giving a total of $739 per month.
- Property would rent for approximately $585 per month.
- Negative cash flow is $254 per month prior to considering tax savings. Individuals with taxable incomes of between $20,000 to $25,000 could easily afford this purchase.

METHOD 7—NEW MORTGAGE, USE SECOND PROPERTY AS COLLATERAL

- Used when property has large equity.
- New mortgage approximately 60% or less of the sell price.

- Second trust must have interest rates less than first trust.
- Down payment not required since property to be purchased is free of secondary financing (second trust mortgage).

The lending institution may not advance the money for the first trust if the down payment has been borrowed. The best way I have found to deal with the situation is, if asked, to state that the down payment has been arranged between you and the seller through an exchange of properties, or simply to state that the seller has received full consideration for the remaining equity. If necessary, draft a letter stating that the required down payment has been arranged between you and seller. Sign the letter (both you and the seller) and submit with the loan application. Be sure to emphasize that the value of the property above their loan is free and clear. Since there should be a large equity, there should be no problems. Remember, loan officers do not write those fancy jingles on TV commercials. They are in business to make money at minimum risk. They do not like the idea of an investor buying an investment property with no money down. (See Figure 3-8 for a detailed explanation of this method.)

Properties that offer the best possibilities are those with unassumable loans. Remember you are buying from a "must seller," who is strongly motivated to sell his or her property. Borrow as little as possible of the new money. Have the seller deal directly with the lending institution holding the first trust and negotiate for favorable interest rates. Not all lending in-

FIGURE 3-8
Method 7: New mortgage, use second property as collateral.

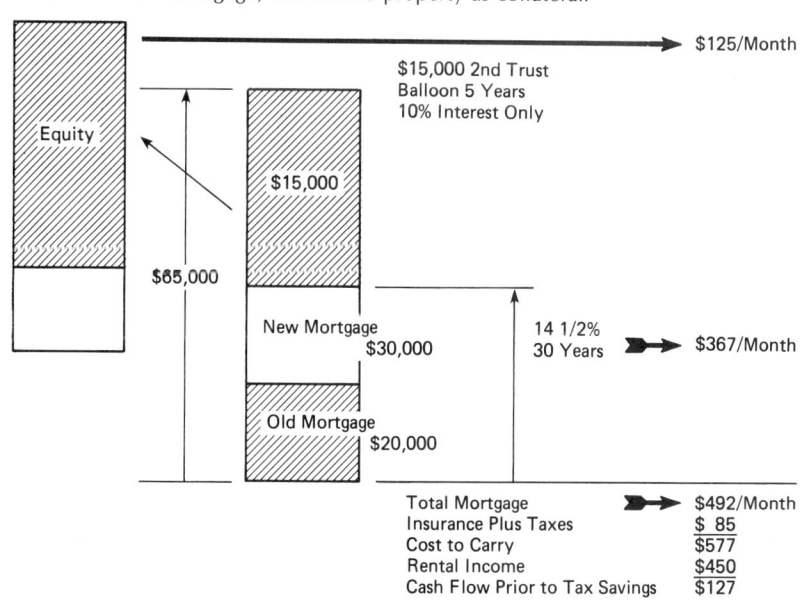

$15,000 2nd Trust Balloon 5 Years 10% Interest Only	$125/Month
New Mortgage $30,000 at 14 1/2% 30 Years	$367/Month
Old Mortgage $20,000	
Equity $65,000 / $15,000	
Total Mortgage	$492/Month
Insurance Plus Taxes	$ 85
Cost to Carry	$577
Rental Income	$450
Cash Flow Prior to Tax Savings	$127

112 THE HUNT

stitutions will negotiate the new money interest rates below prime. However, do remember that there are thousands of homes in any given city of America that fit these conditions. You are interested in just one investment property, and one motivated seller, and one motivated lending institution.

Summary of Method 7
- Similar to Method 5, there is *no* down payment.
- Must have second property (your house), which serves as collateral.
- At five years you may wish to refinance and pay off the balloon (see Method 11).
- Negotiate the new mortgage ($30,000) to as low as possible and at an interest rate below prime. Remember, you are doing the holder of the first trust note (old mortgage) a favor, since you are removing a low-interest loan from their portfolio.

METHOD 8—BORROW DOWN PAYMENT FROM SELLER

- Works best when the old mortgage is small.
- Seller lends the buyer $5,000 for the down payment with second property as collateral; for example, a second trust on the investor's home.
- Seller takes back a second trust of $5,000 after raising the cost of the home by $5,000.
- Seller takes back the remaining equity as third trust.

Since the value of the property was raised $5,000, the return after the first year may be small. (See Figure 3-9.) However, this is an excellent tech-

FIGURE 3-9
Method 8: Borrow down payment from seller.

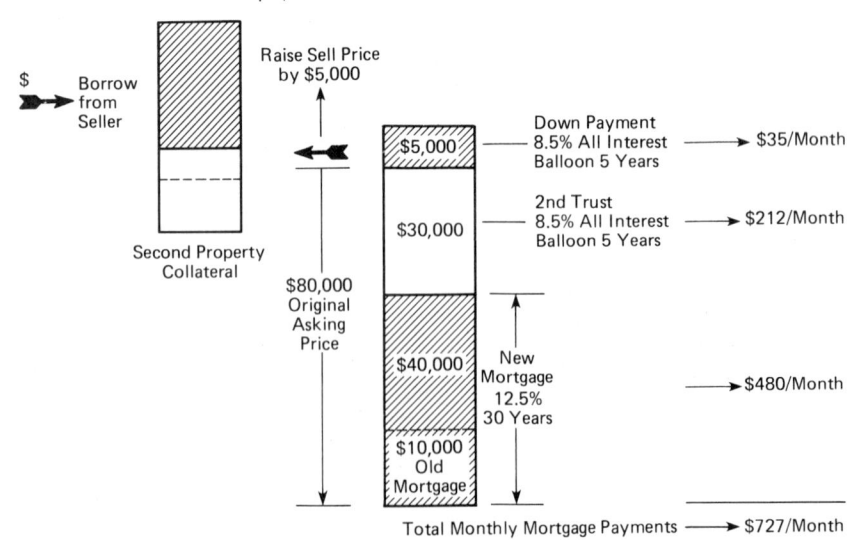

nique for undervalued property. A beautiful example of this type of situation is a builder who is having problems with his or her construction loan and is selling the property at a discounted price.

Technically, this type of purchase is nothing more than a buy down. A word of caution: Lending institutions do not like the idea of a part of their money being used as down payment. A method that can be used to successfully complete the above transaction would be to raise the purchase price by $5,000 or $10,000. Borrow the required down payment as a short-term loan. After settlement, the seller would return the down payment from the borrowed money. Since this method requires trust between the seller and the buyer, it is important that a knowledgeable realtor be involved in the transaction. Preferably, the same realtor should represent both the seller and buyer.

Summary of Method 8
- In this example, the seller receives $30,000 cash at settlement plus $247 per month for the second and third trusts. The $35,000 in secondary financing would be due in five years.
- Be sure to explain the advantages of the second trust. Find second trust buyers if needed.
- A technique with balloon second trusts that I have employed successfully is to refinance the property after two or three years of ownership. Obtain written permission from the holder of the second trust money to buy a discounted second trust in a third investment property. When refinancing, you must pay off the second trust holders. It is to their advantage to allow you to use a portion of the paid-off second trust, since they receive a percentage of the second trust in hard cash.

METHOD 9—ALL-INCLUSIVE DEED OF TRUST (WRAPAROUND)

- Property has an assumable VA, FHA, or negotiable first trust.
- First trust remains with original owner (seller), or the lending institution assumes the responsibility for payment of first trust.
- New loan (all-inclusive deed of trust) is at an interest rate below prime (negotiable) based on the total sell price less down payment.
- Lending institution or individual financing the all-inclusive trust receives payments at an effective interest rate that is higher than new mortgage loan.
- New loan financed over same period as years remaining on the original loan.
- Small down payment required.

I have found lending institutions that will allow wraparounds with the new mortgage loans as high as 100% of the value of the first trust. With investors, the lending institution usually requires a certain percentage of the

FIGURE 3-10
Method 9: All-inclusive deed of trust (wraparound).

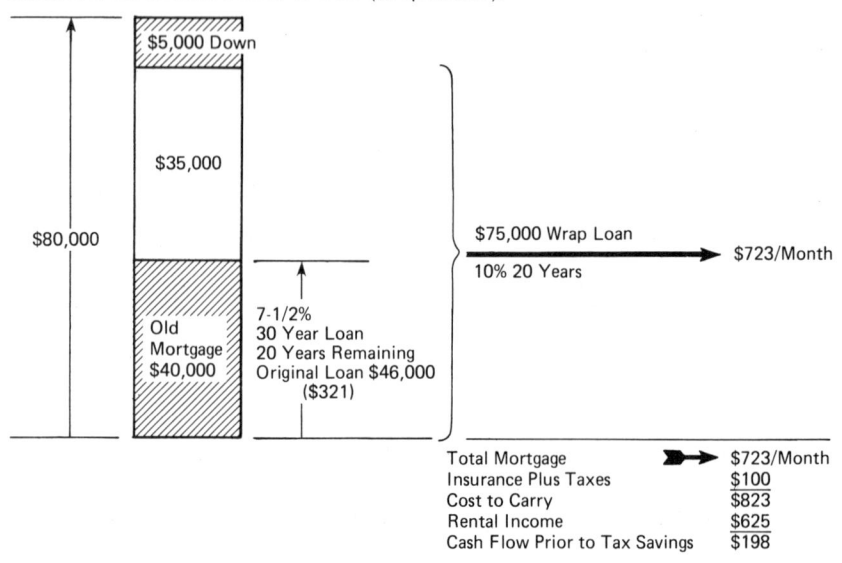

```
                                    $75,000 Wrap Loan
$80,000    $5,000 Down              ─────────────────→ $723/Month
           $35,000                  10% 20 Years

           Old           7-1/2%
           Mortgage      30 Year Loan
           $40,000       20 Years Remaining
                         Original Loan $46,000
                         ($321)

                         Total Mortgage              ▶ $723/Month
                         Insurance Plus Taxes          $100
                         Cost to Carry                 $823
                         Rental Income                 $625
                         Cash Flow Prior to Tax Savings $198
```

property to be free and clear (down payment). Method 10 discusses moving the mortgage to a second property. Thus there is no down payment.

The reason lending institutions have wraparound programs is that they only finance a portion of the new mortgage. In the example shown in Figure 3–10, only $35,000 of the $75,000 is new money. Thus, $40,000 of the lending institution's funds are now available to finance a second new loan at prime rate. The lending institution will simply pick up the assumable loan and continue to pay it off. Notice that $75,000 was borrowed at 10% interest. However, the effective interest returned is 13.8%. Remember, lending institutions are in business to make money.

Summary of Method 9

- Buyer pays seller (individual or mortgage institution having wraparound plan) $75,000 at 10% over 20 years. This amounts to $723.77 per month, or $8,685.24 per year.
- Seller pays first trust, 7½% original 30-year loan, which totals $321 per month, or $3,859 per year.
- Seller has positive cash flow ($8,685 − 3,859 = $4,826 per year).
- For new money (75,000 − $40,000 = $35,000).
- It is extremely important that any individual who is serious about purchasing an investment property understand the above. Learn how to calculate for the true interest rate. I have found lending institutions with wrap financing programs yielding true interest rates two or three points above prime. Do your own calculations, clearly understand the true interest rate and negotiate for the best terms. Shop around, you may also find that a straight second trust loan is in your best interest.

METHOD 10—ALL-INCLUSIVE DEED OF TRUST WITH NO DOWN PAYMENT

- First trust remains with seller.
- Second trust remains with seller.
- Equity becomes part of wraparound.
- An additional second (third) trust is generated with a second property serving as collateral.

Moving the mortgage to a second property results in freeing the top part of the property, thus increasing the probability of new mortgage money. If an individual is financing the wraparound, then it is best to include the entire equity within the wraparound.

When the first trust remains with an individual, it is best to protect yourself against nonpayment by arranging for first (second) trust insurance and tax payments through a bank or escrow company. Also, be sure that your interest in the property cannot be jeopardized by the nonpayment of the mortgage remaining with the seller. Make arrangements with the bank that you be notified in case of nonpayment. Have a clear and definitive understanding concerning what constitutes default. It is best that the investment-homebuyer obtain the services of a competent lawyer when purchasing a property involving an all-inclusive deed of trust. See Figure 3-11 for a graphic explanation of this method.

Summary of Method 10
- Seller pays first trust at 8½%, loan equals $50,000, payments are $384 per month.
- Seller pays second trust at 9½%, loan equals $25,000, payments are $210 per month.
- Total payments are $594 per month.
- Seller's positive cash flow is $833 − 594 = $239 per month, or $2,868 per year.
- True interest (first year) = $2,868 ÷ $20,000 = 14.3%

METHOD 11—REFINANCE, A FORM OF WRAPAROUND

- Investor currently owns a property with an assumable first trust.
- Property has second trust, balloon in five years.
- Property has been held for a period of four years.
- Original value of property is $45,000.
- Current value of property is $84,970.
- Equity in property is $32,490 ($84,970 − $52,480).

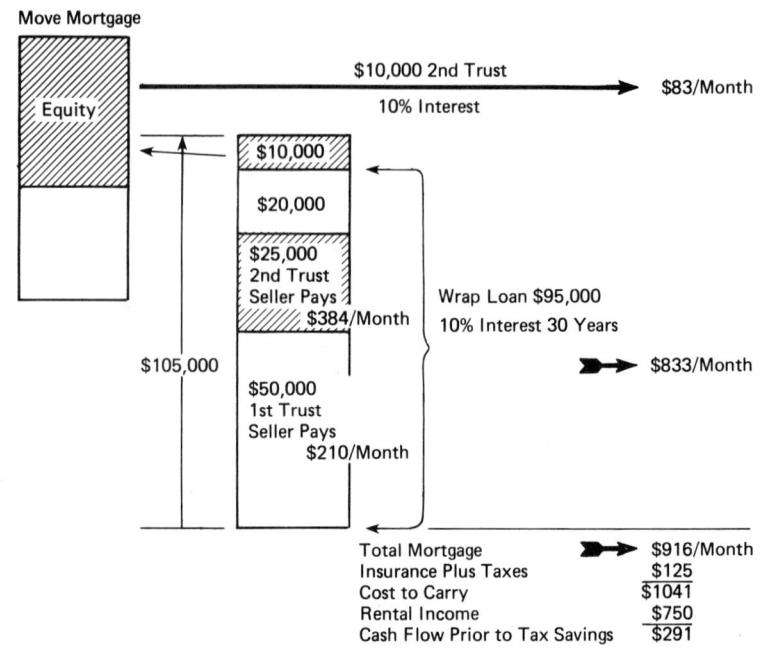

FIGURE 3-11
Method 10: All-inclusive deed of trust with no down payment.

Move Mortgage

Equity

$105,000

$10,000 2nd Trust
10% Interest
→ $83/Month

$10,000

$20,000

$25,000
2nd Trust
Seller Pays
$384/Month

$50,000
1st Trust
Seller Pays
$210/Month

Wrap Loan $95,000
10% Interest 30 Years
→ $833/Month

Total Mortgage	→ $916/Month
Insurance Plus Taxes	$125
Cost to Carry	$1041
Rental Income	$750
Cash Flow Prior to Tax Savings	$291

You, the investor, purchased the property four years ago. The second trust note (balloon) is due in one year. You must pay off the second trust, but you wish to retain the property. First, you need to find a lending institution with a wraparound loan program. Borrow $67,976. (See Figure 3–12.) Allow the lending institution to assume the first trust (they will pay it off). A total of $11,845 is required to pay off the original second trust. Cash in your pocket is $15,496 (less loan origination points). Use a portion of the cash to purchase a second property. The remaining $16,994 ($84,970 − $67,976) remains as equity in the property. (See Table 3–2.)

Before you pay off the second trust, ask the holder of the second trust if he or she would be interested in purchasing a discounted second on an additional property with a portion of the current second trust. Make this a condition for the refinance. This technique works most effectively if you refinance as soon after the purchase of the investment property as possible. The reason is simple: The holder of the second trust receives cash and buys a discounted second trust with a higher yield. This technique has never failed me; it should work more often than not. The key is knowledge and being able to properly explain and articulate the benefits of buying a discounted second trust.

FIGURE 3-12
Method 11: Refinance "a form of a wraparound."

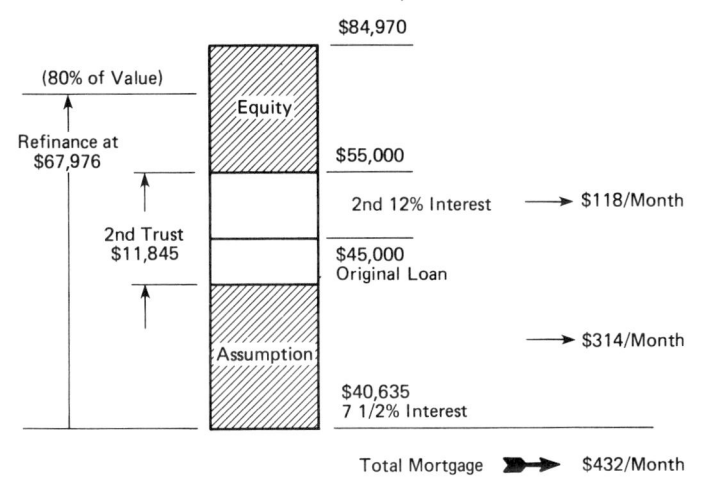

```
                                    $84,970
     (80% of Value)          ┌──────────────┐
          ▲                  │////Equity////│
   Refinance at              │              │
     $67,976                 ├──────────────┤ $55,000
          │                  │              │
          │                  │  2nd 12% Interest ──▶ $118/Month
          │   2nd Trust      │              │
          │    $11,845       ├──────────────┤ $45,000
          │                  │              │  Original Loan
          ▼                  │              │
                             │//Assumption//│              ──▶ $314/Month
                             │              │
                             └──────────────┘ $40,635
                                               7 1/2% Interest

                              Total Mortgage ▶▶ $432/Month
```

Summary of Method 11
- The lending institution assumes the $40,635 loan, providing you, the investor, with $69,976 at approximately 10% interest. New monthly payments equal $596.53. The lending institution will have an effective interest rate of approximately 13% on the new money amount of $27,341.
- Value of first trust when the property was purchased was $43,155.

METHOD 12—INDIVIDUAL PARTNER TO HELP FINANCE (SPLIT PROFITS AT SELL)

- Down payment comes from individual partner (silent).
- Buyer (investor) depreciates property.
- Investor (principal) manages property and cash flow.
- Principal and silent partner split profits at sell.
- Works excellently with relatives or friends who do not wish to manage property.

This method (see Figure 3–13) is a form of the equity participation mortgage (also see Method 14). The difference is that your partner provides all or a portion of the down payment. An agreement is made that you as the active investor manage and receive the full benefits of the tax write offs. Your silent partner has a maintenance free investment period and receives a percentage of the equity gain when the investment property is sold. The

TABLE 3-2.

AGE OF PROPERTY	APPRECIATION RATE (INFLATION)	VALUE OF PROPERTY
0		$45,000
1	.06	47,700
2	.06	50,562
3	.06	53,595
4	.06	56,810
	You purchase investment	
5	.08	61,354
6	.10	67,489
7	.10	74,238
8	.14	84,970

biggest problem you will have is your partner's need to overcome the psychological barrier. You must help him or her to overcome by knowledge. Do your homework, present clear facts, such as expected profits, good location, rent money, and so forth, projecting the expected return. Commit the agreement to writing, signed by you, your partner, and witnessed by a third individual. Treat your partner as you would a bank by keeping your commitment.

Consider reversing positions with your partner, the principal becomes the silent and vice versa. This is an excellent method of holding multiple

FIGURE 3-13
Method 12: Individual partner to help finance (split profits at sell).

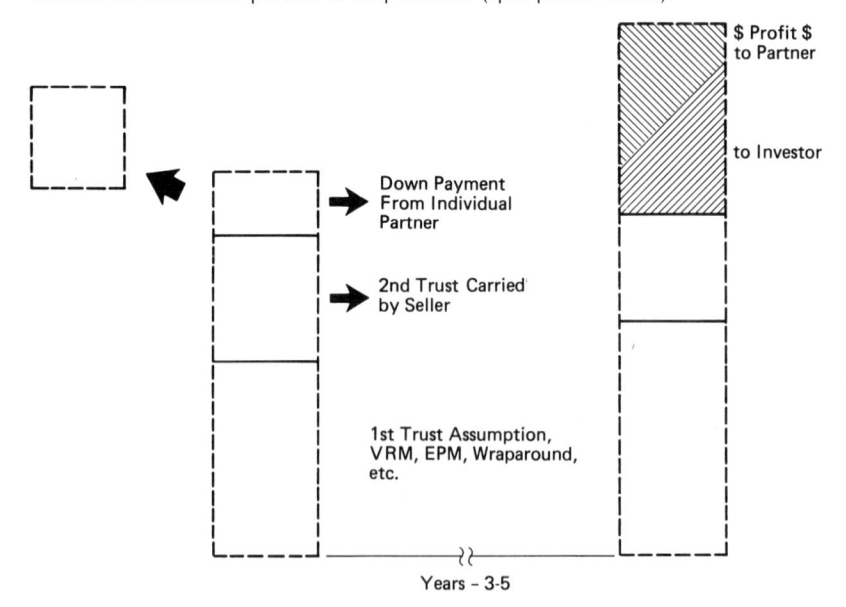

investments and at the same time decreasing management responsibilities.

If you don't know an individual who would assist you with the down payment, research the possibility of an investment corporation providing the equity sharing partner. I know of several both on the East and West Coasts that provide either direct money or the service of finding an investment partner. Young couples just getting started should seriously look into this arrangement.

Summary of Method 12
- Consider moving the equity to a second property if new money is used.
- Profit split should reflect percentage of down payment monies with adjustment for property management (to five points).
- Maintenance costs should be deducted before determination of profits.
- Agree on all terms and conditions *before* signing the agreement.
- Assuming the equity split is 50-50, remember that 50% of something is better than 100% of nothing.

METHOD 13—BUY OFF MORTGAGES AT DISCOUNTED PRICES

- Short term—fast turnaround profits.
- Need cash for short period of time.
- Works best in the slow periods of the year (December through February). During this period you have a higher concentration of "must sellers." See discussion on "must sellers" later in this phase.
- Ideal for investors who have developed their real estate portfolios over a period of three or more years.
- Works best in cold weather climates. Traditionally, winter is a slow period. Property appreciates faster in summer months.

This is a great method to generate large profits in relatively short periods of time. My recommendation is to be aware of this possibility as you hunt for properties. The situation is most likely to present itself with a property that has multiple liens at relatively low interest rates—for example, a property selling for $75,000 with a $45,000 assumable first trust and a $16,000 second trust. Make the offer to purchase the property contingent on assuming the first trust and paying off the second trust for $12,000 (25% discount). The current holder of the second trust would in most probabilities accept the discounted price if the second trust note was long term (over five years) and at a fairly low interest rate.

Summary of Method 13
- Excellent program for investor who has a developed investment portfolio.
- Discounted notes plus appreciation of property will generate $20,000 to $30,000 within 18 months with properties in the $75,000 range.

FIGURE 3-14
Method 13: Buy off mortgages at discounted prices.

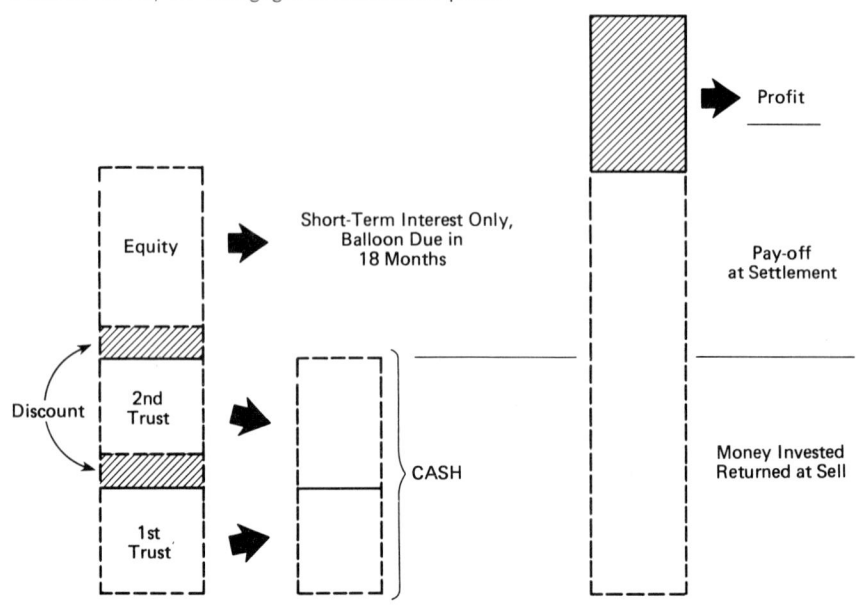

- Cash required to purchase the discounted trusts can be OPM. Borrow money from the credit union, banks, commercial lenders, or individuals with other investment properties as collateral.

METHOD 14—VARIABLE-RATE MORTGAGE (RENEGOTIABLE-RATE MORTGAGE)

- Negotiate all details at the beginning of the loan. Interest rates will be outlined in the original agreement.
- Interest is usually lower at the start of loan. Amount of rate increase or decrease is negotiable.
- There is no prepayment penalty, and these mortgages can be refinanced any time.
- Possible that loan may be assumed, however, it is usually raised to the interest rate of the next time period.
- Federal regulations have directed that loan rates can only change every three years (ideal for investor).
- Specify renegotiable periods. Be sure agreement outlines that interest rate will not exceed an agreed-to rate, usually the increase cannot exceed 1.5 points.
- If the prime rate is lower than the initial rate at the time of renegotiation, the rate will automatically fall to a lower rate.
- No new loan origination fees.
- Remember, all negotiating is done at the beginning of the loan. Be sure to negotiate the most favorable terms possible.

FIGURE 3-15
Method 14: Variable rate mortgages (renegotiable rate mortgage).

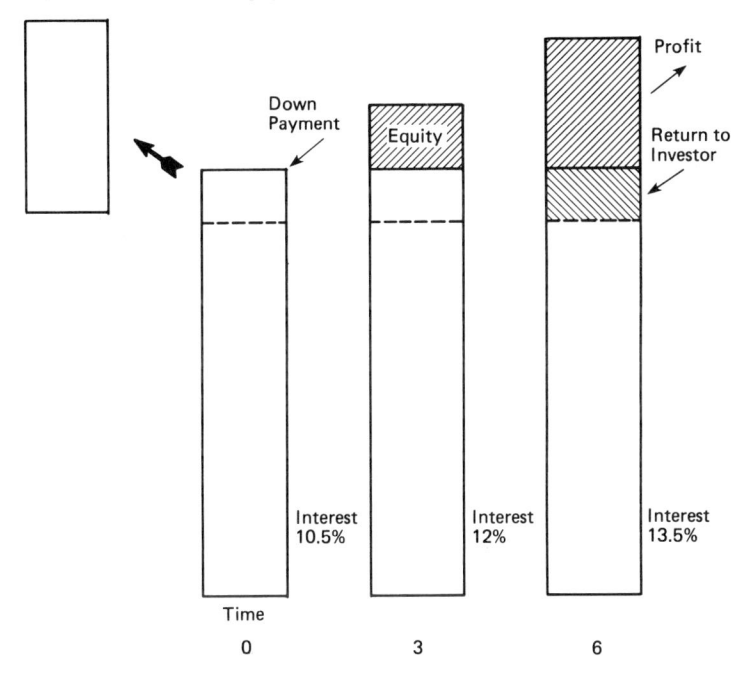

VRMs are not the exclusive right of lending institutions. Any direct financing (subordinate notes) between the seller and buyer may be structured similar to a VRM. See Figure 3-15 for a graphic illustration of this method.

Summary of Method 14
- Consider making the down payment a second trust, with collateral being equity in a second property.
- At the time this book was in the making, the FHLBB announced that time periods during which interest rates can be adjusted are completely negotiable between lender and borrower. Be sure to specify limits on how often the rate can be adjusted and the maximum increase in the rate.

METHOD 15—EQUITY PARTICIPATION MORTGAGE (EPM)

- Partnership with mortgage institution or individual.
- Mortgage rate some percentage below prime (usually two-thirds).
- Owner (investor) depreciates property.
- Profit split can be 50-50, 33-66, 25-75, or whatever appropriate. EPMs are extremely negotiable.
- Investor's profit is taxed as long-term capital gain.

FIGURE 3-16
Method 15: Equity participation mortgage (EPM).

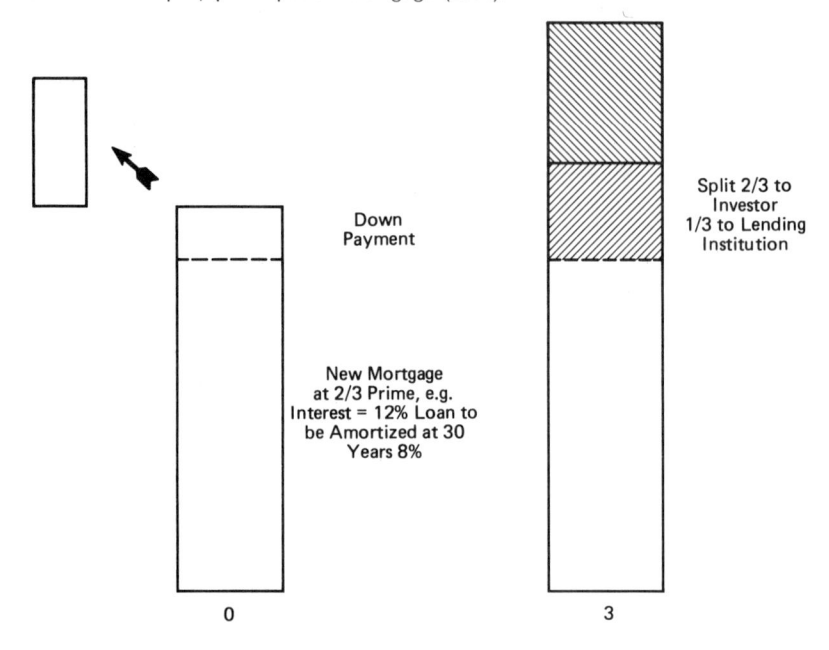

Down Payment

New Mortgage at 2/3 Prime, e.g. Interest = 12% Loan to be Amortized at 30 Years 8%

Split 2/3 to Investor
1/3 to Lending Institution

- The profit made by the mortgage institution must be declared as a short-term taxable gain.

The problem involved with this type of loan is that homeowners must refinance in five or ten years. (See Figure 3-16.) Home buyers tend to think of themselves as remaining on the property for a lifetime. Additionally, lending institutions that receive high profits might be subject to state unconscionability laws, which protect borrowers. Also, lending institutions may desire to invest in high appreciation neighborhoods, thus indirectly discriminating against certain individuals.

Currently EPMs are limited to owner occupied homes. You should consider using your present home as collateral for a down payment (second trust) on a new home. Your present home becomes your investment property. It is excellent for beginners. I did this with a renegotiable-rate mortgage.

METHOD 16—SHORT- TO LONG-TERM ROLLOVER

- Obtain deferred, short-term construction loan from builder.
- Upon completion of construction, roll the construction loan to mortgage.
- Usually done with large custom-building contractors.

- Ideal for first-time buyers.
- Have duplex or small attached apartment built for rental property.
- Can be multifamily rental income property for pure investment purposes.

Method 16 involves new money; however, it does guarantee the eventual purchase of either an investment property or an owner-occupied home for no money down. The builder advances the construction money for the building of a custom home to the buyer. Monthly payments are deferred for a period of 6 to 12 months after the start of the construction. The construction can either be outside shell only or a completely finished home.

The ideal situation is to purchase a lot (owner financed, no money down) in an area with expensive homes, for example, homes valued at $150,000 to $175,000. The custom home can be built for approximately $100,000. Keep your present home as an investment. If you are a renter, have a duplex or a triplex built. Rent the other units; the rent money will pay for the mortgage. For example, mortgage payments on $100,000 at 14%, amortized over 30 years, is $1,184 per month. Half of the property will rent for $500. All of the interest is tax deductible. Net result is positive cash, with $150,000 worth of property!

Note that one of two things must be done with the purchase of the lot before the lending institution advances the first trust money: (1) The lot must be owned by the investor free and clear. Or (2) The owner of the lot must accept a second trust on the custom-built home as collateral for the lot. The latter option should not be a problem, since failure to pay the monthly payments would result in the lot owner acquiring the property at a large discount. Generally the lending institution will not advance the first trust monies if they are not recorded as the first institution to collect money in case of foreclosure. One additional note—be prepared to shop around, since this technique, although technically and financially sound and legal, will be unconventional to the majority of lending institutions. Nevertheless, the time required to shop around will be well worth the effort. See Figure 3-17 for a graphic description of this method.

Summary of Method 16
- A construction loan of $100,000 is rolled into a long-term mortgage at 11%, amortized over 30 years. Mortgage payments are $1,184 per month.
- One-half of investment home (duplex) rents for five hundred dollars ... cash flow negative $684 per month before taxes.
- With mortgage interest and rental property tax deductions, the investor will have a net negative cash flow of $300 to $400 per month. If the investor is currently renting at $500 per month, he or she will actually have a *positive* cash flow!
- Remember the home (duplex) will easily appraise at 150% of the roll over construction loan. In this example, the immediate equity is $50,000.
- Note that in order to obtain financing for the building of the custom home, the lending institution will require that the lot have a clear title. This is not

FIGURE 3-17
Method 16: Short to long-term rollover.

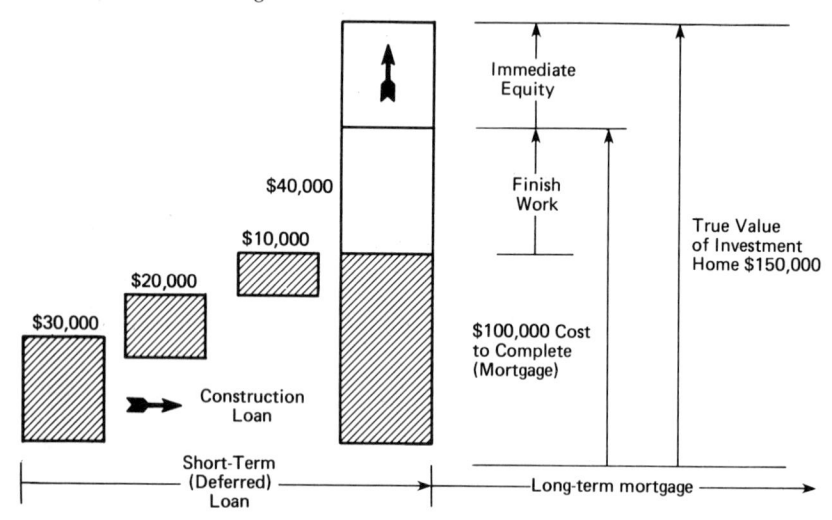

a problem. Have the seller of the lot finance the true value of the lot with a second property as collateral, or have the owner of the lot assume a second trust in the custom-built home.

METHOD 17—BUY BELOW MARKET VALUE AND REFINANCE TO MAXIMUM ALLOWABLE

- Assumable first trust (VA or FHA).
- Must seller.
- Preferably the property should be for sale by the owner.
- Offer cash to assume loan, discounted 30% to 40% of the cash value (discounted approximately 10% of the total property value).

Properties with assumable loans and $20,000 to $30,000 cash to assume are ideal candidates. (See Figure 3–18.) Offer to buy out the equity if the seller is willing to discount the cash requirement. In essence, the investor is buying the property at a wholesale price. If the owner were to take back the equity in a second trust, then the sale price would be the asking value. When you enter Phase 3, The Hunt, you will be pleasantly surprised to find hundreds of properties in this category. Make offers on the best five or six possibilities, the worst that can happen is that they say no. Remember, you are looking for only *one* investment property. In less than a year, you can refinance and recover the cash sum invested.

When hunting for properties, it is best if you purchase an assumption

FIGURE 3-18
Method 17: Buy below market value and refinance to maximum allowable.

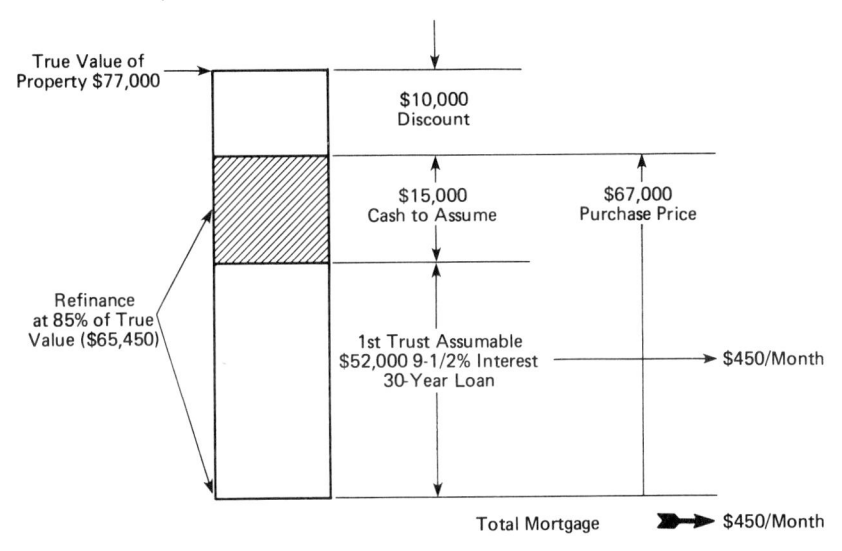

```
True Value of
Property $77,000 ─┐
                  │        ↓
                  │   $10,000
                  │   Discount
                  │          ↑             ↑
                  │     $15,000         $67,000
                  │     Cash to Assume  Purchase Price
                  │          ↓
Refinance
at 85% of True
Value ($65,450)
                     1st Trust Assumable
                     $52,000 9-1/2% Interest  ──→ $450/Month
                     30-Year Loan

                     Total Mortgage  ══► $450/Month
```

held by the Federal National Mortgage Association, nicknamed Fannie Mae. Fannie Mae will refinance the trust at extremely favorable rates, since it is currently attempting to clear the books of low-interest-bearing accounts.

A favorite technique of mine is to purchase the investment property at 10% or 15% below the market value (purchase in the dead of winter), wait for one good year of appreciation, and refinance. At 18% inflation, the property will appraise for $84,700 one year after the purchase date. With an 80% refinance loan, total cash to the investor is $67,760 (80% of $84,700) less loan origination fees. Approximately $52,000 is used to pay off the first trust. Total cash in hand is approximately $13,000, which can be used to buy a second investment property. With approximately $15,000 in cash (yours or OPM), a wise investor should be able to purchase one property per year with no money down (all OPM). It is best if the assumable first trust is carried by the Federal National Mortgage Association, as it can be refinanced or sold as a wraparound program.

METHOD 18—UNDERVALUED PROPERTY IN GOOD LOCATION

- This method works best for property that is undervalued due to general neglect and that has been on the market for some time.
- The property should have a small first trust compared with the total asking price. For example, the first trust may be 25% or less of the asking price.
- Obtain a new loan to cover the first trust, the cash requirements of the seller, and the cash required to repair the property.

126 THE HUNT

- The seller will carry back a sizable second trust. If necessary balloon over a short period. For example, three or five years and pay interest only. The method will work best for property that has been owned for some period of time by the present owner, since the discounted sale price will cut down his or her equity gain. To the seller, the sale price is actually $70,000, since $10,000 of the new money is being used to fix the property. (See Figure 3-19.)

I used the method described in Figure 3-19 to purchase a duplex. The rental was $400 per unit, total $800 per month. Negative cash flow was $252 prior to accounting for tax savings. An investor with a taxable income of $25,000 per year could easily carry the property. Generally properties being sold that are undervalued because of neglect remain on the market for some period of time. A method that could be used to identify a must seller is to make offers to purchase properties that have been on the market longer than 3 months and are vacant. The sell price is already reduced plus your offer to purchase would be 10% below the asking price. Remember to deal with numbers, make ten offers and the odds are in your favor that one will say yes.

Summary of Method 18
- The $20,000 first trust will be paid off with the new loan.
- The $15,000 will be used to meet the cash requirements of the seller.
- $5,000 is for closing costs, and $10,000 is for fixing the property.
- The seller takes back a second trust worth $30,000.

FIGURE 3-19
Method 18: Undervalued property in good location.

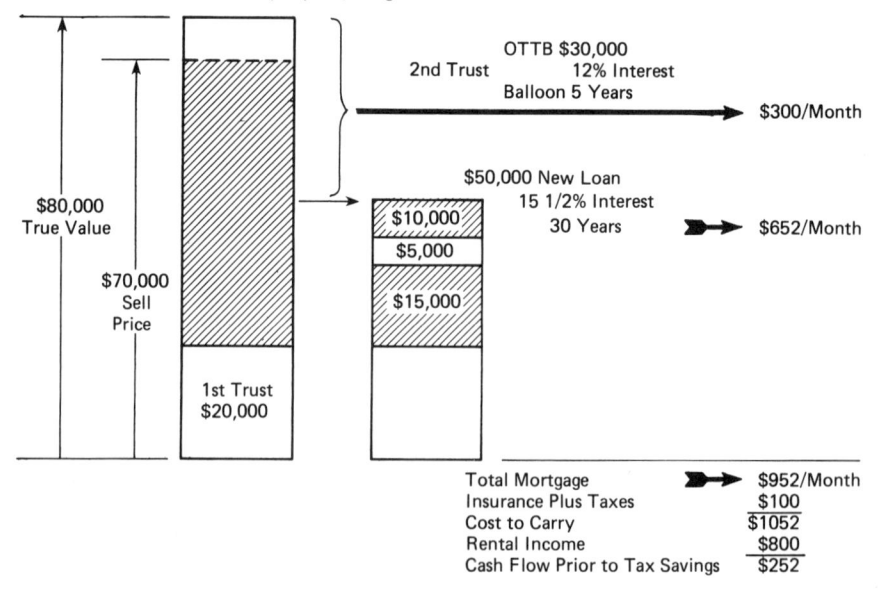

$80,000 True Value
$70,000 Sell Price

1st Trust $20,000

2nd Trust — OTTB $30,000, 12% Interest, Balloon 5 Years → $300/Month

$50,000 New Loan, 15 1/2% Interest, 30 Years → $652/Month
$10,000
$5,000
$15,000

Total Mortgage	$952/Month
Insurance Plus Taxes	$100
Cost to Carry	$1052
Rental Income	$800
Cash Flow Prior to Tax Savings	$252

FIGURE 3-20
Method 19: Small 1st trust/owner financed.

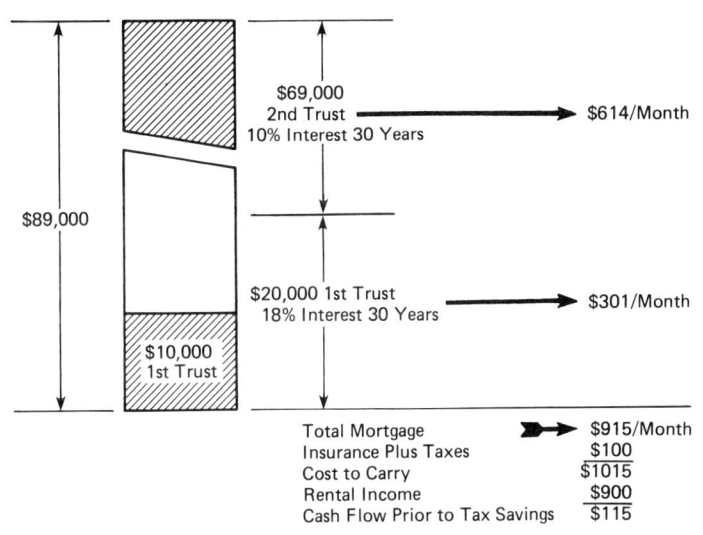

```
$89,000  {  $69,000
            2nd Trust            ———▶  $614/Month
            10% Interest 30 Years

            $20,000 1st Trust
            18% Interest 30 Years  ———▶  $301/Month

            $10,000
            1st Trust
```

Total Mortgage	$915/Month
Insurance Plus Taxes	$100
Cost to Carry	$1015
Rental Income	$900
Cash Flow Prior to Tax Savings	$115

METHOD 19—OWNER FINANCED SMALL FIRST TRUST

- Small first trust.
- Obtain investor loan for first trust.
- Indicate down payment is property exchange.
- Owner carries back second trust at interest rate below prevailing rate.

The property has large equity and the owner is willing to carry back a sizable portion as a second trust. (See Figure 3-20.) The first trust is obtained from a mortgage corporation as an investor loan at prevailing rates. The second trust is negotiated at below prevailing rates. The down payment is in the form of a second trust on a second property. Another method of obtaining the down payment could be money borrowed as a second trust loan from your current home of residence or any other investment properties.

Recently a business partner of mine and I were hunting for properties. I had just completed two no money down transactions when we found a four-unit apartment complex selling for $89,000. The owner was willing to carry back $86,000 as a second trust at 10%, amortized over 30 years. Needless to say, we put down the $3,000 and purchased the property. All four units were rented and the PITI was $850 per month. The total rent was $995 per month. Total depreciation on the property was in excess of $10,000 per year.

These opportunities do exist, just keep searching and always cultivate new sensors (realtors).

Summary of Method 19
- In the actual case, the $89,000 apartment complex rented for a total of $995 per month.
- An immediate cash flow was realized.
- A single family home would rent for approximately $600.
- The $315 negative cash flow could easily be carried by anyone with a taxable income over $30,000 per year.

METHOD 20—YOUR IMAGINATION IS YOUR ONLY LIMIT

- Move all individually held mortgages to free the property.
- Consider second trust owner financing for a portion of equity.
- Once a good portion of the property is free, obtain new financing via a wraparound loan.
- Any combination of the previously discussed methods can be used. (See Figure 3-21.) Remember, strive for minimum cash down and use borrowed money at the lowest possible interest rate, amortized over longest period of time.

This method pertains to investors with established real estate portfolios. There are an infinite number of methods to buy clean properties in move-in condition at affordable prices. Your imagination is your unique tool. Learn to be creative. Acquire a distaste for the conventional. Give yourself a challenge, and see what other methods you can create.

FIGURE 3-21
Method 20: Your imagination is your limit.

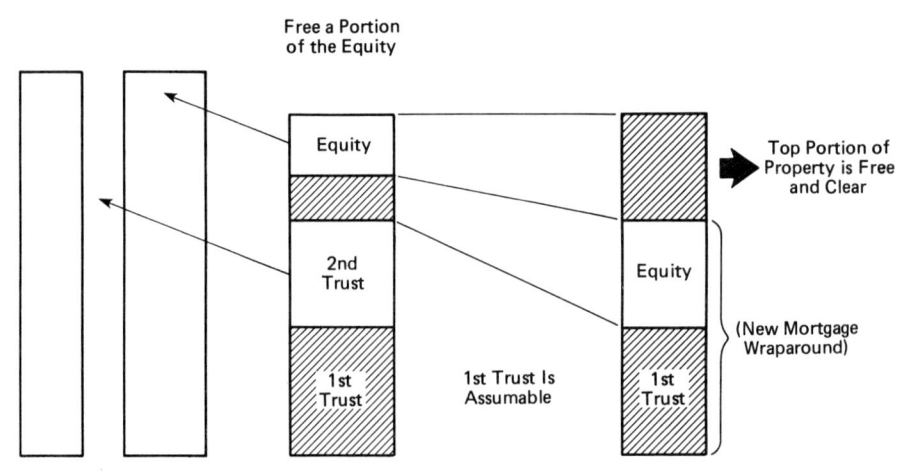

Summary of Method 20
- The new mortgage is used to pay off the first trust and a portion of the equity.
- The second trust and a portion of the equity are moved to other properties.
- Allows purchase with no down payment.
- Negotiate the second trusts (using the other properties as collateral) at low interest rate, since seller receives cash at settlement.

METHOD 21—USE THE RENT AS A DOWN PAYMENT

- Assumption.
- Must seller because of divorce or other reason.
- To be sold to investor only.
- Willing to carry back equity.

Awhile ago I dedicated one weekend to the purchase of two investment properties. Both properties were purchased using absolutely *no money down.* I had called a realtor whom I had met in one of my previous purchases, and we spent one afternoon inspecting approximately 20 properties. All the properties were assumptions, with owners already stating that they would carry back a portion of the equity. One of the two properties I chose from the 20 we visited was owned by a divorcing couple. The wife wanted to remain on the property.

The offer to purchase was structured as follows: first trust to be assumed; second trust to be from a commercial lender; third trust to be split into two equal parts—the first part would be in the form of the seller being able to remain in the investment property rent free for 12 months, the second part of the remaining equity would be moved to a second investment property and carried back as an interest-only balloon loan in five years.

See Figure 3-22 for a graphic description of this method. Note that, although there will be *no* rental income the first year, for income tax purposes $400 ($4,800 divided by 12) will be claimed as rental income. Tax deductions will be $176 × 12 ($2,112) plus depreciation of the building. Depreciation equals $55,600 × 13/16 divided by 15 and multiplied by 1.75 ($5,270). Total deductions equal $7,382 ($2,112 plus $5,270). An individual in the 35% tax bracket would save $2,583 ($7,382 × 0.35) in the first year of property ownership. His or her out-of-pocket expenses would be the total cost to carry ($6,912) minus tax savings ($2,583). Total monies required to sustain the property the first year would be $4,329. After the first year, a rental income of $440 per month ($5,280 per year) would be realized, offsetting all negative cash flow. An investor who cannot sustain an out-of-pocket expense of $4,329 the first year should consider using a partnership to help finance (see Method 23).

FIGURE 3-22
Method 21: Using your imagination. Use the rent as the down payment.

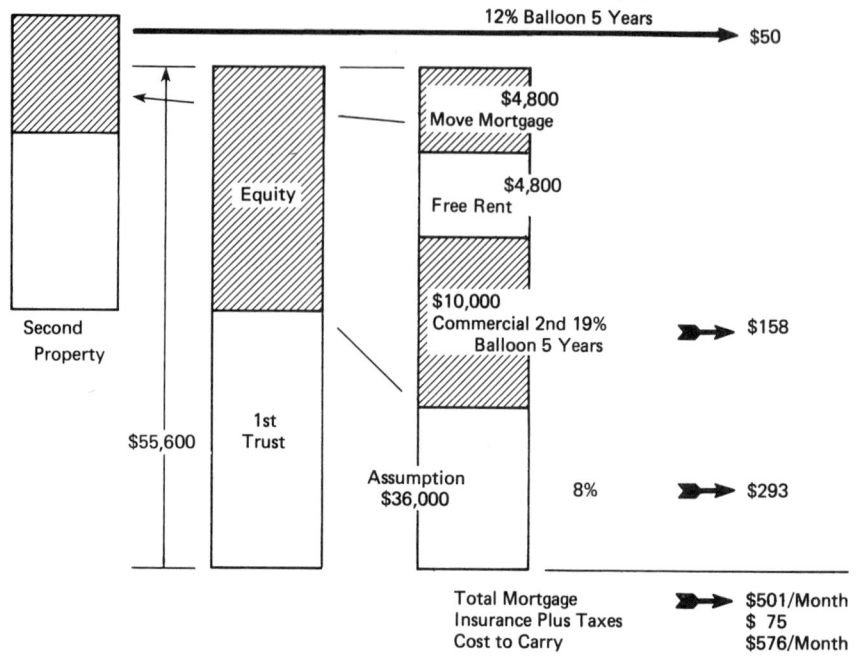

```
                    12% Balloon 5 Years            $50
                    
                         $4,800
                         Move Mortgage
                         
                         $4,800
              Equity     Free Rent
              
                         $10,000
Second                   Commercial 2nd 19%       $158
Property                 Balloon 5 Years
              
              1st
$55,600       Trust
                         Assumption
                         $36,000        8%        $293
                         
                         Total Mortgage           $501/Month
                         Insurance Plus Taxes     $ 75
                         Cost to Carry            $576/Month
```

METHOD 22—MOVING MORTGAGES

- Assumption.
- Investor owns property.
- Existing second trust (assumable by owner only).
- Seller willing to carry portion of the equity.
- Realtor will take commission as a third trust.

When purchasing the investment property using free rent as the down payment (Method 21), I also came across a property (townhouse) that carried an assumable first trust and a second trust that was assumable only by the current owner. The seller was willing to carry a good portion of the equity in the form of a second trust only. She would not carry a third trust because her exposure would be too high. The realtor had agreed to take his commission in the form of a third trust on a second investment property. The take back trust by the realtor would be increased by $1,000 in order to allow him to sell the note at a discount rate.

From Figure 3-23, note that the property is rented for $395 per month. The negative cash flow is $183 and easily carries itself since depreciation on the property is in excess of $7,500 per year. An investor with a

FIGURE 3-23
Method 22: Using your imagination. Moving mortgages.

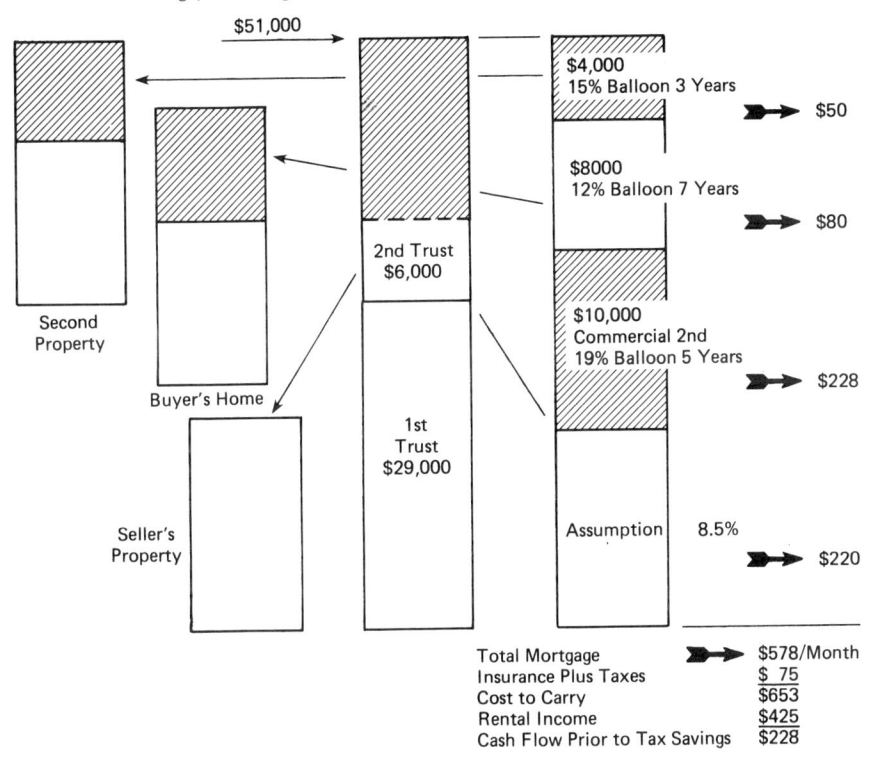

```
                    $51,000
Second Property  →                      $4,000
                                        15% Balloon 3 Years    →  $50

                                        $8000
                                        12% Balloon 7 Years    →  $80

                 Buyer's Home   2nd Trust
                                $6,000
                                        $10,000
                                        Commercial 2nd
                                        19% Balloon 5 Years    →  $228

                                1st
                                Trust
                                $29,000
 Seller's
 Property                               Assumption   8.5%      →  $220


                        Total Mortgage              →  $578/Month
                        Insurance Plus Taxes           $ 75
                        Cost to Carry                  $653
                        Rental Income                  $425
                        Cash Flow Prior to Tax Savings $228
```

taxable income of $30,000 would save over $2,200 per year due to the reduced taxable income ($22,500). Soon after purchasing the property (6 to 12 months), you can refinance with the holder of the first trust. For example, the property could be refinanced for $44,000 at 12% interest, resulting in a new mortgage on the investment property of $463 per month. So for a few more dollars per month ($463 − $448), you, the investor, would realize $4,000 to $5,000 dollars.

METHOD 23—A PARTNERSHIP

- Assumption.
- Commercial second trust.
- OTTB, third trust.
- Seller takes back remaining equity with collateral on second property.

The investor purchases a property with a sizable negative cash flow. The investor has already purchased a sufficient number of properties (three to

132 THE HUNT

five) and has reduced his or her taxable income to below $15,000. The purchase of an additional property with any amount of negative cash flow would cause a problem, since there are no longer any savings to be realized due to the property depreciation. A solution is to have a second party (partner) finance all or part of the negative cash flow. The partner borrows the money. An adjustment is made in the partnership arrangement to allow the tax savings to pay for the borrowed money. Also all interest on the borrowed money is tax deductible.

See Figure 3-24 for a graphic illustration of this method. To simplify the computations, taxes and insurance are not taken into account. The key is simply knowing the cost of carrying the property (in this example, $346 per month) and calculating the partnership to allow the investor's partner the required tax savings to provide for a zero cash flow. The calculations for this method are as follows:

Summary of Method 23
- Rent is $600 per month.
- Negative cash flow equals $346 per month.
- The partner supports the partnership with $250 per month. The partner should have a current taxable yearly income of $34,000.
- Investment property will have a total of $13,157 of allowable tax deductions. Calculations follow: $95,000 × 13/16 divided by 15 and multiplied by 1.75 equals $9,005. All interest is also tax deductible: $346 × 12 equals $4,152. Thus allowable tax deduction equals $9,005 plus $4,152 ($13,157).
- The partner borrows $5,000 to allow for the $250 per month support for a

FIGURE 3-24
Method 23: A partnership.

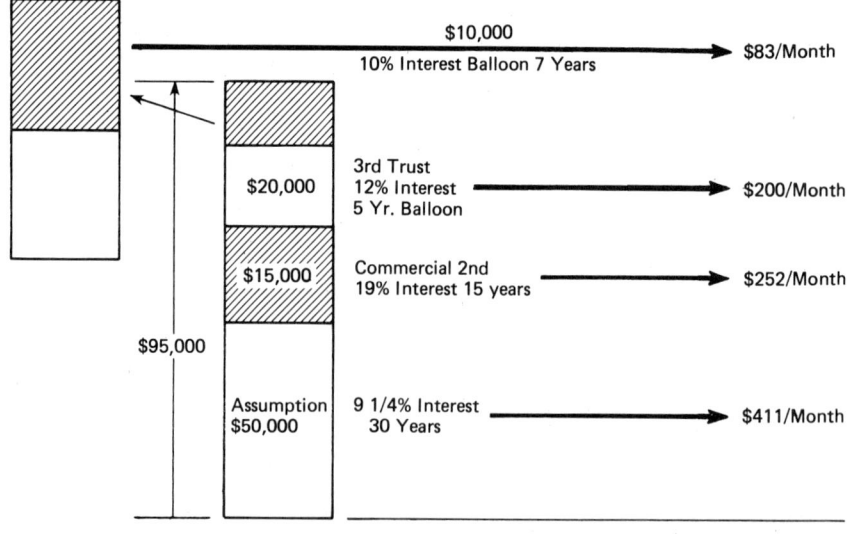

period of two years. $5,000 loan is at 15% and is amortized over eight years. Monthly payments are $89 per month. In order to offset the monthly payments, the partner must realize a yearly total of $1,068 per year ($89 × 12) due to tax savings.
- To realize a savings of $1,068 (from taxes), the partner with the $34,000 taxable income must reduce his or her taxable base from $34,000 to $30,650. Difference in taxes paid is $1,178 ($6,987 − $5,809). Thus, the partner needs a total of $3,350 worth of deductions.
- Total amount of the first year's tax deduction equals $13,157. Ratio of $3,350 to $13,157 determines the partnership arrangement.

$$\frac{\$\ 3{,}350}{\$13{,}157} \times 100 = 25\%$$

- Profit split is 75% to the investor and 25% to the partner.
- Remember, the partner borrowed the $5,000, thus all money is OPM, and the *leverage is infinite!*

METHOD 24—THE LEASE OPTION

- Conventional or assumable mortgage on the property.
- Tight money situation prevails (high interest rates).
- Price of property captured for reasonable period of time (negotiable) for small sum of money.
- Real estate agents can use this very effectively to increase their sales in the near future.
- If the intent is to purchase, the IRS considers the property to have been sold upon the signing of the lease option.
- Conventional lenders do not normally consider lease options to be formal transfers of property, thus the value of the loan is not required to be paid upon signing the lease option.

In a tight money situation, homebuyers and investors generally look for homes with assumable loans. Unfortunately, the majority of homes that are currently on the market do not have assumable loans. A great percentage of these loans are held by federally chartered savings and loan associations. These savings and loans aggressively pursue the policy of not allowing their loans to be assumed.

The lease option is unquestionably the most underused of all creative financing techniques. The reason is that realtors generally do not understand them and that they do not receive their commission until the sales contract is exercised. The waiting period may be one, two, or three years. Unfortunately, the realtor does not understand that the lease option is so powerful that the total number that could be written in tight money situations is easily five or six times (or more) greater than straight-sales contracts. When the interest rates come down, the majority of the options will be exercised, providing the creative realtor with a bonanza of sales contracts.

The lease option also offers a great method of selling properties. A few of the benefits are:

1. Eliminates negative cash flow.
2. Houses rent quickly.
3. Quality tenants.
4. Tax-free option money.

If the intent is truly to purchase the property during the option period, the IRS considers the sale to have occurred at the time the lease was signed. IRS publication 527, *Rental Property*, recognizes that a lease with an option to buy *may be* a purchase contract. The publication specifically states that any payments made during the option period that are to be applied against the purchase price are *not* to be treated as rental income. Thus when purchasing an investment property using a lease option, the investor may depreciate the property starting with the date of the lease agreement.

Savings and loan institutions, however, do not recognize the signing of a lease with option to buy as transfer of ownership. When either buying or selling a property using the option lease, structure the lease option agreement through a lawyer who understands lease options. The agreement should be a formal written commitment by both parties and should *clearly* outline all conditions of the transaction. For example, the purchase price, owner financing, length of the option, escalation clauses, no further liens on the property by the current owner, plus others. The principal advantage to the leasing party (ultimately the buyer) is that the purchase price is captured and all equity gained during the option period belongs to the buyer.

From Figure 3–25, we see the following:

Summary of Method 24
- Seller continues to pay the first trust of $345 per month.
- Buyer pays the seller a total monthly payment of $695 per month.
- The lease option is written for two years. The sale price is captured at $75,000.
- At the end of two years, the property will have a market value of $90,750. All of the equity build belongs to the buyer.
- All expenses to maintain the property during the option period are the responsibility of the buyer.
- The lease option should state in writing how the equity will be financed, for example, $10,000 cash and the seller to carry back a subordinate note of $15,000. The $10,000 cash will be obtained from a commercial second trust.

FIGURE 3-25
Method 24: The lease option.

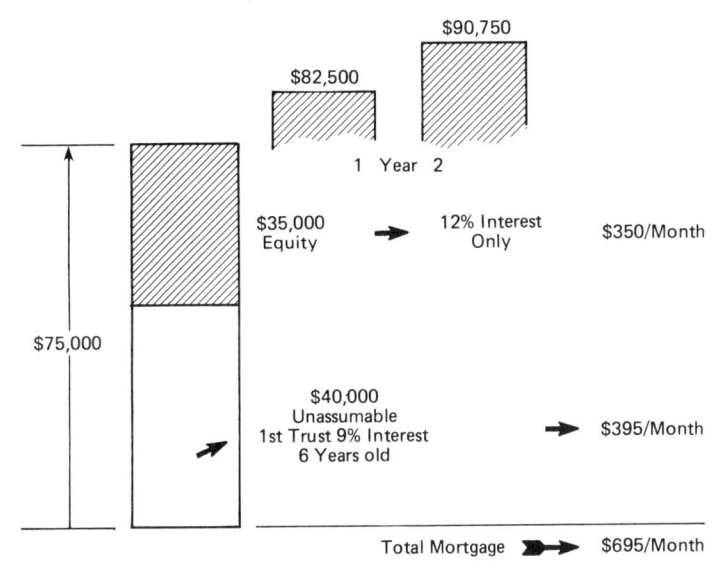

$90,750

$82,500

1 Year 2

$75,000

$35,000 Equity → 12% Interest Only $350/Month

$40,000
Unassumable
1st Trust 9% Interest
6 Years old   → $395/Month

Total Mortgage ➤➤ $695/Month

METHOD 25—LAND INSTALLMENT CONTRACT

- Property has an assumable VA, FHA, or negotiable first trust or property is owned outright by the seller.
- The seller is interested in a steady income.
- The seller wishes to spread out the taxable gain over several future years.
- The seller has little or no need for a large amount of cash.
- The property will usually bring in top price with little or no down payment.

A land installment contract can be a very beneficial arrangement for a couple nearing retirement age or for any seller who does not wish to receive a lump sum of cash in any one taxable year. Receiving the equity in one lump sum would propel the seller into an unacceptably high income tax bracket. For a seller in this position, the land installment contract may be the answer.

A few words on the land installment contract. It is a legal contract that declares that the seller retains legal title to the property until some time in the future. Usually this agreed-to time is related to some percentage of the purchase price having been paid off. The buyer receives equitable title to the property upon execution of the land installment contract.

In 1980 Congress enacted the Installment Sales Revision Act. Under this law, all sales (principal home of residence and investments) may qual-

FIGURE 3-26
Method 25: Land installment contract.

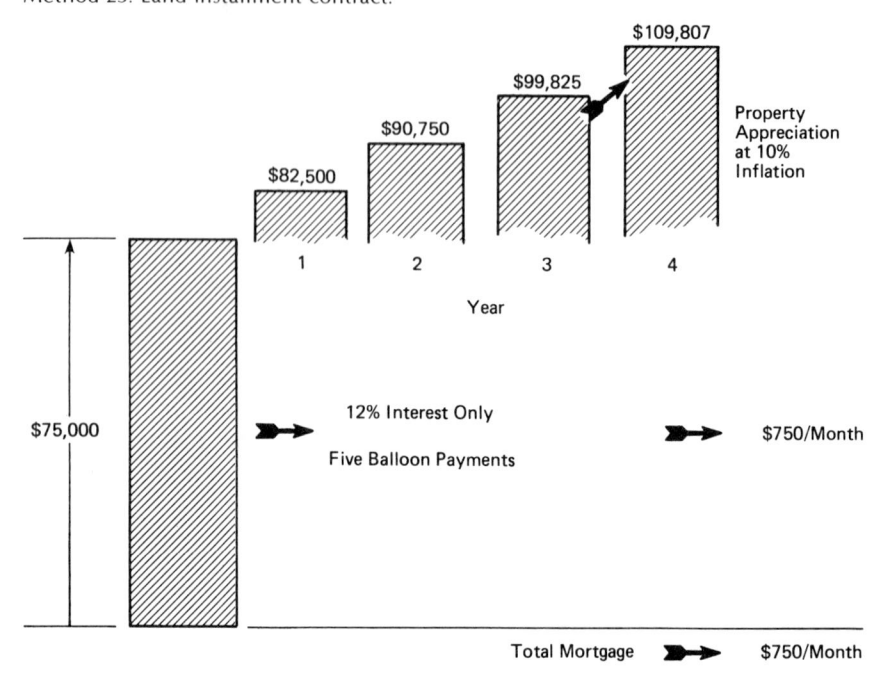

```
                                                            $109,807
                                                 $99,825
                                      $90,750                         Property
                                                                      Appreciation
                            $82,500                                   at 10%
                                                                      Inflation

                              1          2          3          4
                                           Year


                              12% Interest Only
$75,000                                                        $750/Month
                              Five Balloon Payments


                                         Total Mortgage  ▶  $750/Month
```

ify for future installment payments, thus preventing the seller from being pushed into a higher tax bracket in any given year. Simply stated, an installment sale occurs when the payment for the purchase of a home is not fully received in the year of sale. The payment of the equity can be in any form. For example, the payments could be structured in a series of balloon payments (see Figure 3–26), or, if an assumable loan existed, a wraparound mortgage could be structured. The payments could be structured so that the interest and principal would not be covered, thus increasing the value of the outstanding loan. This technique should suit individuals nearing retirement age, since the structure of the purchase agreement would serve as a savings account to be used in future years.

Summary of Method 25
- First balloon payment is due in four years. At this time, the market value of the property shall be $109,807 (at 10% inflation). Each succeeding balloon payment is spaced three years apart. Total time to complete the purchase is 16 years.
- Seller will release the $75,000 note for a new note of $60,000 and a cash payment of $15,000.
- Buyer obtains the $15,000 as a second trust, with the investment property acting as collateral. The value of the first trust is $60,000, and the market value of the property will be $109,807. Thus a $15,000 commercial second trust will not be a problem.

- At each of the three-year periods, the buyer would refinance the trust and pay off the maturing balloon. All equity exceeding $75,000 belongs to the buyer.

SHOPPING FOR SECOND TRUST MONEY

The best source of second trust buyers are friends or relatives who currently hold CDs, bonds, or have money in saving accounts. A return of 22.6% minimum and a potential of 49.6% return per year on a discounted second at 12% interest is significantly better than the 5¾% to 12% that savings, bonds, and CDs traditionally pay. Your task is to convince them that the second trust is a solid investment. However, having failed to convince your friends or relatives or not knowing anyone with these types of investments, you can find individual buyers of second trusts in your newspapers. Look in the classified section under the listings, business opportunities, money to lend, or mortgages. Individuals in the market of buying discounted second trusts are generally more flexible than the traditional lending institution. Call a few and see what terms they will apply. The discount rate is extremely negotiable. Generally speaking, the buyer of the discounted second trust will want some cushion between the appraised property value and the top part of his or her trust. Try to negotiate this difference to zero.

I have found it extremely helpful to have a credit report done on my financial status in any negotiations I have with second trust buyers. Obtain your credit report from the local credit bureau and provide a copy to any potential buyers of the discounted second trust. As I previously mentioned, it is important that you have a good credit rating. Remember it is you *and* the property that are the investments to the second trust buyer. Also provide all the pertinent information (appreciation schedule, photographs, and so forth) on the investment property. Once having initiated your investment program, current holders of second trusts on your own investment properties are excellent sources of money! Simply refinance and arrange for a portion of the second trust to be used for a second investment property.

Mortgage Institutions

If a second trust cannot be arranged with the seller and if an individual cannot be found to purchase the second trust at a discount rate, investigate the possibility of obtaining the necessary financing from a commercial second-mortgage lender. The newspapers are filled with numerous lending institutions that offer special packages of second trust loans. Once when I was in Los Angeles, I noted 12 before I stopped counting. In the tight money market of 1980 and 1981, I obtained a 12% second trust on one of my investment properties. The prime rate at the time was 15%. This particular bank was just entering the creative financing field and had a limited offer of 12% for 30 days or until they ran out of funds. They were out of funds within one week (five days) of their initial advertisement. Incidentally, I knew about this particular offer *before* the bank advertised. Why? Because in my shopping around for money I came in contact with various bankers and loan officers, who directed me to this particular bank. My friend who had money to invest in discounted second trusts also took out $10,000 at 12% and invested that in the purchase of discounted second trusts.

Lending institutions dealing in the second mortgage market can be found in the Yellow Pages under *Mortgages*. The commercial lender can become a valuable source of money, since, most likely, the amount you require to purchase the investment property will be small when compared with the overall sell price. For example, if the property has an equity of $20,000 and the seller is willing to carry back a second trust of only $10,000, it may be in your best interest to seek the required $10,000 from a commercial lender. Try to negotiate the collateral on the seller's second trust to be on a second property (for example, your present home of residence). Moving the mortgage and having 5% to 10% of the investment property clear will increase your chances of obtaining the required secondary financing.

As you increase the total number of investment properties and start to pyramid your assets, be aware of the commercial lender. They are capable of providing quick sums of money in excess of normal first-mortgage lending limits. However, also note that the interest rates they charge are higher since their risk is greater. In general the commercial lending rate will be two to four points above first-mortgage lending rates. The interest charged by the secondary market may vary by as much as two to ten points from lender to lender! Be sure to shop around. The few days taken to call several lenders and the subsequent discussions may save you a sizable sum of money. Table 3-3 outlines the various loan packages offered by commercial lenders in the winter of 1982. By the winter of 1983 the interest rates had been reduced by three to four points.

Obtain Second Trust from the Realtor

Remember it is in the agent's best interest that there be plenty of cash on the table and that the investment property be purchased in the most straightforward of financing methods possible. When you approach a real estate agent with your desire to purchase an investment property with no money down, he or she will probably come to the incorrect conclusion that the commission will be directly affected. You must explain that "no money down" means not using your *own* money, that you will use *other* people's money. Generally you will need to educate the realtor concerning your in-

TABLE 3-3. Commercial Loans

Institution	Interest %	Amortization Period	Loan Limitations
1. Columbia	20	10-yr. straight	75% of appraisal less liens
2. Fairview	18	5-yr. balloon	75% of appraisal less liens
3. Metro	19.5	10-yr. straight	75%
4. K. K. Brown	21	15-yr. straight	80%
5. Credit Union	16	12-yr. straight	75% appraisal (no investment props)
6. Virginia	16	5-yr. balloon	80% investment 85% home of residence
7. Omni	18.25	10-yr. straight	75% investment 80% home of residence
8. Community	18	15-yr. straight	75%
9. ATC	19	3-yr. straight	75%
10. Westfield	15.1	15-yr. straight	80% home of residence
11. Northern Virg	18.5	5-yr. straight	80% home of residence
12. Home Loans	18.5	12-yr. straight	75%
13. P. H. Salk	21.5	5-yr. balloon	70%
14. Metro Equity	15	5-yr. straight	75% home of residence
15. Frederick	17.5	10-yr. straight	75%

novative, creative, and imaginative methods of financing and your specific terms. If you know your material, especially the methods of buying as previously discussed, you will quickly find the most knowledgeable realtors. Learning the different techniques of creative financing will allow you to put these agents to good use. If second mortgage money is to be required, ask the realtor if he or she knows of individuals who are interested in purchasing discounted second trusts. Does he or she know of any commercial secondary mortgage institutions? Ask where you can find the best rates, and ask if his or her real estate firm purchases discounted second trusts. Occasionally real estate firms do purchase second trusts; however, they do not advertise this service.

Approach four or five realtors with the following conditions and terms for an investment property: purchase price—$50,000 to $70,000; location—within two miles from shopping center to be completed by 1983; assumption of at least 55% of asking price; interest rate on assumption 9% or less; owner will carry back second trust of $10,000 at 12% interest, balloon at five years; the collateral on the second trust will be on your (the investor's) home of residence; and find a mortgage institution that will finance new money using the wraparound plan (all-inclusive deed of trust) for 100% of the existing assumable loan—for example, $60,000 property, $35,000 first trust, the lending institution will finance a wraparound loan at a maximum value of $60,000. Note that the interest rate on the wraparound depends on the interest rate of the assumable loan (see Method 9).

Explain to the realtor that the conditions and terms are to be used as a *guide* and may slightly deviate. The realtor must understand, however, that the money on the settlement table will come from the wraparound loan and that he or she will get a commission.

The financial picture of the purchase described above will be as follows: Assuming the investment property is purchased at $60,000 and the wraparound loan is $50,000 amortized at 10.5% over the same time frame as the existing assumable loan (25 years), the monthly payments on the wraparound will be $472 per month. The seller will carry back a $10,000 second trust with a second property as collateral, financed at 12%, balloon payment at five years. Monthly payment equals $100 per month. Total payment per month equals $572 ($472 + $100). Rental in the area would be $500 per month. If the conditions and terms described above can be met, the investor will have a $72 per month negative cash flow before taxes are taken into account. All perfectly legal. The $50,000 from the mortgage company wraps around the existing loan, which is equal to $35,000. The owner will walk away with the difference between the wraparound loan and the value of the first trust. If the first trust was $35,000, he or she would receive $15,000 cash (less settlement costs) and a $10,000 second trust.

If the seller is not willing to carry back a second trust, ask the realtor if his or her real estate company would buy a second trust on your investment property. You may find yourself a second trust buyer. To any readers who currently have an investment property with the former owner holding a second trust, consider refinancing the second trust two or three years before the balloon payment is due, contingent on the holder of the second allowing you to use a portion of the second trust money to purchase an additional property. To anyone purchasing an investment property with the owner carrying a second trust, be sure to pay your payments promptly. The holder of the second trust will become a most valuable source of money. Remember also that the return on the discounted second is more than 22% at 12% interest discounted 25%. At 14% or 16% interest, the discounted second trust returns at a value greater than 25%. The section on the advantages of a discounted second trust included in Method 4 describes this transaction.

Current Holders of Second Trusts

Once having initiated your investment program, current holders of second trusts are an excellent source of money. The technique outlined here will work a majority of the time. (See Figure 3–27 for a graphic outline of this technique.) Let us assume that you have purchased an investment property with an assumable trust of $35,000. The owner takes back a second trust of $15,000, with payments on interest only and with a balloon payment in

FIGURE 3-27
Refinance an investment property with a 2nd trust.

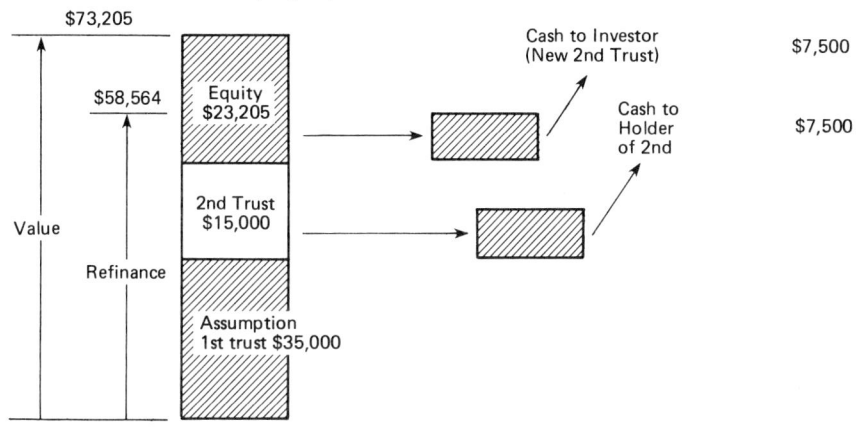

five years. The property was originally purchased for $55,000. In three years the property will be worth $73,205 at 10% inflation. Write a letter to the current holder of the second trust, stating that you are considering refinancing the property contingent on him or her agreeing to release the $15,000 second trust for $7,500. The remaining $7,500 will be carried back as a new second trust note at any new negotiable rate, over any negotiable period.

Generally this technique will work because the holder of the second trust note is receiving one-half of the value of the note prior to the note becoming due and the remaining portion (in our example, 50%) is carried back on the same property. The risk is minimal. The investor should encounter no problems refinancing the property at 80% of current value ($73,205). Total refinanced value will be $58,564 less refinance expenses. The amount of $42,500 of the refinance monies is to be used to pay off the first trust ($35,000) and the second trust ($7,500). Cash in hand to the investor will be $16,064 ($58,564 − $42,500), less refinance charges. The beauty of this technique is that you are using 50% of the second trust holder's money to purchase an additional investment. All the money is OPM, thus you are purchasing an investment property with *no money down!*

Note the following from Figure 3-27:

- First trust is paid off or, if refinanced, is a wrap loan. With a wrap loan, the lending institution will simply be assuming the loan.
- When refinancing, the second trust ($15,000) is required to be fully paid off. Make arrangements through a lawyer (after you have contacted the second trust holder) to release the $15,000 second trust for $7,500. The remaining $7,500 of the second trust is carried back on the property as a new second trust.

- Holder of second trust receives $7,500 in cash.
- The investor receives $16,064 less loan origination charges as tax-free pocket money.

Important Facts about the Second Trust Note

When a seller has carried back a second trust, explain to him or her that the second trust is an extremely negotiable note. It can be sold at a discount from the face value. Basically what it means to you, the investor, is that if the seller decides to sell his or her second trust note, your payments on the second trust shall be to a third party. In order to allow the holder of the second trust the opportunity to market his or her note, the following documents should be provided:

- Contract of sale.
- Description of property (collateral).
- Appraisal of property. Have this done yourself, since it will appraise higher than the bank's appraisal.
- Copy of the first deed of trust.
- Settlement transactions (signed by attorney or escrow company).
- Copy of the recorder's receipt of the second deed of trust from the courthouse.
- Insurance policy covering both the first and second trust notes.
- Your credit report.

Any good real estate lawyer or escrow company can prepare the items listed above.

Having these documents will allow any holder of the second trust to market the note. I have found that the majority of sellers taking back a second trust know little or nothing about the secondary market. It is best if the seller's attorney (or an attorney) explains the legal aspects of the market value of the second trust. In reality, however, I believe I do a much better job of explaining to sellers how they can market their second trust notes. But in all honesty, the psychological barrier may be tremendous, thus it is best if they not only hear it from you, the investor, but also from the settlement attorney. One final note, prepare the attorney about having him or her explain the marketability of the second trust. Attorneys are human and there are some things they do not do well. More on this subject in Phase 4, The Buy.

Figure 3–28 shows the total return on a second trust note purchased at a discounted price of 25%. Assuming that the interest rate on the full value of the note is 12%, the rate of return after five years will be 22.7%.

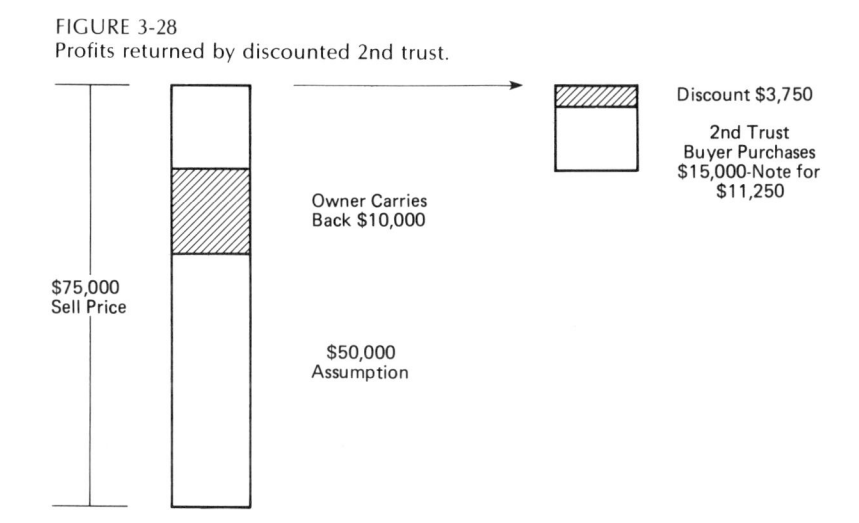

FIGURE 3-28
Profits returned by discounted 2nd trust.

- $75,000 Sell Price
  - $50,000 Assumption
  - Owner Carries Back $10,000
- 2nd Trust Buyer Purchases $15,000-Note for $11,250
- Discount $3,750

HUNTING FOR PROPERTIES

You are now ready to start the actual process of the drive-around-the-block phase of the investment process. Recall that I stated earlier, always seek to maintain presence of mind; know where you stand. Be alert and learn all you can from all people you come in contact with. Ask the same questions to different realtors, bankers, loan officers, and sellers. Before long, you can consider yourself an expert in the field. Recently I was involved in assisting two business partners (and former students of mine) use the approach of surveying a wide field of possibilities before selecting their investment properties. During the hunt, they came in contact with realtors, loan officers, bankers, lawyers, other investors, and a multitude of sellers. After reviewing the newspaper and selecting approximately 20 potential properties, the possibilities were quickly reduced to eight. The eight that were selected had proper financial terms surrounding the purchase of the property in question. The first five properties we inspected required large quantities of cash to assume the loans. The sixth property was ideal. The realtor representing the seller met us at the townhouse. During the inspection, the realtor mentioned that the owners were anxious to sell since they had purchased a home and were carrying two mortgages. However, the total cash to assume the mortgage was $31,000 (assumable first trust was $37,000 at 8%). The realtor absolutely insisted that the seller required $15,000 cash. I discussed the situation with my business partner and we decided to structure the sales contract asking the seller to carry all the equity as a second trust, interest only payments with a balloon payment in five years. We also offered the option of finding a buyer for $10,000 of the equity discounted by $2,500. The end result was that the property was bought with $5,000 down, and an additional $10,000 (total $15,000). The realtor had found one buyer and she in turn offered her commission in the form of a subordinate note on the property. Both subordinate notes were later sold on the open market for the discounted prices. Total cash to the seller at settlement was $13,500. The point is that the seller received close to his cash requirement. Nonetheless, with the exception of the $5,000, the cash on the settlement table was OPM.

The same weekend that we located the townhouse noted above we also located another property with a $31,900 assumption and a second trust note. We asked the realtor (different from the one above) if he could find a commercial lending institution that would advance us $8,000 with the property to be purchased acting as collateral. The realtor insisted that all lending institutions would require 10% down before they would advance the required loan. We simply kept asking different realtors the same question until we found one who said, "No problem, but you'll have to pay 19% interest." My business partner assumed the first trust, the second trust, moved 10% of the equity to a different property, and used the borrowed $8,000 as the cash on the settlement table. The same realtor who found us the commercial money then directed us to a property that required only $3,000 down and the owner would finance the remaining $97,000 as owner financing. The property was a four-unit apartment complex, and the owner guaranteed a positive cash flow from initial buy. My business partner submitted a sales contract. Thirty days after buying the first property, he refinanced (paid off the 19% commercial loan), and realized a profit of $4,000. $3,000 of the $4,000 was advanced against the purchase of the apartment complex. He had purchased close to $200,000 worth of real estate with absolutely nothing down.

The examples above emphasize my opening remarks in this book—you will come in contact with realtors, loan officers, sellers, lawyers, and others who will tell you it absolutely cannot be done! Do not believe it! Just keep asking the question, and you will be pleasantly surprised at how many times the answer will be yes.

The Start of the Hunt

Since having been successful in the purchase of my investment properties, the question that I am asked most frequently is, "How do I get started?" Start hunting for your investment property utilizing a top-down investigation process. Try to visualize the entire city, county, or metropolitan area where you presently live as an Easter egg field. You are told that hundreds of Easter eggs do exist, and your task is to find them. As children having fun at an Easter egg hunt, you as an investor should have fun in attempting to find your investment property. Do not get discouraged! Believe that the investment properties *do* exist. As I learned when I was a kid, there were certain areas in the yard where my parents always hid the Easter eggs. After two or three Easter egg hunts, you automatically go to the far tree behind the evergreen because you develop the base knowledge of where the Easter egg bunny (your mom) hides the eggs. Finding an investment property is perhaps more complex but involves the same technique.

Go out and scout around. Take two or three hours on a Saturday or Sunday and look at different neighborhoods. Learn where the *f*orward *e*dge of *bu*ilding (FEBI) is presently located. Investigate good neighborhoods and bad neighborhoods. Try to determine why some neighborhoods look simply vanquished and raped after 10 to 15 years and yet other neighborhoods look splendid after 15 or even 20 years. What caused one neighborhood to deteriorate and the other to appreciate in value and appearance?

Adopt the position of a neutral third party observer who is simply investigating the value of real estate properties as a function of location. If you have lived in a particular area for a long period of time, you may have emotional ties to that section of the city or county. Try not to let this interfere with objective and factual reasoning. Do not get emotionally involved with a given area. Analyze potential neighborhoods based strictly on facts. Does the neighborhood have new professional buildings (doctors, lawyers, and so forth), new shopping centers, new stores, and new residential developments? Savings and loan institutions and banks will totally investigate a given neighborhood before establishing a new branch there. Are there any new banks in the area? If there are new savings and loans or banks, stop by and talk to a loan officer. Loan officers are excellent sources of information for the quality of the neighborhood. Begin your conversation with questions concerning their lending rates. Ask questions concerning new mortgages, second trusts, home improvement loans, construction loans, signature loans, and so forth. It has been my experience that asking these questions from the standpoint of an owner-occupied home produces the best results.

After obtaining the loan package information on an owner occupied home, ask the loan officer questions concerning lending rates for investment properties. Having obtained a wealth of knowledge on loan packages, ask about the neighborhood surrounding the bank. What does he or she think about purchasing a home within one or two miles of the bank? If the loan officer lives in another section of the city, ask him or her questions concerning the particular neighborhood. I generally make it a policy to stop by a different savings and loan every Friday, since most of them have late hours on Fridays. Incidentally, I have found excellent second trust loan packages using this technique. Most loan officers will tell you if another bank has better rates, especially if they are currently not lending money for that particular type of purchase.

Be aware that some areas may look run down but are on their upward cycle again. This phenomenon is occurring throughout America because of the interstate highway system built during the 1960s. When the interstate highways were completed, entire sections of some cities dried up since most of the traffic was carried by the interstate. Major arteries that ran parallel to the interstates suffered devastating blows, and it is not unusual to see many old restaurants and tourist shops boarded and closed up. With the population explosion of the 1950s (post–World War II baby boom) and the general move of the suburbs to the major metropolitan areas of America, the major arteries that suffered such devastating blows in the 1960s and 1970s are now returning to life. This phenomenon can easily be seen along the major eastern corridor of Virginia Beach to Boston. Areas such as Dallas, Atlanta, Los Angeles, San Francisco, and so forth are no exceptions. What has happened is that the FEBI has extended to the areas that suffered major setbacks. These are now on their way back to recovery.

When hunting for your ideal investment property, put yourself in the correct frame of mind. Understand that it will take time. However, also understand that the second investment and the third investment will take only a fraction of the time required for the initial investment. Be prepared to sacrifice that football game or that vacation in your first year. I did, and I quite honestly do not remember who won or lost the second game of the NFL schedule between Dallas and Washington in 1978. However, I do remember that the investment property I bought in the winter of 1977–1978 now has equity worth $40,000!

After performing the initial analysis to purchase your first investment property, you will find that you develop a nose for good investments. Generally people tend to think that successful investors somehow have that certain stroke of luck or the MIDAS touch. Most successful investors, however, do not have any more luck or MIDAS touch than anybody else. What they *do* have is determination, persistence, vigor, gusto, and a dream.

Must Sellers and Unloaders

Before I discuss the actual process of hunting for your investment property, it is important that you understand what type of seller you are interested in finding. Think of it this way—there are hundreds of Easter eggs hidden in the backyard but you want to find the one type of special egg with the special candy. The key is to recognize these special eggs. The type of seller you are looking for is called in the real estate trade a "don't wanter." In the purchase of my investment properties I have refined in the "don't wanter" category of seller what I believe to be a subtle but important difference. There are two types of "don't wanters"—the must seller and the unloader.

Must sellers have circumstances surrounding them that place them in a situation that pressures them to sell. The property is in excellent condition (move-in) and in a good location. Generally the circumstances creating the must sell situation are job transfers or high interest rates (tight money). You want to purchase your properties from must sellers, since this increases your chances for no money down, and thus for infinite leverage. I have purchased all my investment properties from must sellers. *Unloaders* are selling the property because the property itself is causing the "don't wanter" situation, for example, low rent causing high negative cash flow, decaying neighborhood, maintenance headaches, and so forth. If you purchase a property in the unloader category, be sure you can correct the problem!

I can best describe the must seller and the unloader categories by providing examples of properties I selected to purchase and those I selected not to purchase. First, the unloader category: I answered an advertisement in the real estate section of the Sunday paper, and the realtor on the floor assigned to answer the phone provided me the details of the property being advertised. As usual, the property did not meet my conditions and terms, so I asked if she knew of any properties that generally fitted the conditions I had outlined. She did her homework and returned my call in a few hours, outlining five properties that had potential. All the properties were townhouses with assumptions, and the owners were all willing to consider holding a second trust. One property in particular showed promise. It was not on the multiple listing since it had been listed with the real estate agency that very morning. The PITI was approximately $490 with the rental $400 per month. What was even more interesting was that the market value was listed at $59,000 and the asking price was $56,000. We went over and inspected the property. The property was in terrible condition—writing on the walls, wet spots on the ceilings, holes in the walls, and appliances in state of general disrepair. I found that the sell price was being discounted $3,000 because of the repair work required. I reviewed the general terrain and neighborhood and found that the area was scheduled for further development of apartments and multifamily dwellings. Two huge apartment complexes were within a quarter of a mile, and I asked for information on the rental prices. The realtor did not know. After we left the potential investment property, I went over to the apartments and simply asked for information. I found that the apartments were subsidized by the government, had a waiting list of two years, and the worker in the office did not see any relief until the new apartments that were scheduled to be built were completed. I then drove over to the library, used a real estate guide, and in 15 minutes did a property appreciation on the townhouses in the complex where the potential investment property was located. The properties were seven to eight years old and had appreciated approximately 3% per year. When I drove around the neighborhood, I noticed a high number of "for sale" signs. I surmised that the neighborhood was merely a holding place for families interested in the subsidized housing apartments. I had not only found one unloader, I had found a cluster of bad investments. Needless to say, I did not purchase the property.

A few days later, another realtor called (I had also inspected properties with him), and he told me, "Get ready to purchase, I believe I have found exactly what you are interested in." The details of the property were assumption, seven years old, market value $62,500, asking price $58,000. The owner had had a contract written on the property, however, the prospective purchaser could not qualify for the required new money. The seller was now willing to allow the loan to be assumed. The problem was that the first trust was slightly less than half the purchase price. A significant amount of new money would be required to assume the loan. I had recently been discussing my real estate investments with a friend of mine, and he had expressed a strong interest in purchasing discounted second trusts. Immediately after my realtor called, I called my friend and asked him if he desired to purchase a second trust of $10,000 discounted 25%. His return would be a minimum of 22.6%; it would be more if I sold the property before the five-year balloon. He said, "Definitely, as long as I know it is you who will be paying the second trust. No problem, I'll buy the discounted second." Armed with this important tool, my realtor and I went off to view the property.

The property was excellent and was located in a small cluster of townhouses with single-family homes surrounding the row of townhouses. The investment property was in showcase condition with a finished full basement, three bedrooms, family room, work room, wash room, kitchen, dining room, with a brook and a park directly behind the townhouse. When inspecting the property, I found that the owner was an officer in the U.S. Army and was rotating to Germany for three years. I happen to know from my years in Germany that military personnel rotating to Germany have their housing fully paid for by the government. During our negotiations I asked him to take back the entire second trust with a small down payment (less than $1,000) to cover settlement and realtor fees. I then stated that if he required cash I would find a buyer for $10,000 of the second trust. We explained (my realtor, his realtor, and I) that he would receive $7,500 cash. However, his second trust would be reduced by $10,000. He said he would think it over for a day and let us know if he really wanted to sell any part of the second trust. We had done our job so well that he correctly calculated that he was better off with the entire second trust. He would receive interest-only payments, and the full note ($27,000) would be due in five years. If I had given him $27,000 cash, he was going to buy CDs that would pay less than the second trust! When he returns from Europe, he will have the full value of the second trust and receive regular payments from me every month. My total PITI for the property is $495 per month and I rent for $425. My cash flow is minus $70 prior to tax savings. After I depreciate the property plus deduct interest on payments, my cash flow is positive!

During the same search I also found another excellent opportunity. Because of the high interest rates, a particular builder was having problems with his construction loan. Interest rates were going up; the bank would not advance him additional funds until he paid his overdue monthly payments. The builder could not find a buyer because the interest rates would cause high monthly mortgage payments. I quickly talked to the loan officer of the bank and to a few realtors and had an appraisal made on the property. It had over 3,200 square feet of living space, six bedrooms, family room, fireplace, living room, dining room, bar, three-car garage, and a wine cellar!

The construction loan was approximately 30% below the appraised value. I offered the builder the value of his construction loan plus a few thousand in profit. He accepted, the bank advanced him the required monies to complete the house, and I had myself a home for 30% under the market value. Needless to say, it became my family home. The house in which we were living at the time had a first trust of $68,000, and it was valued at $105,000. I took out a second trust on the equity of my former residence and purchased another property.

I have used the examples cited above to emphasize the difference between a must seller and an unloader. The two properties I described were excellent examples of clean move-in properties. The owners were caught in a set of circumstances that were beyond their control. In both cases, they were just as happy to sell their properties as I was to purchase them. To this date, I correspond with both the former owner and the builder. With the former owner, I offered to refinance the property, contingent on him allowing me to use $10,000 of the $27,000 to purchase a discounted second trust in an additional second investment property. As I explained to him, "If you can trust me with $27,000, you can certainly trust me with $10,000." After refinancing, I used the $10,000 to purchase an additional investment. The former owner received $17,000 cash, and he was simply elated. With the custom builder, I have discussed the potential of building residential homes and selling at a profit. The venture would be funded not by my personal funds but by my corporation, Aaron-Armen, that I presently head as president and chairman of the board.

Specifics for Starting Your Hunt

Start hunting for your potential investment property in a parallel manner—investigate *all* possibilities. Research the areas listed below:

- Realtors
- Newspapers
- Home owner associations

150   THE HUNT

- Cluster concept
- Owner for sale signs
- Friends and relatives
- Foreclosures and bankruptcies
- Seminars

Realtors   Even if you think you have a good realtor, go out and search for yourself. Increase your total number of sensors. Figure 3-29 illustrates my recommended approach to using realtors. Pick a main street or location that has a cluster of real estate agencies, simply walk in, and ask to speak to the person on the floor about possible investment opportunities. Prepare a list of questions. Even if you know the answers, ask them anyway. Compare the answers given by 10 or 15 realtors. Believe me, you will know when you have found a good realtor. Listed below are questions you can ask a realtor:

1. What would you recommend as an investment property?
2. How many properties are currently on the market within a ten-mile radius (or location) that have assumable loans?
3. Can you provide me with a listing of rental price as a function of location and type of rental property?

FIGURE 3-29
Shotgun approach for using realtors.

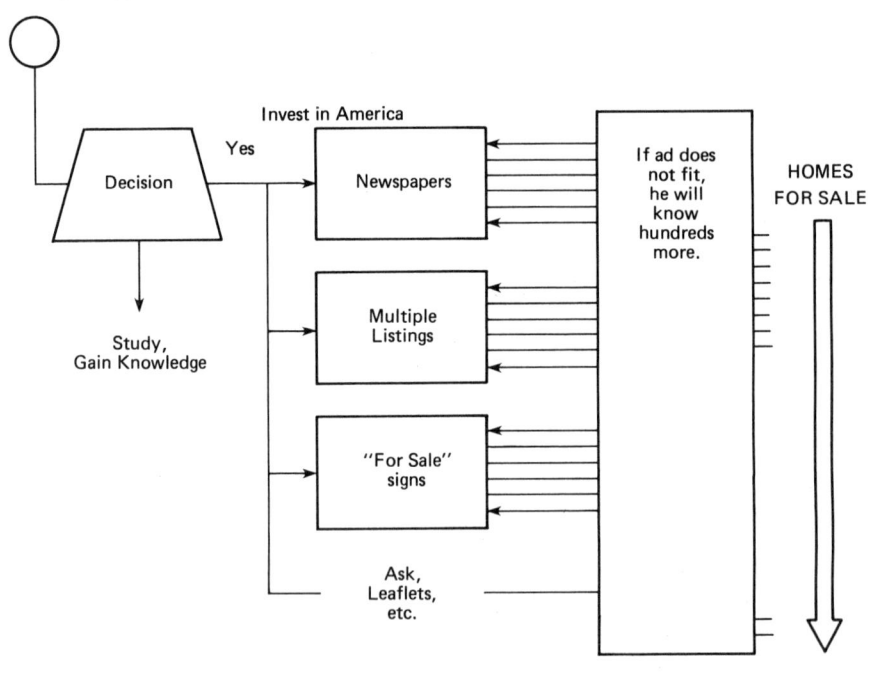

4. Does your computerized multiple listing provide information concerning which sellers are willing to carry back part of equity as a second trust?
5. Will you tell me which mortgage institutions have wraparound programs?
6. Can you give me a computerized investment profile on properties as a function of my taxable income, monthly mortgage payments, and expected rent? Real estate agencies should have this capability.
7. Pick two creative financing techniques and ask that they be explained. For example, I am not sure I understand the relationship between the first and second trust. Can you explain a second trust note? Does the second trust need to remain with the property being sold? For example, can I use my current home as collateral for the second trust?
8. Can you explain a wraparound mortgage to me?
9. Does your real estate firm/agency purchase discounted second trusts? Most will do this; however, they prefer not to advertise it.
10. Do you know of any individuals or institutions that purchase discounted second trusts?
11. Generally what size of negative cash flow can I expect to carry with an investment property?
12. Do you have any information on properties that are in difficulty and may soon be facing foreclosure?
13. If I purchase a property through this agency can the multiple listing service be used to rent the property at no extra charge?
14. Can you provide me with a listing of potential investment properties in location _____ that fits the following terms?
    a. Assumable loan 60% or more of the asking price.
    b. Owner has stated he or she will carry second trust.
    c. Property will rent for at least two-thirds of the monthly mortgage.
    d. Property approximately three to five years old.
15. Are you willing to decrease your commission if needed to strike a contract? (Save this question until you have established a working relationship.)

It has been my experience that you will quickly be referred to either the most knowledgeable realtor within the office or the manager/owner of the real estate franchise. Your questions have considerable depth, and as a general rule the agent manning the floor will not be able to answer them all. After having obtained your information, if you feel that this particular agent has potential, arrange for an inspection of properties some time in the future. I review the listing properties and arrange to call back and inspect only those I can afford. The arrangement to call back also serves the purpose of allowing time to select the most knowledgeable agent. Also keep in mind that he or she will become a negotiator, so be selective in whom you choose. It is *your* borrowed money that will be dealt around the settlement table, so the least you should do is select the players!

As previously stated, in order to allow you to maximize your profits, you desire to have none of your own money used as a down payment, but to have all monies used in the purchase of your investment property to be borrowed. Generally, if you approach a realtor with the proposition that you desire to buy an investment property with *no money down,* he or she will immediately think there will be no commission. It has been my experience that four out of five realtors will not accept the challenge of pursuing the purchase of an investment property using all borrowed money. The reason that they choose not to play is *lack of knowledge.* Roughly one-half of the one out of five realtors who do accept the challenge have sufficient knowledge about the tax laws of this nation to be able to explain to any investor and/or seller that borrowing money and/or taking back subordinate notes may be in their best interest. Additionally, the truly knowledgeable realtor will also have sources of money that provide second trust loans, with the sellers carrying a third trust. I am simply amazed at the number of realtors who know little or next to nothing concerning who will lend money at what rates, the amount that can be borrowed relative to the sell price (exposure factor) and allowed values over the exposure factor to be in the form of seller take back notes. The realtor must understand that a property with an assumption, a commercial second, and the owner carrying back the remaining equity in the form of a third trust can be purchased using all borrowed monies. His or her commission will come from the commercial second.

Another method that may be used by the realtor is for the seller to carry back all of the equity as a second trust and for the realtor to find a third party to purchase the second trust from the seller at a discount value. The realtor's commission comes from the cash used to purchase the discounted second. I have used this quite successfully numerous times.

Another method that may be used by the realtor is to purposely structure the seller carry back equity as two subordinate notes. Raise the value of one of the notes by the discounted amount and then sell the note on the open market. The realtor can even structure the discounted value of the note to be equal to his or her commission. For example, if the realtor's commission equals $3,000, part of the carry back equity can be structured in the form of a $4,000 subordinate note. Discount the note $1,000 and then sell the note on the open market for $3,000. The realtor realizes $3,000 at the time he or she sells the note.

An additional method should by now be obvious. The realtor simply takes his or her commission in the form of a note on the purchased property. Receiving $50 to $100 per month and the full value of the note upon maturing may be in the best interest of the realtor, since the chances are quite favorable that reducing the cash requirements of the buyer will greatly improve the realtor's total number of sales.

Additional methods and/or items that the knowledgeable and creative realtor should consider accepting as his or her commission are services rendered by the buyer; for example, dental work, construction work, brick laying, home repairs, car repairs, automobiles, stereos, boats, travel tickets, or anything of value. Use your imagination! Have a distaste for the conventional.

Newspapers The newspaper is one of the most important tools in developing your investment portfolio. It is a cross section of the real estate market in your city or county. I have recommended the use of the library throughout this book, however, the newspaper is equally important. Scan the real estate section and pick what appear to be good investment properties. Call 15 or 20 sellers or realtors and ask questions similar to the 15 realtor questions listed above. When asking the question concerning the willingness of carrying back a second trust, ask only if the owner will consider carrying back a portion of the equity. Do not negotiate or ask specifics on the amount of the second trust.

When scanning the want ads, look for properties that fit your particular terms. Be aware that the real estate sections of the major newspapers of America are nothing more than an extension of the advertising departments of the real estate agencies, Madison Avenue frills and all. Remember, their intent is to catch your eye. I have nothing against the flashy advertising, just remember to dig through the entire section and pull out the properties that appear to fit *your* terms. As I mentioned in the section on methods of buying, owner financing is new money, but the terms are fully negotiable. Call on all possibilities.

Following are a few tips on listings. In general the listings will not have the street and address. If the terms appear to be favorable, ask the lister for the address. If the listing is through a realtor, he or she may not wish to give you the address. If this situation develops, tell the realtor that location is an all-important issue and that there is no need to waste your time or the realtor's. Usually this works. If not, you will have sufficient information to obtain the address from the next realtor you call. Remember, the world of realtors is extremely competitive. Learn to use this competition between realtors to your advantage.

Listed below is a sample of homes for sale. The locations have been slightly edited. However, all terms are as they appeared in the newspaper. The advertisements were taken from a small suburban newspaper in northern Virginia, just south of the Washington, D.C., metropolitan area.

Advertisements
GOLDEN ACRES—Owner will finance. Princess style with addition of 20×32 family room & 24×24 garage, 5 bedrooms, $10,000 down, balance $60,000 at 12%, terms flexible. 3pJan19.

Remarks
Possibility, terms are flexible. Negotiate the $10,000 down. Excellent with second trust buyer.

Advertisements	Remarks
MOUNTAIN RIDGE—New 3, 4 & 5 bedroom homes. Immediate availability. Consider trades, VA, second trusts. One at 11½% interest.	Appears to be builder. Area is VA approved. Excellent for first-time buyers.
PENNY HILL — 3-acre wooded homesites on Davis Ford Rd. From $15,750. Call developer.	No comment.
SELL OR TRADE—2 lots off Allison Rd. City water & sewer. SpJan 21.	No comment.
TOWNHOUSE OAK TREES—Emerson model, end unit. 8½% assumption available. By owner flexible equity financing. 7Jan22.	Possibility, flexible equity financing. Wraparound with second trust in different property appears possible. Good rental.
STONEBRIDGE—Townhouse, $49,500. All closing costs paid. Will accept auto as down payment. Realtors welcome. 7Jan23.	This is a real "must seller" or "unloader." Pursue!
STONEBRIDGE—Snug brick rambler; low utilities & taxes; storm windows & doors; 4 bedrooms; finished basement; close to shopping & schools. $62,000. No agents. 5pJan23.	NOTE: No agents, owner is selling. Appears to be an inflexible seller. Call but do not expect good results.
A CHANCE TO ASSUME an 8% VA loan. Balance $35,215, principal & interest $268 for 26 years. Leased until July 1982 at $345 per month. Nice property & tenants. 3BRs, 1½ baths, family room, $59,950.	Good assumption. Either a wraparound or OTTB will work. A new wraparound for 55,000 at 10½% for 26 years will be $515 per month.
ASSUME 10%—FHA mortgage. 3-story 3-bedroom brick end unit. Convenient. Park off Allison. By owner. 7Jan21.	Good assumption. At 10%, first trust is good percentage of sell price, small equity. Find what rentals are in the area. Pursue!
ASSUMPTION—or trade for smaller house. $15,000 cash will assume 11.5% interest with approximate PITI $743. Like new with lots of extras. 4 bedrooms, 2 baths, rec. room, dining room, eat-in kitchen, large utility room. 7 rtc.	Good possibility for first-time home buyers, appears that PITI is too high for rental. Note also the possibility of an exchange.

The data above are a snapshot of 15 minutes of newspaper scanning time. If I were to scan the *Washington Post,* I would have a list of over 100. Remember, you are looking for only *one* investment property. Surely you can find one move-in that fits your terms. After calling the listers, I will make up a matrix as shown in Table 3–4 and keep track of all information.

TABLE 3-4. Potential Investments

DATE	DESCRIPTION OF PROPERTY	TERMS	PHONE CONTACT	APPROX. RENT	LOCATION	REMARKS
1. Jan. 5	Townhouse	Assumption OWC	D. Lewis 723–24XX	$425	Woodbridge	Cul-de-sac (clean)
2. Jan. 7	Single Detached	VA Assumption	J. Allen 821–82XX	$550	Springfield	Neg. cash $250
3. Jan. 8	Duplex	Conventional Assumption	P. Pappas 727–23XX	$450	Richardson	Good Neighborhood
4. Jan. 13	Townhouse	FHA Assumption	K. Willis	$375	Eastwood	Less than $3,000 down
5. Jan. 13	Townhouse	VA Assumption	T. Henry 941–23XX	$575	Mount Vernon	Fannie Mae Loan
6. Jan. 14	Townhouse	VA Assumption	G. Kirk	$595	Alexandria	Owner for Sale

I only keep notes on properties that have potential. After reviewing the list and reducing the number to approximately three or five, I am ready to inspect. Do not get discouraged if the first time you inspect the properties they do not fit your conditions or terms. If you do your homework and perform all of your analyses ahead of time, you should have no difficulty in finding the ideal investment in less than two weekends!

In Phase 1 I mentioned the value of group discussions and group participation. Reducing properties to a list of three to five, splitting the number, and having two teams inspect is recommended as a good way to share responsibilities. Obviously any other responsibilities could be split as well; for example, calling realtors, scanning newspapers, finding OPM, or interviewing loan officers.

Homeowners Associations Homeowners associations are generally found in every major city of America. Information available at the associations is extremely useful, such as sale prices, terms of sales, prices versus locations, and homes that are owner financed. In all cases I have found that their employees are extremely helpful and that they are, like the employees of a library, in the business of providing information. Take advantage of their helpfulness! These associations offer an excellent opportunity to review listings and gain valued experience in dealing directly with sellers. In general, you will find that individuals who list with homeowners associations are fairly knowledgeable about financing.

Before you approach a seller, be sure you do a thorough analysis of the selling price of homes in the seller's neighborhood, which can be done in the library. Homeowners that are selling their own properties tend to list the sell price at a higher than average level. Be prepared to show the figures and negotiate the price and terms. In all fairness, I should mention that the probabilities of finding a must seller using homeowner associations is possible but remote. When the seller gets in a tight situation, he or she will first advertise in the local newspaper and then will list with a realtor. Given that the seller is in no rush to sell, he or she will list with a homeowners association and wait for his or her terms. The key to purchasing an investment property directly from an owner is to make your offer during that critical transition period between selling the property him- or herself and listing with a realtor.

After inspecting a property being sold by an owner and having decided that the physical conditions are acceptable, that is, location, state of repair, good rental, and so forth, discuss the financial terms with the seller. Generally, the seller will want his or her equity all in cash, with new financing. Discuss the possibility of you assuming the loan and the seller financing a second trust. Do not negotiate the details. Prepare a formal offer and explain all of the details of the offer *in writing*. Deliver the offer to the seller and give him or her 30 to 60 days to accept the offer. If during your discussions, the seller indicates that he or she would not be willing to take back a second trust of more than $5,000, do not let that discourage you from asking him or her to take back more than $5,000. For example, you could ask the seller to take back a $10,000 three year balloon with favorable interest rates. Chances are that he or she will also reject this offer. However, do this ten times, and the law of averages is on your side that one of the ten will accept!

I came upon the technique described above early in the development of my investment portfolio, because I would notice that properties that were being sold by the owners would remain on the market for one or two months before being listed with a realtor. I found that if I made my offer in writing, a certain percentage would call me back in one or two months to ask if I was still interested. Because it never takes me more than a couple of weekends to find an investment property, it would turn out that I had already purchased my investment property for that particular time period and I was no longer interested. On several occasions, I arranged for other investors to purchase the properties; in all cases, the properties were purchased with the conditions and terms similar to my written offer. I am convinced that any investor who is willing to take the time to investigate all properties at the homeowners association and who makes written offers on all properties with reasonable chance of success, could easily develop his or her investment portfolio of five to ten houses within five years.

Visit your homeowners association. At the very least, you shall gain valuable experience and add to that all-important area—your base of knowledge. Who knows, you just might find that investment opportunity!

Cluster Concept   A method that has worked for me is to make about 100 copies of a typed sheet of paper stating your name, address, phone number, and the fact that you are interested in purchasing a home. You can list any number of conditions or terms on the information sheet. Distribute the sheets in a particular neighborhood that has a high probability of having properties that fit your conditions and terms.

I came upon the cluster concept one Saturday afternoon at the library while I was conducting neighborhood appreciation rates. I noted that a particular neighborhood I was quite familiar with because I did all my jogging in that area had a large concentration of VA loans. The properties were four to six years old, and at any given period of time 1 out of 30 would be on the market. I was mainly interested to see if my technique of shotgunning leaflets would work, so I made a master copy using a marker, had a hundred made up, and took an extra half an hour on my next weekend jog. Sure enough, I got five or six return calls. Within a week I had purchased an investment property.

158   THE HUNT

An example of an excellent neighborhood is one that is three to five years old. It is generally located slightly behind the forward edge of building, thus new properties will continuously pull the price of your investment skyward. The interest rates in the 1976 to 1978 period were 8% to 9½% for FHA and VA loans. Since the property is fairly new, the first trust will be no greater than 60% or 70% of the sell price. A small down payment with a second trust works excellently here. If you have a buyer of the discounted second trust, you can probably purchase as many properties as you desire. Remember, there is no realtor involved, and the commission now goes to the seller. If the realtor's commission were 6%, the additional cash to the seller will be more than the 25% that the second trust will be discounted (depends on size of second trust). For example, assume a sell price of $80,000. The commission would equal $4,800 (6% of the sale price). A second trust of $19,200 with a buyer purchasing at the discounted rate of 25% would net the seller an equal amount of cash (25% of $19,200 equals $4,800). (See Figure 3-30.) Using either method shown in Figure 3-30 will provide seller with $14,400 of his or her equity. Be sure to do a property appraisal using sell prices over the last six months, and be aware that seller will generally ask for more than the property is worth.

One word of strong advice when distributing your leaflets. When you do get a return call from potential customers, proceed slowly and gain the confidence of the sellers. Remember, they do not know who they are dealing with. You need to assure them that you are not a con artist and that you are serious about purchasing a property. It is best if you talk to them face to face after you have established that there is potential for negotiations. I thoroughly explain to potential sellers the financial aspect of the terms (second trusts, wraparounds, moving the mortgage, and so forth), leave the information with them plus personal and credit references, and

FIGURE 3-30
Purchasing investment without realtor and using discounted 2nd.

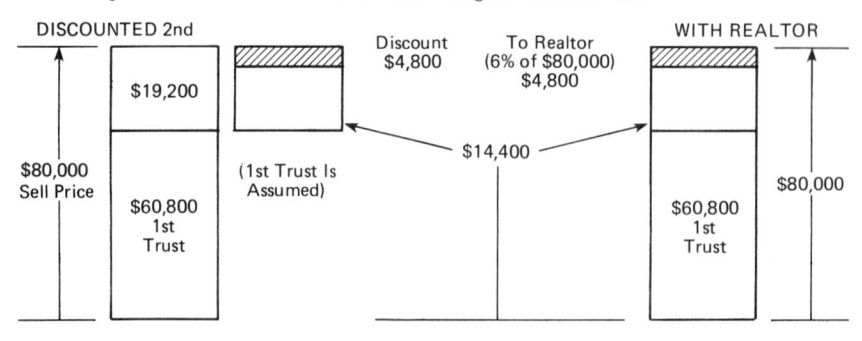

Using either method will provide seller with $14,400 of his equity.

wait for a return call. I have found that the seller will generally call me back within one or two weeks after our face-to-face discussion.

In order to best explain the financial terms of the purchase, I develop graphic representations of my creative financing techniques. The section on methods of buying is a result of these graphics. It is quite natural for buyers to ask and indeed expect all cash up front. However, because of the income tax laws, it may not be in their best interests to receive a lump sum of cash. Explain to them that it would be more beneficial if they received their payments distributed over the next few years, since a lump sum will push them into a higher tax bracket.

One of your biggest problems will be that sellers often require a truck load of cash for the home they will be purchasing. They generally feel that they would like to transfer the majority of the equity on their present home against the down payment on the new home. This is perfectly natural. But is it the proper thing to do? The answer is *no!* They would be better off by purchasing their new home with as small a down payment as possible and carrying back the majority of equity on their present home (*your* investment property). It is true that their monthly mortgage payments will be higher because of the small down payment. However, all interest on the mortgage loan is deductible and you will be paying them for the second trust. Throughout this book I have used a balloon second, but actually you could amortize the second trust over a period of time. Either way is acceptable. Your payment on the second trust would offset their higher monthly payments. The problem sellers are confronted with is managing their cash-flow position.

When taking all factors into account, all parties can make money on the transaction! However, in all fairness, I must emphasize that the largest percentage of sellers will simply not understand your reasoning. The psychological barrier is simply too big to overcome in one afternoon of discussions. This is one instance when using a realtor would tend to simplify the transaction. You could explain the entire investment process to the seller's realtor, who has the seller's confidence, who will then go over the numbers after you have presented your offer. However, when the owner is selling the property, you will not have this advantage. The best thing to do is to be prepared to explain your offer using clearly understood explanations coupled with graphics. For example, you could use my explanation of the discounted second trust paying 22.6% with interest on the loan at 12%. (See Method 4.) Without the graphics and the numbers to support the figures, it becomes next to impossible to explain to someone that cash is not always the best alternative.

Remember when dealing directly with sellers, gain their confidence *before* you go into creative financing techniques. Go slowly and be sure they understand prior to explaining the next step. Do not attempt to force a decision. Leave the data, personal references, your credit report, and your phone number. If they are serious, they will call. When they call back, you know you have yourself an investment property.

RENTAL PRICES BY AREA

Knowing what rent to expect is vitally important. Your best source of information comes directly from realtors. However, use your newspapers to get a good idea of the rental prices as a function of area and type of home. The problem, however, is that simply obtaining the data from the paper is not sufficient. You have not seen the condition of the home. I have found that the best way to obtain complete data is to call the real estate firm that has a property for rent after you have seen the home and neighborhood. Simply state that you are interested in inspecting the home. After inspecting two or three rentals, you will have a good idea of the rent that can be expected in a given area. When discussing the rental with the realtor, ask questions concerning other areas and types of homes. With this base, check the rental prices in the newspapers to provide a wider picture of the rental market. As you comb down the rental want advertisements, call a few at the top, middle, and low price range to obtain the addresses. The expected rent is required to calculate your cash-flow position in Phase 4, The Buy.

FORECLOSURES AND BANKRUPTCIES

The investor should continuously be aware of the existence of foreclosures and bankruptcies. A foreclosure is not difficult to find. The Sunday classified edition of any major newspaper carries numerous announcements of public auctions on properties that are to be foreclosed. However, 99% of all properties that require an announcement for auction are not good investment opportunities. The bankers, mortgage companies, or second trust holders will usually take the property if it is in decent shape and sell it outright at a profit. A good percentage of the time, the bank may refer the property to preferred customers (done indirectly through the bank's law firm), and the preferred bank customers will clean up the delinquent loans or back taxes, pay off the owner at a negotiated discount price, and sell the property some time later at a sizable profit. Your task as a small-time investor is difficult; however, it is not impossible. I have found that the best source of information concerning properties that are at the beginning of financial problems is from real estate agents, lawyers, and bankers.

Since the majority of beginning investors do not have contacts with law firms, nor have they developed personal or business relationships with bankers, I will concentrate on sources outside of the lawyer-banker area. I find it amusing and frustrating when I pay $16.75 for a book on how to find investment properties and the writer refers me to a lawyer. If I had my own real estate lawyer or law firm, I probably wouldn't have bought the book to begin with!

Small-money investors should be aware of the potential opportunity that results from properties undergoing the initial financial difficulties. You need to understand and research foreclosure properties. This, of course, will require some effort on your part to ensure a sound investment in property well below true market value. Be aware that there are investors who are only interested in properties scheduled for foreclosure, and at various times the competition can be much greater than you would anticipate. This competition is there because of the potential profits. The extra effort on your part can be well worth your time and trouble. I do not, however, recommend foreclosure investment as a sole means of acquiring properties. But you should be aware of the foreclosure process and procedures to be in a position to act when you are offered the opportunity for investment in property below true market value.

A few words on the circumstances surrounding a foreclosure. A property is generally undergoing foreclosure proceedings due to the failure on the part of the individual in managing the property, in managing his or her own life style, or in being negligent of the financial responsibilities associated with home ownership. There are exceptions to this, of course, such as if the major breadwinner (the owner) can no longer meet the financial arrangements previously made with a lender or if there has been a death in the family and no one is available to take over the maintenance of the family and the property.

In some instances, individuals will simply walk away from a property, considering their payments as having been little more than average monthly rent. This will normally happen when there is an FHA or VA mortgage. Of course, the owners normally remain on the property for a number of months without paying the mortgage prior to the walk out. In some instances, this could be a 9- to 12-month period of time, which they consider to be rent free. Individuals do strange things when they are out of work and when the responsibilities for family maintenance cannot be met. This often results in a breakup of the family. Seldom can the property in question be saved from foreclosure and bad credit ratings for the lendee will result unless you, as an investor, can provide financial assistance.

The investor may find it appropriate to enter into negotiations with either the lender or lendee at several different points during the foreclosure process. To identify the better points, let us first discuss the foreclosure process. The foreclosure process is a process under law that the lender has available when a lendee defaults on a loan secured by a property. The laws in each state establish a process for foreclosure that protects the lender and permits him or her to regain financial interest in the property by a foreclosure action. This same law, of course, supports the lendee. In a foreclosure action, there are four well-defined steps that must be followed for it to be legally sound.

Step one is the nonpayment period during which the lendee does not make the payments agreed upon when he or she acquired the property. This nonpayment period is specified in the initial contract, which states that foreclosure action will be taken if the lendee does not make the payments within the agreed time period. The lender is under obligation to formally notify the lendee that if payment is not received, foreclosure action will be initiated.

Step two in the foreclosure process is recording a notice of default at the county recorder's office. The *notice of default* gives notice to the public that a loan on a specific property is in default, and it must remain in effect for a specific period, during which time the owner or lendee may reinstate the loan by simply making all overdue payments and penalties. On the twenty-first day after the notice of default period, the lender may advertise the property for foreclosure sale but must not have the sale for 21 days. The owner or lendee may redeem his or her property within that 21 days by payment in full of the money owed the lender. These time periods do vary from state to state, however, the 3 or 4 week time period discussed above is average.

Step three in the foreclosure process is the advertised foreclosure sale. This will occur as advertised if the lendee takes no action during the last 21 days when the sale is advertised. At the foreclosure sale, the lender or trust holder (first, second, or third) is permitted to establish a minimum bid that would cover the outstanding debt. If the debt in question is the first trust, the first trust holder may set the bid to cover only the first trust. If the property is sold at the minimum bid, then the holders of the second, third, or fourth trusts (and so on), if any, would not be paid. A difficulty, of course, is that the bid must be paid in cash at the auction, and few individuals have large amounts of cash available. If there are no bids at or above the minimum established by the first trust holder, then the foreclosure action continues. In actuality, the normal process would be that for properties involving more than one trust (for example, first and second), the first trust holder will more than gladly allow the second trust holder to assume the debt obligation. Thus, the second trust holder will pick up a property at a value considerably under market value.

Step four is the final stage of the foreclosure process. If the auction is unsuccessful in producing a buyer at the minimum bid price or higher, the ownership of the property then reverts to the lending institution at cost of the outstanding loan balance. This property is then designated as REO (real estate owned) property, which is somewhat of a nuisance to most lending institutions. They attempt to unload the REO properties as soon as possible at very acceptable prices and terms. However, there is considerable competition for REOs. Obviously, in selling properties, the lending institutions provide most of the legal expertise required for establishing the mortgage and transfer of title to the property, and so forth. This, of course, is at no cost to you, the buyer.

The ideal time for the investor to enter into the picture is before the first step of the foreclosure action. That is, during the nonpayment period prior to the lender's lawyer recording a notice of default. During this period, you are free to deal only with the lendee, who obviously needs the money you can provide. After this point in time, there may be others involved with the pricing and purchasing.

Once the action has been turned over to a lawyer to initiate and record a notice of default, the information concerning this property is available to the public. The competition may be heavy. Note, however, that information concerning notice of default actions is available at the recording office and that anyone has the right to inspect county records. This means that all notice of defaults are available to you. In some instances, enterprising individuals publish and sell the listings of notice of defaults recorded in any given week. This is often for sale at a cheaper price than the cost in time and transportation to the court house to inspect the records. Keep in mind that during the default (nonpayment) period, you deal with the lendee. After that, you must deal with the lender.

During my search for investment properties I never purposely look for a foreclosure. However, I do maintain that continuously being aware that they *do* exist often directs me to a possible foreclosure. For example, an investment that I currently own was purchased from a developer who was simply caught in the tight money market of 1980 and 1981. The savings and loan that had granted him the construction loan was applying pressure for back payments. I negotiated directly with the lending institution after we had settled on a price and obtained favorable interest rates. I heard about the property through a realtor whom I had just met a month earlier. He called me at 11:30 P.M., and we presented the contract by 8:30 the next morning.

Remember, when you find the property with the terms and conditions, you must act fast. In the winter of 1980 I was on business in Los Angeles and I found myself with two or three hours of free time on my way to the airport. I drove by a couple of real estate agencies and quickly developed a good working relationship with the manager of a national real estate franchise. After discussing potential investment properties with him, he indicated that he had some information from "reliable sources" that a particular condominium could be purchased with some $3,000 to $5,000 to clean up the second trust and assume the first trust. The first trust was $58,000, and the property could be sold for $90,000 after some minor repair work. Unfortunately, I had to rush back to the East Coast, and I did not have time to pursue the issue. However, I did call a friend of mine in the

Huntington Beach area of southern California and provided him with the details. He contacted the realtor, cleaned up the second trust with $5,000, assumed the first trust, and paid the realtor a finder's fee. His total initial investment was $6,500, and his only payment is the first trust loan. He now rents with a positive cash flow of over $150 per month, and the equity in the property is over $25,000. My West Coast friend and I have an agreement to split the profits on the condominium after sale. I discuss principal–silent partner arrangements in Method 12.

I complete this section by reemphasizing that you should always be aware of owners with financial problems. As a general rule, properties that are advertised in the newspapers for public auction are not good investment properties. Find the properties *before* the lending institutions initiate formal proceedings. Your realtors (you should have 10 to 15 working for you) are your best source of this type of information.

FUTURE TRENDS

Inflation *will* continue! Regardless of what the federal government does concerning the budget deficit, inflation will continue. The only question is, at what rate? Even if the federal government should cure its appetite for creating new money with no standard to back it (deficit spending), inflation will still continue in the housing market. The reasons are simple—the supply cannot keep up with the demand and a percentage of the raw materials required in the housing industry must be imported from price increasing foreign markets. As previously stated, the demand for housing through the year 2000 will simply outnumber the supply. The crest of the baby boom tidal wave will peak in 1985 (age group 26 to 34) and only slightly decrease through the next ten years. Raw materials required to produce the basic building blocks of the housing industry must be imported. We have little control over these vital resources, for example, oil.

Forty percent of our oil requirement comes from abroad. The majority of that oil comes from the volatile Middle East, primarily Saudi Arabia. The tremendous wealth that the Saudis have created is causing major problems within their kingdom. Arab nationalists are pressuring for solidarity among all Middle East oil producers. Religious Moslem conservatives are planting the seeds for an Iran-type revolution. Even the educated technocrats are resisting the Saudi policy of producing an oversupply of oil; they caution against a waste in the country's natural wealth. Saudi Arabia's oil production in 1980 and 1981 was approximately 10 million barrels a day. A simple reduction of 2 million barrels per day would result in world oil shortages. It is inconceivable that the Saudis will continue to oversupply the world with oil. Their internal political and social problems will simply not allow such waste in their natural resources. A revolution that overthrows the reigning monarchy will be simply devastating to Western oil requirements. It is only a question of time before the second stage of rampant oil price increases.

Oil is used either directly or indirectly in over 75% of all items required to build a home. These include shingles for the roof, vinyl for the floors, synthetic rugs, insulation material, asphalt roads, plastic inserts, rubber moldings, appliances, bathroom fixtures, and so forth. Also, all the lumber, bricks, stones, shrubbery, and so forth must be transported in oil-consuming trucks.

With the world recession of the early 1980s the price of oil has decreased from $36.00 to $29.00 per barrel—a decrease of approximately 10%. Once the recession is but a memory, the highly industrialized western economies will demand a considerable supply of energy. The cost of oil will stabilize and then rise to new heights surpassing the record costs of $36.00 per barrel. As the cost of oil rises, the cost of house construction will follow! Admirably the federal government is tackling the inflation problem head-on by proposing cutbacks in government spending. Unfortunately, the problem is tremendously more complex than simply reducing deficit spending! Don't wages contribute to inflation when they rise rapidly? What about all the decontrol legislation that the present administration has initiated? Will the decontrol of natural gas contribute to inflation? Do you think that the much-publicized and highly paid professional athletes will not continue to push for sky-high bonuses and salaries? What about food costs? Will not the world population explosion continue to increase the demand for food?

Additionally, the United States is more than 50% dependent on foreign sources for more than half of the 40 minerals considered essential to the nation's $2.3 trillion economy. The United States is more than 90% dependent on foreign sources of magnesium, aluminum, chromium, cobalt, titanium, and platinum. These materials are considered essential to the production of high-technology items, such as permanent magnets, drill bits, catalysts for chemicals, mining tools, electronic components, and parts for many other industrial applications. The vast majority of these minerals are located in either the African continent or the Soviet Union. Any disruption of these essential minerals will result in the increase of prices for a wide spectrum of basic materials and items, for example, televisions, radios, fertilizers, jet planes, automobiles, toys, microwave ovens, hand tools, and hundreds of other items.

Adding to the problem of holding inflation down is the fact that America has become a nation that is service versus production oriented. Bankers, lawyers, doctors, fast-food workers, government workers, real estate agents, and publishers do not add direct wealth to the nation. These vocations, however much needed, provide a service. Miners, auto workers, construction workers, steel workers, farmers, lumberjacks, and engineers provide the nation its real wealth. Unfortunately, the shift since World War II has been from production to service. The less goods we produce the more expensive they become. Individuals working in the service fields merely add to the problem. They are pure consumers and directly contribute to the increased demand. The problem of service versus production can best be explained as overhead versus direct labor. Too much overhead will drive any company to bankruptcy. A simpler analogy is to think of a nation as having ten citizens. Eight of the ten are farmers, miners, and lumberjacks. Two of the ten are government workers—the mayor and one staff member. Taxes from the eight producers pay the mayor and the staff member. If the ratio is reversed, two of the ten are producers (one farmer and one lumberjack), and the price of food and lumber will sky-rocket. Why? Because the eight people that perform services are competing for the basic raw materials of food and lumber produced by two people. Also, the only citizens that produce real wealth are the producers. When 80% of the population is performing services, the government would in all likelihood print money with no standard to back it (fiat money). The money would be used by all citizens freely, but in order to have true value it would require a producible standard to back the printed paper (for example, four potatoes equals one dollar). Money printed freely would simply result in runaway inflation.

I have purposely digressed ever so slightly on some highly complex issues that plague not only America but the world as a whole. Individuals who are serious about investments must understand the world around them. Knowledge is the key.

Certainly all of the factors noted above will ensure that we continue with inflation. Again the question is, at what rate? The federal government chooses not to discuss these points simply because it does not wish to get pushed into a complex cash-flow analysis policy (vector forces at the national level). The single item that is most directly controllable by the government is the federal budget. Reducing deficit spending to zero is an admirable and noble goal. However, let's not fool ourselves. A person who thinks that inflation will ever be less than 2% through the 1980s probably also believes that gasoline will return to the 1958 price of 28 cents per gallon. If inflation can be controlled to slightly less than 10%, it will be a totally workable inflationary rate. Even with 8% to 10% inflation, analysts predict that the median price of a home will rise from the 1980 level of $66,000 to over $400,000 by 1990! Difficult to believe? Well, from 1960 to 1980 prices increased from $20,000 to $66,000—an increase of over 300% in a fairly low inflationary period. Remember, inflation was below 5% throughout the 1960s and 1970s.

During the 1980s, the 30-year fixed-rate mortgage, long the cornerstone of home financing, will appear less frequently. Lending institutions will be reluctant to lend money at long-term fixed rates, afraid that they will be caught in lending money at below prime interest rates over long periods of time. The preferred alternative will be to lend money at interest rates that fluctuate with the prevailing interest rates. Because of more frequent fluctuations in the interest rates, aggressive thrift institutions and mortgage bankers will offer mortgage packages that are imaginative, innovative, and increasingly more complex. New mortgage loans will benefit the knowledgeable owner, home buyer, or investor. Loans will be offered below prime and at discounted points with no prepayment penalties. However, these conditions are negotiable. The price for the discounted rates and favorable conditions will be an adjustment of the interest rate every three to five years, or less. As an investor, this would not be a problem, since the equity in a $65,000 home would increase to over $90,000 within three years at inflation rates about 10%. A recent study by the U.S. Housing Industry reported the following:

- Record demand for housing will press against a limited supply of mortgage funds. As a result, mortgage rates throughout the decade will be higher than in the past, even if inflation levels off.
- Mortgage rates will accelerate quickly in periods of economic expansion and fall slowly in times of recession.
- Mortgages will be steeper. However, money will continue to be available. This situation will exist because lending institutions will mount aggressive and competitive programs that will yield apparent high returns (but less than inflation) to investors in the money market certificates.
- Construction loans will be tied directly to prime. During periods of accelerating interest rates, builders will face ever increasing payments with no home buyers. The end result will be foreclosures, bankruptcies, and must sellers.

During the 1979 to 1980 and 1980 to 1981 accelerating interest rate periods, it was reported that over 30% of the independent builders went out of business. The long-term result is that there are less builders, less homes, increased demand, and faster appreciation rates on homes. The trend will be to smaller and higher density homes (condominiums and townhouses are ideal investment properties). Also, an increasing number of institutions will introduce graduated payment mortgages in order to qualify the buyer. I shall discuss these new innovations later in this section. The demand for rental properties will also increase, driving the price of rentals skyward. The Reagan administration strongly favors the relaxation of rent controls. (President Carter favored rent control.) This is an important issue, as the rent is used to offset the mortgage payment.

Forecast

In the late 1970s, a 10% mortgage rate was considered to be an insurmountable barrier. In the high interest rate periods of 1979 to 1980 and

1980 to 1981, the interest rates climbed to 15% and slowly declined to 12%. The heavy fluctuations of the interest rates caused by the Federal Reserve's battle against inflation have conditioned the American public to interest rates above 10%. By the summer of 1981, the prime interest rate had again risen to over 15%. In the summer of 1982 the Federal Reserve reversed its tight money policy causing the prime rate to fall below 12% by early 1983. In order to continue with the economic recovery it is highly unlikely that the Federal Reserve will return to its tight money policy. Most likely congressional pressure will cause the Federal Reserve to adopt a policy that will produce a prime interest rate in the neighborhood of 10%.

As a result of the high interest rates and high inflation, lending institutions will seek a part of the profit action and at the same time provide mortgage money below prime lending rates. The program is referred to as the *equity participation mortgage* (EPM) or the *shared appreciation mortgage* (SAM) plan. The mortgage plans are quite simple but yet complex in how they are administered. Basically, a mortgage institution provides money at two-thirds the prime rate. For the discounted interest rate, the homeowner agrees that the lending institution will share in the profits resulting from inflation. Additionally, the homeowner must agree that he or she will sell or refinance within a ten-year period. The EPMs or SAMs have been received by potential home buyers with mixed feelings because of the fear of having to refinance or sell in ten years. Actually, they are great programs, since they allow a home buyer to purchase a $75,000 home at 8% interest with monthly payments of $550 (30-year amortization period). Without the SAM, the owner pays $771 per month at 12%. The additional monthly payment may make the homeowner ineligible for the loan. Refinancing in ten years should be no problem, since two-thirds of the equity will be worth more than the original price of the home! A second trust or refinancing the one-third of the equity over the original price would pay off the lending institution. Remember, without the partnership of the lending institution, the homeowner could not have bought the house in the first place, and certainly two-thirds of *something* (equity in $75,000 home will be over $100,000 in ten years) is better than three-thirds of *nothing*.

During late 1980 and through 1981, the Advanced Mortgage Corporation, a subsidiary of Oppenheimer Corporation of Detroit, Michigan, launched experimental SAM programs in Arizona, Colorado, Florida, and Washington, D.C. Unfortunately, as of this writing, the SAMs continue to be experimental since the Federal Home Loan Bank Board (FHLBB), which regulates the mortgage institutions, has put the program on hold pending review. The problem appears to be political. Criticisms from public-interest groups have been negative and have been aimed at lending institutions making too much profit. What these groups fail to realize is that without the favorable interest rates the home buyer could not afford the home in the first place! Remember, banks and lending institutions are in the business of making money!

I have been forming a similar type of partnership since I started in my investment program. I called it a principal-silent partnership. The principal holds the property and receives all tax benefits, the silent assists in the original purchase price (down payment) and receives a share of the profits. The silent must pay short-term gains in the year of sell. However, if the partnership is structured as a corporation with actual transfer of shares, the investment becomes long-term capital gains, and the profits enjoyed by the silent partner can be claimed as long-term capital gains. The principal-silent partnership coupled with a corporation is complex but inexpensive! You generally can form a corporation anywhere in America for under $65. There are several books on this subject.

Returning to the SAM, the lending institution would not share in the real estate equity. Technically and legally the profit shared by the lending institution is known as a deferred payoff of "contingent interest." That deferred payoff would be taxable as ordinary income and not as long-term capital gains. However, this is workable, since paying a high percentage of taxes on something is better than not paying taxes on anything!

Problems of the more serious nature concerning SAMs stem from state unconscionability laws that protect borrowers from loan arrangements that are written in favor of the lenders. For example, the Chicago-based U.S. League of Savings Associations reported, "We can see a homeowner faced with having to pay out 40% of a 10-year, $100,000 gain on a property. The homeowner's lawyer tells him or her that the deal was 'unconscionable,' and they file suit, tying up the loan for the next two years." This is a serious issue but can be overcome by slight changes in state usury laws and written agreements *before* the loans are made. Remember, the happy homeowner has a profit of $60,000. The problem is probably more likely to be the lawyer who convinces the homeowner to sue because he or she wants a piece of the action too!

The future of EPMs and SAMs, although temporarily at a standstill, looks extremely good. Problems that are inherent in the program are primarily split of profits and modification or rewriting of existing laws. All of these problems can be solved! However, the driving force toward using some type of SAM or EPM will be the continued high rates of interest on mortgage monies. The price of homes will continue to increase with inflation, demand will be greater in the 1980s than ever before, high costs of energy will drive building prices up, and the anti-inflation tactics of the federal government will create tight money. Because of the multiple forces driving the cost of homes to ever-increasing dimensions, SAM and EPM partnerships with lending institutions will continue to develop. Learn all you can, read as much as possible, know where you stand, be first in line, and act fast! Knowledge is your most important tool!

LOANS FOR THE 1980s

The homebuyer or investor of the 1980s must be more educated in creative financing. Following are examples of the types of loans that are developing for the 1980s.

Variable-Rate Mortgage (VRM)

Variable-rate mortgages are also known as *renegotiable-rate mortgages* (RRM). With a VRM or RRM, interest rates are adjusted up or down every three or five years and within specified limits. The interest rate is adjusted at the specified time to the national index of home borrowing costs. The lending institutions refer to these mortgage packages as *renegotiable*. However, all the negotiations are done at the beginning of the loan. As this book goes to press, the FHLBB has authorized all federally chartered savings and loan institutions the right to offer totally negotiable variable-rate mortgages. These loans are not restricted to specified limits in either time or interest rates. In theory, the mortgage payments could fluctuate between 10% and 20% over a period of one year. This type of loan is currently known as an *adjustable-rate mortgage*. In all likelihood, savings and loan institutions will impose self regulations on maximum increases as a function of time periods and interest rates. These instruments will be extremely competitive among the different lending institutions. As with the three-year RRMs, be sure you settle the full arrangements at the beginning of the loan. Following are negotiable issues for the RRM, VRM, and adjustable-rate mortgage.

Interest Rate Changes. No more than one-half of 1% per year. For a three-year loan, the allowable rate change would be 1.5%. The rate cannot go up by more than 1.5%, however, if the interest rate is less than the original by more than 1.5%, be sure to negotiate that the new interest rate will automatically drop to the lower rate regardless of the differential. *Warning:* The interest rates for the adjustable-rate mortgage over any period are *completely* negotiable. Interest rates can change on a monthly basis! Negotiate for terms similar to those of a VRM.

Prepayment and Lending Periods. Negotiate these mortgages for no prepayment penalty. If the interest rate drops substantially below the original interest rate, you may wish to refinance at the lower rate. Negotiate lending periods when applying for the loan.

Additional facts about the VRM and RRM:

- The original interest rates are generally below the national average for long-term loans. The lending institutions provide discount points because they know that the interest rate will change at specified periods.
- Who can make VRMs and RRMs? All federally chartered savings and loan associations were authorized by the Federal Home Loan Bank Board on April 3, 1980 to make VRMs and RRMs. Some state-chartered institutions are also authorized to make these loans. It is interesting to note that a very few years ago VRMs and RRMs were considered to be too revolutionary and were receiving general criticism similar to that received by EPMs and SAMS. This is one reason why I predict the eventual acceptance of the EPMs and SAMs.
- Who determines the national interest index? The index is computed by the Federal Home Loan Bank Board and is published monthly by the FHLBB journal.
- Must the mortgage be renewed at the end of the specified period? Yes. FHLBB regulations are extremely tight on this issue. The lending institution *must renew the mortgage* at the negotiated interest rate. Remember, we have come a long way since the banker-lurking-in-the-barnyard syndrome.
- Does the borrower pay loan origination fees at the time of a new loan? No. Any costs connected with the renewal are to be paid *by the lender*.
- Mortgage loan periods are, in actuality, balloon mortgages. The agreed rate will be renegotiated at the end of the agreed time. Make sure that the amortization period is long term, for example, 30 years or longer if the lending institution allows.

Silent Seconds

In California, imaginative investors have created innovative techniques termed *silent seconds*. An investor or partner (silent second) pays the down payment or a percentage of the down payment for a split in the appreciation. This is similar to my own principal-silent partner method that I outline in Method 12. Partners can be used in any number of ways, however, I emphasize that before you start searching for partnership money be fully knowledgeable and conversant on the subject of value of investing in Real Estate. When I started my own investment program, I assumed that others would clearly see the benefits of investing in residential properties. It came as a setback to me when potential partners were hesitant to invest in real estate. The psychological barrier in some cases is simply just too great to overcome. I have now adopted the same philosophy toward partnerships as I have toward sellers. Do not waste time with reluctant partners! Believe me, there is an infinite supply of individuals who will clearly see that residential real estate investments are gold mines.

Graduated-Payment Mortgage (GPM)

The graduated-payment mortgage is a form of the VRM. However, the mortgage is not renegotiated at specified periods. It is designed primarily for young people who expect their income to increase. GPMs are insured by the FHA and have been available since 1978 and 1979. Of the FHA-insured mortgages made from 1979 to 1980, fully 25% are GPMs. Generally GPMs are not available to investors. However, on occasion you will find a GPM assumable loan. If you do, great, but be sure you understand the graduated schedule. Since it is a fairly new loan, it will be a good assumption. Federally chartered savings and loan associations are also authorized to write conventional (non-FHA) GPMs. However, these loans are generally not assumable.

Flip Mortgages

In a *flip mortgage,* all or part of the down payment is kept in an interest-bearing escrow account. During the initial years of the mortgage, money is withdrawn from the escrow account to make up the monthly payments. The end result can be quite noticeable. For example, a house bought for $50,000, with $10,000 down, a flip mortgage at 10% interest, and amortized over 30 years would result in monthly payments of $290.86 the first year. By the sixth year the monthly payment would level off to $440 per month. Generally, lending institutions do not favor flip mortgages. The reason is obvious—the escrow account is tied up and they would rather be using the money elsewhere.

With the high interest rates of the 1980s, innovative techniques such as this will allow buyers to qualify for their potential homes. As an investor, if you can swing a down payment to the seller as a second trust on a second property (move the mortgage), pick up a wraparound loan on the existing assumable first, and arrange for a flip payment or GPM repayment schedule, you could potentially have an investment property for nothing down and discounted mortgage payments through the initial years of the investment property. With all the new techniques that will undoubtedly spring up in the 1980s, the methods of buying an investment property will increase to double infinity. Your imagination is your only limitation!

Rollover Mortgages

Basically, they are the same as VRMs and the RRMs. The difference is that if an increase in interest rate is in order, the borrower has an option of making higher monthly payments or extending the term of the loan. Extending the term of the loan would result in no increase in the monthly payments. Generally, the amortization period cannot extend beyond 40 years.

Institutional Buying of First and Second Trusts

As I write this book, articles have appeared in the newspaper of the possibility of the Federal National Mortgage Association (Fannie Mae) purchasing owner-held first and second trusts. Fannie Mae is strongly considering purchasing seller-financed trusts. However, the trusts must conform to the nationally prescribed standards.

Fannie Mae will buy deeds of trust or mortgages between individuals in a home sale transaction if they conform to the following:

- Originates with the professional help of mortgage bankers, savings and loan associations, or commercial banks that normally deal with Fannie Mae. Your best bet is to arrange for the trust through your lawyer or escrow company. Be sure that the first or second trust abides by all federally prescribed regulations. If the holder of the trust wishes to cash in his or her note, you have generated a second trust buyer. If this proposal by Fannie Mae comes through, and if the investor does his or her homework, it could prove to be a windfall for the solution of finding buyers of second trusts.
- Complies with sound lending principles regarding appraisal of the property's market value and the credit worthiness of the home purchasers. Remember your good credit is vital!
- Carries regular 20- to 30-year monthly payment terms, no balloon provisions. This is only a problem if you don't know about this provision. Generally, holders of second trusts want balloon provisions. They want their money as soon as possible. Fannie Mae is interested in long-term gains, thus the seller of the property who is to take back a second must understand that if he or she is to sell the note to Fannie Mae, the trust must be amortized over 20 or 30 years. To solve this problem, a provision should be written into the purchase contract that states that if the seller cannot find a buyer of the second trust within two years (or any agreed period) from the settlement date, the purchaser agrees to pay the note in full five years from settlement (it becomes balloon).

The buying back of the owner-financed note, although financed by Fannie Mae, will be carried out by a local federally chartered savings and loan. The lending institution does everything it normally does for a normal loan transaction, except provide money from its vault. It will use the standard documents required by Fannie Mae and handle all the paperwork. The lender will also service the loan. They will collect the payments from you and keep track of taxes, insurance, principal, interest, and so forth. Why do they do this if the money does not come from their vault? Simple—they charge Fannie Mae a service charge for handling the loan transactions.

Fannie Mae pays lenders three-eighths of 1% of the loan principal balance for loans serviced on the corporation behalf. Now you may be asking, "Why is Fannie Mae doing all this for me?" If the seller is reluctant to take back the second, why isn't Fannie Mae also reluctant? The difference is simple: Fannie Mae is a sophisticated institution that is in the business of making money. If you held a second trust at 12% in a 15% market, Fannie Mae would buy the note from you at roughly 85% of its face value. However, if the market was 11%, it would buy the second trust at face value plus a slight discount and still make a return of 12% on their investment. It is much like the insurance companies that I mentioned in Phase 1. The members of the Federal National Mortgage Association have been investing in America for years and they are quite prosperous. I am recommending that you do likewise.

Partners and Corporations

Frequently I have mentioned a method that is uniquely mine—principal-silent partnerships. I have used this method, and it has been most beneficial. My silent partners have now become principals in other properties, and several of them are currently serving on my corporation's board of directors. The idea of the principal-silent partner relationship came to me because of the continuous problems that occur in dual property management. This method clearly defines where the lines of responsibilities are drawn. The principal holds the property and receives all tax benefits, and the silent partner shares in the split of the appreciation. The silent partner must declare his or her earnings as ordinary income and not long-term capital gains. There is, however, a remedy to this problem. The principal-silent partners can form a corporation. The initial investment by the silent partner is backed by stock certificates. Upon the sale of the property, the stock certificates will now reflect growth that is long-term capital gain. Another way of looking at the problem facing the silent partner is: $X\%$ of some profit is better than 100% of *no* profit. In other words, being in the position of having to pay too much in tax dollars because of a windfall profit is a good position to be in.

I have chosen to briefly mention partners and corporations in order to stimulate the minds of all my readers. To properly treat this subject in depth, it would require a project similar to the writing of this book. I leave the entire area of partners and the effective use of partners as an open challenge for all of you to pursue and investigate.

We now leave Phase 3 and enter Phase 4, The Buy.

Phase 4
The Buy

PHASE 4 OBJECTIVES

- Learn how to negotiate for the best terms.
- Always maintain an even balance.
- Learn what is negotiable.
- Understand that the seller's interest is directly opposite to yours.
- Keep in mind that the basic negotiable items are price, down payment, length and interest rate of loans.
- Consider additional items in the negotiations; for example, lights, TV antenna, painting, new doors and so forth.
- Study the forces affecting the negotiations.
- Always be fair and honest.
- Keep in mind that you are truly the only individual in your corner of the ring.
- Understand that for the seller it may be an emotional experience.
- Learn to negotiate through your realtor.
- Understand that when interest rates are high it is a buyer's market.
- Remember, his or her price, your terms; his or her terms, your price.
- Learn that seller financing is extremely negotiable.
- Understand the sales contract.
- Be quick, but don't hurry.
- Understand the closing process (settlement).
- Study sample contracts.

MAINTAIN YOUR BALANCE

You have now completed your hunt for potential investment properties. During your search you have completed thorough analyses of the many alternatives. Always maintain an even balance. Be continuously aware of your goal, your end objective. Do not be discouraged when you encounter setbacks. Indeed, anticipate and plan for a certain number of setbacks. For example, an ideal property is sold to another individual as you prepare your contract, or all sellers require cash, or realtors stating that a property cannot be bought with anything other than $10,000, and so on. Steady on course, hands on the helm, maintain that precious and delicate balance.

The location or locations have been selected. You have decided on single-family homes, townhouses, condominiums, duplexes, triplexes, and so forth. Along with the location and type of property is how each property can be financed. Each property that you carry to the buy phase is potentially a good investment. Your task is to obtain the most favorable terms possible. Each property presents various methods of financing, some are good—straight assumptions—and others may be best if you obtain a wraparound loan. If the owner is willing to finance—great! Investigate the possibility of a land installment contract. As you perform your analyses of alternatives (location, type of investment property, and number of investments), you must also bracket the seller's position. If your initial position in comparison with the seller's requirement is too far removed, it is best to move on.

Deal with all potential investment properties as statistics. As a beginning investor, you must guard yourself against a traumatic letdown. Several of my former students have been pumped super high after taking my seminar, and they charge on with their investment programs. This is good, however, do not be greatly concerned when you find the ideal investment and it is sold before you conclude your negotiations. It will happen; it has happened to me many times, and it will happen in the future. Do not allow the disappointment to affect the investment process. Pick up your thoughts, ideas, and imagination, and keep on rolling. You will find your property.

Since the investor is interested in maximum leverage and a seller in a must-sell situation, it is best to be negotiating on a number of properties at the same time. When you have reduced the number of potential properties to a manageable five or six, write a contract on all of them. Describe the conditions and terms (using OPM), and be ready to negotiate. Remember, you are interested in only *one* property. If all six refuse your offer and if the sellers' positions are too far removed, carry on. Find five or six more properties. The process can best be compared to a 36-stroke golf handicapper (highest allowable handicap in golf), who will par at least 1 hole in the course of 18 holes. The reason is simple—statistics are on his or her side.

After playing 18 holes, the chances are good that he or she will par at least 1 hole. It is the same in the investment process, write contracts on 18 properties and the chances are good that one will accept.

Before you write a contract on any property, you should complete the Abbreviated Vector Cash-Flow Analysis! The calculations should not take more than 10 or 15 minutes per property. Actually, only the first analysis should take that long. The remaining five or so should be done in less than a minute. Remember the three variables are (1) mortgage payments, (2) rent income, and (3) tax savings. Also complete a projected appreciation schedule on all the properties that have potential. The realtor can also complete the schedule, however, it is best to use information from the library, since you are certain it is correct and is related to the specific neighborhood of the investment property. Remember, maintain your presence of mind. Be fully aware of your cash-flow situation and your projected profits one year, two years, three years, four years, and five years from the purchase date.

ITEMS TO NEGOTIATE

In your negotiations with the seller, the following items should be considered as negotiable (they are listed in order of priority):

- Down payment
- Assumption
- Owner to carry back
- Move the mortgage
- Length of carry-back loan
- Interest (second or wrap)
- Seller financing
- Price
- Property items
- Additional items to consider

Down Payment

Notice that the actual price of the property, although important, must be considered only as it directly affects your cash-flow position. Of greater importance is the required down payment. Ideally, you desire a property with *no* down payment or as low an amount as possible. The interests of the seller are directly opposite to yours, since he or she most likely wants *maximum* price with *all* cash over the table. In reality the seller may think that all cash is needed, but the true need may simply be one of managing his or her cash flow. For example, individuals who are selling their homes in order to move into a better home believe that they want all cash in order to advance the equity in their present home toward the down payment of their new home. The idea of doubling their mortgage payments is simply staggering. However, if you can get them to *understand* that your payments on the second trust will offset their new mortgage payments, their total negative cash flow will be identical to having paid a large down payment! In fact, they may be better off since your second trust payments may actually provide the seller a better cash-flow position. Again, as I have stated throughout this book, it is a question of cash flow. As an investor, it is important that you understand this point as all sellers are moving elsewhere and they need money to finance their new purchase. Remember, knowledge is the key, explain to them (through the realtors if possible) that a second trust might be in their best interest.

Assumption

Usually the assumption is not a problem. The seller has either stated that he or she is willing to allow the loan to be assumed (does not need to be paid off with new money) or he or she refuses to allow the loan to be assumed. In all honesty, the number of assumable loans on the market are so numerous that as a general rule I do not recommend that the investor waste his or her valuable time attempting to convince the seller to allow his or her loan to be assumed. As stated previously, simply make this condition a must, and go after assumptions only.

Owner to Carry Back

When you purchase an investment property with an assumption, all your energies in the negotiation process should be focused on the equity. Ideally, your desire is to have the seller carry the entire equity as a second trust. Since you are negotiating with a motivated seller whose main concern is to sell the property, his or her cash requirements should be a secondary concern. For example, if the investment property is currently vacant, the seller has already met his or her cash requirements for the purchase of a second home. The main concern is to eliminate the burden of carrying two mortgages. Additionally, owner-occupied homes require small down payments—it is quite customary to find 90% to 95% financing for owner-occupied homes. The seller's greatest fear is that he or she will have to carry a sizable mortgage payment if the equity of the present home is not advanced against the new property. Your task is to convince him or her that the payment on the second trust will offset the larger mortgage. Senior citizens who are retiring can most benefit by taking back a good portion of the equity as a second trust. However, due to the fact that they have been conditioned in the 1930s to owning their own home as an all-important item, they will generally demand cash. In turn, they will pay cash for their retirement home. I have witnessed this characteristic in the great majority of senior citizens. Try to convince the seller that taking back a second trust may be in his or her best interest, since it will pay 12%, 14%, or 16% interest, with a balloon in five years. If the seller does have a small cash requirement, arrange to have a third party purchase a portion of the equity at a discounted price.

There is one additional note on the seller (owner) taking back the entire equity as a second trust. Realtors will not take the lead charge on this technique. The reason should be obvious. Where is the commission coming from? For example, if you purchase a $100,000 investment with a $65,000 assumable first trust and the seller carries back $35,000 in a subordinate trust note, where does the $6,000 (6% of $100,000) come from to pay the realtor's commission? Ask the realtor to allow you to finance his or her commission over the next three years. If he or she so desires, the property can be used as collateral in the form of a second trust. Will the realtor do it? It does not hurt to ask. Remember, you are dealing with a motivated seller, and chances are his or her realtor is also motivated to sell the property, as the listing may be nearing the contracted period. I recommend that you not present this option until the negotiations are well underway. If necessary, raise the value of the note by the discounted price. This will allow the realtor to go out on the open market and sell the note.

In Phase 3, I mentioned homeowner associations through which sellers are selling their homes directly to buyers. These sellers offer possibilities for purchasing an investment property with small down payments. However, in general, they do not fit the mold of must sellers. Only after they find that they cannot sell their properties do they turn to realtors. Nevertheless, pursue all possibilities.

The total number of possibilities available to the investor in structuring the carry-back subordinate notes (seconds or thirds) is infinite. The following are a few of the many methods of structuring the notes:

- Move the mortgage.
- Increase the amortization period.
- Interest only.
- Balloon mortgage.
- Seasonal adjustments.
- Reverse paper (value of loan increases).
- Stair step interest (VRMs).
- No interest until sometime in the future.
- No payment until sometime in the future.
- Convert balloon to amortization schedule.
- Sell note at discount price.

180   THE BUY

- Payment constant—vary interest to principal.
- Increase mortgage payment, equity increases.

Move the Mortgage

Moving the mortgage to a second property can be one of your most effective techniques for acquiring your investment property with no money down! This is especially true if you use Method 10—a wraparound loan with the owner taking back a second trust on your present home of residence or on a second investment property. There are problems in utilizing this method: (1) The owner (seller) may not wish to move the mortgage to a second property since he or she does not know what it is worth. (2) The lending institution with the wrap financing may require that you put down cash for the top 10% or 20% of the investment property. There are an infinite number of solutions. I will briefly outline several.

In order to provide the seller the security that he or she desires when the mortgage is moved to a second property, have a professional appraisal done on your present home or on your investment property. Emphasize to the appraiser that you want top appraisal value since you will be using the equity as collateral on a second trust. The appraisal will provide the seller the security that he or she requires. A few notes on appraisals: The appraisal value of a particular home *will* vary. If the appraiser is working for a lending institution, he or she will tend to appraise the value of the property on the low side. On the other hand, if the appraiser is working for you, he or she will appraise on the high side, since that is your desire. Once there is a signed appraisal, a second appraisal will tend to reflect the appraisal value of the first. The reason is that the second appraiser (from the lending institution) will cite the original appraisal as a reference. Having referenced the original appraisal, he or she now has protection from possible bank losses in any foreclosure proceedings, since the responsibility of the appraisal is, in essence, transferred to the original appraiser. I have found that appraisers are extremely conservative people. When in doubt, they will appraise low. I suggest that you be there when the appraisal is made. Influence his or her decision in the direction that is to your benefit.

Once you have a completed appraisal on the second property, provide a copy to the present owner of the investment property. Invite the owner to inspect the property. Explain that (if the collateral is to be your current place of residence) he or she can legally foreclose on the property if you do not pay the mortgage payments. Remind the seller that a second trust on your current home of residence is in actuality better than a second trust on the investment property, since your failure to pay the second trust mortgage can result in his or her foreclosing on your present home of residence.

As stated above, many lending institutions require that the investor put down cash for the top 10% or 20% of the purchase price. The loan officer is actually saying that the top 10% or 20% of the investment property must be *free and clear*. *Great!* Instead of having the current owner take a second trust on the investment property, move the mortgage to a second property. If you currently own a home with $10,000 or $20,000 of equity, there is absolutely no reason why you cannot purchase your investment property with no money down. As soon as the current investment property builds sufficient equity, you are ready to go again. In Phase 6, Sell/Profits, we see just how easy it is to pyramid your assets using infinite leverage! One final word: If the lending institution asks you how you are paying the down payment, simply state that it has been arranged through an exchange of properties. In all likelihood, they will not ask, but it is best to be prepared.

Length of the Carry-Back Loan

Ideally you desire the amortization period of the carry-back loan to be as long as possible. However, if you propose a 100-year amortization period on a $15,000 second trust at 14% interest, I doubt that you will find very many interested sellers. I have found that what works best is to write all of the carry-back loans as balloons. Structure the balloon with an infinite amortization schedule, paying only interest and with the balance due in three, five, or seven years. The due date is extremely negotiable. The majority of my second trust notes are written with due dates in five years. I generally pay off carry-back loans prior to the five-year period. The reason is simple—it is an excellent method for automatically generating buyers of discounted second trusts. Here's how you proceed. Assume that you have bought an investment two years ago with the owner carrying back a second trust of $27,000 (interest only and due in five years). (Impossible? Not really, I have done exactly that.) The investment property was purchased for $56,000 with a $29,000 assumable first trust. The property is then appraised at $66,000. I refinance using wrap financing. The new loan is $60,000. This is done using Method 9. Prior to refinancing, I write to the present holder of the second trust ($27,000) and tell him or her of my plan to refinance, subject to him or her allowing me to use all or a portion (for example, $15,000) of the second trust to purchase discounted second trusts in additional investment properties. He or she receives $12,000 in cash and the $15,000 is used to purchase a discounted second trust of $20,000. His or her return shall be 22.6% minimum! See the section on the advantages of buying discounted second trusts in Method 4.

Interest (Second or Wrap)

Interest on carry-back second trusts may be set by the state usury laws. There is, however, a general trend in all states to either remove the maxi-

182   THE BUY

mum interest rate or allow higher interest in second trusts financed by individuals. In the state of Maryland, a land installment contract may not exceed 8% interest. This low interest rate can easily be overcome by writing balloon notes. The seller receives his or her money within a reasonable time span. In some states, for example, California, where the second trusts between the seller and buyer are completely negotiable, the investor has great leverage in convincing the owner to carry back all of the equity. Obviously, as an investor, you must perform the Vector Cash-Flow Analysis with any possible interest rate over the amortization period. The beauty of the interest-only balloon mortgage is that the monthly payments are smaller and all the interest is tax deductible. In any negotiations between you and the seller concerning owner-financed second trusts, be prepared to show him or her that the monthly payments you pay can be used to offset any possible higher mortgage payments. Once you understand the seller's financial po-

FIGURE 4-1
Effective interest rate.

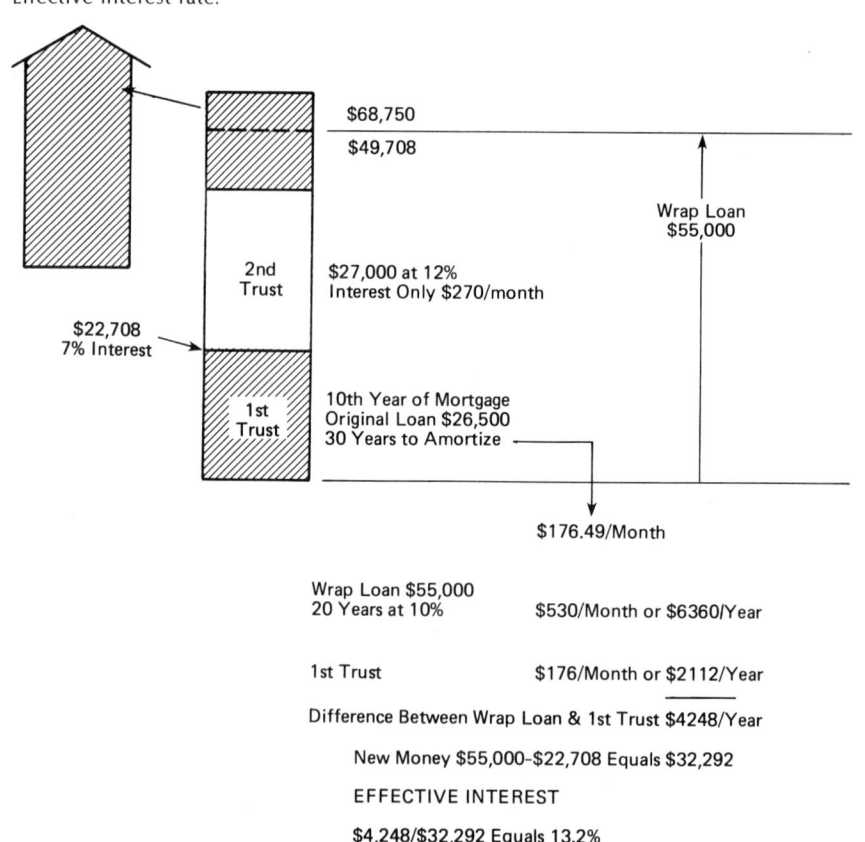

$68,750
$49,708

2nd Trust $27,000 at 12%
             Interest Only $270/month

$22,708
7% Interest

1st Trust   10th Year of Mortgage
             Original Loan $26,500
             30 Years to Amortize

Wrap Loan
$55,000

$176.49/Month

Wrap Loan $55,000
20 Years at 10% $530/Month or $6360/Year

1st Trust $176/Month or $2112/Year

Difference Between Wrap Loan & 1st Trust $4248/Year

New Money $55,000−$22,708 Equals $32,292

EFFECTIVE INTEREST

$4,248/$32,292 Equals 13.2%

sition, be prepared to adjust the interest rate up or down to ensure making the purchase.

Concerning the effective interest rate on wraparound loans, you must learn to deal from a position of strength. Learn and understand how to use Methods 9 and 10. It is vital that you clearly understand how the effective interest rate is determined. Take the initiative and perform all calculations yourself. Whether the current owner will continue carrying the first trust or whether a lending institution advances you wrap financing, prepare a clearly written financial analysis with all calculations, clearly showing the effective interest rate on the new money (see Figure 4-1). All monthly payments to amortize the loans (first and wraparound) can easily be obtained from paperbacks listing amortization tables. The second trust that is currently on the property would be paid off with the new wraparound money. The example can also be used to explain the benefits of refinancing your investment properties that have assumables with former owner-holding second trusts. Note that the sum of the first and second trusts equals $446.49 per month. The wraparound would be $530.77 per month. However, the new loan provides $5,000 in ready cash, and the current holder of the second trust would in all probability become a buyer of discounted second trusts.

Seller Financing

Properties that are owned outright by the seller are excellent investment properties for negotiating loans. The loans are a form of new money; the interest rate and down payment requirements are extremely negotiable. In general, properties that are owner-financed fall into the must-seller category or the seller requires a minimum of cash. Seller-financed properties will surface in greater numbers during periods of tight money. These properties offer excellent opportunities for small down payments and for balloon payment schedules. The owner can then be paid in full three or five years from the date of purchase by simply refinancing the property. Since the property is owned free and clear by the current owner, the property will in most likelihood be a minimum of 15 to 20 years old. The seller's greatest need will most likely be a steady income protected against inflation. Attempt to negotiate a no down payment, variable-rate mortgage (VRM) or a small down payment with a balloon first trust. With the VRM, the interest rate of the loan would automatically be adjusted to the prime lending rate, less one point every three years. This would provide him or her an excellent hedge against inflation. If the seller requires some cash, arrange for a first trust loan from a lending institution. Have the seller carry back a portion of the equity in a second property. For example, if the property sell price is $75,000, obtain a first trust of $20,000 and have the owner carry back $55,000 (the property acting as collateral for $35,000 and a second property acting as collateral on $20,000). Be sure to complete your Vector Cash-Flow Analysis, as the first trust will be a couple of points above prime (investment loan). The total monthly payments may cause more of a negative cash flow than you can afford. Again it depends on projected rental income and the investor's tax savings. Nevertheless, owner-financed properties offer golden opportunities to purchase an investment with little or no money down. Pursue all that you see advertised.

Price

Negotiating the price as related to the overall cash flow position is important. Obviously if you can negotiate a price 20% or 30% below market value, which requires a sizable down payment ($20,000 or $30,000), you should pursue. The reason should be obvious—the property can be turned around in one year with a $30,000 profit! (See Method 17.) However, an opportunity of this nature may occur only once or twice in your investment life, depending on how much time you devote to the investment process. The more time you spend, the more sensors you cultivate in real estate properties. An increase in the number of sensors enhances your probabilities of purchasing a property at 20% or 30% below market value. The problem here may be the $20,000 or $30,000 required for the down payment. Finding $20,000 to $30,000 of OPM, however, is not difficult once you have been active in the investment field and have achieved one or two successful purchases.

Finding partners also comes naturally. Remember the old adage, everybody likes a winner. It especially applies to making money. If you can clearly show that the property is indeed worth $20,000 or $30,000 over the purchase price and if the seller is in the a must-sell-now category, you should have no problem finding partners. Method 12 concerning principal–silent partner arrangements discusses the details of the arrangements. A partnership could also be structured as all partners sharing equal rights. However, as I explained in Phase 3, I personally do not prefer this type of arrangement, as there is no clear definition of property maintenance responsibilities.

Returning to the purchase price, always strive for no money down. If necessary offer the seller a slightly higher price for the property, if he or she is willing to lower the down payment requirements. For example, you are negotiating to purchase an assumption. The owner is to carry back all of the equity as a second trust. You have offered to find a purchaser of the second trust, discounted 25%. However, the seller has a higher cash requirement than 75% of the second trust. One solution is to simply raise the price of the investment property. The carry-back equity will now be higher, thus

FIGURE 4-2
Normal discounted 2nd.

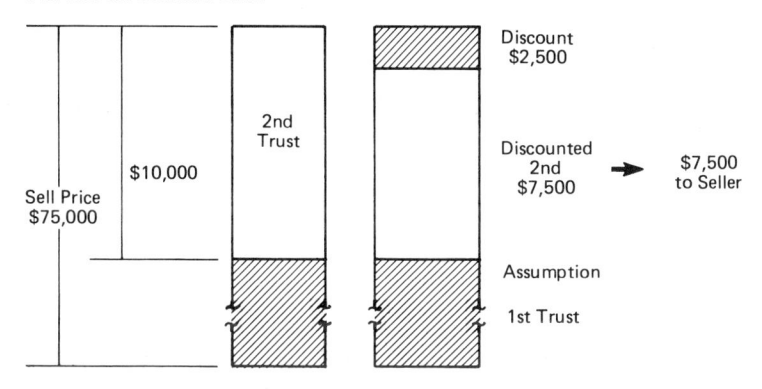

75% of the second trust will provide more immediate cash. Figure 4-2 illustrates this method. However, the cash requirements of the seller are $8,500, not $7,500. The solution is to raise the price of the investment property and in turn the amount of the second trust. (See Figure 4-3.)

Property Items

In your negotiations you can often include other items, such as drapes, a crystal chandelier, lawn furniture, TV antenna, fireplace equipment, anything you believe could come with the house. These items might prove valuable when negotiating the terms. For example, the seller's counter offer might not include the small items. However, the financing terms might be acceptable. If you had not included the small items, the seller may have countered by modifying the terms. Adding small tangible property items to the sales contract has the benefit of distraction. Your main objectives are the terms and conditions.

FIGURE 4-3
Adjusted discounted 2nd.

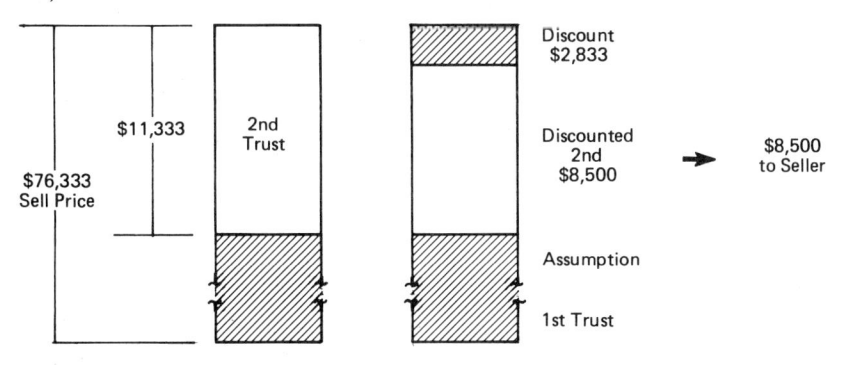

Additional Items to Consider

Consider the following items in your negotiations:

- Overall condition of the home. It may need minor repairs. I prefer to stay away from the "specials," requiring many repairs. Buy clean properties in move-in condition.
- Energy costs. Remember you will be renting, the renters will be very interested in this item.
- Proximity to major arteries and public transportation. Good rentals and high appreciation rates are found in these areas.
- Quality of schools. Anyone having children will be interested in the school system. Be prepared to answer this question when renting your property.
- Property taxes. Be aware of the taxes you must pay when you purchase the home.
- Be sure that the community is not a no growth area. No growth areas have slow property appreciation rates. The ideal situation is to have your slightly used property surrounded by a new housing development. The new homes will pull your investment property to the sell prices of the new property.
- General neighborhood quality. What is the general condition of the surrounding properties? Is the neighborhood safe? What about factories, noise, litter, smoke, smell, trains, and so forth?
- Are major businesses and stores locating in the area?
- Are houses and other buildings in a state of disrepair? Are some houses vacant and boarded up?
- What is the ratio of owner-occupied housing and rentals? Stay away from heavy concentrations of rental properties.
- Are home prices increasing, decreasing, or maintaining an even level? Do your analyses, using information available at the library or county courthouse.

FORCES AFFECTING THE NEGOTIATIONS

Before you start negotiations on your investment properties establish a sound understanding of the psychological, emotional, and physical forces (vector forces) affecting the outcome of the negotiations. When dealing with residential real estate, most sellers with whom you come in contact will have little or no experience in selling a home. At the most, they have sold one or two of their former homes; relatively speaking, they are amateurs in the field of negotiating. Also remember that this book is written primarily for the first-time and small-money investor. Therefore, the two principal parties (seller and buyer) will in most likelihood both be amateurs in the negotiation process. However, do not be concerned about this. The fact that you are both amateurs does not mean that the final outcome will not be in your favor. Remember, you are negotiating with a must seller and are applying the techniques written in this book. Knowledge and the ability to explain the financial conditions with clarity and understanding will automatically propel you into a position of strength. I continue to be amazed at the total number of sellers who do not understand that cash flow is really the important issue. Approach all negotiations with an honest and total concern for all parties. Do not try to skim or cheat the seller. Be honest and straightforward. A good understanding of the items listed below will add to your required information base to provide you, the investor, with an understanding of the investment field as a total picture. Again, I emphasize, maintain your presence of mind *at all times*.

> *Forces Affecting the Negotiations*
> - You are the only individual in your corner of the ring.
> - For the seller, it is an emotional experience.
> - Ask, "Why are you selling your home?" Find a must seller.
> - Find out what the current owner paid for the property.
> - Negotiate through your real estate agent.
> - Real estate commission is not a "sacred cow."
> - It is a buyer's market when mortgage rates are high.
> - How long has the property been on the market?
> - Financing available. Seller has arranged for terms.
> - Remember, seller's price, your terms; seller's terms, your price.

You Are the Only Individual in Your Corner of the Ring

All individuals you come in contact with throughout the purchase of your property are "against" you, in the sense that it is in their vested interest that the property sell for as high a price as possible, with the largest amount of cash on the table and purchased in the least complex of financing methods. Earlier in this book, I mentioned Newton's law of dynamics when dealing with inertia. There is another law that states, "The shortest distance between two points is a straight line." Translating this phrase into the purchase of your investment property would read, "All individuals involved in the purchasing of a property, with the exception of the buyer, will do the least amount necessary to produce the top price and the highest down payment to assure the sell of the property." The reason is that all personnel stand to make more money in less time if the purchase is top dollar and all cash. Your interest is the opposite of theirs. You want lowest price with minimum down payment. Remember this very important point throughout your investment program. In time it will even itself out, as the straphangers will shift to your side when you get ready to sell. I know that the above sounds rather harsh, but I am also aware of the pledge that real estate agents and lawyers make to always protect the interests of their customers. But believe me, lawyers and real estate agents are not in the business for the love of the home buyer or the investor. They are in the business to make money. Remember that!

For the Seller It Is an Emotional Experience

You are interested in nice, clean, move-in properties. They are clean and basically in good shape because the present owners cared. I offer the following advice—*do not* insult an owner by emphasizing everything that is wrong with the property. All the books I find on the market that deal with investing in real estate recommend that you destroy all expectations of the seller making a huge profit. Other investment books recommend that you find every crack, emphasize every defect, and ask embarrassing questions. *I do not recommend this approach.* Gain the confidence of the seller by complimenting him or her on the rose garden or by commenting on how well the property has been kept. Take time to sit down and chat about the neighborhood. Ask questions about the schools and the neighbors. Develop a good friendly relationship with the owner of any potential investment. After you have thoroughly inspected the property, discuss it with your real estate agent. Remember, even though I came down hard on real estate agents in the last paragraph, I *do* recommend that you deal through an agent.

Do a property appreciation on the neighborhood using both the realtor's figures and your own (from the library). Take the figures that best represent your position (lowest price). Using these figures, discuss with your realtor what you are willing to offer for the property—highest price, maximum down payment, and the amount that you will ask the owner to carry back. If you find any faults in the property, have your realtor point these out to the seller's realtor and use them in the negotiation process to lower the price. You do not need to be present during the negotiations. Tell your realtor exactly where you will draw the line. If you are dealing with only one realtor and he or she also represents the seller, give him or her your limit with a few dollars to spare. Remember, the realtor represents the seller, and will by law look after the seller's best interest and his or her own cash requirements. Whether there is one realtor or two realtors, remind them that if the only thing that stands in the way of a deal is a percentage or two, you expect them to negotiate their commission to a lesser figure. This point is discussed in greater detail later in this chapter.

In all honesty, when I started on my investment program, I too read all the books and tried that theory of "emphasizing every fault." It did not work, and I personally find it not to my taste. I found that what works for me is to gather my wife and children (and dog if you have one) and go over and inspect the property. Gain the confidence of the seller. Let them (especially the wife) know that you truly care about the property. Allow time to sit down and have a cup of coffee. Chat about anything. While you are being the nice person, let the realtors earn their commission, let them be the "heavies." Don't involve yourself with the dirty work. I came upon this technique quite by accident, as early in my investment program it became apparent to me that sellers were reluctant to sell to me because I was an "investor." Remember, *selling a home is an emotional experience*. Let the seller know that you are human and really care about the property. Since the largest percentage of my investment properties carry owner-financed second trusts, I continue to communicate with the sellers. In all cases, we have developed a remote but personal relationship. The exceptions to this are my investment properties with wraparound loans from lending institutions. Remember with a wraparound, the lending institution picks up the assumption, pays off the seller, and you deal directly with the mortgage company.

The most interesting phenomenon about owner-financed second trusts is that these individuals will become your future buyers of discounted second trusts! It is an extremely good arrangement. However, you must have at least one investment property with an assumable VA or FHA first trust. I discussed this point several times earlier, but I believe it is an item of such importance that it is worthy of reemphasis. Refinance the investment property after about one or two years. Find a lending institution with a wrap financing plan. The lending institution will pick up the assumption and pay off the second trust held by the former owner with the refinance money. Prior to refinance, arrange with the former owner to have all or a portion of the second trust money used to purchase a discounted second to purchase additional investment properties. I wish to emphasize at this point that during your negotiations regarding a property that has an assumption with the owner taking back a second, that you keep in mind that the seller is a potential second trust buyer, so present yourself as a solid, responsible citizen who offers minimum risk for the seller.

Ask, "Why Are You Selling Your Home?" Find the Must Seller

In your preliminary discussions with sellers, attempt to find out as much as you can about them. Where do they work? What hobbies do they have? Where are they moving? Why are they moving? How many kids do they have? How long have they owned the property? Appear interested, but not overly so. Let them know that you are interested in an investment and that this is one of several properties you will be inspecting. Tell them who you are, and give them a good impression of yourself. The majority of investment books currently on the market provide the following advice: Learn all you can about the seller, but tell him little about yourself. I agree with the first point, and I *disagree* with the second. If a certain property has potential, you will be asking the seller to take back the equity as a second trust. Next to his or her cash requirements, the single greatest concern will be your ability to pay the monthly payments on the second trust. The seller will thus be as interested in you as you are in him or her. Once I have reduced my potential investments to a manageable number, I give the potential sellers a copy of my credit report. This is absolutely invaluable. The seller wants to know that he or she is lending money (the second trust) to an individual who has a history of good credit!

Following is a list of general questions or seller categories that produce must sellers.

Find Out the Seller's Cash Requirements
- Buying new home? Where?
- Moving within city or county? Why?
- Divorce or separation?
- Cannot afford present home?
- Moving down or moving up?
- Property too large or too small?
- Involuntary transfer?
- Carrying two mortgages?
- Near foreclosure or bankruptcy?
- Death, liquidation of assets?

Before you investigate to the lowest level of detail, try to find out why the owner is selling. Ask the question with sincerity. I have never found anyone not willing to answer the question. This is one of the most important questions, as it helps you determine the willingness of the seller to negotiate favorable terms. When you visit properties (during Phase 3), you will find that houses listed by a realtor will in general not have the owner at home during the open house. Only the realtor representing the seller will be at the home. Try to pick up any clues. For example, a few months ago I was helping my uncle analyze investment properties in Bakersfield, California, and it was obvious that there were marital problems with one condominium that we inspected. We noted pictures of a complete family, but there was little furniture and only men's clothes in the home. The asking price was $56,000, but we offered $51,000. Records at the courthouse and information from the realtor revealed that the condominium had been purchased five years ago (new) for $36,000 and that the sell price for comparables in the neighborhood was $56,000 to $60,000. We had found ourselves a must seller. The property was rented one week after settlement and easily carries itself.

I do not discuss all of the items listed above, since they speak for themselves. In general, the must-sell situation is caused by a set of circumstances that are beyond the control of the seller. Do not purchase a property that is being sold because the property itself is causing the "don't wanter" situation. This would be an "unloader," and you wish to purchase from a must seller.

I reemphasize that the best technique to reduce the seller's cash requirement is a thorough knowledge of the investment process. An individual purchasing a new home with a larger mortgage payment can use your monthly payment on the second trust to offset his or her new mortgage. The problem is merely one of cash-flow management. Of particular importance and worthy of special mention is the involuntary transfer within the military. Usually, when a military family is being transferred to a new location, the government will pay for his or her new housing requirement. If the rotation is to an overseas area, for example, Germany, all housing will be paid by the government. His or her cash requirements will be minimal, although the individual may think that $20,000 or $30,000 in cash is needed. Your task is to convince him or her to take back all of the equity as a second trust. The interest you pay would be higher than the current rate at any savings and loan or banking institution.

Find Out What the Current Owner Paid for the Property

Generally the seller will know exactly what the homes are selling for in the neighborhood. If not, the realtor will. To fix the sell price, the seller and the realtor will take the highest comparable and add an inflated value. Your task is to find the same data. Having reduced your potential properties to a manageable number, use the information available at the library or the county courthouse to run a property appreciation rate of the neighborhood and the sell prices of all comparable homes in the neighborhood. If you are using a realtor, have him or her run a computer scan on comparable prices. Note of caution: the realtor printout will provide a computer listing of *all* homes in a general area. The information from major subdivisions can be good or bad. It is best to have the sell price of all homes on the street of purchase, followed by the model of home. Second, investigate and study the methods that were used to finance. Information available from realtors is extremely useful, however it tends to be extremely broad and too general Because this information is so general, I prefer to supplement data on the realtor's computer printouts with information available at the library. Having obtained all information, average the sell price of all sales over the last six months, and make this your starting point of the negotiations.

If you stop to think about it, averaging the sell price of comparables is a reasonable approach, since you are not offering the lowest price and you are not offering the highest. It makes for a reasonable argument that is strongly supported by factual data. I have found this method to work, and it generally saves me between $3,000 to $6,000 off the top price. It might be interesting to note that I have not found a realtor who uses this technique. The reason is, of course, that they want top price. Remember, their commission is based on a percentage of the sell price.

Negotiate Through Your Real Estate Agent

Either your agent or the agent who represents the seller becomes your intermediary. Do not enter into direct negotiations with the seller. It is best that you provide the final line to the realtor and allow him or her to be the negotiator. In Phase 3, The Hunt, you went through an extensive search for properties. During your search you came into contact with dozens of realtors and should have found a knowledgeable one. Make sure that the realtor understands *financing* and *income tax laws*. Real estate agents who understand financing are most successful when interest rates are high and money is tight. The reason is simple: They help the buyer with the financing. A good realtor should know about all the methods discussed in the section in Phase 3 entitled the Method of Buys. However, do not be surprised to find that nine out of ten realtors cannot explain why a discounted second trust pays back 22.6% per year if the interest rate is 12%, discounted 25% over a five-year balloon with interest-only payments. I would also be willing to wager that three out of four realtors in Maryland would tell me that a land installment contract is not legal in the state of Maryland. It *is* legal in the state of Maryland, but the truth of the matter is that realtors today are not being trained on the most important issue—financing.

Second, realtors should be thoroughly familiar with the tax laws. However, they are not, neither are lawyers. On one occasion when I was buying an investment property and there was a lull in the settlement process, I asked a question on recaptured depreciation of properties. I had asked a question on mortgage insurance and the lawyer's secretary was researching the question. The lawyer referred me to the seller's realtor, who was sitting at the table. The realtor answered the question incorrectly; then he said he would research the answer. I then proceeded to ask the lawyer to explain the legalities of a wraparound loan. He answered superficially and quickly excused himself to assist his secretary with the research. Needless to say, I never had my questions answered.

Returning to the use of the realtor as your intermediary, select the best realtor, and train him or her if you have to. Make sure the realtor understands exactly what your terms are, and then negotiate through him or her. This process also allows you some time to think about your counter offer. If you are working with other properties at the same time, the use of the realtor as an intermediary provides you valuable logistical support in writing contracts, counter offers, subject-to clauses, and so forth. The realtor, as a knowledgeable person, can also comment on your creative packages. Hopefully, he or she will offer constructive criticism. Some may even assist you in finding individuals interested in purchasing discounted second trusts.

If you are working on more than one property at the same time, I strongly recommend the approach outlined above. Analyze all counter proposals before you return with your counter proposal. In all likelihood, if you are to purchase one of the investment properties for which you are negotiating, you will know almost immediately. Major concessions are generally made at the initial start of the negotiation process. Working properties in parallel may sound complex, but actually it is quite simple and straightforward. Most of the leg work will be done by the realtor; I simply direct the action from the comfort of my home. I never found myself in the position where, after I found three or four good properties, I did not buy at least one. The only time I failed was when I once waited too long, and the properties were sold before I could make an offer. This occurred early in my investment program when I had not yet refined my cash-flow analysis and appreciation schedule to a matter of a few minutes. This is precisely why I strongly recommend that you do all of your analyses at the very beginning. Recognize a good buy, and be ready to act. The really good buys do not stay on the market long. But be sure you buy because your analyses indicate a good buy and not because of pressure tactics by a real estate agent.

Inform the Real Estate Agent That His or Her Commission Is Not a "Sacred Cow"

There may come a time when the acceptance of a sales contract (purchase agreement) is separated by only a few thousand dollars. Ask the realtor if he or she is willing to give up a point or two in order to guarantee the signing of the contract. I usually ask something like this: "Are you willing to discount your commission a point or two to ensure a sale?" The best and the most solid answer I received to this question was, "Let us consider that to be the last resort, allow me to use my negotiator expertise to gain acceptance of the contract as written."

It is best to deal only with full-time professional real estate agents. You want someone who is continuously looking and searching. You also want maximum time devoted to searching. Part-time agents do not provide this benefit. Full-time professionals who are knowledgeable and dedicated *will earn every penny of their commission.* However, they will not object to giving up part of their commission if they know that it will guarantee a sale. The professional agents will work to 100% of their capabilities before they have to give up $500 or $1,000 of their hard-earned commission.

Buyer's Market, When Mortgage Rates Are High

The time to buy is when everyone else is staying home. Contrary to popular belief, the two best times to buy in the last five years occurred in the winter of 1979–1980 and again in the winter of 1980–1981. Interest rates went up to approximately 15%, and anyone engineering the writing of creative packages could buy investment properties at bargain prices. The reason—there were many sellers, and few buyers. There is a time to buy and a time to sell. Each section of the country is unique. For example, in the Washington, D.C., area because of the high volume of military and federal personnel, properties turn over at higher rates in the summer months. Both the military and government workers can control their job rotations, and they generally wait until the children's school year is over before they move to their next assignment. In the northern climates I have found that the properties appreciate in the spring and summer months and hold steady in the winter. Properties that go up for sale in November stay on the market longer since people prefer not to move in December, January, and February. This is the type of situation that creates must sellers. Because of situations arising that are beyond their control, sellers that list in November will not have a high demand on their properties until the summer months. Buy in the winter and sell late in the summer. The warm climate areas of Florida and California do not reflect this pattern. However, I would venture to say that every area of the country has its own unique pattern. Learn what it is, and take advantage of the seasonal trends.

How Long Has the Home Been on the Market?

Find out how long the home has been for sale. The two extremes here are ideal—either when the property first comes on the market or after it has been on the market for some time. Either situation favors the investor. Homes that are selling with good terms, assumptions, and owners willing to carry part of the equity will not last long on the market. The key is to be there when they are first listed. If the property is in a good location, is clean, and is in move-in condition, offer the seller his or her asking price but on *your* terms. The worst that can happen is that he or she will refuse. The best that can happen is that you have an investment property. Having good working relationships with realtors helps, since they generally know about good buys before they are listed. The other extreme can also be good if the home has been on the market for some time. Find out why. If it is clean and in move-in condition, offer the seller 20% below the asking price. Do this with ten different properties. All you are looking for is one seller to say yes. When you hear yes, you have an investment property. Even if you have to ask the question 18 times, your chances are extremely good that you will get one positive answer.

Financing Available, Seller Has Arranged for Terms

Homes that are listed as "seller has arranged for terms" are excellent prospects. In general, it means that the seller has arranged with a lending institution to finance the selling of the home. Usually it is with the mortgage company that is the holder of the present note. The lending institution may approve the new mortgage at favorable rates. When you stop and reflect upon this, it is nothing more than a type of wraparound program. The lending institution will be making near prime interest on the new money required for the new mortgage.

In Some Situations, Cash May Be the Answer

When initially starting on your investment program, you will want to concentrate on the seller's price or terms, by giving the price he or she wants if a second trust is carried back. You may even give the seller a higher price if he or she takes back the entire equity as a second trust and if you arrange for a buyer to purchase the second trust at a discounted price. Later in your investment program as you generate equity in your properties, you can borrow the required down payments using the investment properties as collateral. However, if you start providing cash over the table, negotiate the initial price down, by 10% or 20%. For example, if you find a property selling for $65,000 with an assumable VA loan at $45,000, pay $15,000 cash to assume the loan. The $15,000 would be borrowed using a second property as collateral. The $65,000 property could be kept one year and a nice little profit of $10,000 could easily be realized. There are a few points of note about this technique: First, borrowing $15,000 using a second property as collateral will require that you have equity in the property that is greater than $15,000. A lending institution will not lend you the full equity in the property. However, this is a good technique if you have a home that has a good equity built up. Remember that the payments on the money you borrow for the cash down payment will be tax deductible. Be sure you take this into account. Second, an assumption with cash (or owner carrying the equity as a second trust) results in settlement costs of less than $1,000. There is no new money involved, hence no large dollar items involving loan origination fees.

NEGOTIATING FOR NEW MONEY

The last major item that I will briefly discuss is negotiations for *new money*. These negotiations are extremely important and take place between you and the lending institutions, not the seller. I have continuously stressed the purchasing of your investment properties utilizing old money (assumptions) and owner-financed second trusts. However, in some cases (for example, wrap financing) new money may be a requirement. Always shop around for the best terms. Even during the tight money periods of 1979–1980 and 1980–1981, rates varied by two or three percentage points. Advertisements appeared in the newspapers for 80% to 90% investment financing. With a written request, with solid data on the property, and with a good credit rating on the investor's part, you may be able to obtain up to 95% financing on a wraparound loan. Again, the point is to shop around.

In finding new money lenders, use the same technique used in utilizing realtors: Shotgun the lending institutions; talk to as many as time permits. As with your investment properties, do your ground work *before* you start. Know who is offering what and when. Draw up a plan and stick to it. For example, here is a suggestion. Every Friday afternoon on your way home from work, stop at a bank or a savings and loan institution and ask questions concerning loans. Do not approach the loan officer with the statement that you are interested in "investment loans." Approach the loan officers with questions concerning owner-occupied homes (first trusts). Savings and loans and mortgage institutions will offer long-term loans. Banks will offer short-term notes of lesser value, shorter amortization periods, and higher interest rates. A mortgage house will obtain money from all sources (money market certificates, large daily loans, treasury bills, mutual funds, individuals, life insurance companies, and so forth) at one rate and lend money at a higher rate to the interested borrower. Savings and loan institutions obtain funds from the individual depositors of the savings and loan. Knowing which lending institutions lend what type of money helps as it allows you to ask the correct questions. At the savings and loans and mortgage houses, ask about long-term lending packages. What are the interest rate and amortization period? Do they have VRMs and RRMs? Have they heard about equity participation mortgages? Do they have graduated payment mortgages? Do they have prepayment penalties? As you can clearly see, the questions are infinite. Depending on the answer to any one question, you may wish to explore the subject further. Once having developed a good rapport with the loan officer, then you can state that you are also interested in investment loans. What is the maximum amount of financing? May I obtain 90% or 95%? What if I buy mortgage insurance, can I then obtain more than 80% financing? (Mortgage insurance is discussed in the next section of this phase.) Ask about wrap financing. If they do not have any of the creative financing packages, ask if they know who does.

At the banking institutions, which handle short-term notes, ask about second trust loans. What percentage of the equity can you borrow? What is the amortization period? What is the interest rate? What is the maximum amount that you can borrow? Since the banks generally deal with only short-term notes, start your conversations with your desire to borrow money using the equity in your present home for a home improvement loan. Once you gain the confidence of the loan officer, start asking your investment questions.

Try following the procedure described above at least once a week for one hour, and within a month you will quickly find yourself an expert in loan packages. As you gain knowledge, you will feel more and more comfortable with the various loan officers. It wasn't long before I knew more about what other lending institutions were offering than any one loan officer. Once this happened, it became apparent that the loan officers were as interested in *my* knowledge of the lending rates and plans as I was in their knowledge. As I so frequently mentioned in Phases 1, 2, and 3—*knowledge is your most important tool,* always increase your knowledge base. It is free; learn to harness and cherish it dearly!

THE SALES CONTRACT

The *sales contract* is a formal written commitment of the intent to purchase the investment property. Depending on the state or locality, the sales contract may also be referred to as an *agreement of sale, contract of purchase, sales agreement, purchase agreement, intent to purchase,* and so forth. The *conditions* and *terms* of the sale are outlined in writing in the sales contract. Any subject-to clauses or contingencies must also be written into the contract. Both the seller and the buyer sign the contract.

Clearly Outline All Terms   Before you sign the sales contract negotiate all terms and conditions. Be specific. Clearly outline the sell price, the down payment, the amount of the second trust, the interest rate, and any subject-to clauses. Leave nothing to memory; commit it to writing.

Understand the Sales Contract   Read the sales contract carefully and understand exactly what it states. If you are to pay any unusual settlement costs or pay part of the seller customary fees, be sure it is stated in the contract.

Be Quick But Don't Hurry   Be quick but don't hurry. Remember, you have completed all your analyses ahead of time. You are not buying on the spur of the moment. By a carefully laid out plan you have methodically reduced your potential investments to a manageable number. You know your exact position, cash flow, and projected profits. Once you have located your investment property with the right terms and proper conditions—*be ready to act fast!*

Once the sales contract is negotiated and in writing, sign it as soon as possible. Remember, you have negotiated a price and terms that are favorable to your investment program. Do not allow the seller to rethink the situation. You may find that the next buyer will offer all cash.

Early in my investment program I had located two beautiful investment properties. They provided a zero cash flow with the price and terms extremely favorable. One in particular was a beautiful townhouse in a new neighborhood with a must seller. I inspected the property on a Saturday afternoon, conducted preliminary probing negotiations with the seller and the seller's real estate agent that same afternoon. The property was a three-level townhouse having three bedrooms, a family room, a living room, and 2½ baths in mint condition. The PITI was $595 per month with rentals in the area between $450 and $500. My negative cash flow could be absorbed by my tax savings. I decided to think it over for a few days. Monday night I called the realtor. The property had sold Sunday afternoon. A couple of weeks later I was doing some research in the library and did a quick scan on the terms and conditions of the sell. I had explained the second trust so well that the eventual buyer had assumed the first trust and received support in financing the equity by the owner taking back a second. The sell price was slightly higher than what I was initially prepared to offer. I learned my lesson well. The next property I bought, my real estate agent and I had inspected the property at 9:00 P.M. and had a signed sales contract at 11:30 P.M. Remember, you are not buying on the blind; do your analysis (cost, financial, location, and appreciation) ahead of time. When you find the ideal investment, be prepared to act quickly. When you first get started on your investment program, this will be a difficult hurdle to overcome. The psychological vectors associated with the banker-in-the-barnyard syndrome may resurface. You must know your position, be ready to act, and charge on.

Be Realistic   If you have a taxable income of $10,000 to $15,000 per year, you may not be able to afford a property with a negative cash flow of $200 per month. Your sacrifice may be too high. On the other hand, a professional with a $50,000 a year salary can well afford a $300 to $400 monthly negative cash flow. Avoid a negative cash flow you cannot afford. Bracket your position and always know where you stand.

Items Included in the Sales Contract
- Price of the investment property.
- Name(s) and address of buyer (you) and seller(s) (owner).
- Proper description of the property.

- Terms of the mortgage—interest rate and years to amortize.
- Owner financing—balloon mortgage, graduated mortgage, flip mortgage, and so forth should all be included.
- Date and time of closing. I prefer to make all my closings late in the month, since there is less interest to pay at closing and the property will be easier to rent.
- Where the closing will take place.
- Real estate agent's commission.
- Inspections—any required inspections, for example, termite and appraisal inspections.
- All subject-to clauses (contingencies).
- Earnest money—always put down as little earnest money as possible. If for any reason the purchase is not finalized, it is usually difficult to have your money returned.
- Other items included in the sale (furniture, fixtures, antennas, appliances, and so forth).

I shall highlight some of the additional contract items listed above that I have not previously discussed.

Earnest Money   *Earnest money* is a cash deposit to assure the seller that you are serious about the purchase of the property. Once the sales contract is signed, the earnest money binds you and the seller to the terms of the contract. The earnest money is applied to the sell price of the investment.

The earnest money is usually held by the real estate agent or an escrow company. Also the seller's lawyer may hold the deposit. You lose your deposit if you, the buyer, do not carry through with the purchase for reasons not specifically outlined in the sales contract. If you are purchasing an investment property on the condition that you will find financing below a certain value, be sure to include the specifics in the sales contract. For example, specify that you will purchase the property provided that you can obtain financing with a purchase money second at 85% of the appraised value. If the loan cannot be obtained, you should be able to retrieve your earnest money. The problem occurs when the seller's lawyers state that you simply did not try hard enough. The best thing to remember is put down as little as possible, especially if you are financing using a complex method that may not materialize.

Offer to Purchase   The *offer to purchase* is a formal offer to buy the investment property. The price is fixed at the offered price once the offer to purchase is signed. You are now free to negotiate conditions and terms of the actual purchase. Usually an offer to purchase is only valid for a few days. A sales contract or agreement must be signed by both parties before the terms become fixed. The advantage of using the offer to purchase is that you have an intermediate step that allows for negotiations and protects your potential investment from other buyers.

Option to Buy   The *option to buy* provides the exclusive right to buy a piece of property for a certain price within a specific time period. You pay the seller a small percentage of the asking price, for example, 2% to 5%, for the exclusive right to buy the property. The option to buy is extremely useful to the investor when you wish to purchase an investment property with the use of partners. The option to buy provides you sufficient time to find partners for your real estate investment. Early in my investment program, I had problems with this only because I was not sufficiently knowledgeable concerning the values of investing in real estate. Once having completed my initial analyses clearly showing the benefits of residential real estate, I have no problems finding partners.

THE CLOSING PROCESS (SETTLEMENT)

At the *closing* or *settlement* of your investment property, all players—principals and juniors—will meet face to face. The closing process is a business meeting usually held at the office of the seller's lawyer. In attendance are the buyer (that's you), the seller, your respective lawyers and real estate agents, representatives of the title insurance company (not in all cases), and the representative of the escrow companies (not in all cases). I previously made mention of the fact that all individuals involved in your purchase of an investment property have interests that are directly opposite to yours. Remember, it is your money that is being distributed around the table. The purpose of the meeting is to transfer title (ownership) of the property from the seller to the buyer.

Take advantage of the rare opportunity offered by the settlement meeting, and ask every question that is of importance to your investment portfolio. Ask why specific charges and costs are being made on taxes, interest, mortgage title insurance, loan origination fees, and so forth. At the settlement of one investment property, I used the opportunity to question the real estate lawyer about wraparound loan property transfers. Because of the conversation, I found a particular mortgage company that was initiating a new wraparound program. I tipped off one of my second trust buyers about the mortgage company (he had happened to have his first trust with the same mortgage company), and he refinanced several of his investments at extremely favorable rates. Use every available opportunity to question the professionals (lawyers, bankers, escrow agents, and real estate agents) about their business. You will soon have a good handle on the complete investment process.

Some Points about the Closing Process
- Bring your paid insurance policy.
- If the property is to be held jointly by you and your spouse or partner, all have to be present to sign the deed of trust.
- The mortgage note—your promise to the mortgage company—will also require signatures.
- The Title to the property will pass from the seller to you, the buyer.
- Be sure you receive a loan disclosure statement containing all closing costs. These costs will be added to the cost basis of the property for depreciation allowance.
- The deed and mortgage plus all financial transactions will be recorded for public record in the town or county registry of deeds. Recall all of the information that is available at the library. This is exactly how it gets there.

Typical Closing Costs

When buying a home with new money, the closing costs can add 2% to 10% to the cost of the home. If you purchase an investment property with an assumption and the equity is financed by the owner carrying a second trust, the reduction in costs is significant. For example, my present home was purchased with a variable-rate mortgage, which is a form of new money. (I discussed this purchase in Phase 3.) The closing costs were over $3,000. The last investment property I purchased (an assumption with the owner financing the equity) had a total settlement cost of $795. The reason was that there was no new money, thus there were no loan origination points.

Legal Fees   *Legal fees* constitute lending institution charges for preparing and recording the legal documents, searching the title, and other services performed to protect the interest of the lender.

Origination Fees   *Origination fees* are the fees charged by the lender to make the loan (1% to 10%). This charge varies according to the money situation and is probably the one item that adds the most to the cost. The loan origination fee for my investment property purchased in 1978 was 1%. In 1981, the cost increased to 4% to 6%. By the spring of 1983 the cost had decreased to 2% to 4%.

Appraisal Fees   *Appraisal fees* are charges to appraise the property, typically $100 to $200. The lending institution will appraise the property to protect their interest.

Inspection Fees   Inspections are required by local housing codes, government agencies, or lenders, for example, termite inspections.

Credit Report All lending institutions require a credit report. Next to a stable job and imagination, your good credit is vital. If you do not have good credit, take steps to adjust any bad credit records. The lending institutions are investing in *you;* they want assurances that the money from their vaults will be repaid.

Application Fees The cost of processing your loan application is the *application fee.* This fee is really no different from the loan origination fee. Both costs are incurred by the buyer for the privilege of doing business with the lending institution.

Survey Fees *Survey fees* are the costs of having a professional survey made on the purchased property. The survey includes the location of the home on the property and the boundaries of the property.

Real Estate Taxes Taxes paid to the city or county on the property are called *real estate taxes.* The lending institution requires all taxes to be paid in advance and to be held in escrow to protect it against foreclosures of the property due to delinquent taxes.

Mortgage Title Insurance *Mortgage title insurance* is insurance required by the lending institution if the amount to be borrowed is in excess of a stated amount of the appraised value of the property. Usually if you borrow over 80% of the appraised value of the property, the lending institution will require mortgage insurance. Be aware of this, as it can add $500 to $1,000 to the settlement cost.

INVESTMENT OWNERSHIP

You are now the proud owner of an investment property. Treat it with care and affection. In time it will reward you with magnificent profits. Welcome to the world of investing in America! We now turn our attention to the management and maintenance of our investment property. It should be trouble free and without worry. All of my properties have been excellent buys with very little maintenance required (normal maintenance) and no major problems with my renters. The key is simple—initial analyses, knowledge, and a continuous presence of mind.

Sample Contracts

The following pages contain samples of contracts and agreements in use in the investment process. Samples of these and other contracts can be purchased in any business office store.

- Sales contract—state of Virginia.
- Proposal to purchase memorandum.
- Sample of deed—state of Virginia.
- Example of HUD's lease with option to purchase.
- Example of HUD's lender's estimate of settlement charges.

SALES CONTRACT

THIS AGREEMENT of Sale made in triplicate this _____ day of _____ 19_____, between _____ (hereinafter known as the Vendee) and _____ (hereinafter known as the Vendor) and _____ (hereinafter known as the Agent).

WITNESSETH: That for and in consideration of the sum of _____ _____ Dollars ($_____), by cash/check in hand paid, receipt of which is hereby acknowledged, the Vendee agrees to buy and the Vendor agrees to sell for the sum of _____ Dollars ($_____), all that certain piece, parcel, or lot of land described as follows, to wit: _____
_____
_____

Terms of sale: _____
_____
_____

The Vendor agrees to convey the above property with a General Warranty Deed. Examination of title, conveyancing, notary fees, transfer taxes, and all recording charges, including those for purchase money trust, if any, are to be at the cost of the Vendee.

Where trustees are to be named in a deed of trust or trusts, the said trustees are to be named by the party respectively secured thereby.

All taxes, insurance, rents, and interest are to be adjusted at the time of closing.

The Vendee agrees to comply with the terms of sale herein within _____ days from the date of acceptance by owner or the deposit will be forfeited, in which even one-half of said deposit shall be paid to _____

It is understood that the title is to be free of all encumbrances or no sale. However, a reasonable time shall be allowed the Vendor to correct any defects reported by the title examiner.

It is understood that the property is to be conveyed subject to any restrictions now thereon.

Possession is to be given _____

The Vendor agrees to pay to the Agent cash or check for his or her services a commission on the sale price of the property at the following rate:

The following signatures and seals this _____ day of _____, 19_____.

_____ (SEAL)

_____ (SEAL)

_____ (SEAL)

_____ (SEAL)

PROPOSAL TO PURCHASE MEMORANDUM

_____

hereinafter referred to as Buyer, hereby authorizes _____
to present the following proposal to purchase premises situated: _____

for the sum of _____ $_____
   SUMS PAID HEREWITH _____ $_____
BUYER AGREES TO MAKE AN ADDITIONAL PAYMENT OF
_____ $_____
   at the time of signing of Agreement of Sale and
   Buyer and Seller agree to execute Agreement
   of Sale on or before _____ $_____

BUYER HEREBY AGREES TO PAY
_____ $_____
   in cash or certified check at time of final
   settlement _____ $_____

THE AGREEMENT OF SALE shall provide the same,
   subject to Buyer obtaining a _____ VA,
   _____ FHA, _____ Conventional Mortgage
   maturing in _____ years in the amount of
   _____ $_____

OR

   that title to be conveyed shall be subject to
   existing mortgage with approximate balance of
   _____ $_____
   maturing in approximately _____ years at a rate of _____%

FINAL SETTLEMENT is to be held on or before _____
_____, at the office of _____
_____ or at the office of any reputable Title Company, as shall be provided under said Agreement of Sale.

THIS PROPOSAL TO PURCHASE is made on the following Terms and Conditions:

THIS PROPOSAL TO PURCHASE INCLUDES all fixtures permanently attached to the building or buildings herein described; and appurtenances. The following items now in use or in storage at premises are also included in sale price; all screens, storm doors, shades and/or blinds, shutters, electrical fixtures, plumbing and heating equipment and kitchen range; together with all items of landscaping and planting. ALSO INCLUDED OR EXCLUDED ARE: _____

_____
_____

IT IS ALSO UNDERSTOOD AND AGREED under the Agreement of Sale that Sellers shall provide Buyers with a negative termite report, or be responsible for the arrest of such activity if prevailing.

THIS PROPOSAL TO PURCHASE HAS BEEN RECEIVED BY _____ as agents for the Seller and subject to the approval of the Seller. If this Proposal to Purchase is not approved by the Seller within _____ days, then said payment herewith made will be returned to Buyer.

This instrument is only a stage in the transaction until an Agreement of Sale is executed between the parties.

IN WITNESS WHEREOF, the parties hereto have hereunto set their hands and seals.

Date _____

_____

hereby acknowledges receipt of the above-mentioned sums paid herewith.

BY: _____

BROKER:

_____

Phone _____

Signed _____ (LS)

BUYER

Signed _____ (LS)

Address _____
_____

Phone _____

APPROVED:

Date _____
Seller Signed _____ (LS)
Signed _____ (LS)

DEED

THIS DEED made this _____ day of _____, 19_____, between _____,
parties of the first part, and _____,
his or her spouse, as tenants by the entirety, parties of the second part.

WITNESSETH

That for and in consideration of the sum _____ in hand paid, the receipt of which is hereby acknowledged, the parties of the first part do grant and convey, with General Warranty of Title, unto the parties of the second part, as tenants by the entirety, with the full common law right of survivorship to the survivor of either of the parties of the second part, the following described property situated and being in the _____ of _____, the state of _____.

This conveyance is made subject to the restrictions and conditions contained in the deeds forming the chain of title to this property.

The grantors covenant that they have the right to convey the aforesaid property unto the grantees; that the grantees shall have quiet possession thereof; that the said grantors have done no act to encumber said land and that they will execute such further assurances of the land as may be requisite.

WITNESS the following signatures and seals:

_____ (SEAL)

_____ (SEAL)

STATE OF VIRGINIA,
COUNTY OF _____, to wit: _____
I, _____, a Notary Public in and for the County aforesaid, in the State of _____, do _____ hereby certify that _____ whose names are signed to the above writing, bearing date on the _____ day of _____, 19_____, have personally appeared before me in my County aforesaid and acknowledged the same.

GIVEN under my hand this _____ day of _____, 19 _____.

My commission expires on the _____ day of _____, 19_____.

_____
Notary Public

LEASE WITH OPTION TO PURCHASE
(OBTAINED FROM HUD)

THIS AGREEMENT, made this _____ day of _____, 19_____ between the _____ as LANDLORD, and _____ as TENANT.

WITNESSETH, that the LANDLORD leases to the TENANT, and the TENANT hires from the LANDLORD, premises known as _____ for the term commencing on the _____ day of _____, 19_____, and ending on the last calendar day _____, 19____, at the rental of _____ dollars ($_____) per month. Said rent shall be payable monthly in advance on or before the first calendar day of each month during the term. In the event the TENANT shall, with the consent of the LANDLORD, hold over after the term of this lease, he or she shall become a hold-over TENANT of said premises for a further definite term of one month only at the same rental, payable in advance on the first day of said renewed term, which renewed term shall expire of its own limitation at midnight on the last day of said term. As long as said TENANT shall continue to occupy said premises, with the consent of the LANDLORD, he or she shall be a hold-over TENANT for a definite term of one month, said tenancy expiring without notice as aforesaid at the end of each renewed term. Said rent shall be payable at the office of _____

or to such other person and at such other place as the LANDLORD shall, from time to time, by written notice designate.

1. The TENANT for him or herself and his or her heirs, executors, administrators, and assigns, agrees as follows: (a) To pay the rent herein stated promptly when due, without any deductions whatsoever and without any obligation on the part of the LANDLORD to make any demand for the same. (b) To pay all charges for utilities, except as noted hereinafter, as they become due. (c) To use the premises for no unlawful purposes, but to occupy the same only as a dwelling. (d) Not to assign or sublet the premises without the LANDLORD's written consent. (e) Not to use said premises for any purposes deemed hazardous by insurance companies carrying homeowner's insurance thereon. (f) That if any damage to the property shall be caused by his or her acts or neglect, the TENANT shall forthwith repair such damage at his or her own expense, to the LANDLORD's satisfaction and should the TENANT fail or refuse damage, the LANDLORD may at his or her option make such repairs and charge the cost thereof to the TENANT, and the TENANT shall thereupon reimburse the LANDLORD, for the total cost of all damages so caused. (g) To permit the LANDLORD, or his or her agents, to post "FOR RENT" and "FOR SALE" signs and to exhibit the premises to prospective purchasers or tenants at reasonable hours and to enter the premises for the purpose of making reasonable inspections and repairs.

2. The TENANT further agrees to properly maintain the premises in good condition at all times and to comply with all laws, health and policy requirements, with respect to said premises and appurtenances, and to save the LANDLORD harmless from all fines, penalties, and costs for violation or noncompliance with any of said laws, requirements, or regulations, and from all liability arising out of any such violation or noncompliance.

3. The TENANT by the execution of this agreement admits that the premises are in tenantable condition and agrees that at the end of said term to deliver up and surrender said premises to the LANDLORD in as good condition as when received, reasonable wear and tear thereof, excepted.

4. It is further agreed that the LANDLORD will make all necessary repairs to said property except repairs necessary to be made caused by the

acts or neglect of the TENANT. No alteration, addition, or improvements shall be made in or to the premises without the consent of the LANDLORD in writing, and all additions and improvements made by the TENANT shall belong to the LANDLORD.

5. The TENANT further agrees that if he or she should fail to pay the rent herein stipulated promptly when due or should fail to comply with any and all other provisions of this agreement, then in any of said cases, it shall be lawful for the LANDLORD, at his or her election of option, upon 30 days' notice, to reenter and take possession, and thereupon this lease agreement shall be terminated; however, nothing in this agreement shall constitute or be construed as a waiver or relinquishment of any right accruing to the LANDLORD under this agreement by virtue of law.

6. All goods and chattels placed or stored in or about the premises are at the risk of the TENANT.

7. The failure of the LANDLORD to insist upon the strict performance of the terms, covenants, agreements, and conditions herein contained, or any of them, shall not constitute or be construed as a waive or relinquishment of the LANDLORD's right thereafter to enforce any such term, covenant, agreement, or condition, but the same shall continue in full force and effect.

8. The TENANT warrants that no person or agency has been employed or retained to solicit or secure this lease upon an agreement or understanding for a commission, percentage, brokerage, or contingent fee, excepting bona fide employees or bona fide established commercial agencies maintained by the TENANT for the purpose of securing business. For breach or violation of this warranty, the LANDLORD shall have the right to annul this lease without liability or in its discretion to require the TENANT to pay, in addition to the rentals and other amounts payable hereunder, the full amount of such commission, percentage, brokerage, or contingent fee.

9. It is further agreed that if TENANT purchases said premises in his or her own name, at or prior to the termination of this lease, LANDLORD will credit _____ of the rent paid, first, toward down payment, second, for payment of allowable prepaid items, and third, toward the purchase price of the premises in increments of $50.00. This credit will be given only to the TENANT named herein and is not assignable. In the event TENANT holds over after the term of this lease, with the consent of the LANDLORD, the credit provided herein will be granted for such renewed term only with the specific written agreement of the LANDLORD.

10. It is further agreed that TENANT shall have an option to purchase said premises for a purchase price of _____. TENANT may exercise this option at any time during the term of this lease, but said option shall expire on the last day of _____, 19_____. TENANT shall exercise this option only by execution and delivery of _____ Sales Contract. The term of this Lease with option to Purchase Agreement may be extended at the discretion of the LANDLORD.

11. The exercise of this option by TENANT in no way obligates the LANDLORD to sell premises other than on an all cash basis. In the event _____ Sales Contract, submitted by TENANT in the exercise of this option, is contingent upon the closing of a loan, LANDLORD, in his or her sole discretion, may reject such contract where the credit history, financial condition, and income of TENANT do not meet minimum qualifications for such loan. TENANT, by signing this lease, expressly acknowledges he or she understands that his or her credit history, financial condition, and income must be found acceptable to LANDLORD before he or she shall be eligible to purchase said premises through the use of an owner-financed loan.

12. This option to purchase is revoked and rescinded in the event that:
    a. TENANT fails to exercise said option within the time and in the manner required and the LANDLORD has not extended the lease option term;
    b. TENANT fails to comply with any or all provisions in this agreement;
    c. The premises are damaged by fire or other casualty and LANDLORD elects not to repair or rebuild, or are condemned by public authority for public use;
    d. TENANT transfers or assigns this lease or this option without the written consent of LANDLORD; and
    e. LANDLORD is unable to convey good marketable title to TENANT.

13. This lease is nontransferable and runs to the benefit of the signatory only with the exception that with the prior approval of the LANDLORD this lease may inure to the benefit of the spouse of the signatory. No other assignment of this lease is permissible without prior approval of the LANDLORD.

14. This lease contains the entire agreement between the parties hereto, and neither party is bound by representations or agreements of any kind except herein:

WITNESS:

_____ BY _____

_____   _____
                                               TENANT

AGREEMENT

This agreement made this _____ day of _____, 19_____, between _____
part _____ of the first part _____
part _____ of the second part:

WITNESSETH, that _____
_____
_____
_____

AND IT IS FURTHER AGREED between said parties hereto, that the part _____ that shall fail to perform this agreement on _____ part, will pay to the other the full sum of _____ dollars, as liquidated damages.

IN TESTIMONY WHEREOF, said parties have hereunto set their hands and seals the day and year first above written.

Witness:

_____   _____ (SEAL)

_____   _____ (SEAL)

_____   _____ (SEAL)

_____   _____ (SEAL)

AMENDMENT TO APPLICATION—LENDER'S ESTIMATE OF SETTLEMENT CHARGES
(HUD Example)

Date _____

NOTE: You may apply for the loan in your own name or you may wish your spouse (if any) to be co-applicant. There is no requirement for your spouse (if any) to apply or otherwise become obligated to repay the debt except to the extent that your spouse's income and/or assets are necessary to qualify you for the loan. However, your spouse may be required to execute the security instrument (i.e., Mortgage or Deed of Trust).

1. Title will be vested in what names? _____

2. How will title be held? (Tenancy) _____

3. Note will be signed by? _____

GOOD FAITH ESTIMATES

This list gives an estimate of most of the charges you will have to pay at the settlement of your loan. The figures shown, as *estimates*, are subject to change. The figures shown are computed based on sales price and proposed mortgage amount as stated on your loan application. The numbers listed on the left correspond with those on the HUD-1 Uniform Settlement Form you will be required to execute at settlement. For further information about these charges, consult your Special Information Booklet.

Estimate Settlement Charges

801	Loan Origination Fee	$
805	Inspection Fee	
806	Mortgage Application Fee	
901	Interest[a]	
902	Mortgage Insurance Premium	
1107	Attorney's Fees	
1108	Title Insurance	
1201	Recording Fees	
1202	City/County Tax/Stamps	
1203	State Tax/Stamps	
1301	Survey	

[a] This interest calculation represents the greatest amount of interest you could be required to pay at settlement. The actual amount will be determined by which day of the month your settlement is conducted. To determine the amount you will have to pay, multiply the number of days remaining in the month in which you settle times the daily interest charge for your loan.

"THIS FORM DOES NOT COVER ALL ITEMS YOU WILL BE REQUIRED TO PAY IN CASH AT SETTLEMENT, FOR EXAMPLE, DEPOSIT IN ESCROW FOR REAL ESTATE TAXES AND INSURANCE. YOU MAY WISH TO INQUIRE AS TO THE AMOUNTS OF SUCH OTHER ITEMS. YOU MAY BE REQUIRED TO PAY OTHER ADDITIONAL AMOUNTS AT SETTLEMENT."

In accordance with the Real Estate Settlement Procedure Act of 1974, I/we acknowledge receipt of the Settlement Costs Booklet. I/we also acknowledge receipt of the notice required by the Equal Credit Opportunity Act, which is located on the inside back cover of the Settlement Cost Booklet. By signing this form, we acknowledge receipt this date of a duplicate copy of this form including the "Good Faith Estimates" of settlement costs, the Settlement Costs Booklet with the notice required by the Equal Credit Opportunity Act.

_____   _____
           Applicant   Co-Applicant

Phase 5

Your Investment Property

PHASE 5 OBJECTIVES

Finding Good Renters

- Write creative advertisements, make your rental property stand out.
- The preferred alternative is to rent the property yourself; stay involved.
- The selection of the renter is all important, since he or she shall be entrusted with the maintenance of your investment.
- If you select to use a realtor, advertise through an open listing.
- Learn how to price the rent by calling and inspecting other rentals.
- Advertise 30 days prior to availability, start high and decrease slowly.
- Understanding the selection process of finding the ideal renter.
- Always attempt to inspect the potential renter's current place of residence.
- Good renters appreciate and respect their living quarters; they are proud of where they live.
- Find responsible, stable renters.
- Reduce the number of potential renters to a manageable number, and then interview.
- Learn to say *no* politely.
- Do not stop interviewing until the rent money is in hand (deposit plus first month's rent).
- You may wish to purchase an investment for a specific group of good renters.

The Rental Contract

- The ideal contract is for one year with continuation of a two-month to two-month basis.

- Make other agreements outside the basic rental contract.
- The advantage of a rent with option to buy.

The Maintenance of Your Property
- How to manage your property; use of the banks.
- Do not collect the rent yourself; arrange for automatic bank transfers.
- How to arrange for your mortgage payments and managing your money.
- How to keep track of expenses and good records.

FINDING GOOD RENTERS

Having purchased your investment property, your task is now to find a renter to whom you shall entrust the responsibility of maintaining your property. You have purchased a clean property in good condition and in a good location, and, as such, you should encounter little or no difficulty in renting the property. Once your property is viewed by potential renters, your only problem should be renter selection.

Treat your investment property with tender loving care. It shall reward you handsomely. Thus, since the day-to-day care and maintenance of your investment property shall be entrusted to a renter and since it is highly probable that the renter will be a complete stranger, it is imperative that you choose the renter with care and deliberation.

As owner of the property, you should be directly involved in the selection of your renter for the following reasons: (1) Only you have the total interest in the proper maintenance of the property. (2) Through an interview you can determine if you can get along with the renter. (3) Staying directly involved in the investment process adds tremendously to your base knowledge. You have invested valuable time and energy to perform the initial analyses, cash-flow analyses, hunting/searching, purchasing, and closing, so you should spend just a few more days to advertise and select your renter. It can make the difference between continuing or terminating your investment program.

Rent the property yourself. Only on rare occasions (I shall discuss this later) should you enlist the aid of a professional real estate firm. The selection of a renter is vitally important. Through good advertising and a well-thought-out selection process you can increase the probability of finding a responsible renter. I shall discuss the selection process later in this phase. First, let us return to the advertisement of the investment property.

Advertising

The start of the process of finding a good renter is to have a large selection base. You generate a large base by advertising. Advertise in every media you can think of, for example, newspapers, supermarket bulletin boards, library bulletin boards, suburban newspapers, factories, plants, housing referrals, military bases, and other forms of advertisement.

Make your advertisement or bulletin board notice stand out—be different. The human eye will catch the advertisement that is written differently. Be complete and thorough. Do not abbreviate. List all the main features—price, location, size—and use adjectives. Emphasize the unusual. For example, if your property has a stream running behind the backyard, advertise the stream. If a large city or county park is located across the street, advertise the park. If the property has a pool, advertise the pool. Other unusual features are sewing room, study adjacent to master bedroom, three-car garage, large wooded lot, mother-in-law suite, three fireplaces, three decks, complete privacy, modern kitchen with microwave oven, and so forth—anything to catch the eye.

An example of advertising the unusual was a townhouse that was located on a cul-de-sac (dead-end road). Certainly you need to include the number of bedrooms, baths, and the other main features. However, all of the other rental ads will do the same; your task is to make your advertisement stand out. Once potential renters see your well-kept property, you should have no problems finding renters.

Advertising Through a Realtor

At times it may not be in your best interest to handle the advertisement of your investment property yourself. You may select to have a realtor advertise it via the multiple listing service. Tell the realtor to list your property as an open listing. An *open listing* gives all real estate agents the right to rent your property for a finder's fee. Generally, the finder's fee is one-half of the first month's rent for a one-year lease, three-fourths of the first month's rent for a two-year lease, and a full month's rent for a three-year lease. Be sure that the open listing also provides you with the right to find a renter yourself. Should you find a renter, have an agreement with the listing realtor that there will be no charge for the rental of the property.

I generally close on the purchase of the investment property (settlement date) 45 to 60 days from the date of the sales contract. I include in the contract that the buyer has the right to advertise the rental of the property 30 days from settlement. Also, I include that the buyer or a designated representative (realtor) has the right to show the property to any prospective renter, giving the seller at least one hour's notification. From the time the sales contract is signed, I obtain a key to the property and if I choose to rent through a realtor, I have a real estate lock box installed on the home. Advertise your property at least 30 days from the date of availability. Since, as a general rule, renters are interested in finding a property immediately, do not be concerned when only one or two people inquire about your property. If the property has not been rented by the realtor by one week prior to the settlement date, I usually spring into action and advertise in every available newspaper. I usually receive at least three to four times more inquiries via the newspapers than realtors obtain via the multiple listing. The reason is that most renters look first in the newspaper before obtaining the services of a realtor (the exception to this are people from out of town who are shopping for a rental on a weekend trip). When the realtor finds a prospective renter who qualifies, *always interview the person or family.* Remember, always stay involved and always maintain complete presence of mind.

With all the creative and imaginative methods that are available to purchase properties, always view the renter as a potential buyer of your investment property. If your investment property has an assumable first trust (VA or FHA), the renter will be able to purchase the home after a two- or three-year equity build with wrap financing to 95% of the sell price. Take back 5% as a second trust, and pocket the remaining portion of the equity as profit. Sounds simple? It is, if you know what must be done. Remember, knowledge, presence of mind, and be sure that the renter can qualify for the loan.

PRICING THE RENT

In order to complete your cash-flow analysis in Phase 2 (Critical Decision) and Phase 4 (The Buy), it was necessary to estimate the rental income for specific investment properties. The estimate of the rental income was based on factual data. Research was completed by telephoning owners and/or realtors and asking for the rental price of specific properties. Newspapers and rental agencies were researched to give you a good understanding of the rental prices as a function of location and type of property.

Now that you have bought your investment, the specific rental price relative to the property must be determined. Assuming that you are to rent the property yourself and not through a realtor, proceed as follows: Take a Sunday afternoon and drive around the area of your investment property. All you need to do is to find one property that is currently renting and that is similar in size to your own property. Write down the name of the listing agent. Telephone the agent and ask for the specifics—price, length of lease, deposit, and all particulars. I prefer to tell the agent that I am compiling a list of potential rental properties for a friend of mine who will be moving to this area in a couple of weeks. I then ask the agent for any other properties that fit the description of the first property, and I may also ask if he or she is aware of any investment opportunities. After completing a list of six to ten rentals, arrange to inspect the properties. It is important that you understand what other properties have to offer compared with your own property. This type of information will prove invaluable when you are discussing the rental of your property with prospective renters. Having inspected the competition, you can now determine a fair market rental price. I always determine the base rental price to be the average rental of the properties I have inspected and researched through newspapers, phone calls, and other information sources. Starting with the base price, add approximately 20% to the rental price. Start advertising your rental property 30 days before settlement date. If your property has not rented within 15 days, drop the rent 10%. Maintain the rental price approximately 10% above the base price until the closing day of your property. After closing, drop the rent to the base price. For example, I determined that the base price on one of my investments was $525 per month (five-bedroom detached home). Thirty days prior to availability date, I advertised the property for $695. I came within a whisker of renting the property at that figure. Two weeks later I dropped the rental price to $575, and within three days the property was rented. Thus, I rented the property at $50 above my base, improving my overall cash-flow position. (See the discussion on the Vector Cash-Flow Analysis.)

SELECTION OF THE RENTER

Next to the financial terms and location, the selection of the renter is the most important decision you will make in the investment process. Do not treat this subject lightly, since you will be entrusting your investment to an individual with whom you shall have met for one hour or so. The selection of the renter can produce a trouble-free investment period or it can be a nightmare. As you have conducted your initial analyses of the selection and purchase of your investment property, so give the same level of forethought to the decision-flow process concerning the selection of a renter. You desire the following qualities in a renter:

- Appreciation of living quarters.
- Responsible.
- Stable.
- Good credit.
- Good, steady income.
- No destructive elements (children or pets).
- Maintains his or her living quarters.

The question is, how do I find the ideal renter, given the fact that I shall meet him or her for only a fraction of an hour? It is a valid question, and I give you here the benefit of my hard-learned experience. The following applies when you are renting the property directly. I shall later discuss some points if you decide to rent the property through a realtor. When I started my investment program, I heard my share of horror stories concerning destructive renters. However, I and a number of my friends and business partners have at one time or another been renters. I know that good renters do exist. The question is, how do I screen all potential renters in a minimum amount of time to guarantee the greatest possibility of finding the ideal renter?

Let us review the bidding: We have offered a sales contract (purchase agreement) on our investment property and the seller has accepted. Written into the sales contract is the right of the buyer (yourself) to show the property to any prospective renter provided you give the seller one hour's notice. You advertise the property and start receiving phone calls 30 days prior to settlement. Using the telephone, you answer any additional questions in regard to the rental property. The advertisement you placed in the newspaper cannot possibly contain all of the required information (school district, street address, bus routes, livable floor space, and so on). After providing the information to prospective renters, if they are interested, arrange for an inspection of the property. Remember, the owner still lives in the property.

I always ask for the address of the interested renter. I then make arrangements to pick them up myself in my car and drive them to the rental property. I came upon this technique by accident. Initially, I would arrange to meet them at the rental property. Four things can happen, three of which are bad—(1) they do not show up; (2) they are early, (3) they are late, or (4) they are on time. All I needed was to have the prospective renter not show up one time to decide that there had to be a better way, *and there is!* Arrange to meet them at their current place of residence. This technique offers a wonderful advantage, since you have the opportunity to inspect their current place of residence. When you arrive at their current place of residence, make every effort to inspect the inside of their rental home or apartment. Ask to use the telephone or, better yet, ask to use the bathroom. Most likely, you will not be in their rental home any great length of time, but be observant and determine the state of care. If the walls are dirty, the kitchen greasy, the living room in a state of disarray, the floors dirty, crayon markings on the walls, or pet odors—beware! Moving to a new property (yours) will not change their living habits. I have never found the current residence of a prospective renter to be in such a poor state of care that I have decided not to show my investment property. However, the cleanliness of the current residence plays an all-important factor in my selection of a renter. I usually suggest that the entire family inspect the rental property. This is generally not a problem since all members of the family are interested in the new rental property. As you drive to the rental property, ask general questions: How long have you lived at your current residence? Where do you work? How long? What part of the country are you from? Have you been in the armed service? Mix these questions with general conversation and small talk. Basically, you want to know everything about the renter and if he or she is responsible and has a fair amount of stability. Stay away from drifters, families with undisciplined children, renters with no record of steady work habits, or anyone not having a steady source of income.

Once you inspect the property and you drive back, the conversation will tend to be concentrated on the property itself, especially if they remain interested. During the time you are with the prospective renters, observe the general behavior of any children under the age of ten. Are they disciplined? Are they squirming, twisting, and turning in the car? Do they run wild at their current home of residence? How do they behave at the rental property? Children (and pets) are potentially the greatest threat to your investment property. The ideal situation is to have a slightly older family with children beyond the destructive years. A family with children in their teens usually consists of a single responsible individual (husband or wife) as the major breadwinner and children to help with the maintenance of the property (cutting grass, trimming edges, cleaning the kitchen, and so forth). I might add that I invariably have groups of two or three adults interested in renting; I tend to stay away from these types of groups of individuals for three reasons: (1) there is no single responsible individual; (2) if one moves, rent money problems arise; and (3) there is a high frequency of parties and disorderly conduct.

Once I have picked up the prospective renters and driven them to the rental property, I allow them ample time to inspect the property, answer any questions, and let the property speak for itself. Remember, you have bought a clean, well-kept property, thus you should encounter no problems in renting your investment purchase. When the potential renters complete the inspection, I generally know if they are interested. If they *are* interested and *do not* meet my approval, I simply state that the property will be "open house" for one (or two) weeks, and that at the end of the "open house" period, I will make a decision on the renter. I need not offer any further explanations. When I first tried this technique, it was a little difficult, since prospective renters were often prepared to offer me a check. However, because of various reasons, I felt that my investment property could not be entrusted to a particular renter. If, after inspecting the property, prospective renters are interested and if they initially meet my approval, I drive back to their place of residence and conduct a much more thorough interview. Do not get the wrong idea, you are not to conduct a third-degree cross-examination. Sit down in the comfort of their present residence and continue your conversations about anything—politics, sports, travel, jobs, real estate, or even inflation. Be careful not to control the conversation; remember, you are trying to get to know the renter and vice versa. If you cannot get along with them in one evening of conversation, chances are you will have problems when they become your renters. Proceed with caution.

Let us assume that all lights are green. Explain to them that the property will continue to be on the market until a cash deposit plus the first month's rent are advanced. *Do not* under any circumstances take the property off the rental market until the money is in hand. Listen to the voice of experience: Prospective renters are simply ecstatic about the property, and they are totally convinced that they will rent it. They say, "Take the property off the market; we know definitely we will rent!" I then ask for the deposit and the first month's rent. There is a pause in the conversation; they do not have their checkbook, or they must confer with another member of the family. They require more time to think. They say they will advance me the money within the next 24 hours, but they never even bother to phone about a change of mind. Initially, I could not understand how people could flatly state one thing and mean something totally different. The reason is simple—the hard commitment to advance the money.

Returning to the selection process, assuming that the deposit plus first month's rental is advanced, I obtain the following information from the prospective renter:

- Present address
- How long at present address
- Landlord's name and address
- Previous landlord's name and address
- Present job (how long)
- Supervisor on present job
- Income
- Credit references
- Personal references
- Banking

Generally, although I accept the deposit and the first month's rental money, we do not sign a rental contract that very night. The reason I choose not to draw the contract is that it will take a few minutes to outline the terms and conditions, and the time it takes to draft the contract creates an unusual lull in the discussions. I obtain all the information, provide a receipt for the advance money, explain the terms and conditions of the rental (subject to verification of the qualifying information), draft the contract the next day, and obtain signatures one or two days later. This also gives me the benefit of calling their present landlord, supervisor, and personal references.

In closing this discussion, it is only fair to add that the steps outlined above for the selection of a renter do not always fit the process. For example, a good percentage of prospective renters may be from out of town, thus their current place of residence will be a motel. Pick them up at the motel, and then you basically follow the same process outlined above. Secondly, you may select to rent your property through a realtor.

If you rent through a real estate agency, tell the realtor to perform a credit rating on any potential renter. Should you decide to rent the property without using a realtor, a credit rating can still be obtained from a local credit bureau. You will need the consent of the prospective renter. The cost to having a credit rating run on any potential renter is generally from $15 to $30. I strongly recommend that the rental contract be subject to the renter having a good credit rating. Although I generally try not to rent through a realtor, I have done it on occasion and will continue to do so when I believe it is in my best interest, for example, when the investment property is more than one hour's drive from my home. When I rent through a realtor, I leave strict and specific instructions in regard to qualifying data. Any signed rental contract is subject to my approval after conducting a personal interview with the prospective renter. All interviews are conducted in my home, and I generally ask the same questions I would ask if I were renting the property without a realtor. I also use the initial interview to discuss the future monthly rental payments. The majority of my renters pay directly into interest-bearing checking accounts. In some cases the rents are handled either via allotments from the renters' pay checks or direct bank-to-bank transfers. It makes for excellent records. Later in this phase, I discuss the management of the rental income.

RENTING TO A SPECIFIC GROUP OF PEOPLE

Every city across America has good renters. Indeed you may wish to purchase your investment property in a specific location because good renters are found in the area of the investment property. Through the 1980s, any metropolitan area that has a high concentration of electronics firms, especially those with contracts from the U.S. Department of Defense, are excellent locations. Norfolk, Virginia, will boom because of shipbuilding; north Dallas, Texas, will continue to grow because of the high density of electronics companies; San Jose and Santa Clara, California, will continue to offer good investments, Tucson and Phoenix, Arizona, also have large concentrations of electronics firms that are Department of Defense–related corporations. The majority of these companies produce good renters because their professional people (young engineers) make good money.

In the Washington, D.C., metropolitan area (northern Virginia), I prefer to rent to military personnel. My properties rent for prices higher than the average rental, thus I tend to attract families with good incomes. A high price automatically discourages low-income families. Because I understand the military structure, I prefer to rent to GIs, since they find it natural to have allotments taken directly from their paycheck.

Every area in the nation is different. Your task is to find the good renters in your area. Indeed, you may even wish to buy your investment property based purely on the fact that a particular property rents to good solid renters. For example, recently on one of my trips across America, an investor friend of mine was telling me of great investment properties in El Paso, Texas. He had purchased two condominiums near Fort Bliss and listed his properties with a realtor who handles the majority of the German Luftwaffe families. He told me that the Germans were insulted when only one month's deposit was required. My friend also explained that, without exception, every German family left the condominium *in better shape* than when they moved in. I remembered my own experiences in Germany, where it is indeed required to pay a security deposit of three months' rent and the renter is expected to keep up the house and yard. Thus my friend in El Paso had not only found a good renter, he had found a cluster of good rental customers.

An interesting story related to the above occurred on this particular trip to El Paso. On the same day that I had talked to my investor friend about the German renters, I had dinner with another good friend of mine and his wife. Most of my friends know that I "invest in America," and everybody is interested in real estate. During the course of our dinner, the conversation turned to real estate and my friend indicated to me that in the southwest there simply weren't any opportunities to buy investment properties. No assumptions, bad rentals, low appreciation rates—all the reasons why investing in El Paso was poor business. I told him that only by coincidence had I met an investor friend of mine and that he was having marvelous success in north El Paso. My friend refused to believe that it could be done, so we made a wager. I told him that based strictly on the Sunday edition of the *El Paso Times,* I could find at least two assumptions that were five years or less in age and that provided a negative cash flow of less than $150 before tax deductions and depreciation allowances. The next day we reviewed the paper and found ten before we stopped counting. We inspected two of the ten properties. Both would have rented with no problems.

Another group of potentially good renters are American senior citizens. I have not concentrated on this market simply because the cost of living in northern Virginia is too high for this group of individuals. My brother in southern California has several properties in Hemet, California, and he has been most successful in renting to retired Americans.

I wish to emphasize that good investment properties and good renters are found in every city of every county of every state all across America. Just do your homework—be determined, persistent, and pursue your goal with vigor.

THE RENTAL CONTRACT

The rental contract should be in writing and signed by both the renter and the owner (you, the investor) of the property. There follows a sample rental contract. Such a rental contract can be purchased at any business store. If you are renting through a real estate agency, the realtor will not only supply you with the contract, he or she will ensure that all the details are properly filled out and the forms signed. The rental contract should be for one year with an option to extend. At the end of the year, the lease automatically remains in effect in specified increments of time.

SAMPLE RENTAL CONTRACT

Made this _____ day of _____, 19____, between _____, Tenant, and _____, Landlord.

Witnesseth, That the said Landlord does demise unto the said Tenant, his or her personal representatives, the premises known as _____

from the _____ day of _____, 19____, for the term of _____ from thence ensuing; and to expire on the FIRST day of _____, 19____, yielding therefore during the said term to rent of _____ Dollars ($_____) payable as follows, to wit: $_____ per month, the first installment to become due on the FIRST day of _____ next. (If the term begins on a day other than the first of a month, Tenant shall pay pro-rata for the balance of the month and the lease shall run for (12) twelve months from the first day of the next month.) At the end of the term of this lease, the lease shall be deemed automatically renewed for one month, under the same terms and conditions, and thereafter from month to month, unless either party notifies the other, in writing, at least 30 days prior to the expiration of this term, of his or her intention not to renew.

1. Security Deposit in the amount of $_____ received. ____ cash ____ check ____ M.O. Interest will be paid on this deposit in accordance with any applicable state statutes or local ordinances. Rent from _____ to _____ in the total amount of $_____, due on or before the date of occupancy.

2. Any and all monthly payments are to be made in advance on or before the first day of each month. Tenant herewith deposits with Landlord/Agent one month's rent to secure his or her full and faithful performance of all covenants and conditions of this lease. This sum shall be returned to Tenant within thirty (30) days after the end of the lease term, less any expenses caused by the breach of any conditions of this lease and any sums due from Tenant. This deposit is not to be used or applied by Tenant as a substitute for rent due any month.

3. In consideration of the terms herein stated, the premises are rented to the above tenants to be used only by them and for living quarters only, and is not to be sublet or assigned.

4. The premises are rented unfurnished, and are equipped with _____ _____ and are to be returned to the owner or agent at the expiration of occupancy, in as good condition as received (reasonable wear and tear excepted).

5. The occupants are to keep premises neat and clean and free from objectionable features, nuisances, and hazards. The lawns, shrubs, and grounds are to be kept in trim by tenant. Sidewalks are to be kept clean by the tenant, to include snow removal.

6. The Tenant shall promptly pay all bills for utilities charged to the premises, including sewerage charges. Tenant shall assume expenses for maintenance of portable dishwasher, washing machine, dryer, window or wall air conditioners, humidifiers, unclogging drains, or freeing jammed disposals or dishwasher pumps. Tenant shall assume full responsibility for all minor repairs under $50.00.

7. The Owner or Agent shall give the Tenants quiet enjoyment for the term of lease. The Tenant is responsible for loss or damage from freezing of water pipes or plumbing fixtures in cold weather or from the stoppage of water drains, which shall be repaired at the expense of the Tenants.

8. Time is a critical element in this agreement, and if the Tenant fails to make foregoing payments or any of them on time, or uses the premises for any other purposes than herein stated, or fails to maintain the premises in the condition herein specified, or shall vacate the premises, each or any of the foregoing acts (among others) shall constitute a violation of this agreement; in which case the Owner or Agent hereby reserves the right to terminate the lease and is hereby expressly given the right to enter the premises and remove any and all belongings and property of the said Tenants and thereby repossess the premises without let or hindrance or any right of damage against them or either of them by said Tenant or anyone occupying said premises with him or her or by his or her consent for so doing.

9. Any expenses incurred in collecting Tenant's past due obligations, including attorney's fees, shall be paid by Tenant.

10. It is also understood and agreed that in case of the violation of this agreement in any way by said Tenant, or occupants, the Owner or Agent hereby reserves and hereby is expressly given the right to take any other action than that specified which is allowable by law for the enforcement of this agreement or otherwise.

11. The Tenant agrees to allow the Landlord or his or her representatives at any reasonable hour, to enter the said premises for the purpose of inspecting the same, for making any repairs that they may deem necessary or desirable, or for showing the premises to any parties; and one month preceding the expiration of said term will allow the usual notice of "for rent" or "for sale" to be placed in front of the said premises and remain thereon without hindrance or molestation.

12. The Tenant has no authority to incur any debt or make any charge against the Landlord or assign or create any lien upon the said leased property.

13. It is further agreed that no waiver of any breach of any covenant, condition, or agreement herein shall operate as a waiver of the covenant, condition, or agreement itself.

14. If Tenant is in military service and is transferred out of the area during the lease term, he or she may terminate this lease by giving the Landlord *30 days' written notice* to that effect, together with a copy of his or her transfer orders. Such notice shall cancel this lease on the last day of the following month, provided that the notice is accompanied by the rent for such following month.

15. All rents not paid by due date are subject to a late payment charge of $25.00.

16. Tenant agrees to have the property de-flead and de-ticked by a professional exterminator at the end of the term of the lease, and the Tenant agrees to fill the oil tank at the end of the lease term.

17. When the property is equipped with an oil tank, the Landlord agrees to fill the oil tank at the beginning of the term of the lease and the Tenant agrees to fill the oil tank at the end of the lease term.

18. All of the terms, covenants, agreements, and provisions herein contained shall bind and inure to the benefit of Landlord, Tenant, and Agent, their heirs, executors, administrators, personal representatives, successors, trustees, receivers, and assigns as applicable, except as otherwise provided herein.

19. Tenant agrees to provide the Landlord/Agent with a copy of final water and sewer service payment receipts at the termination of this lease.

20. Special considerations

_____
_____
_____
_____
_____

21. This lease is valid only when ratified by all parties or duly authorized representatives. It contains the entire agreement between all parties hereto and shall not be changed or modified in any manner except by an instrument in writing executed by parties hereto.

WITNESS the following signatures and seals this _____ day of _____, 19____.

Tenant _____ (SEAL) Landlord _____ (SEAL)

Tenant _____ (SEAL) Landlord _____ (SEAL)

At the completion of one year, either the renter or the owner has the option to terminate the lease given two months' written notice. If the lease is terminated by either party, the owner retains the right to show the property to any prospective new renters during the last month of the rental period. It is best not to write a new contract after one year, since you have achieved your long-term capital investment period; the ideal situation is to be able to sell if the need arises.

Agreements

Agreements between you and the renter outside of the basic rental contract should be made independent of the rental agreement. For example, if you agree to sell the renter furniture or appliances left in the house, agree on the terms separately from the rental contract. The same applies to personal property that is affixed to the house but is to be purchased by the renter. For example, if the renter decides to install thermo-insulated windows in order to reduce his or her heating bills, do not include the financial terms of the arrangement in the rental contract. You may change your mind and decide to purchase the thermo windows if he or she installs them. Remember, you may claim tax deductions on all maintenance costs. Also, all improvements related to energy conservation can be claimed as tax credits.

Should you decide to sell the renter the investment property during the investment period, agree on the terms and conditions outside of the rental agreement. In general, restrict the rental contract to the basic requirement of fixing the rent and the conditions and terms surrounding the rental of the property. All other items should be kept separate and independent. I recommend this because, should a disagreement arise, it can easily be settled. If the rental agreement and all other agreements are separate, it is much easier to discuss the separate and independent responsibilities.

Rent with Option to Buy

One exception to the rental agreement is that you may wish to consider an option to buy with the original rental contract. This arrangement works very well when the house you currently own is to become your investment property. Let us assume that you have owned your house for five years and have a first trust of $45,000 with equity of $30,000. Market value of the home is $75,000. You refinance your home at $60,000 and use one of the methods discussed in Phase 3 to purchase a second home and an additional investment property. With $15,000 you should have no problem purchasing two additional properties. The house you bought for yourself is purchased at $90,000 and the investment property at $60,000 (townhouse or condominium). Overnight you own three properties. One is your new house—the wife is happy because you moved up, the children are happy since they have bigger bedrooms and a bigger yard. Your former house still has $15,000 ($75,000 − $60,000) of equity. All the interest you are paying on the three loans is tax deductible. New home, refinanced home, and new investment property are now yours. Your total cash flow situation should be zero or a small positive cash flow. You can rent your old home with an option to buy, returning to the renter 30% of the total rent money paid during the rental period. In two years, your old home will be valued at approximately $90,000 (10% inflation). Your home currently valued at $75,000 will rent for approximately $625 per month. In two years the total rent paid will equal $15,000 ($625 × 24). Thirty percent of $15,000 is $4,500. You return $4,500 to the buyer (your renter) against the sale price. If you plan ahead and select a renter with VA rights, he or she can purchase your former home with no money down. The $4,500 that you advance the renter will probably bring the required mortgage under the VA appraisal. The renter will be able to borrow all of the required money to finance the purchase. Your *total profit* is $85,500 ($90,000 − $4,500) minus $60,000 (refinanced mortgage balance) equals $25,500.

You now have $25,500 to reinvest. Since you had the foresight to include an option to buy, you sold the property without the 5% to 6% commission to the realtor. The renters know from the moment they sign the rental contract that the house is to become theirs, so they would be more likely to properly maintain the house. You win, the renter wins, everybody is happy. Even the lending institutions are elated because you have paid off the loans in full. The losers? All the folks who never overcome the psychological barrier of investing in real estate. Those who run to the bank and invest their money in 5¾% savings accounts and 10% CDs. Renting with an option to buy also has the added benefit of creating a large base of interested renters. I have advertised properties for over two weeks with little results. Inserting the phrase "option to buy" always produces results.

MANAGING YOUR PROPERTY

To manage your properties personally or to obtain the services of a professional management firm is entirely your decision. I recommend that, during the initial years of your investment portfolio, you personally manage your properties. Initially you should stay involved. The management of the first four to six properties will be valuable experience in the harvest years of your investment portfolio. Since you have purchased clean properties in good condition, in good locations, and renting for values above the average, your renters will have a sound financial base. Since embarking on my own investment program, I visit the properties about once every four months. I generally do a little repair work or hire professional help to do some basic work on the home in the springtime. My greatest involvement, however, occurs during the selection of the renter.

Initially, it is important that you stay involved. Learn from my experience. Purchasing six investment properties in three years can easily be done (I discuss pyramiding your assets in Phase 6, Sell/Profits. Within three to five years, you may wish to propel yourself to larger, multifamily rental units. The experience gained in the management of your initial six investment properties will be invaluable. When to hire a professional management firm will depend on the type of properties (condominiums, townhouses, duplexes, and so forth) and the distance between your investment properties and your home. After purchasing between four to six investment properties, you may consider shifting to a professional management firm. Management firms are listed in the telephone directories under real estate management. Also any knowledgeable real estate agent can direct you to numerous management firms. Managing your properties initially also has the big advantage of producing a better cash-flow position. Management firms charge from 10% to 15% of the rent for the management services. If you have followed the recommendations of Phases 3, 4, and 5 (good renter), you would be paying a nice sum of money to a management firm simply to strip 10% to 15% off the rent before transferring the funds to your account.

Management firms do provide nice, clean records concerning the maintenance of your investment property. However, good records can also be generated by all those bankers who you have interviewed in shopping for money. Not only will they maintain your records, they will pay *you* for the service! More on the subject later in the section entitled Collecting Your Rent.

Real estate management firms can be extremely helpful if you have more than six properties or if you purchase multifamily rental units. If you find a 10- or 20-unit apartment building having all the desired conditions and terms, by all means purchase it. However, if you are a novice, proceed cautiously. After having purchased, consult a real estate management firm to manage the property. The management of a 20-unit apartment complex does require continuous professional management, and in this case, the management fee will be well earned by the management company. You may also run across a multifamily rental unit that has a manager's apartment. This situation is ideal, since you can hire a manager to live on the premises and look after your properties on a continuous basis.

Collecting Your Rent

Arrange for the method of rent payment during the signing of the rental contract. Indeed, discuss your preferred method during the initial interviews as discussed earlier in this phase. If possible, arrange for allotments to be taken directly from the renter's paycheck and deposited into your checking account. If this is not possible, arrange for automatic bank-to-bank transfers. This method can be arranged with any bank by simply filling out transfer forms. Your renter's bank account number and his or her signature providing consent is required. Provide this information to both your bank and the renter's bank. The transfer of funds will occur automatically on the specified date. I prefer this method since it removes the requirement of directly handling the rent money. Second, the bank-to-bank transfer elevates the payment of the rent to a professional financial transaction. The renter knows that the automatic transfer will occur on a specified date. Failure to cover the required transfer amount will result in a reminder from the bank of an overdraft with the resultant penalty fee. The system does have a definite built-in advantage. Third and probably most important, the use of a separate bank account to handle every investment property provides a beautiful bookkeeping system to record all transactions. I receive my monthly statements from the banks and file them by month and property. Any maintenance costs incurred on a particular property are paid using a check from the property requiring the maintenance. At the end of the year, I simply review all monthly bank statements, transfer all expenses to my tax forms, and submit my yearly income tax return. This year I completed my total federal and state tax returns working one evening for approximately two hours. I have infinitely more deductions, exemptions, forms, and so forth than I had before I started on my investment program. Nevertheless, I complete my tax return in half the time of before. My wife comments, "Gee, why didn't you do that several years ago?" The key is *knowledge* and keeping good records. Let the banks do all your bookkeeping. Having good, clean, explainable records is invaluable if the IRS selects to audit your return on any given year.

Making Your Mortgage Payments and Managing Your Money

Handle all your mortgage payments exactly in the reverse order of collecting your rent. Transfer directly from your property accounts to the mortgage companies. All mortgage companies have preprinted forms that you sign and return to the mortgage company. The mortgage company will then send a copy of the preprinted form to your bank informing the bank that it has your permission to issue a draft for the mortgage payment on a monthly basis. The mortgage payment is now automatic, and you are sent a receipt of the draft on a monthly basis. The transfer of funds is indicated on your monthly banking statement. Remember, the renters are paying directly into the interest-bearing account (positive cash). The positive cash from the rents should equal or be greater than the outgoing (negative cash flow) mortgage payments. If the mortgage payments are larger (initially, chances are they will be), you will need to subsidize your checking account. The required amount to sustain your investment property will come from your tax savings. The cash-flow analysis on the property you purchase was performed during Phases 2 and 3. Using the Vector Cash-Flow Analysis, you computed the resultant tax savings due to interest on the loan and depreciation allowance. The amount of savings due to the payment of less taxes should be automatically transferred from your regular take-home pay to your investment property accounts. Again, the bank will automatically handle these transactions. I hope it is not starting to sound too complex, because it really is not. Just remember, do all your cash-flow analyses *before* your purchase, and be sure you can sustain any negative cash flow. I have purposely opened different accounts with different banks to handle my investment properties because I want maximum exposure to the financial world. The amount of funds that revolve through any one account in one year is approximately $10,000.

When applying for loans for the purchase of additional investment properties, I expect and receive preferred treatment, since the branch managers know me on a first name basis. Recall I mentioned earlier that it was vital that you establish good credit. The establishment of numerous accounts with thousands of dollars revolving through the bank vaults makes a nice sound to all bankers; and your credit rating will continue to be strengthened. Also make it a point to do a certain percentage of your banking on a person-to-person basis. As you continue to pyramid your investment properties, you will automatically become more and more knowledgeable about the financial world. Chat with the loan officer about the prevailing interest rates. Ask him or her to let you know in advance of any special "bargain basement" second trust loans. My list of second trust buyers (discounted second trusts) was built using information provided by loan officers at banks where I do my banking business. Learn to take advantage of every opportunity. As you become more and more knowledgeable about who is lending what type of money and at what lending rates, you will find that the loan officers will be as interested in you as you are in them.

Keeping Track of Expenses and Maintaining Good Records

Besides the rent money, mortgage payments, insurance, and taxes, you will have additional expenses to maintain your properties, for example, termite insurance, providing paint to the renter, lawn service, appliance repair, general hardware items, and so forth. Pay all expenses using the investment checking account. Even if you have to transfer from your personal account to the investment account, do it! Learn to separate your expenses. Keeping good records is an absolute must. Reflect any major items purchased for the investment property as independent entries in the investment account, for example, a stove or refrigerator. These items may be depreciated in five years independent of the investment property. The initial value of the equipment should also be reflected in the account. Maintain accurate bookkeeping in case you are ever questioned by the IRS.

230   YOUR INVESTMENT PROPERTY

A Bookkeeping System   I recommend that when you first start your investment program you should keep all your own records for two major reasons: (1) to cut down on expenses, and (2) to gain knowledge.

I previously recommended that separate checking accounts be opened for each property. Consider having no more than two accounts at any one bank. Banks occasionally make mistakes and having too many (three or more) accounts at the same bank under the same name does cause problems at times. However, there is an easy solution to this problem. Open checking accounts at different banks. As mentioned above, an extremely important side benefit to having numerous checking accounts at

Table 5-1. First Virginia Bank

Gil Armen

SUMMARY OF ACTIVITY

Scat	1,800.13	4,767.15	3,278.21	3,289.07

SUMMARY OF ACTIVITY
SCAT ACCOUNTS 4378-8882

DESCRIPTION OF ACTIVITY

PREVIOUS BALANCE					4-10	1,800.13
CHECK	B	223	2nd Mortgage Payment	86.78−	4-16	1,713.35
CHECK	A	224	2nd Mortgage Payment	277.00−	4-20	1,436.35
CHECK	B		Mortage Payment (Auto)	676.00−	4-20	760.35
DEPOSIT	B		ADVANCE RENT	4,375.00+	4-21	5,135.35
CHECK	B	225	R.E. Commission	150.00−	4-21	4,985.35
DEPOSIT	A		RENT	375.00+	4-28	5,360.35
CHECK	B	226	Hardware Expenses	27.57−	4-29	5,332.78
CHECK	A	227	Hardware Expenses	36.61−	4-29	5,296.17
CHECK	B	228	Hardware Expenses	75.13−	4-29	5,221.04
CHECK	B	229	Pool Supplies	100.86−	4-30	5,120.18
CHECK	A	236	Homeowners Association	30.00−	5-05	5,090.18
CHECK	B	234	Paint	42.00−	5-06	5,048.18
CHECK	B	232	Paint	26.38−	5-06	5,021.80
CHECK	B	231	Pool Supplies	54.58−	5-06	4,967.22
CHECK	B	230	New Dishwasher	271.30−	5-06	4,695.92
CHECK	B	237	New Carpeting	1,424.00−	5-11	3,271.92
*INTEREST EARNED				17.15+	5-12	3,289.07

*****AVERAGE BALANCE FOR STATEMENT PERIOD IS	3,973.58
*****INTEREST EARNED YEAR-TO-DATE	41.78

TABLE 5-2. Property B

RENT ($8,880)	JAN 750	FEB 750	MAR 750	APR 750	MAY[a] 730	JUN 730	JUL 730	AUG 730	SEP 730	OCT 730	NOV 750	DEC 750	TOTAL $8,880
Expenses													11,941.08
Advertising				32									32
Auto and travel	25	20	0	35	65	55	0	0	0	15	25	0	240
Cleaning and maintenance	0	0	0	65	0	0	0	0	0	0	0	0	65
Commissions					150								150
Insurance[b]												225	225
Interest[c]												7489	7489
Prof. fees[d]							309						309
Repairs					589								589
Supplies					363.18								363.18
Taxes												1,298	1,298
Utilities													0
Wages				75									75
Other													
Dishwasher					271.30								271.30
Carpeting					835								835

[a] Six months' advance rent, resulted in a discount of $20 per month.
[b] Insurance, total for year = $225.
[c] Interest, total for year = $7,439, mortgage company will provide.
[d] Obtained a second trust loan of $14,400, lawyer's fees = $309.

NOTE: Total deductions for the year will be $8,880 − $11,941.08 = −Depreciation of property. In this particular case, the amount of depreciation was $5,731.20, thus allowable tax write-off was $8,792.28. In order to break even in the taxable year, the investor would need to incur a tax savings of $3,061.08 (negative cash flow equals $8,880 − $11,941.08). With a tax write-off of $8,792.28, the investor would need to be in the 35% tax bracket ($3,061.08 divided by $8,792.28) to break even. I would, however, like to emphasize that the property had an unusually high cost associated with repairs and supplies in April and May. These repairs (new carpeting, dishwasher, painting, and so forth) are done entirely at the discretion of the investor. This particular property is in an outstanding location with an extremely good appreciation schedule. It is my intent to sell the property within one year, thus new carpeting, dishwasher, painting, and pool supplies are necessary to bring in a good sell price.

FIGURE 5-1
A bookkeeping system.

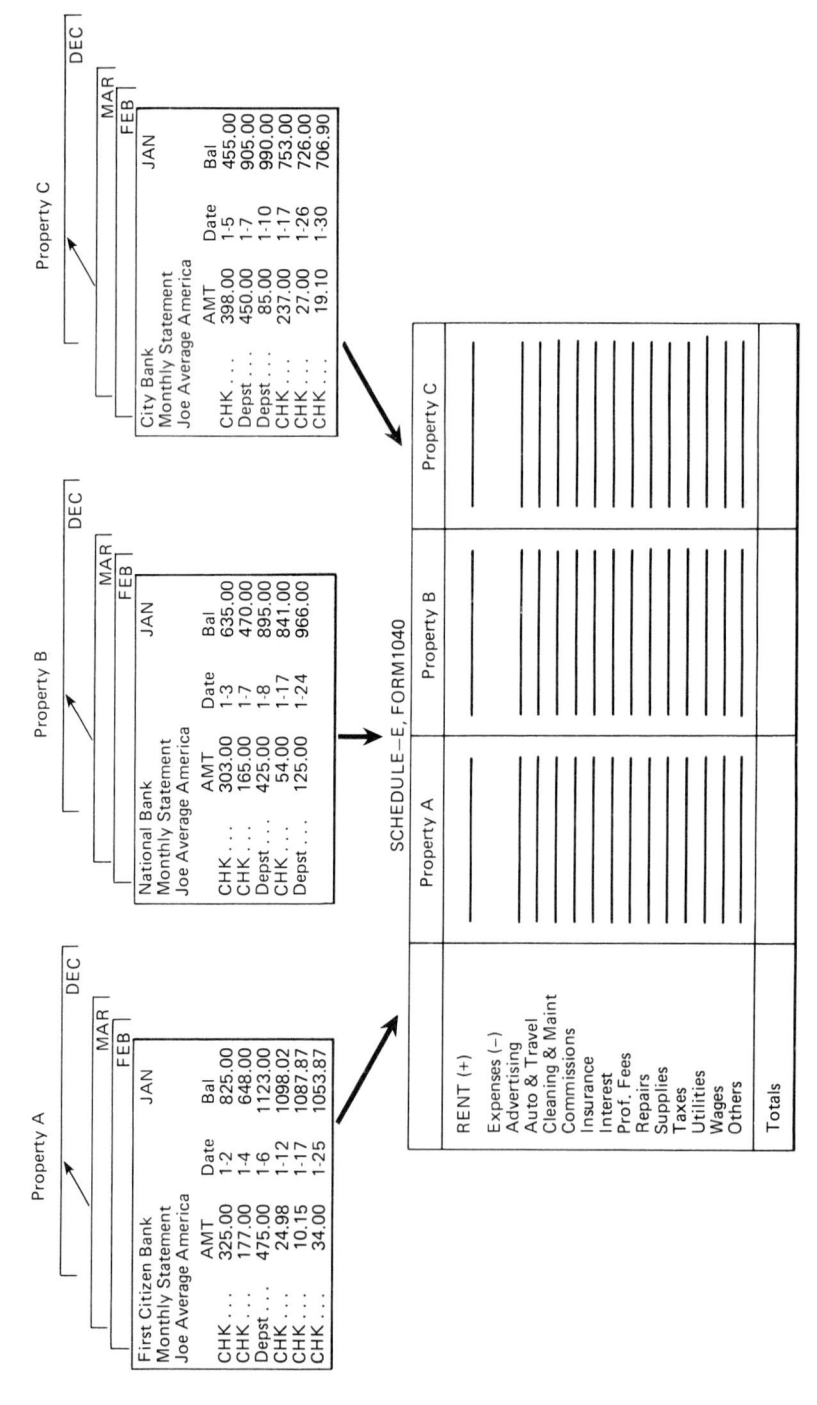

different banks is having a broader base to borrow money when purchasing any additional investment properties. Banks give their customers preferred treatment.

Table 5-1 is a record of one of my checking accounts that handles two properties. The bank statement is for the period of April 4 to May 12, 1981. The letters A and B immediately following either check or deposit signify either property A or property B. Notice the first deposit listed on the fourth line down showing a deposit of $4,375.00. The property was rented in April with the rental period to start on the first day of May. Considerable expenses are shown here for property B, as I chose to do some painting and general repairs between tenants. The last two items, checks 230 and 237, are for a new dishwasher and new carpeting on the bottom floor of the investment property. The total cost of $1,424.00 for the new carpeting includes labor and materials. All labor and repairs are deductible in a given tax year. The value of the carpet ($835.00) will be depreciated over five years at 200% declining balance.

Once you have received all monthly bank statements, simply transfer all maintenance expenses to a table as shown in Table 5-2.

Figure 5-1 is an indication of how the different property checking account figures can be used at the end of the tax year. The expenses as indicated on bank statements of properties A, B, and C are transferred to Schedule E, of tax Form 1040. This technique provides you a clean record of all expenses related to your investment properties.

Phase 6
Sell/Profits

PHASE 6 OBJECTIVES

Learn that there are three basic methods of depreciation, (1) straight-line, (2) declining balance, and (3) sum of years' digits. Understand that the declining balance depreciation method is best suited for residential real estate.

- Learn how to figure your taxable gain.
- How to report a sale.
- Understand how to use Schedule E, Form 1040.
- How to report rental income, depreciation and expenses to the IRS.
- Calculating for the adjusted basis.
- How to report your investment profits to the IRS.
- When to exchange or trade.
- Understand how to use income tax Form 4797.
- Learn to pyramid your investments.
- That you are the cornerstone to your future.
- Why the 1980s is an investor's paradise.
- The power of positive thinking.
- Why you need to continue your thirst for knowledge.

FORMING A PARTNERSHIP WITH THE IRS

The tax laws of this country are written to favor investors. Investments can be depreciated, and the amount of depreciation is subtracted from the investor's taxable income. The reason is that the investor's property depreciates in value, thus the investor is rewarded for the loss in value by a reduction in his or her taxable income base. For example, if an entrepreneur is in the truck hauling business, he or she is allowed to deduct the depreciation of the dump trucks from his or her taxable earnings. These laws are not only required, they are essential to the free, capitalistic system of our nation. Without the depreciation tax laws, large and small corporations and business enterprises would find it difficult if not impossible to continue to do business. The system rewards those who are willing to invest in new machinery and property. With the purchasing of new equipment and the construction of new buildings and plants come the required jobs to feed and clothe the American population. The chief advantage of real estate is that the investor is allowed to *depreciate* an investment property that, in the majority of cases, *appreciates* in value. (However, recall from Phase 3 that real estate *can* depreciate in value.) It is essential that any investor understand the tax laws of this country. Learn to live within the system; it is indeed a beautiful one. Properly used and thoroughly understood, it can bring most favorable results.

The tax laws of this country, as they pertain to residential real estate, are indeed complex. However, to obtain a good working knowledge of the essentials is totally doable. One must remember that the tax laws are written by the Congress of the United States. They are the result of a political process, thus they are subject to give and take and compromise and agreements. There are literally hundreds of books available offering advice on the tax laws. No one person thoroughly understands the tax laws of this country since they are subject to interpretation by the investor, tax consultants, and the IRS. I have asked several "tax experts" the same question, and the answers have represented a wide spectrum of opinions. Because the final decision on any tax question ultimately resides with you, it is in your best interest to have a sound understanding of the tax laws. When questions arise, ask the tax experts (consultants) specific questions that require specific answers. The IRS can also help; however IRS consultants tend to be more knowledgeable in the common everyday questions regarding the proper completion of Form 1040. Nonetheless, I have had extremely good assistance from the IRS in providing me with packets of information regarding investment properties. As you have done in finding your investment property and in shopping for money, *address questions* to anyone having knowledge about the tax structure, and read as much as you can consume.

236 SELL/PROFITS

The following pages provide an excellent base for understanding the tax laws as they pertain to income-producing real estate. Remember, you and only you have a 100% vested interest in your investment program. Knowledge is the key: Read, ask questions, be your own tax consultant. You'll probably find that you are not all that bad at it, and the rewards can be most enjoyable.

Paper Depreciation of Your Investment Property

The depreciation of your investment property is tax deductible. The amount of dollar savings due to the depreciation can be significant. Indeed, depreciation allowances coupled with the property appreciation (which follows inflation) forms the cornerstone of the value of investing in residential real estate. It is vital that you understand the process.

Depreciation of investment property occurs over the useful life of the property. In February 1981, the Reagan administration, through its economic recovery package (*America's New Beginning*), presented to Congress specific depreciation periods which would *not* be subject to audit by the IRS. They would be accepted and not questioned, and would be used regardless of the condition of the property when purchased. All depreciation would be on a straight-life basis and would become effective for all properties purchased after December 31, 1980. In August 1981, Congress enacted the Economic Recovery Tax Act, which provides for 15-year, 175% declining balance, accelerated depreciation for all income producing real estate. This law is outstanding for the investor, as the law prior to August 1981

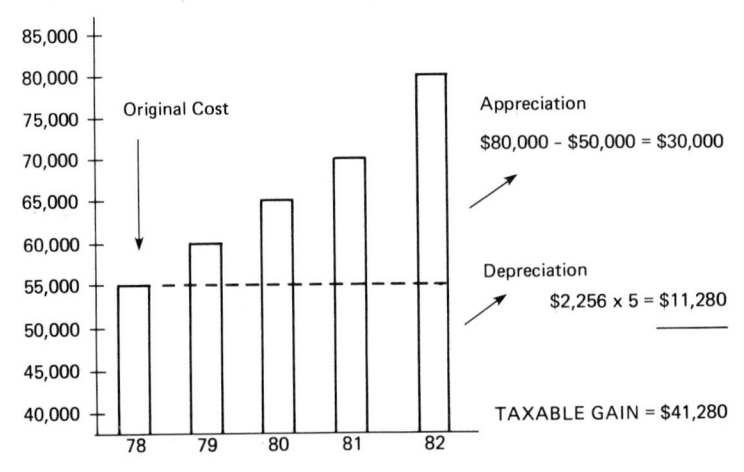

FIGURE 6-1
Depreciation added to appreciation to compute taxable gain.

Appreciation
$80,000 − $50,000 = $30,000

Depreciation
$2,256 × 5 = $11,280

TAXABLE GAIN = $41,280

was vague and subject to interpretation by both the investor and the IRS. The old law was to depreciate new residential property over 30 years and used residential property over approximately 25 years. With the 15-year, 175% declining balance depreciation allowance, no questions are asked, and due to accelerated depreciation the amount of tax deductions will be almost four times greater. For an investment property of a building valued at $100,000, straight-line depreciation allowance over 30 years is $3,333 per year. The same investment property depreciated over 15 years, 175% declining balance allows for a depreciation allowance of $11,666 per year. The amount of tax deductions is almost quadrupled. For an investor in the 50% tax bracket, the additional savings will be $5,833 per year, thus an investment property with a $486 per month negative cash flow could be sustained!

The 1981 Economic Recovery Tax Act has greatly simplified the depreciation process. Items within your investment property, for example, dishwashers, heating systems, and so forth, can be depreciated independently of the property itself. It is in your best interest to understand all three allowable methods (a) straight-line, (b) declining balance, and (c) sum of years' digits. I shall discuss all three methods in more detail later in this phase, but first I describe some important items concerning how your long-term capital gains are taxed.

Depreciation Added to Appreciation to Compute Taxable Gain

Depreciation allows you to reduce the amount of your taxable income on a given year. However, the total amount of depreciation will increase your taxable gain or decrease your loss on a later sale or exchange. This point is important, since the depreciation is added to the difference between original purchase price and sell price (less expenses) to determine long-term capital gain. Depreciation claimed in excess of straight-line (recaptured depreciation) is taxed as ordinary income, and all other gain is taxed as long-term gain provided you hold your investment longer than one year.

See Figure 6-1. Note that the taxable gain when you sell in 1982 is $41,280, that is, the sum of the appreciation and the depreciation, which will be taxed as long-term capital gain. Think of the depreciation as borrowing money (your tax money) at negative interest rates! Of the $41,280, 60%, or $24,768 ($41,280 × .60) will be tax free and is straight pocket money. Forty percent of $41,280, or $16,512, is added to your regular income before taxes are computed. If the $16,512 pushes your taxable income to the 50% tax bracket, no problem, simply buy more investment properties, take the first-year depreciation, and reduce your taxable income!

Methods of Depreciation

I shall now discuss the three methods of depreciation: (1) straight-line, (2) declining balance, and (3) sum of years' digits.

Straight-Line Method Under the *straight-line method,* you deduct an equal part of the cost of the investment property less the salvage value over the useful life. For example: An investor purchases a property with a total cost of $75,000. The estimated useful life is determined to be 15 years. The value of the structure equals 13/16 of $75,000, or $60,940. Salvage value is estimated at $5,000. Annual depreciation (rounded to nearest dollar) over the 15-year period is

$$\frac{\$60,940 - \$5,000}{15} = \$3,729$$

Thus, $3,729 is depreciated every year of the investment period. See Figure 6–2 for a graphic illustration of this example. Theoretically, if your investment period was 15 years, the final value of your investment would be $5,000, the salvage value.

Declining Balance Method The *declining balance method* allows for a higher percentage of the straight-line depreciation to be depreciated over the initial years of the investment period. The depreciation taken each year is then subtracted from the adjusted value of the property before the depreciation allowance is determined for the coming year. An equal depreciation rate applies to a smaller adjusted value each year. Since there is a large balance at the start of the depreciation, a larger deduction is taken for the first

FIGURE 6-2
Depreciation—straight line method.

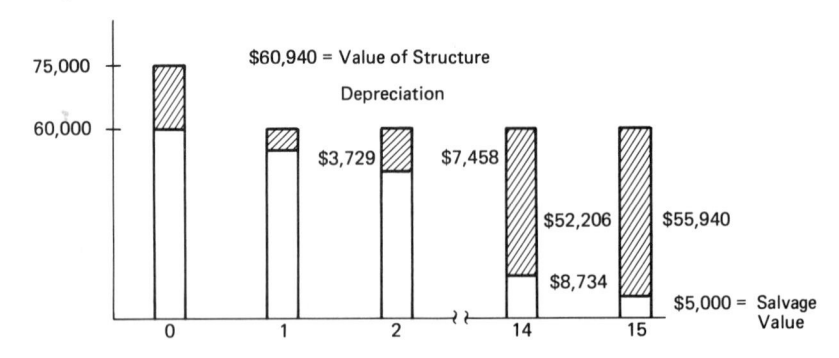

year and gradually smaller deductions are taken each succeeding year, hence the term "declining balance."

Prior to August 1981, allowable rates were 200%, 150%, or 125% of the straight-line depreciation. Only new residential property could be deducted at the 150% or 200% rate. Used residential (all assumptions) could be deducted at the 125% rate.

With the 1981 Economic Recovery Tax Act, all rental properties regardless of age can be depreciated by the 15-year, straight-line, 175% declining balance method. Salvage value is not deducted from the cost of the property when determining depreciation. However, the property may not be depreciated below a reasonable salvage value. The salvage value should be of no concern to the investor, since it is strongly recommended that the investment property be sold long before it reaches its salvage value. And remember, newer property located in the forward edge of new construction areas appreciates faster.

Let us calculate the declining balance method of depreciation for the same property that was used in the straight-line depreciation method. The value of the structure equals $60,940 (13/16 of $75,000). We shall use 175% declining balance.

$$\text{Depreciation for first year} = \frac{\$60{,}940}{15} \times 1.75 = \$7{,}109$$

$$\text{Depreciation for second year} = \frac{(\$60{,}940 - \$7{,}109)}{15} \times 1.75 = \$6{,}280$$

Depreciation for third year =

$$\frac{(\$60{,}940 - \$7{,}109 - \$6{,}280)}{15} \times 1.75 = \$5{,}547$$

Depreciation for fourth year =

$$\frac{(\$60{,}940 - \$7{,}109 - \$6{,}280 - \$5{,}547)}{15} - 1.75 = \$4{,}900$$

Depreciation for fifth year =

$$\frac{(\$60{,}940 - \$7{,}109 - \$6{,}280 - \$5{,}547 - \$4{,}900)}{15} \times 1.75 = \$4{,}328$$

Another computation method is to divide the declining percentage (200%, 175%, 150%, or 125%) by the useful life to determine the declining application rate. For example, using 175:

$$\frac{175}{15} = 11.67\%$$

240   SELL/PROFITS

The multiplication factor is 0.1167. To determine the allowable depreciation for a given tax year, multiply the declining balance (value of property) by the multiplication factor, for example:

Depreciation for first year = $60,940 × .1167 = $7,111
Depreciation for second year = ($60,940 − $7,111) × .1167 = $6,281
Depreciation for third year = ($60,940 − $7,111 − $6,281) × .1167 = $5,548 and so on.

There is one additional point of interest concerning the 175% declining balance. When I am conducting my seminars, I am often asked, why 175% declining balance? The reason 175% was decided on is that the bill introduced by the House Ways and Means Committee recommended a 15-year depreciation period and a 150% declining balance, whereas Congressmen Barber B. Conable, Jr. and Kent Hance recommended a depreciation schedule essentially the same as the Ways and Means Committee's bill, except that they recommended a 200% declining balance. The end result was a compromise. Remember that the laws of this country are the result of the political process, and it is necessary to anticipate continued changes in the tax laws.

Sum of Years' Digits Method   The *sum of years' digits method* of depreciation is determined by multiplying the cost of the property less its salvage value by a different fraction each year. It is based on the application of a diminishing rate to a constant value (base). The number of the years of the useful life is added to form the base (sum of years' digit). For example, if the useful life of the property is five years, the constant basis is 1 + 2 + 3 + 4 + 5 = 15. Thus, if the useful life is 15 years, the constant base is 1 + 2 + 3 + 4 + 5 + 6 + 7 + 8 + 9 + 10 + 11 + 12 + 13 + 14 + 15 = 120. An easier method of computing the constant base is the following formula:

$$\frac{n(n+1)}{2}$$

where n is the number of years of useful life. The depreciation as a function of year is then computed as follows:

$$\text{Depreciation for first year} = \frac{\text{useful life}}{\text{constant base}} (\text{cost} - \text{salvage value})$$

$$\text{Depreciation for second year} = \frac{\text{useful life} - 1}{\text{constant base}} (\text{cost} - \text{salvage value})$$

$$\text{Depreciation for third year} = \frac{\text{useful life} - 2}{\text{constant base}} (\text{cost} - \text{salvage value})$$

Let us use the same property that was used in the straight-line and declining balance methods. Assume the useful life equals 15.

$$\text{Depreciation for first year} = \frac{15-0}{120} (\$60{,}940 - \$5{,}000) = \$6{,}992$$

$$\text{Depreciation for second year} = \frac{15-1}{120} (60{,}940 - \$5{,}000) = \$6{,}526$$

$$\text{Depreciation for third year} = \frac{15-2}{120} (\$60{,}940 - \$5{,}000) = \$6{,}060$$

Comparison of Depreciation Methods

Let us compare the three depreciation methods on a property described as follows:

Initial cost of property = $75,000
Value of structure = $75,000 (13/16) = $60,940
Salvage value = $5,000
Useful life = 15 years

Note that both the straight-line and sum of years' digits methods reduce the adjusted value of the property to the salvage value if allowed to depreciate the entire 15 years. The declining balance method (175%) starts out fast, with the depreciation allowance for the sixth year equaling the straight-line depreciation allowance. Using the declining balance method, the adjusted value of the property will never depreciate to zero. The reason that the property will never have an adjusted value of zero is that the depreciation is always a fixed percentage of the remaining balance. Mathematically, you will never reduce the property to zero.

As an investor, I strongly recommend using the declining balance method, since it depreciates quickly at the beginning and tapers off toward the latter half of the property's useful life. If you maintain your investment property beyond the recommended three to five years, the adjusted long-term capital gain is reduced because the depreciation stabilizes. Remember, when you sell the property, the depreciation is added to the equity to determine your long-term gain. We shall discuss this point in the pages to follow.

How to Figure Your Taxable Gain

The *taxable gain* on an investment property is defined as the amount realized from a sale or exchange over the adjusted basis of the property. Notice the key words *exchange* and *adjusted basis*. If you exchange your investment property, taxes are deferred on that portion that was used as an exchange.

242   SELL/PROFITS

Taxes are paid on the portion of the sell that was realized as cash profit. For example, a $75,000 property with equity of $30,000 was exchanged for a $100,000 property with equity of $25,000 plus $5,000 cash. Tax is computed on only the $5,000 cash profit. The $25,000 equity exchange would be deferred to a later tax year. Exchanges are discussed later in this phase.

The key phrase *adjusted basis* is very important. Depreciation (straight-line) of your investment property is added to the appreciation gain to determine the adjusted basis (sell price − original cost + depreciation). Depreciation is considered a gain since you recapture your depreciation loss during the sell. Excess depreciation, referred to as *recaptured depreciation,* is taxed as ordinary income. Both the straight-line and sum of years' digits depreciation methods will theoretically reduce the value of an investment property to the salvage value at the end of its useful life, whereas the 175% declining balance method will not. See Table 6–1. The depreciation of an investment property using the 175% declining balance method shows little or no depreciation in the last half of the depreciation period. Using the declining balance method allows the investor to depreciate the majority of the investment property during the initial investment period. Selling the property immediately following the accelerated years (0 through 5) results in the excess depreciation being taxed as ordinary income. On the surface, paying excess depreciation as ordinary income may sound unfavorable. However, if you stop to think about it, it is a very good way to borrow money. In essence, you are borrowing money during the initial period of your investment. You repay the IRS after you sell at no interest and in inflated dollars. The advantage is on the investor's side. Later in this phase I shall discuss the actual reporting of this gain.

Reporting Rental Income, Depreciation, and Expenses to the IRS

Rental income, to include depreciation of the building and expenses related to the investment property, is reported using Schedule E (Form 1040). (See Figures 6–3 and 6–4.) Total income, expenses, and depreciation for each property are reported in Part I, lines 3 through 18 of Schedule E. The depreciation of the investment properties are indicated on Depreciation Form 4562. Form 1040 is discussed in more detail later in this discussion under the section entitled, Example of Schedule E, Form 1040.

An example is provided to illustrate the reporting of rental income, depreciation, and expenses of an investment property. The properties used in Phase 0 are used to explain the process. Our investor's name is Miss Jamison.

TABLE 6-1. Depreciation Allowances

YEAR	STRAIGHT-LINE Adjusted Basis	STRAIGHT-LINE Depreciation	175% DECLINING BALANCE Adjusted Basis	175% DECLINING BALANCE Depreciation	SUM-OF-YEARS' DIGITS Adjusted Basis	SUM-OF-YEARS' DIGITS Depreciation
0	$60,940		$60,940		$60,940	
1	57,211	$3,729	60,940	$7,109	53,948	$6,992
2	53,482	3,729	53,831	6,280	47,422	6,526
3	49,753	3,729	47,551	5,547	41,362	6,060
4	46,024	3,729	42,004	4,900	35,768	5,594
5	42,295	3,729	37,104	4,328	30,641	5,127
6	38,566	3,729	32,776	3,823	25,980	4,661
7	34,837	3,729	28,953	3,377	21,785	4,195
8	31,108	3,729	25,576	2,983	18,056	3,729
9	27,379	3,729	22,593	2,635	14,793	3,263
10	23,650	3,729	19,958	2,328	11,996	2,797
11	19,921	3,729	17,630	2,056	9,666	2,330
12	16,192	3,729	15,574	1,816	7,802	1,864
13	12,463	3,729	13,758	1,605	6,404	1,398
14	8,734	3,729	12,153	1,417	5,472	932
15	5,000	3,729	10,736	1,252	5,006	466

FIGURE 6-3
SCHEDULE E (page 1).

SCHEDULE E (Form 1040) Department of the Treasury Internal Revenue Service (2)	**Supplemental Income Schedule** (From rents and royalties, partnerships, estates and trusts, etc.) ▶ Attach to Form 1040. ▶ See Instructions for Schedule E (Form 1040).	OMB No. 1545-0074 **19** 15
Name(s) as shown on Form 1040	MISS JAMISON	Your social security number

Part I   Rent and Royalty Income or Loss

1 Are any of the expenses listed below for a vacation home or other recreational unit (see Instructions)? . . . . . ☐ Yes ☐ No
2 If you checked "Yes" to question 1, did you or a member of your family occupy the vacation home or other recreational unit for more than the greater of 14 days or 10% of the total days rented at fair rental value during the tax year? . ☐ Yes ☐ No

Description of Properties
Property A (Show kind and location) _____
Property B (Show kind and location) _____
Property C (Show kind and location) _____

Rental and Royalty Income		Properties			Totals (Add columns A, B, C, and D)
		A	B	C	D	
3 a Rents received		5400 00	5400 00	6000 00	6900 00	3 23,700 00
b Royalties received					ITEM 5	
Rental and Royalty Expenses						
4 Advertising	4					
5 Auto and travel	5					
6 Cleaning and maintenance . . .	6					
7 Commissions	7	125 00				
8 Insurance	8	175 00	175 00	175 00	175 00	
9 Interest	9	4500 00	5100 00	5520 00	8400 00	
10 Legal and other professional fees . .	10					
11 Repairs ★	11					
12 Supplies	12					
13 Taxes (Do NOT include Windfall Profit Tax here. See Part III, line 35.) . . .	13	850 00	850 00	850 00	750 00	
14 Utilities	14					
15 Wages and salaries	15					
16 Other (list) ▶						
★ REPAIRS						
FENCE		175 00				
PAINT		75 00	65 00	125 00		
PROF. LAWN MAINT		150 00	65 00	—	75 00	
ELECTRICIAN		65 00	—	75 00	100 00	
PLUMBER		85 00	95 00	—	50 00	
					ITEM 6	ITEM 7
17 Total expenses other than depreciation and depletion. Add lines 4 through 16	17	6200 00	6350 00	6840 00	9550 00	17 28,940 00
18 Depreciation expense (see Instructions), or Depletion	18	4532 00	5267 00	6909 00	9049 00	18 25,757 00
19 Total. Add lines 17 and 18 . . .	19	10,732 00	11,617 00	13,749 00	18,599 00	**E**
20 Income or (loss) from rental or royalty properties. Subtract line 19 from line 3a (rents) or 3b (royalties) . . .	20	5332 00	6217 00	7749 00	11,699 00	
21 Add properties with profits on line 20, and write the total profits here					21	
22 Add properties with losses on line 20, and write the total (losses) here					22 (30,997) 00	
23 Combine amounts on lines 21 and 22, and write the net profit or (loss) here					23	
24 Net farm rental profit or (loss) from Form 4835, line 50					24	
25 Total rental or royalty income or (loss). Combine amounts on lines 23 and 24, and write the total here. If Parts II, III, and IV on page 2 do not apply to you, write the amount from line 25 on Form 1040, line 18. Otherwise, include the amount in line 37 of Schedule E					25	

For Paperwork Reduction Act Notice, see Form 1040 Instructions.   ITEM 8

FIGURE 6-4
SCHEDULE E (page 2).

Schedule E (Form 1040) 19 Page **2**

Part II — Income or Losses from Partnerships, Estates or Trusts, or Small Business Corporations

If you report a loss below, do you have amounts invested in that activity for which you are not "at risk" (see Instructions)? ☐ Yes ☐ No
If "Yes," and your loss exceeded your amount "at risk," did you limit your loss to your amount "at risk?" . . . . ☐ Yes ☐ No

(a) Name	(b) Employer identification number	(c) Net loss (see instructions for "at risk" limitations)	(d) Net income

Partnerships

26 Add amounts in columns (c) and (d) and write here . . . . | 26 |( )
27 Combine amounts in columns (c) and (d), line 26, and write net income or (loss) . . . . . | 27 |
28 Expense deduction for section 179 property, (Form 1065, Schedule K-1, line 11). Do not enter more than $5,000 ($2,500 if married filing separately) . . . . | 28 |( )
29 Total partnership income or (loss). Combine amounts on lines 27 and 28. Write here and include in line 37 below . . . . | 29 |

Estates or Trusts

30 Add amounts in columns (c) and (d) and write here . . . . | 30 |( )
31 Total estate or trust income or (loss). Combine amounts in columns (c) and (d), line 30. Write here and include in line 37 below . . . . | 31 |

Small Business Corporations

32 Add amounts in columns (c) and (d) and write here . . . . | 32 |( )
33 Total small business corporation income or (loss). Combine amounts in columns (c) and (d), line 32. Write here and include in line 37 below . . . . | 33 |

Part III — Windfall Profit Tax Summary

34 Windfall profit tax credit or refund received in 1982 (see Instructions) . . . . | 34 |
35 Windfall profit tax withheld in 1982 (see Instructions) . . . . | 35 |( )
36 Combine amounts on lines 34 and 35. Write here and include in line 37 below . . . . . . | 36 |

Part IV — Summary

37 TOTAL income or (loss). Combine lines 25, 29, 31, 33, and 36. Write here and on Form 1040, line 18. ▶ | 37 | 30,997 | 00
38 Farmers and fishermen: Write your share of GROSS FARMING AND FISHING INCOME applicable to Parts I and II . . . . | 38 |

Part V — Depreciation Claimed in Part I
Complete only if property was placed in service before January 1, 1981. For more space, use Form 4562. If you placed any property in service after December 31, 1980, use Form 4562 for all property; do NOT complete Part V.

(a) Description of property	(b) Date acquired	(c) Cost or other basis	(d) Depreciation allowed or allowable in prior years	(e) Depreciation method	(f) Life or rate	(g) Depreciation for this year
Property A HOUSE	1-1-81	71,230	24,544	175% DB	15 Yr	4457 00
DISHWASHER	2-1-85			S.L.	5 Yr	75 00
Totals (Property A)						4532 00
Property B HOUSE	1-5-82	80,615	20,352	175% DB	15 Yr	5267 00
Totals (Property B)						5267 00
Property C HOUSE	6-25-83	87,630	11,976	175% DB	15 Yr	6909 00
				NOTE 2, TABLE 6-3		6909 00
Property D HOUSE	10-1-84	98,338	2330	175% DB	15 Yr	9049 00
Totals (Property C)						9049 00

☆ U.S. GOVERNMENT PRINTING OFFICE: 1982—O-363-315   52-0906127

TABLE 6-2. Pertinent Tax Figures for 1985 Tax Return

Property	Value of Structure	Month/Year Purchased	Prior Depreciation (81–84)	Recaptured[b] (81–85)	175% this year[c]
A ($ 77,230)	$62,750	1-81	$24,544	$9,751	$4,457
B ($ 80,615)	65,500	1-82	20,352	9,487	5,267
C ($ 87,630)	71,200	6-83	11,976	7,853	6,909
D ($ 98,338)	79,900	10-84	2,330	5,138	9,049
E ($116,923)	95,000	1-86	—	—	

DEPRECIATION[a]

[a] See Table 6-3 for depreciation by year.
[b] Recaptured depreciation is used when computing profit. See Figure 6-5, Supplemental Schedule of Gains and Losses, Form 4797 later in this phase.
[c] Depreciation for the taxable year. Used in Schedule E, Form 1040. (See Figure 6-3.)

Example of Schedule E, Form 1040 Using the data from Tables 6-2 and 6-3, we shall now complete Schedule E, Form 1040.

line 3: Amount from rents is considered positive cash flow.

line 17: True expenses. This is the actual cash you must pay out (negative cash flow) in order to pay the mortgage and maintain the property.

line 18: Depreciation of investment properties. Remember this is primarily a paper deduction. In reality, the property will appreciate in value.

line 22: Net loss due to depreciation and expenses. With a taxable income of $40,000 and two exemptions, your tax bite equals $9,355. With a tax deduction of $30,997, your taxable income becomes $40,000 − $30,997 = $9,003. The tax dollars on a taxable income of $9,003 equals $538. Total savings equals $8,817 ($9,355 − $538).

Figure 6-3, Schedule E, Form 1040 is interesting. Note that line 37 of Schedule E equals $30,997. This is the amount that Miss Jamison can deduct from her 1985 taxable income. Assuming that she earned $40,000 in 1985, her taxable income will be reduced to $9,003. Her tax savings are in excess of $8,000 per year. Note that line 17 of Schedule E indicates an actual cash expense of $6,200, $6,350, $6,840, and $9,550 for properties A, B, C, and D respectively. Her expense to carry the investments for the year was $28,940. Her rental income for the properties was $5,400, $5,400, $6,000 and $6,900. Total incoming cash was $23,700. Her resulting cash flow position prior to tax savings was a negative $5,240. However, after she takes the tax savings of $8,000 into account, her resulting cash flow position will be a positive $2,760.

Miss Jamison shall be rewarded handsomely. We are now ready to harvest our crops. We shall sell property A and calculate for our profits. For purposes of simplicity, we shall sell property A and realize the full profits as long-term capital gains. In reality, the investor may wish to borrow on the

TABLE 6-3. Depreciation of Properties

Property (Purchase date)	Value of Structure Declining Balance 175%		First (81)	Second (82)	Third (83)	Fourth (84)	Fifth (85)	Total
A (1-81)	$62,750	Depreciation	$62,750 7,320	$55,430 6,466	$48,964 5,712	$43,252 5,046	$38,206 4,457	$29,001
		Recaptured depreciation	3,470	2,616	1,862	1,196	607	9,751
B (1-82)	$65,500	Dep. —— note 3		65,500 7,640	57,860 6,750	51,110 5,962	45,148 5,267	25,619
		Recap dep		3,607	2,717	1,929	1,234	9,487
C (6-83)	$71,200	Dep		(property held for 6 months in 1983)	71,200 4,154	67,046 7,822	59,224 6,909	18,885
		Recap dep ——— note 4 ——→			1,948	3,409	2,496	7,853
D (10-84)	$79,900	Dep				79,900 2,330	77,570 9,049	11,379
		Recap dep				1,082	4,056	5,138
E (1-86)	$95,000	Dep	(will be reflected in 1986 tax return)				note 2	

Note 1: Recaptured depreciation will be used when computing profit. (See Supplemental Schedule of Gains and Losses, Form 4797, later in this phase.)
Note 2: Depreciation for the taxable year. Used in Part VI, Schedule E, Form 1040. (See Figure 6-4.)
Note 3: Depreciation of property in tax year. Note the declining amount of allowable depreciation.
Note 4: Amount of depreciation over the straight-line method. The addition of excess depreciation becomes the recaptured depreciation. We shall see later that, when you sell your property, it will be taxed as ordinary income.
PROPERTY A—Straight-line depreciation = $62,750 − $5,000 ÷ 15 = $3,850
PROPERTY B—Straight-line depreciation = $65,500 − $5,000 ÷ 15 = $4,033
PROPERTY C—Straight-line depreciation = $71,200 − $5,000 ÷ 15 = $4,413
PROPERTY D—Straight-line depreciation = $79,900 − $5,000 ÷ 15 = $4,993

equity or exchange the property and defer tax gains to a later year. Don't forget to use your imagination, innovation, and determination.

Selling Your Investment Property

First we discuss *selling* the investment property. Later, we discuss *exchanging* the investment property. In the last section of this phase, by means of case studies, we review the many options that are available to the investor, depending on his or her financial position. In order to qualify for long-term capital gains, the investor is required to retain his or her investment property for one year plus one day. Before discussing the sell of your investment property, some important terms need to be defined.

Long-term gains are profits to be taxed at favorable rates. Only 40% of the long-term gain is figured in your taxable income; 60% of the gain is tax free. Investment must be held for a minimum of one year.

Your *gain* is the amount you realize from a sale minus the adjusted basis of the property. The adjusted basis of the property is the original cost plus improvements minus depreciation. Think of it this way: If you bought an investment property in 1950 for $10,000, depreciated the property over 30 years to $2,000, but sold the property in 1980 for $50,000, your gain would be $48,000. $48,000 is computed as follows: $40,000 (appreciation) + 8,000 (depreciation) = $48,000.

The basis of your investment property is the purchase price plus all items charged to you at closing settlement. The settlement charges that may be subtracted from the basis are attorney fees, surveys, transfer taxes, title insurance, initial utility connections (electricity, water, and so forth), and any amounts normally paid by the seller but that you have agreed to pay. In general, any charges that were levied against you to purchase the property are added to the initial basis. Settlement costs must be added to the initial cost and depreciated over the life of the property. On your home of residence, settlement costs are directly deductible in the tax year of purchase.

The *adjusted basis* is the original cost increased by improvements and decreased by the depreciation.

Your Profit Having now made some basic definitions, let us compute the profit of Property A shown on Table 6-3. Property A was purchased in January 1981 for $62,750 and sold in December 1985 for $98,000. First we shall calculate our gains.

Original cost of house and land	$ 77,230
Improvements made during investment period	$ 2,000
Total investment	$ 79,230

Now subtract the depreciation taken during the investment period from table 6–3.

Total depreciation was	−$29,001
Adjusted basis	$50,229
Sale price	$120,000
Gain ($120,000 − $50,229)	$ 69,771

At this time in our calculations we have simply figured a gain. We will not be required to pay taxes on the total gain of $69,771. Let's carry on and figure the tax. Form 4797, Supplemental Schedule of Gains and Losses (Figures 6–5 and 6–6) shows the total gain plus amount to be taxed as ordinary income.

Upon selling your investment property, you report your gain as real estate property used in a trade or business. To report profits, you are required to use IRS Form 4797, Supplemental Schedule of Gains and Losses. (See Figures 6–5 and 6–6.) I will quote directly from paragraph B of Instructions for Form 4997.

Use this form to report the following:
1. The sale or exchange of:
   a. *Trade or business property,*
   b. Some kinds of depreciable and amortizable property,
   c. Some kinds of oil, gas, and geothermal property,
   d. Section 126 property.
2. The involuntary conversion (other than casualty or theft) of trade or business property and certain capital assets.
3. Disposition of other noncapital assets not mentioned in 1 or 2.

Note paragraph 1a says, *"trade or business property."* Thus, Form 4797 is used to report the sale of *rental* property, a type of business property.

Example Using Form 4797—Reporting Your Profits   Part I of Form 4797 is used to report your long-term capital gains. The sale of your investment property will produce both ordinary and long-term gains (60-40 tax law already discussed). Also, if you have used accelerated depreciation, the excess depreciation is taxed at ordinary rates. Part II of Form 4797 is used to compute and report ordinary gains, and Part III is used to compute ordinary and long-term gains of the investment property. Let us illustrate by using an example. See Part III of Form 4797 in Figures 6–5 and 6–6. Let us assume that property A is purchased in January 1981 for $77,230 and is sold in December 1985 for $120,000 (approximately 8% inflation).

Items 1 through 6 on Form 4797 require the following information:

   Item 1: Total gain of the investment—sell price minus original cost minus depreciation.

   Item 2: Excess depreciation taken between 1 January 1976 to sell date.

FIGURE 6-5
IRS FORM 4797 (page 1).

Form 4797 — Supplemental Schedule of Gains and Losses

(Includes Gains and Losses From Sales or Exchanges of Assets Used in a Trade or Business and Involuntary Conversions)
To be filed with Form 1040, 1041, 1065, 1120, etc.—See Separate Instructions

Department of the Treasury / Internal Revenue Service

OMB No. 1545-0184

19___ 31

Name(s) as shown on return | Identifying number

Part I — Sales or Exchanges of Property Used in a Trade or Business, and Involuntary Conversions From Other Than Casualty and Theft—Property Held More Than 1 Year (Except for Certain Livestock)

Note: Use Form 4684 to report involuntary conversions from casualty and theft.
Caution: If you sold property on which you claimed the investment credit, you may be liable for recapture of that credit. See Form 4255 for additional information.

a. Kind of property and description	b. Date acquired (mo., day, yr.)	c. Date sold (mo., day, yr.)	d. Gross sales price minus expense of sale	e. Depreciation allowed (or allowable) since acquisition	f. Cost or other basis, plus improvements	g. LOSS (f minus the sum of d and e)	h. GAIN (d plus e minus f)
1 LAND-RENTAL PROPERTY	JAN 1, 1981	DEC. 27, 85	14,480	—	22,500		8020
			← APPRECIATION OF LAND				

2 (a) Gain, if any, from Form 4684, line 25 . . . .
   (b) Section 1231 gain from installment sales from Form 6252, line 21 or 29 . . . . .
3 Gain, if any, from line 26, Part III, on back of this form from other than casualty and theft . . .
4 Add lines 1 through 3 in column g and column h . . . . ( ) **52,000**
5 Combine line 4, column g and line 4, column h. Enter gain or (loss) here, and on the appropriate line as follows: **60,020**
   (a) For all except partnership returns:
      (1) If line 5 is a gain, enter the gain as a long-term capital gain on Schedule D. See instruction E.
      (2) If line 5 is zero or a loss, enter that amount on line 6.
   (b) For partnership returns: Enter the amount from line 5 above, on Schedule K (Form 1065), line 8.

Part II — Ordinary Gains and Losses

a. Kind of property and description	b. Date acquired (mo., day, yr.)	c. Date sold (mo., day, yr.)	d. Gross sales price minus expense of sale	e. Depreciation allowed (or allowable) since acquisition	f. Cost or other basis, plus improvements	g. LOSS (f minus the sum of d and e)	h. GAIN (d plus e minus f)

6 Loss, if any, from line 5(a)(2) . . . .
7 Gain, if any, from line 25, Part III on back of this form **9751**
8 (a) Net gain or (loss) from Form 4684, lines 17 and 24a . . . .
   (b) Ordinary gain from installment sales from Form 6252, line 20 or 28 . . . . . .
9 Other ordinary gains and losses (include property held 1 year or less): . . . . . .

ITEM 6 ● TOTAL LONG TERM CAPITAL GAIN
        ● 60% TAX FREE ($36012)
        ● $33,759 ORDINARY INCOME
          ($24,008 PLUS $9751 (EXCESS DEP)

10 Add lines 6 through 9 in column g and column h . . . . ( ) **9751**
11 Combine line 10, column g and line 10, column h. Enter gain or (loss) here, and on the appropriate line as follows: **9,751**
   (a) For all except individual returns: Enter the gain or (loss) from line 11, on the return being filed. See instruction F for specific line reference.
   (b) For individual returns:
      (1) If the loss on line 6 includes a loss from Form 4684, Part II, column B(ii), enter that part of the loss here and on line 24 of Schedule A (Form 1040). Identify as from "Form 4797, line 11(b)(1)" . . . . .
      (2) Redetermine the gain or (loss) on line 11, excluding the loss (if any) on line 11(b)(1). Enter here and on Form 1040, line 15 . . . . **9,751**

For Paperwork Reduction Act Notice, see page 1 of separate instructions.   Form **4797** (1982)

250

FIGURE 6-6
IRS FORM 4797 (page 2).

Form 4797 (1982)   Page **2**

Part III   Gain From Disposition of Property Under Sections 1245, 1250, 1251, 1252, 1254, 1255
Skip lines 20 and 21 if you did not dispose of farm property or farmland, or if a partnership files this form.

12 Description of sections 1245, 1250, 1251, 1252, 1254, and 1255 property:	Date acquired (mo., day, yr.)	Date sold (mo., day, yr.)
(A) HOUSE RENTAL PROPERTY	1-1-81	12-27-85
(B)		
(C)		
(D)		

Relate lines 12(A) through 12(D) to these columns ▶▶▶	Property (A)	Property (B)	
13 Gross sales price minus expense of sale	97,500		**ORIGINAL COST PLUS IMPROVEMENTS (ONLY STRUCTURE)**
14 Cost or other basis	64,750		
15 Depreciation (or depletion) allowed (or allowable)	29,001		
16 Adjusted basis, subtract line 15 from line 14	35,749		
17 Total gain, subtract line 16 from line 13	61,751		**ITEM 1**
18 If section 1245 property: (a) Depreciation allowed (or allowable) after applicable date (see instructions) (b) Enter smaller of line 17 or 18(a)			**TOTAL DEPRECIATION**
19 If section 1250 property: (If straight line depreciation used, enter zero on line 19(f).) (a) Additional depreciation after 12/31/75	9751		**ITEM 2**
(b) Applicable percentage times the smaller of line 17 or line 19(a) (see instruction G.4)	9751		
(c) Subtract line 19(a) from line 17. If line 17 is not more than line 19(a), skip lines 19(d) and 19(e)	52000		
(d) Additional depreciation after 12/31/69 and before 1/1/76			
(e) Applicable percentage times the smaller of line 19(c) or 19(d) (see instruction G.4)			
(f) Add lines 19(b), and 19(e)	9751		**ITEM 3**
20 If section 1251 property: (a) If farmland, enter soil, water, and land clearing expenses for current year and the four preceding years (b) If farm property other than land, subtract line 18(b) from line 17; if farmland, enter smaller of line 17 or 20(a)			
(c) Excess deductions account (see instruction G.5)			
(d) Enter smaller of line 20(b) or 20(c)			
21 If section 1252 property: (a) Soil, water, and land clearing expenses			
(b) Amount from line 20(d), if none enter zero			
(c) Subtract line 21(b) from line 21(a). If line 21(b) is more than line 21(a), enter zero			
(d) Line 21(c) times applicable percentage (see instruction G.5)			
(e) Subtract line 21(b) from line 17			
(f) Enter smaller of line 21(d) or 21(e)			
22 If section 1254 property: (a) Intangible drilling and development costs deducted after 12/31/75 (see instruction G.6)			
(b) Enter smaller of line 17 or 22(a)			
23 If section 1255 property: (a) Applicable percentage of payments excluded from income under section 126 (see instruction G.7)			**ITEM 4**
(b) Enter the smaller of line 17 or 23(a)			

Summary of Part III Gains (Complete Property columns (A) through (D) through line 23(b) before going to line 24)

24 Total gains for all properties (add columns (A) through (D), line 17)		61,751
25 Add columns (A) through (D), lines 18(b), 19(f), 20(d), 21(f), 22(b) and 23(b). Enter here and on Part II, line 7.		9,751
26 Subtract line 25 from line 24. Enter the portion from casualty and theft on Form 4684, line 19; enter the portion from other than casualty and theft on Form 4797, Part I, line 3		52,000

Part IV   Complete this Part Only if You Elect Out of the Installment Method And Report a Note or Other Obligation at Less Than Full Face Value   **ITEM 5**

☐ Check here if you elect out of the installment method.
Enter the face amount of the note or other obligation ▶
Enter the percentage of valuation of the note or other obligation ▶

252   SELL/PROFITS

Item 3: Excess depreciation, will be taxed as ordinary income in the year of sale.
Item 4: Excess depreciation due to 175% declining balance.
Item 5: Gain to be taxed as long-term capital gain (60-40 tax law).
Item 6: Total gain (land plus building) taxed as long-term capital gain (60-40 tax law).

The amounts of ordinary and long-term gains are calculated in Part III of Form 4797. After calculating for ordinary and long term gains, the figures are transferred to Parts I and II of Form 4797.

Part I is used to compute appreciation of land plus long-term capital gain due to the building. Part II reflects the amount of ordinary income. Ordinary income from your investment is transferred directly to Form 1040 and taxed at ordinary rates. Long-term capital gains are transferred to Form 1040, Schedule D. Forty percent (see item 6) of your long-term capital gains is taxed as ordinary income.

A review of the actual profits and taxes indicate the following (data taken from Figures 6–5 and 6–6):

Property A
Gain = $69,771 from January 1981 to December 1985
Long-term capital gain = $60,020
Excess depreciation = $9,751
Tax-free profit = $36,012
Taxed as ordinary income = $33,759 ($24,008 + $9,751)
$24,008 plus $9,751 (excess depreciation) is added to your taxable income for the current year.

Should you be fortunate enough to be in this position, reinvest your taxable profits in additional properties and depreciate the first year, thus lowering your tax base. However, do not lose sight of the fact that the total gain of $69,771 was made possible because of favorable tax laws. Recall that the property used in the example above is one of five that our investor is selling. Earlier in this book it was shown that an investor with a take-home pay of $40,000 would reduce the taxable income to less than $10,000 with the properties listed in the beginning of the example. Adding the ordinary income of $33,759 to the $10,000 results in a tax of approximately $10,000.

Remember, the investor has made a total gain of $69,771. Her total income will be $73,759 ($40,000 + $33,759), minus depreciations. The other four properties that our investor currently owns will reduce her taxable income of $40,000. Remember also that the investor has made a total gain of $40,000. Of the paper gain of $69,771, approximately $43,000 is hard cash. The sell price was $120,000, and the original cost was $77,000. If a down payment was used to purchase the property, that would also be returned.

When you sell an investment property that produces a nice return, be sure to reinvest some of the profits. As a minimum, you should purchase two additional properties. It should be clear that an investment portfolio of ten homes in ten years with the selling (or refinancing) of your investment homes in five years can easily be obtained. Beginning in year five, the amount of profits realized just by selling one house a year provides sufficient money to retire. Remember, to reap a harvest you must start with a seed!

Exchanging or Trading Your Investment Property

We have outlined how the sale of your investment property is reported to the IRS. An exchange of your investment property for a similar property will defer your taxes until the sale of the exchanged property. The advantage is twofold: (1) The tax that you would normally pay on the gain is deferred, thus you are, in reality, borrowing money interest free from Uncle Sam. (2) You exchange your current property for a property that provides you with a much bigger initial base. With the larger initial base, the appreciation rate will be much better.

For example, one of your investment properties is appraised at $100,000 and has $50,000 equity. The property with which it is to be exchanged is new and is worth $100,000. The new property has a higher initial starting point and will probably appreciate faster than the old investment property. Figure 6-7 illustrates this process. In order for the trade to be tax deferred, the following conditions must be met:

- The exchange must be with another *investment* property of a like kind, such as between two investment real estate properties. It cannot be property held for personal use, for example, your home of residence.
- The exchange must occur between *like* properties. The IRS is relaxed on this subject, since any types of investment real estate properties may be exchanged. However, a residential property and a piece of electrical machinery are not considered to be like properties.
- The exchange must be between *tangible* properties; it cannot be between stocks, bonds, notes, or any other paper certificates.
- Properties must be held for investment purposes. You cannot exchange merchandise that you have for sale over the counter.

Receiving Cash Plus Exchange

You may exchange your investment property and also receive cash. The investment profits (the cash received) is taxed as a gain. If the investment

FIGURE 6-7
Exchange for new property.

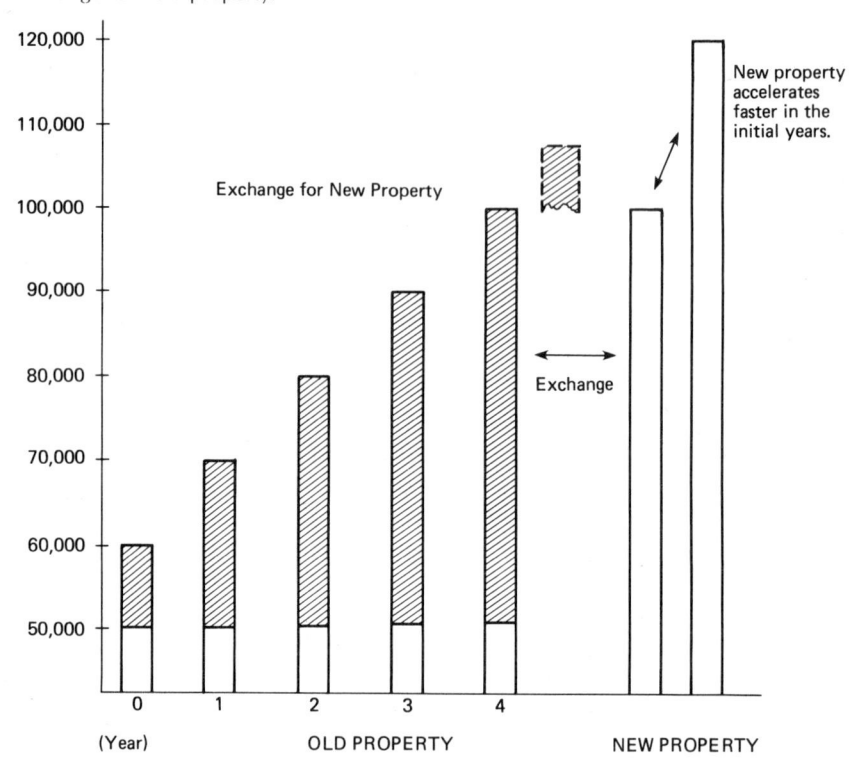

was long-term capital gain, the cash received is reported on Form 4797 similar to an all-cash sale. The basis of the property you received by the exchange (new investment) is the adjusted basis (original cost − depreciation) of the property you trade plus any cash received or minus any loss recognized by the trade. Let's look at an example to illustrate the process. Your investment property has an adjusted basis of $50,000 (original cost − depreciation) and is now valued at $100,000. You exchange the property for another property valued at $100,000. The basis for depreciation of the new property is $50,000. If you had purchased the property outright for $100,000, your tax basis for depreciation would be $100,000, giving you a larger depreciation base. The tax-free exchange is advantageous despite the lower depreciation if, for example, you have no taxable income to offset the depreciation (low taxable dollars). The exchange can also be to the advantage of the investor if he or she is mainly interested in the appreciation of the property. For example, trading the $50,000 property for $50,000 of equity for a property appraised at $100,000 offers more potential for faster appreciation. The new property may also be in a better neighborhood, which will also enhance its appreciation.

To summarize, the chief advantage of an exchange is that the full equity in your present investment property can be used to reinvest in the new property. The postponement of paying the tax you would have paid had you sold the property is equivalent to receiving an *interest-free loan*. This advantage cannot be realized if you sell the investment property and reinvest the profits. In my seminars, I dedicate extensive time to the tax laws. I use multiprojectors, split screens, and multibuild slides and vu-graphs to explain the tax process in a reasonable time period. To learn and understand how to take advantage of the tax laws as they pertain to residential income-producing real estate is well worth the cost of the seminar.

PYRAMIDING YOUR PROPERTIES

Throughout this book I have discussed various investment properties that I have purchased in the last three years. The last section of this book—Case Studies of Potential American Investors—is dedicated to all my readers. I detail eight case studies that provide the profiles of Americans of all walks of life. All individuals in the studies are attempting to achieve flight, however, liftoff is extremely difficult. Their wings may be out of synchronization, they may be pointed in the wrong direction, they may be pulling against each other, they may not have the proper strength, or they may not be willing to accept success! Synchronize your wings, find the proper direction, gain the required strength, add to your strengths, and be willing to achieve flight through knowledge. The case studies are about *you*, the reader, for you shall find a little bit of yourself in each example—the reluctant partner, the advocate of the coming real estate crash, the unknowledgeable homeowner, the person with the banker-lurking-in-the-barnyard syndrome, the person who lives in the past (if only I had bought five houses in 1969), the person who honestly believes that all renters are destructive, and so forth. The greatest majority of Americans do not realize, however, that they can and should invest in America. Learn from each case, and apply any of the methods or techniques that are described. One of the cases or a combination of several cases may best fit your situation.

Before we look at the case studies, I would like to tell you two success stories. The first one is about my cousins, who invested heavily in the Los Angeles area starting in the 1950s. The second story is about a friend of mine from my days of living abroad who invested in the Southeastern United States in the late 1970s. I have selected these two success stories because they illustrate the extremes of the investment life spans of the majority of my readers, and because they serve to drive my point home that residential real estate was a wise investment 30 years ago, was even better several years ago, and will be even better in the coming years. This book has been written to convince potential investors that the coming years shall return an even greater profit in the field of real estate.

First let me tell the story of my cousins—Mac and Anita. Both Mac and Anita were ahead of their time. In the 1950s, Mac was busy buying residential properties in southern California. When I was a young teenager I would journey to Los Angeles for summer vacations. I would usually stay with my brother, but at times I would spend weekends with Mac and Anita. Mac would promptly put me to work cutting the grass and trimming the shrubbery. Mac knew what he was doing, but unfortunately for me, he was not a great communicator. I quite honestly did not understand what he was doing. Why did he have all those houses when the rent would barely pay for the mortgage? The guy must be crazy!

By the mid-1960s, Mac and Anita had amassed over 25 properties with equity in excess of over $1 million. Today my cousins are multimillionaires. Why? Because they clearly saw that residential real estate was the key to financial success. I only briefly mention this success story and choose not to relate the details of all of the financial transactions, because some readers may argue, "Yes, it could be done in the 1950s and 1960s; however, now in the 1980s you simply *cannot* use the same pyramiding technique." Remember, people generally tend to think that the prices of homes have reached their highest peak and that they simply cannot continue to appreciate. *They are wrong!* Homes *will* continue to increase in value. If you are one of those readers who skips around or reads the last chapter first (I do the same thing), I advise you to go back to Phase 1, Overcoming Inertia, and review the figures on the American population by age groups. I can assure you that demand for housing in the 1980s will outpace the 1970s. I quote a recent report published by the U.S. Department of Commerce for the Office of Management and Budget entitled "Housing Affordability in an Inflationary Environment."

> It must be re-emphasized that housing is an asset and, therefore, house prices must be interpreted differently from other prices in the Consumer Price Index. The rise in house prices consequently does not reflect the true after-tax cost of housing services, the implicit rent that a homeowner pays. If the issue of rising house prices were redefined in terms of the costs associated with housing services (implicit rent or net capital cost), the house price problem as currently stated disappears. *The problem would then correctly be defined as a cash flow problem of housing finance.* After adjusting both rates of return and cash flow for distortions introduced by inflation, *homeownership appears to be as affordable today (perhaps more affordable) as it has been in the past.*

The interpretation of the statements cited above in lay terms is as follows: Housing is more affordable today than it was in previous years. The reason is that people are making more money and are being propelled into higher income brackets. Because all interest on loan payments is tax deductible, the true price of housing is less than it was in the past. For example, if you are in the 40% tax bracket, a $1,500 per month mortgage is in reality only $900 per month, as reflected in a wage earner's take-home pay.

Remember the story about my aunt and uncle in El Paso, Texas in Phase 1, who were not able to afford that $5,000 home with the $100 monthly payments. At the time, my uncle was making $200 per month, and a $100 per month mortgage payment was indeed a steep price.

I ask, is there a difference between an individual today making $2,000 per month and having a mortgage payment of $1,000? Indeed there is, because of the tax benefits enjoyed by today's generation of homeowners. I believe housing today is more affordable than at any time in the history of America. The point that the Office of Management and Budget study emphasizes is that the problem is simply one of cash-flow management. Today's homeowner needs to be knowledgeable in creative financing, accounting, and tax laws. Given that today's owner files his or her income tax using the long form (Form 1040) and itemizes his or her deductions, the advantage is definitely with today's generation.

Another point I would like to emphasize is that today's "now generation" wants everything *right now*. Instant everything: biggest cars, best entertainment, best foods, best jobs, highest salaries, and all of the finest trappings. Recently, I presented my seminar to a group of young couples. One couple had indicated to me that they simply could not afford a mortgage payment of $1,050 per month. They were renting for $400 per month and had a combined take-home pay of $35,000 per year! I asked a few questions and quickly found out the following: They had been looking for their instant dream home. Five bedrooms, three-car garage, over 2,500 square feet of livable space, an acre of land, and a swimming pool. I explained to them that it was the wrong way to search. First, look for terms, calculate your cash flow, and buy a starter home. Once they understood the benefits of the tax deductions coupled together with purchasing with an assumption and the owner carrying back the equity in a second trust, they were able to purchase a home with mortgage payments of $850 per month. Their tax savings alone were over $300 per month, and of course the equity in the home they purchased can be used in future years. With the tax benefits, their true monthly payments were $450 a month. The study cited above is correct. Housing today is more affordable than it has ever been in the past.

The next success story is about an investor friend of mine who has invested in the Southwestern United States. In 1977, he purchased a home for his family (first investment) and a duplex (second investment) as an investment property. In 1979, he took out a second trust of $5,000 on his home of residence. With this and $2,000 he had saved, he purchased an additional home (third investment) as a home of residence. The home pur-

FIGURE 6-8
Investment portfolio. Pyramid your assets.

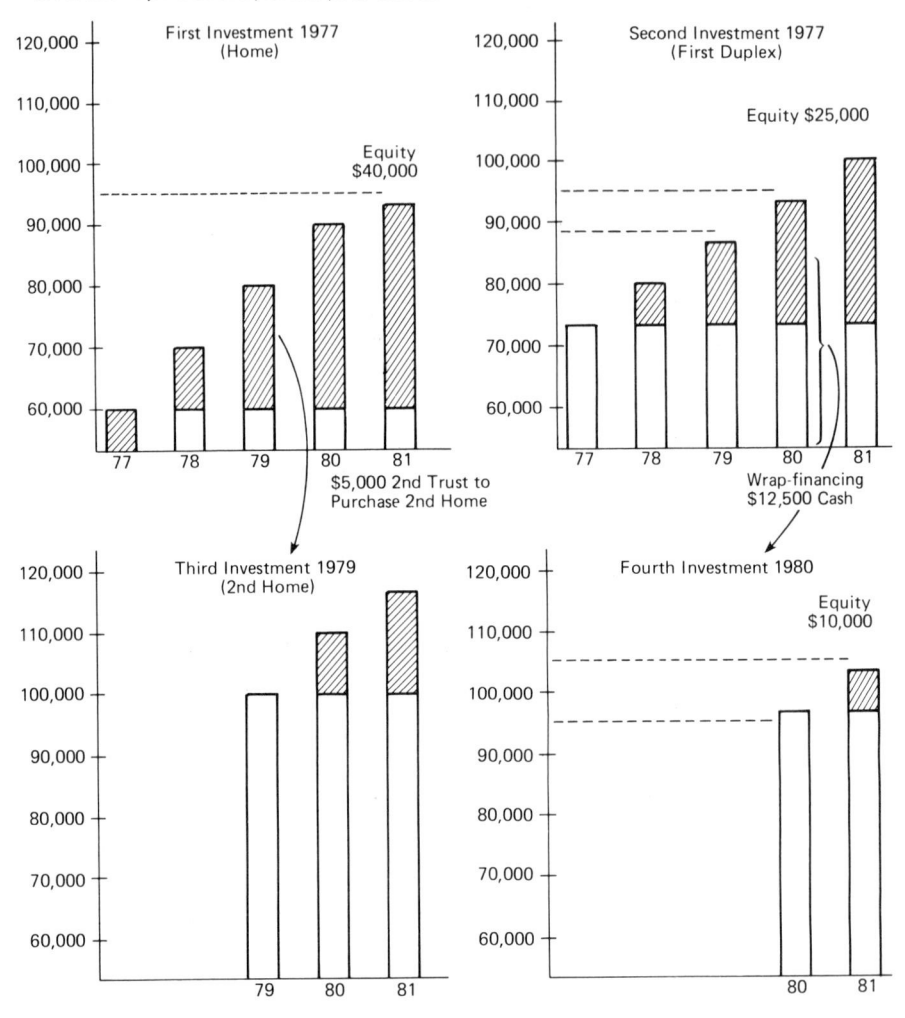

First Investment 1977 (Home) — Equity $40,000; bars for years 77, 78, 79, 80, 81. $5,000 2nd Trust to Purchase 2nd Home.

Second Investment 1977 (First Duplex) — Equity $25,000; bars for years 77, 78, 79, 80, 81. Wrap-financing $12,500 Cash.

Third Investment 1979 (2nd Home) — bars for years 79, 80, 81.

Fourth Investment 1980 — Equity $10,000; bars for years 80, 81.

chased in 1977 was converted to a rental, and it now supports itself. In the fall of 1980, he refinanced the duplex with a wraparound at 10½% (95% of the appraised value) and purchased a second duplex (fourth investment) as an investment property. (See Figure 6–8 for more details.) In 3½ years, he progressed from having no properties to having a home of residence valued at over $115,000; a single-family home (his former residence) valued at $95,000; and two duplex rentals, one valued at $100,000 and the other at $95,000. The initial home of residence now pays for itself (rent plus property depreciation), the first duplex produces a positive cash flow approximately $100 per month), and the second duplex has a negative cash flow of $300 per month. However, when taking the interest on the current home of residence and depreciation of all the investment properties, the net result is a take-home pay of more than $400 per month.

From 1977 to 1981, the total equity in my friend's properties, including the base of his investment properties (his home of residence) is over $50,000. This figure takes into account the $5,000 second trust and the refinancing of the first duplex. By the summer of 1982 when he completed his five-year program, the original home purchased in 1977 for $60,000 was worth approximately $100,000. His equity is over $35,000 ($40,000 minus the $5,000 second trust), and he can choose an infinite number of possibilities to continue with his investment portfolio. He can sell and enjoy the fruits of his wise investments, take that cruise on the Caribbean, ski in St. Moritz, or go trout fishing in the Hindu Kush. When you find yourself in a similar situation, just remember to reinvest some of your hard-earned profit dollars.

Another point that I wish to emphasize is that my friend, like myself, used the leverage of his initial home of residence (second trust money) to purchase his second home of residence. This is an important point, since mortgage rates almost always favor the owner-occupied property. If you currently own a home, think seriously of buying a new home. However, keep your current home as a rental. Depreciate your current home and receive the tax benefits. If you have lived in your current home residence for over five years, be aware that the initial value to be used for depreciation is the price paid when you originally purchased the home. On the other hand, your equity is sizable. There is a delicate balance that must be properly weighed.

Case Studies of Potential American Investors

I shall discuss eight case studies. All the studies guide the reader through the initial years of the investment period, since getting started is always the most difficult. Once the investor purchases his or her initial two or three investment properties, the momentum gained will propel him or her through the investment cycle for the remainder of his or her life. The reason is simple—if the investor currently owns a home, imagine him or her owning not only the present home of residence but two more just like it. It does not take a financial genius to figure out that each of the three houses bought five years ago at $65,000 are now worth over $100,000. Each house has over $35,000 worth of equity. You simply sell, refinance, or exchange to realize your profits! Momentum is automatically created by the profits.

The majority of my case study examples follow very closely the investment experiences of my investor friends and my former students.

Case Study 1

Pertinent Data

- Single, 23-year-old woman who rents.
- Word processor operator (assistant director).
- Salary, $18,000 per year.
- Federal tax is $3,213 per year.

Our 23-year-old single woman is well educated. Her name is Jean Johnston. Jean is a high-school graduate who has two years of business school, three years' experience working as a typist, secretary, and a word processor operator. In two years she has advanced to the position of assistant director. Jean has quickly learned that working with the word processors is the job of the future. The older women can literally "burn up" an electric typewriter, but they are reluctant to try the newly developed word processor. Jean is an intelligent, enterprising individual who welcomes a challenge.

She currently shares a condominium with another woman. Their combined rent is $450 per month, utilities not included. Based on a yearly salary of $18,000, her monthly salary is $1,500. Federal withholding tax is $267 per month, and state, social security, and FICA total $100 per month. Her take-home pay is $1,132 per month. Her rent (one-half of $450) is $225; utilities add up to $60 per month; new car payments are $140 per month. Gasoline for the car plus grocery money total $320 per month. Essential bills total $745 per month. The difference between her take-home pay ($1,132) and essentials ($745) equals $387. The $387 is spent on clothes, eating out, vacations, and entertainment.

The Plan Buy a custom-built duplex as an investment property. Jean will rent one of the properties outright and share the other unit with another woman. Remember, she currently has a roommate and her roommate is paying half the rent. She will use Method 16, the short- to long-term rollover mortgage plan, described in Phase 3. Her two major problems will be qualifying for the loan and purchasing the land. A custom builder (there are numerous throughout America) will qualify her for a property of approximately $60,000 if she has good credit. Jean needs to obtain a cosignature on the loan—either her parents or an investor who is willing to enter into a principal–silent partnership arrangement. The cosigner of the loan does *not* put up any cash. He or she merely offers the lending institution additional assurance that the mortgage will be paid. We will see in the next few paragraphs that Jean can easily afford a $95,000 total property investment. The land can be purchased by asking the owner of the land to take back a second trust on the investment property. The investment property includes the land and the duplex. The title to the property shall be held by the lending institution. The property owner has maximum protection, since failure by Jean to pay either the first or the second will allow the owner of the property to assume ownership of the complete investment property—duplex plus land. Lending institutions will generally agree to this kind of arrangement as long as they hold the first trust.

Cost Figures

INVESTMENT	DEPRECIABLE BASIS	DEPRECIATION[a]	MORTGAGE PAYMENTS	RENTAL INCOME
Duplex (lives in ½ of one unit)	$71,250	$4,750 (1.75) = $8,312	$1,116	$742
Land	—	—	$150	
Totals	$71,250	$8,312	$1,266	$742

[a] Fifteen year, straight line, 175% declining balance.

Computation of Cash Flow

> *Negative Cash*
> Duplex total cost $95,000
> Amortized over 30 years at 14% $1,116 per month
> Land cost = $15,000
> Balloon, 5 years, 12% interest $150 per month
> Total $1,266 per month
>
> *Positive Cash*
> - Rental (one unit) $495 per month
> - Rental (from roommate) $247 per month
> Total $742 per month
> - Tax savings (depreciation—straight-line over 15 years, 175% declining balance):
>
>   (¾ of $95,000) $^{13}/_{16}$ = $4,750 (1.75) = $8,312
> - New Taxable income is $18,000 − $8,312 = $9,688 per year.
> - New tax is $1,109.
> - Tax savings is $3,213 − $1,109 = $2,104 per year ($175 per month).
> - Total positive cash is $917 per month.
> - Total cost is $1,266 − $917 = $349 per month. Jean currently pays $225 per month rental; thus, her additional out-of-pocket cost is $124 per month ($349 − $225).

Now here comes the most interesting part! The duplex with two living quarters of approximately 1,500 square feet of living space per unit will be worth over $150,000 one year after the women move in! The reason is that the rollover plan is initially a construction loan rolled over into a long-term mortgage. Several custom-home builders on the East Coast currently have this plan. The key is to build in a good location. The cost of the duplex will be $95,000, regardless of location. Jean pays for the construction cost only. Needless to say, this is an excellent plan for anyone who is currently renting or who is interested in moving into a new home and has a yearly salary in the $15,000 per year range. If Jean cannot sustain a $124 out-of-pocket expense for one year, either her father or the cosigner of the loan can help pay the mortgage payment. A partnership or principal-silent agreement could be structured to outline the profit split. Within one year from the completion of the duplex, the property could easily be refinanced for $130,000 to $140,000 or could be sold for $150,000.

Case Study 2

Pertinent Data

- Young couple, he is 28 years old, she is 25 years old.
- Professional college graduate.
- Salary is $28,000 per year (taxable income is $22,000).
- Federal tax is $2,751 a year.

Joe is currently employed by the Aerospace Company and works in the sheet metal shop. He has been with Aerospace, Inc. for six years and was married at the age of 23. Soon after marriage, Joe and Diana bought a three-bedroom home. They have no children. Their mortgage is $321 per month; they purchased a $40,000 home five years ago. Their home is currently appraised at $67,000. Joe started a savings plan three years ago by having his employer withdraw $75 per month from his paycheck. They currently have $2,700 saved. Because Joe read that insurance is a must during the early years of the family, he recently purchased a whole life insurance plan costing $110 per month.

Lately Joe and Diana have discussed the subject of preparing for the future. That is the overriding reason for the savings plan of $75.00 per month and the purchase of the life insurance. However, it is clear that at $75 per month the savings plan needs to be strengthened. Diana has recently been reading about investments in general, and the idea has occurred to her to purchase some blue-chip stock with the $2,700 in the savings plan. They have ruled out purchasing real estate because a friend who is a real estate agent told them that they would need $10,000 down and that they might have to take a $300 to $500 negative cash flow.

The Plan Purchase an investment property using Method 10, the wraparound plan, described in Phase 3. Find an investment property with an existing VA or FHA assumable first trust. Borrow up to 85% of the purchase price with a wraparound loan. Have the seller take back a second trust with the collateral on Joe and Diana's current home of residence.

Cost Figures

INVESTMENT	DEPRECIABLE BASIS	DEPRECIATION[a]	MORTGAGE PAYMENTS	RENTAL INCOME
Town house	$60,937	$4,062 (1.75) = $7,108	$648	$450
Home of residence (2nd trust)	—	—	$112	
Totals	$60,937	$7,108	$760	$450

[a] Fifteen year, straight line, 175% declining balance.

Computation of Cash Flow

Negative Cash
Investment property	$75,000
First trust	$45,000 at 9½%
Wrap loan 85% of $75,000	$63,750
Wrap loan 11½% (amortized over 25 years)	$648 per month
Second trust ($75,000 − $63,750)	$11,250
Second trust (interest only, 12%, balloon, 5 years)	$112 per month
Total mortgage	$760 per month

Positive Cash
- Rental income is $450.
- Interest ($761 − $450 = $311 [12]) is $3,732.
- Depreciation allowance:
$$\frac{(^{13}\!/_{16})(75,000)}{15} = \frac{60,937}{15} = \$4,062 \,(1.75) = \$7,108$$
- Total deductible is $10,840
- Tax savings:
Current taxable income is $22,000; tax equals $2,751.
New taxable income is ($22,000 − $10,840) equals $11,160.
New tax is $562.
Tax savings is $2,751 − $562 = $2,189 per year ($182 per month).
- Total positive cash flow is $450 + $182 = $632 per month.
- Net out-of-pocket expenses are $760 − $632 = −$128 per month.

First Joe and Diana should cancel their whole life insurance policy and buy term insurance, which costs $17 per month. The net monthly savings is $93 ($110 − $17). Then they should stop their $75 per month savings plan. This makes a total additional monthly sum of $168 ($93 + $75). Thus, their new monthly cash-flow position is $40 ($168 − $128). Note that the $2,700 is used to pay for the loan origination fees on the wrap loan, which is considered as new money by the lending institution. The cost of the loan origination fee is approximately two or three points ($1,200 to $1,800). In summary, Joe and Diana have an investment property worth $75,000 with their savings of $2,700. Their leverage is fantastic! The $2,700 will easily convert to $30,000 or $50,000 in five years. Sometime between the next one or two years, they will refinance their current home, pay off the second trust, and purchase a second investment with the extra cash.

Case Study 3

Pertinent Data

- Young married couple, he is 29 years old, she is 27 years.
- He is a captain in the U.S. Army; she is an elementary school teacher.
- They have two children, ages 8 and 7.
- Renters, $550 per month.
- Two incomes—his is $26,000 per year and hers is $12,000 per year. Total income is $38,000 per year.
- Federal tax is $8,517 per year.

Ray and Becky have been married for nine years. He has been in the Army for seven years and has been stationed at Fort Bragg, in Germany, and is now in the second year of his current stateside tour. Because the Army has provided Ray and Becky on-base military housing, the thought had never occurred to them to buy a house. However, since returning from Germany, they have had to rent since the area where they are stationed does not have sufficient military housing. Ray and Becky receive $300 housing allowance in addition to his base pay. Ray has just received word that he will most likely remain at his current stateside location for a total of five years. Their current rental, although adequate, does not provide the children sufficient growing space. Becky would also like to have a garden and a big backyard to allow the children ample playing ground. They are definitely interested in buying their own home.

The Plan We shall help Ray and Becky purchase their own home and an investment property as well. The two properties will be purchased using very little of their own money for the down payments by using OPM.

First Ray and Becky borrow $5,000 from the Federal Credit Union on a signature loan. The loan is at 15%, amortized over five years; the payments will be $118.95 per month. Second, Ray and Becky purchase a new home using the VA plan. The cost of the new home was $75,000 at 13% interest and amortized over 30 years. Monthly payments are $829.65. The builder is advertising that he is paying all closing costs. Nevertheless, Ray and Becky use $500 of their $5,000 borrowed from the Credit Union for clean-up settlement costs. Additionally, they order special carpeting and vinyl flooring, for a total cost of $1,000, which leaves them with $3,500.

Third, they locate an investment property selling for $65,000. It has an assumable first trust of $45,000 at 9% with payments of $362 per month. The seller has advertised that he is willing to carry back a portion of the equity as a second trust. Ray and Becky negotiate with the seller, and he agrees to carry back $10,000 of the $20,000 as a second trust at 12%, five-year interest only, balloon payment. Monthly payments are $100.

The task is now to find the remaining $10,000 that the seller desires. Becky finds a buyer for the $10,000 second trust, discounted 25%. The buyers of the discounted note are her parents. Becky's dad currently has over $10,000 in savings. Becky, with the help of the graphs found in Phase 3, explains to her dad that $7,500 will buy a note worth $10,000. Ray and Becky will pay her parents $100 per month with the full value of the note ($10,000) becoming due in five years. Becky's dad and mom were a little reluctant at first, but after Becky explains to them that it is all perfectly legal and over the table, and once they understand the transaction, they agree. Although Becky's dad doesn't admit it, he is also proud of his "little girl"—she has quite a business head.

Cost Figures

INVESTMENT	DEPRECIABLE BASIS	DEPRECIATION[a]	MORTGAGE PAYMENTS	RENTAL INCOME
Signature loan	—	—	$119	
Home of residence (new home)	—	—	$829	
Investment (first trust)	$52,812	$3,520 (1.75) = $6,160	$363	$550
Investment (second trust)	—	—	$100	
Investment (third trust)	—	—	$100	
Totals	$52,812	$6,160	$1,511	$550

[a] Fifteen year, straight line, 175% declining balance.

Computation of Cash Flow

Negative Cash

Signature loan	$119 per month
New home	829 per month
First trust on investment	363 per month
Second trust to seller	100 per month
Third trust to Becky's parents	100 per month
Total	$1,511

266 SELL/PROFITS

Positive Cash
- Rent they are no longer paying is $550 per month.
- Tax savings (all interest is deductible):
  $1,511.35 (12) = $18,136.20
  minus rental income $ 6,600.00
  deductible $11,536.20
- Depreciation (15 years, 175% declining balance):

$$\frac{^{13}/_{16}\,(\$65{,}000)}{15} = \frac{\$52{,}812}{15} = \$3{,}520.00\ (1.75) = \$6{,}160$$

- Total deductions are $11,536.20 + $6,160 = $17,696.
  Current tax based on $38,000 per year is $8,517.
  New tax based on ($38,000 − $17,696.20) $20,304 is $2,343.
- Tax savings per year equals $6,174 ($514 per month).
- Rental income is $500 per month.

Summary of Cash Flow

Rent they are no longer paying	$550
Tax savings	$514
Rent from investment	$550
Total positive cash	$1,614
Total negative cash	−$1,511
Total cash flow	+$103

Summary   Ray and Becky now have their own home, one investment, and $3,500 left over. Their cash-flow position is $103 more per month than when they were renters. The reason for the amazing cash flow is Ray and Becky's high tax bracket. The combined income of $38,000 with no tax shelters results in a heavy tax. The total value of their properties is now $140,000. At 8% inflation, their property appreciation will be $11,200 per year!

Note that the plan described above can be used by any individual currently having VA rights.

Case Study 4

Pertinent Data

- Young executive, single.
- Professional, business degree, employed by chemical company.
- Purchased condominium six years ago in the inner city.
- Salary is $34,000 per year.
- Federal tax is $7,434 per year.

John is a swinger, so he purchased his condominium close to the action. He pursues the "good" things in life (beautiful women, fine clothes, sports cars, and so forth), and he is an aggressive businessman. He is considered to be a comer by the chemical company; he is knowledgeable and is well liked by employees and customers.

Lately John has started thinking more about his long-term goals both with his job (the possibility of transferring within the company or to a new job) and with his personal financial goals. Four years ago he purchased some common stock, and it has sat there like a lump on a log without movement. Calculating for inflation, he has actually lost 20% of his money. He feels that with his salary and being single he should be able to do better with his financial investment plan. He has also been seriously considering moving to a new location. It is getting too noisy in his current neighborhood and there have been several incidents involving purse snatching and street hold-ups.

The Plan Due to six years' inflation, John's condominium is now valued at $90,000. The first trust is $53,000, and the equity is $38,000. He holds a 9% mortgage with payments of $442 per month. John will sell the condominium, move to the forward edge of new construction in his area, buy a duplex, a townhouse, a detached single family home, a Porsche 911 Carrera, and go skiing in Austria in the summer time and golfing in Scotland. Sound unrealistic? Let's see.

Cost Figures John sells his condominium for $90,000 and realizes $35,000 in cash! He purchases a duplex worth $125,000, puts $10,000 down, and the owner carries back $15,000 at 12% interest only, balloon in five years. New money required is $100,000 at 13.5%, amortized over 30 years. John will live in one unit of the duplex and rent the other half for $550 per month. His mortgage payments are $1,145 per month on the new money and $150 on the second trust. $2,500 was required for closing, so John now has $22,500 cash.

John purchases an investment townhouse which costs $55,000. The investment has an assumable mortgage of $36,000 at 8½% interest with payments of $307 per month. The down payment is $7,000. The owner carries back $12,000 at 12% interest, with a balloon payment in five years; payments are $120 per month, rental income is $300 per month. The closing cost is $750. John now has $14,750 remaining ($22,500 − $7,750).

Additionally, John purchases a detached single-family home, which costs $85,000. First trust (assumable) is for $60,000 at 9½% interest, with payments of $546 per month. John puts down $10,000 and the owner carries back $15,000 at 12% interest, five-year balloon. His total payment on the second trust is $150 per month. Rental income is $625 per month. Closing costs are $850. John now has $3,900 remaining ($14,750 − $10,850).

John sells his common stock and realizes $4,500. He adds the $4,500 to the $3,900 ($8,400) and deposits it in an interest-bearing money account. He uses $2,000 of the $8,400 as a down payment on a Porsche Carrera and decides to go skiing in Austria this coming summer and stop off in Scotland en route for one week of golfing at Saint Andrews.

Cost Figures

INVESTMENT	DEPRECIABLE BASIS	DEPRECIATION[a]	MORTGAGE PAYMENTS	RENTAL INCOME
Duplex (lives in one unit)	$60,937	$4,062 (1.75) = $7,108	$1,295	$550
Townhouse	$44,687	$2,979 (1.75) = $5,213	$427	$300
Detached home	$69,062	$4,604 (1.75) = $8,057	$696	$625
Total	—	$20,378	$2,418	$1,475

[a] Fifteen-year, straight-line, 175% declining balance.

Computation of Cash Flow
- Tax deductions = $20,378 (Depreciation + Mortgage − Rent)
  = $20,378 + $2,418 (12) − $1,475 (12)
  = $20,378 + $29,016 − $17,700
  = $31,694
- New taxable income is $34,100 − $31,694 = $2,406.
- Tax savings:
  Previous taxable income was $34,000 (tax = $7,434).
  New taxable income is $2,406 (tax = $0).
  Tax savings is $7,434 per year ($619 per month).
- Adding $619 to the rental income produces positive cash of $2,094 ($1,475 + $619). Additionally, we must add the $442 mortgage payment, which John is no longer paying on the old property. *Net positive cash* is $2,094 + $442 = $2,536 per month. Mortgage payments (negative cash) are $2,418 per month.
- Cash flow is $2,536 − $2,418 = +$118 per month!

Summary John now owns three properties (four, counting the duplex twice) worth $265,000! Even at inflation of 5%, his properties will appreciate at over $13,250 per year. At 10% inflation, his properties will appreciate at $26,500 per year. Notice that in all cases I used sizable down payments ($10,000, $7,000, and $10,000). I did this purposely to show that even with a medium-sized leverage position there is money to be made. If you find yourself in John's position, with $35,000 in cash and with a taxable income of $35,000, always attempt to pay minimum cash down. John could have easily doubled the number of investment buys had he put down only $5,000 of his money per property. The problem would be negative cash flow. With three properties, John has reduced his taxable income to $2,406. Any additional properties would result in no tax savings.

Case Study 5

Pertinent Data

- Married couple, professionals, dual income, he is 38 years old, she is 37. They have two children.
- He works for the government; she is a secretary.
- They had their home custom built; it is 15 years old; they own it free and clear. Its value is $130,000.
- He earns $31,500; she earns $14,300. Combined incomes equal $45,800.
- Federal tax is $12,720 per year.

Robert and Sharon have been married for 16 years. They are both firm believers in the American tradition of hard work. Sharon's parents, who grew up in the Depression, instilled in their daughter that it is best not to have any debts. Robert and Sharon wasted no time after they were married, and in essence used the rollover mortgage plan to go from a construction loan to a long-term mortgage plan to purchase their first home. The mortgage was for 25 years; however, they paid off the loan in 15 years.

They have been saving money all of their adult lives. They currently have a nest egg of $25,000 in a combination of CDs and low-interest savings accounts. Lately, Robert and Sharon seem to be caught up in the "Alice in Wonderland" syndrome—the faster they run, the further they fall behind. Just a few years ago, $20,000 to $25,000 in savings seemed like a sizable amount. Now the entire savings account will be required to send their eldest son to college. Because of the financial requirements of having to send their son to college (he is now 15), Robert and Sharon have been discussing investments. They talked to Sharon's parents about the possibility of investing in real estate. However, her parents recommended that they avoid real estate, because they had purchased an investment property several years ago and the renters were totally destructive. Sharon's dad, however, did everything wrong: He bought in a run-down area, he allowed the realtor to find his renter, and he did not interview the renter himself. Nevertheless, Robert and Sharon have applied their enthusiasm toward gaining knowledge and have been reading about all of the great fortunes that have been made in real estate. They decide to pursue investing in real estate.

The Plan They will purchase three investment properties, having a total value of $245,000. The cash flow will be zero, and we shall not even use a penny of the $25,000 in the savings account.

Fortunately for Robert and Sharon, they have already made the investment of their lives—their present home. After much reading, they have overcome the psychological hurdle of refinancing their home. Remember, they have worked very hard to pay off the mortgage! To most people, the thought of borrowing from the equity on their home is simply contrary to what they have been striving for all their lives. Robert obtains a loan from the Credit Union for $30,000, with their home acting as collateral. The loan is to be amortized in ten years and carries an interest rate of 12%. Monthly payments are $430. They now have $30,000 to invest!

Cost Figures   They buy a single-family detached home for $95,000. The investment home is five years old, with an assumable first trust of $65,000 at 9½%. They first try to have the owner take back all of the equity as a second trust, but the owner has cash requirements.

Robert and Sharon arrange for wrap financing (see Method 10, the wraparound in Phase 3). The wrap loan is for $80,000. Robert and Sharon put down $5,000 of the borrowed $30,000 and ask the owner to carry back $10,000 with the mortgage moved to their present home of residence. This is no problem, since the home is valued at $130,000. The wraparound loan is financed at 11½%, amortized over 25 years. Monthly payments are $559. The $10,000 second trust is at 12%, interest only, balloon in five years. Monthly payments are $100, and closing costs are $2,500. The rental income on the $95,000 home is $600 per month. Their remaining cash equals $22,500 ($30,000 − $7,500).

Second, Robert and Sharon purchase a fairly new townhouse. It is four years old, valued at $75,000, and has an assumable first trust of $59,000 at 10½% interest. Monthly payments are $548. The owner carries back $5,000 at 12% interest, balloon in five years. They put down $10,000 to make up the total asking price of $75,000. The second trust payments are $50 per month. Closing costs are $1,000, and rental income equals $425 per month. Their remaining cash is $11,500 ($22,500 − $11,000).

For purposes of simplicity, the third investment is identical to the second investment property.

Computation of Cash Flow

- Tax deductions = Depreciation + Mortgage − Rental
  = $23,219 + $2,285 (12) − $1,440 (12)
  = $23,219 + $27,420 − $17,280
  = $33,359

- New taxable income is $45,800 − $33,359 = $12,441
- Tax Savings:

Taxable Income	Tax
$45,800	$12,720
$12,441	779

- Tax savings per year is $11,941 ($995 per month).
- Adding the $995 to the rental income produces positive cash of $2,435 per month ($1,440 + $995).
- Cash flow is $2,435 − $2,285 + $150.00 per month.

Cost Figures

INVESTMENT	LOAN	DEPRECIABLE BASIS	DEPRECIATION[a]	MORTGAGE PAYMENTS	RENTAL INCOME
Home	$30,000	—		$430	
Townhouse 1		$77,187	$5,145 (1.75) = $9,003	$659	$600
Townhouse 2		$60,937	$4,062 (1.75) = $7,108	$598	$425
		$60,937	$4,062 (1.75) = $7,108	$598	$425
Total			$23,219	$2,285	$1,440

[a] Fifteen-year, straight-line, 175% declining balance.

Summary   Robert and Sharon have purchased three investment properties valued at over $245,000—one quarter of a million dollars! In reality, they have not used one penny of their own money. All has been borrowed money. This particular example is a good illustration of what can be done when your present home of residence has a large equity. Borrow or refinance, and use the borrowed money to buy investment properties. Just stop and think, if Robert and Sharon had two properties like the one they currently own, they could sell and realize a free profit (less taxes) of $130,000. Needless to say, within one to three years Robert and Sharon can sell, exchange, or refinance an investment property and continue to build on their equity.

One additional point: The second trust loan of $30,000 may have a low interest rate of 12%, depending on the cost of money at the time. Even if their loan is at 15% interest, the monthly payments would be $484, which is only a $54 per month increase. *The key here is the $995 per month tax savings.*

Case Study 6

Pertinent Data

- Married couple, blue-collar worker, housewife. He is 43 years of age, she is 35 years. They have two children.
- Works for maker of auto parts.
- Salary is $25,000.
- Federal tax is $3,504.

Charlie and Rita have been married 15 years. They married after Charlie had served four years in the Air Force. They now have two children, ages 12 and 10. They rented the first five years of their marriage and purchased a home ten years ago. For the first six to eight years of their marriage, Charlie and Rita struggled to make ends meet. About five years ago, they seemed to be doing fine. However, during the last three years they have been in a financial tight squeeze. Charlie is making more money, but inflation has eroded all of Charlie's income. Rita has been thinking of finding a part-time job; however, she is fearful that she has nothing to offer. Charlie needs a new car but believes that he cannot afford the down payment and the resulting payments. Recently a friend of his drove up in a new van. He makes less than Charlie, and Charlie cannot understand how his friend can afford the new van plus a vacation to Bermuda last winter. By asking a few questions, Charlie finds out that his friend has come into some money through a real estate venture. Soon after hearing about the profits made by his friend, Charlie buys several books on real estate investments and decides to "invest in America."

The Plan Charlie and Rita do not even have a savings account. He quickly learns that his present home has $35,000 of equity. He purchased the home on a VA loan ten years ago for $26,500 at 7% interest, amortized over 30 years. His present balance on the first trust is $23,000. His mortgage payment is $183 per month. Charlie and Rita will refinance their present home. They will refinance 90% of $58,000. They will have $29,200 less $3,000 for loan origination fees in cash with which to invest. The new $52,200 loan will be financed at 11% interest, amortized over 20 years. The mortgage payments will be $538 per month. Soon after refinancing their present home, Charlie and Rita will move to a new home. Remember, always refinance *before* you move. You get better terms and higher percentage of home value for owner-occupied homes. Their new home is purchased at $72,000. It has an assumable first trust (VA) at 9% interest. The current balance on the first trust is $56,000, with monthly payments of $482. The equity ($16,000) will be financed as follows: Charlie and Rita put down $5,000, and the owner carries back $11,000 at 12%. The second trust is a five-year balloon with a monthly payment of $110. Total payments for their new house equal $592 per month ($482 + $110). Settlement costs are $950. Charlie and Rita still have $20,250 ($26,200 − $5,950) in cash! Obviously, Charlie and Rita can afford to buy at least one more investment property, however, let's review their cash-flow position.

Computation of Cost Flow
- Refinancing of their present home; $52,200 over 20 years at 11% interest equals $538 per month.
- The old mortgage was $183; therefore, the new mortgage is $355 more per month.
- Interest deduction is $538 per month, $6,456 per year.
- The depreciation of the former residence converted to a rental is based on the original price ($26,500) plus improvements (assume $30,000). Depreciation is $30,000 × 13/16 ÷ 20 × 1.25 = $1,523 per year.[1]
- Rental income per month is $375.
- New home:
    Mortgage equals $592 ($482 + $110).
    Interest deduction equals $7,104 ($592 × 12).
- Tax savings
    Tax deductions = Depreciation + Mortgages − Rent
        = $1,523 + $6,456 + $7,104 − $4,500
        = $10,583
    New taxable income is $25,000 − $10,583 = $14,417
    Tax savings:

Taxable Income	Tax
$25,000	$3,504
$14,417	$1,139
Tax savings per year equals	$2,365 ($197 per month).

---
[1] Home must be depreciated using the pre-1981 tax law.

- Cash flow per month:
    Positive cash − Negative cash = Cash flow
    (Rental income + Old mortgage[2] + Tax savings) − (New mortgages) = Cash flow
    ($375 + $183 + $197) − ($538 + $592) = Cash flow
    $755 − $1,130 = −$375
- Net out-of-pocket expenses are $375 per month.

At first glance, it may seem that a negative cash flow of $375 per month is simply not affordable. But remember that Charlie and Rita still have $20,250 in cash! In a smooth transaction of refinancing and buying a bigger home, Charlie and Rita now have two homes with a value of over $130,000, and $20,250 in the bank. Of the $20,250, Charlie and Rita deposit $7,500 in a high-yield money market to sustain them through two years of $375 negative cash flow per month. The remaining $12,750 will be used to buy a second investment plus provide the down payment on a new car. One extra note of information: Note that Charlie and Rita's former residence had only $1,523 of tax-deductible income. The reason for this small deduction is that the basis for depreciation is based on the *original* cost, and the pre-1981 tax laws. The second investment property will carry a much larger depreciation, however. Charlie and Rita's taxable income is now down to $14,417, and their taxes are $1,139. Any additional tax deductions will not provide tax savings of any significance.

The point I wish to emphasize is that a blue-collar worker with a taxable income between $20,000 and $25,000 and equity in his or her current property can and should invest in America. It pays great profits.

Case Study 7

Pertinent Data

- Husband is professional military; wife is a librarian. He is 33 year old; she is 29. They have two children.
- He is a major in the U.S. Air Force; she works part-time at the public library.
- He earns $33,000; she earns $5,000; combined incomes total $38,000 per year.
- Federal tax on taxable income of $30,000 equals $4,961.
- They own a townhouse for three years. Its value is $75,000, first trust is $52,000 (VA loan).

Case Study 3 was about a military man who was a renter. In Case Study 7, Tom and Sue, who are also a military family, have always purchased a home where they were stationed. Tom has had two stateside tours—one in

---
[2] Charlie and Rita are no longer paying the old mortgage.

Arizona and his current tour in Washington, D.C. He was stationed for three years in Berlin.

Please allow me a brief digression from the particulars concerning Tom and Sue. All career military personnel (especially the officers) should retire after 20 years with a minimum of five houses and $250,000 worth of equity! Individuals who make the military a career are, as a group, in the best position to invest in real estate. Why? Because the military family is conditioned to moving every three years or so anyway. Thus, the single greatest obstacle has been removed—the reluctant partner who does not wish to invest in real estate. Your investment program is automatic—simply purchase a home where you are stationed and rent when you leave. Find the renter yourself, using the technique described in Phase 5, but you must, of course, enlist the aid of a professional management firm when leaving the area. Since military personnel always buy a home that is to be owner occupied, the best financing terms are always available. All moving expenses are paid by the government. Settlement costs, paid by military personnel, are also tax deductible. All areas in which homes are purchased by military personnel have automatic rental populations—other military personnel. Even if the individual in the military wishes to live on post, he or she should always think of buying an investment property. All of his or her utilities and rent are paid by the government. Also all military personnel have VA rights, and they can also join the Federal Credit Union, which generally has the lowest rates in town. Career military personnel should have no problem obtaining a signature loan of $5,000. Unfortunately, 95% of all military personnel do not invest in America, since the military conditions its men and women to think in conventional terms. They must think, look, and act as their peers and superiors. There is little room for creative thinking. I have encountered full colonels with working wives who have had combined incomes of over $68,000 who have never owned their own home. They are renting for $500 per month, and they say they cannot afford a $1,200 per month mortgage! They know next to nothing concerning tax shelters, depreciation, and appreciation of homes. It is odd that most career military personnel have tremendously complex jobs in this age of modern electronic warfare and they tend to be well educated. However, when it comes to their own financial investment plans, they score fairly low grades. They certainly have the base to acquire the knowledge, they simply need to understand the tremendously favorable position that they enjoy. If a young captain would simply convert his or her current home to a rental when rotating and purchase at the new location, within three to five years he or she should be in the position to purchase investment properties in clusters of two or three, and within ten years he or she should have no problem assembling a portfolio of houses with over $500,000 in equity!

Let us return to the particulars concerning our young major and his wife. Tom and Sue have owned their townhousse for three years. The townhouse is valued at $75,000 and has a first trust of $52,000. The equity equals $20,000. Tom is being transferred to Fort Bliss, Texas, and they have decided to keep their townhouse in the Washington, D.C. area as an investment. Upon arriving in El Paso, they wish to purchase another home.

The Plan Tom and Sue will refinance their current home at 90% of the current value ($75,000). The new loan will be $67,500. Loan origination fees are 2 points or $1,350. Total free cash is $14,150 ($15,500 − $1,350). The townhouse will be rented for $550 per month. A second investment will be purchased in the Washington, D.C. area prior to transferring to El Paso. $5,000 will be used for the purchase. Both properties will be managed by a real estate management firm. Upon arriving in El Paso, Tom and Sue will purchase a home with an existing assumption. Equity in both the second investment and the El Paso home will be financed via hard money second trusts. Note, in Texas you can obtain 2nd trust money when purchasing your home. You cannot obtain 2nd trust money for investment purposes after you have purchased your home. Investment properties used as rentals do not have these restrictions.

Cost Figures Their current home will be refinanced. The existing mortgage for $52,000 at 9% has monthly payments equal to $370. The new mortgage for $67,500 at 11½% will be financed over 27 years. Monthly mortgage payments will be $678. The refinancing fee is $1,350. Free cash equals $14,150. Property will be rented for $550 per month. With the existing $14,150, an investment property will be purchased in the Washington, D.C. area. An investment property valued at $60,000 with a $35,000 existing first trust is purchased. The assumable first trust carries a mortgage payment of $288 per month. The equity in the property ($25,000) is financed as follows: Tom and Sue put $5,000 down (from the $14,150); the owner carries back $10,000 at 12% interest, balloon in five years; and Tom's father purchases the remaining $10,000 at a discounted rate of 25%. Payments to Tom's father will be at 12% based on $10,000. The third trust will also be a balloon in five years.

Once Tom and Sue arrive in El Paso, they will buy a $65,000 home, which has an existing first trust of $45,000 at 10% interest. Tom and Sue assume the first trust with payments of $403 per month. The down payment is $4,000 (to cover closing costs), and the owner agrees to take back the remaining equity ($16,000) as a second trust. The second trust is at 12% interest, balloon in five years.

Payments on the second trust are $160 per month. The owner *had* to sell, so he agreed on the large second trust based on the short balloon period. Paying off the balloon in five years will be no problem, since the property can be refinanced or sold.

Cost Figures

INVESTMENT	LOAN	DEPRECIABLE BASIS	DEPRECIATION[a]	MORTGAGE PAYMENTS	RENTAL INCOME
Current home (refinance)	$67,500	$44,687 (13/16 of $53,000)	$2,979 (1.75) = $5,213	$678	$550
Investment A	$35,000 $20,000	$48,750 (13/16 of $60,000)	$3,250 (1.75) = $5,687	$288 $200	$375
New Home	$45,000 $16,000			$403 $160	—
			$10,900	$1,729	$925

[a] Fifteen-year, straight-line, 175% declining balance.

278 SELL/PROFITS

Computation of Cash Flow
- Tax deductions = Depreciation + Mortgage − Rental
  = $10,900 + ($1,729 × 12) − ($925 × 12)
  = $26,977 − $11,100
  = $20,548
- New taxable income is $30,000 − $20,548 = $9,452.
- Tax savings:

Taxable Income	Tax
$30,000	$4,961
$9,452	$291

- Tax savings equals $4,670 ($389 per month).
- Adding the $389 to the rental income of $925 ($550 + $375) produces positive cash of $1,314 per month. Also the old mortgage on the home that was refinanced must be added as positive cash. Total positive cash equals $1,684 ($1,314 + $370).
- Mortgage payments (negative cash) total $1,729 per month ($678 + $288 + $200 + $403 + $160).
- Cash flow is $1,684 − $1,729 = − $45.
- Out-of-pocket expenses are $45 per month.

Summary   Tom and Sue now have two investment properties plus a beautiful home and approximately $5,000 remaining as liquid cash. The total value of their properties is $200,000 ($75,000 + $60,000 + $65,000). At an inflation rate of 10%, the return will be $20,000 per year. Cost for the investment program is only $45 per month!

Case Study 8

Pertinent Data

- Married couple, semiretired, both working, all children grown. He is 57; she is 52.
- He is a technical consultant; she is a secretary. Their incomes are as follows: retirement, $18,000 per year; consulting services, $25,000; secretarial services, $14,000 per year; total income, $57,000 per year.
- Value of present home is $110,000. First trust equals $15,000, 5½% interest, payments are $153 per month.
- Federal tax based on $57,000 equals $18,208 per year, tax is computed as follows: Tax on $45,800 equals $12,720. Amount over $45,800 is taxed at a rate of 49%, thus additional tax is $5,488 [.49 × $11,200]. $11,200 is obtained by subtracting $45,800 from $57,000. Total tax is $12,720 + $5,488 which equals $18,208.

Will and Beth have come a long way from their modest beginning. They married in the late 1940s, and they now have three grown children. All children are on their own and pursuing their careers.

Will semiretired from his job as an air traffic controller. He received a medical retirement due to the stress associated with 25 years of air controller work. He is now doing direct consulting work for corporations involved in assisting the government in writing air traffic regulations.

With her children all grown, Beth started working temporary jobs through a temporary placement service. After working as a temporary for one year, she was offered a job with an engineering firm, which she accepted.

Lately Will and Beth have been having problems paying their federal and state taxes. They earn a sufficient salary, however, a considerable sum of taxes must be paid at the end of each taxable year. Will finally comes to realize that 50% of Beth's salary goes for taxes. Within the next three to five years, Beth would like to stop working in order to spend more time traveling. Will's consulting job will not cause a problem, since the consulting business is result oriented and does not require the punching of a clock. The problem is that they have grown accustomed to the total income of $57,000 per year. They would like to invest some of their monies in order to realize some steady income in their true retirement years.

The Plan After extensive research into stocks, gold, diamonds, commodities, and other investment fields, Will and Beth decide to invest in real estate. Their single biggest problem is overcoming the psychological barriers. They have an unshakable belief that all renters are destructive. They have a morbid fear of receiving phone calls in the middle of the night that the toilets are not functioning. Only after reading several investment books do they come to the realization that there *are* clean, well kept properties available that attract responsible tenants. They will also establish a silent-principal partnership. The silent will manage the property for a percentage of the profits. Will and Beth will deduct the full value of the properties and absorb any negative cash flow.

Their current home with an appraised value of $110,000 will be refinanced for $80,000. The new loan will be at 14% interest, variable-rate mortgage (VRM) with no prepayment penalties. The loan will be based on a 30-year amortization schedule. Monthly payment equals $940. The existing mortgage of $15,000 with the payment of $153 per month is paid off. The difference in monthly payments equals $798 ($948 − $153). However, the new payment is primarily all interest. Since Will and Beth are in the 50% tax bracket, the amount actually required to sustain the loan will be $798 divided by two, or $399 per month. Total amount now in hand to invest equals $80,000 − $15,000 less refinance charges. Conservatively, we shall assume that Will and Beth have $60,000 to invest!

A total of three investment properties shall be purchased with the $60,000—one triplex and two townhouses. A sufficient amount of money shall remain to allow Will and Beth to take a 30-day cruise on the Caribbean and a two-month tour of America.

Cost Figures

INVESTMENT	LOAN	DEPRECIABLE BASIS	DEPRECIATION[a]	MORTGAGE PAYMENTS	RENTAL INCOME
Current home (refinance)	$80,000	—	—	$948	—
Investment A (triplex)	$120,000 (First trust) $25,000 (Second trust, 14%) $15,000 (down)	$125,937 ($^{13}/_{16}$ of $155,000)	$8,395 (1.75) = $14,691	$1,327 $233	$1,125
Investment B (Townhouse 1)	$47,000 (First trust assumption) $20,000 (Second trust) $13,000 (down)	$65,000 ($^{13}/_{16}$ of $80,000)	$4,333 (1.75) = $7,582	$402 $233	$450
Investment C (Townhouse 2)	$74,000 (First trust assumption) $15,000 (Second trust) $6,000 (Down)	$77,187 ($^{13}/_{16}$ of $95,000)	$5,145 (1.75) = $9,003	$630 $175	$600

[a] Fifteen-year, straight-line, 175% declining balance.

Computation of Cash Flow

- Tax deductions = Depreciation + Mortgage − Rental
  = $31,276 + $3,948 (12) − $2,175 (12)
  = $31,276 + $47,376 − $26,100
  = $52,552
- New taxable income is $57,000 − $52,552 = $4,448.
- Tax savings:

Taxable Income	Tax
$47,000	$18,208
$4,448	$ 0

- Tax savings per year equals $18,208 ($1,517 per month).
- Adding the $1,517 to the rental income of $2,175 produces positive cash of $3,692 ($1,519 + $2,175) per month. Also the old mortgage on the home that was refinanced must be added as positive cash. Total positive cash equals $3,845 ($3,692 + $153).
- Total mortgage payments (negative cash flow) are ($948 + $1,327 + $233 + $402 + $233 + $630 + $175) = $3,948.
- Cash flow is $3,845 − $3,948 = −$103 per month.
- Out-of-pocket expenses are $103 per month.

Summary Will and Beth now have four properties (home of residence plus three investments) that total $440,000 in value. The monthly cost of half a million dollars worth of real estate is but $103! Also let us not forget that $26,000 remains of their $60,000 refinanced loan. With a portion of the $26,000, they will take a 30-day cruise to the Caribbean, a two-month trip across America, and most importantly an investment portfolio that increases in value by $50,000 per year.

Will and Beth shall form a silent-principal partnership with their eldest son, Frank. Frank will manage the properties and receive 25% of all profits once the properties are sold or refinanced.

YOU ARE THE CORNERSTONE TO YOUR FUTURE

Throughout this book I have emphasized the necessity of being determined, of gaining the required knowledge, and of being creative and imaginative. All these are valid requirements. However, these items are intangibles—they cannot be measured, weighed, or touched with the hand. They are a state of mind. To give these intangibles meaning and measurable dimensions, *you*, as an individual, must form the cornerstone of your investment program. *You* can be the most knowledgeable, creative, and imaginative person in America, but without the will to act, your dreams will remain fantasies. With the will to act and the ability to actively pursue your goals, your dreams can be translated into reality.

The 1980s, an Investor's Paradise

The early and mid-1980s are an investor's paradise. The high interest rates of the late 1970s and early 1980s have created a buyer's market. Millions of low-interest assumable loans from the 1970s and owner financing will be available throughout the 1980s. The high interest rates keep the average buyer away from the housing market. Knowledgeable home buyers can concentrate on a combination of assumptions and owner financing. Through the use of the assumption, the investor concentrates his or her energies on the remaining equity.

It is only a question of time before the high interest rates will fall. As I am writing this book, the chairman of the Federal Reserve is under considerable pressure from Congress to loosen the tight money policy of the Federal Reserve. The high interest rates cannot continue indefinitely. America's and the free world's economies are directly tied to the ability to borrow money. Small businesses with little or no lines of established credit will go bankrupt. If the tight money policy is maintained it will eventually start to affect larger and larger businesses. The pressure will be on Congress and the President of the United States to force a reversal of the tight money policy. When (not if) the interest rates come down, the price of housing will skyrocket. The reason is simply demand.

Conservative estimates are that between 1980 and 1990 America will require an additional 15 to 20 million new homes. To meet this demand, houses would need to be built at the record-setting pace of 1978—over 2 million new housing starts per year. The housing industry has suffered devastating blows because of high interest rates. Between 1979 and 1980, over 30% of all builders went out of existence. Even if money is made available in any given year, it would take the housing industry at least two or three years to recover. Through the 1980s, housing will be in great demand. The supply will simply not meet the demand.

The population of the world will continue to double itself with each succeeding generation. An increasing number of people will compete for a limited number of vital resources. Oil, gas, wood, stone, coal, and all other raw materials will increase in price. Food prices will also continue to rise.

As mentioned in Phase 4, the U.S. is more than 50% dependent on foreign sources for more than half of the 40 minerals considered essential to the nation's $2.3 trillion economy. These items include magnesium, aluminum, chromium, cobalt, titanium, and platinum. All these items are essentials for the continued production of high technology items, for example, aircraft, electronics, chemicals, mining tools, automobiles, and others. The emerging economies of Third World countries will compete directly for all of these resources. Again it is a matter of supply and demand. Demand increases, supply is limited; the result is increasing prices.

Because of the increasing cost of housing, the ideal investment will be smaller homes, such as townhouses, located in high density neighborhoods. These smaller homes in high density areas are financially within the reach of the majority of Americans, thus renting and selling will not present a problem.

In addition, tax laws approved by Congress strongly favor the investor. Fifteen-year accelerated depreciation periods with 175% declining balance are now allowable. Additional depreciation is allowed in special cases. The new laws allow for 25% tax credit for expenditures to fix up buildings identified as having historical value. Well chosen, these buildings can provide healthy profits within relatively short periods.

Positive Thinking

The one thing that is certain to occur in the 1980s is that residential housing will increase in value. As I state in Phase 0 and again in Phase 3, the only question is at *what rate*. No other field of investment can give you that assurance—not gold, silver, stocks, or even oil—only residential real estate can. The reason is simple—supply and demand. Once having accepted this fact of life, you need only understand leverage and imaginative financing. Through leverage you purchase the maximum amount of property with the least amount of your own money. Remember, no money down does not mean no cash over the settlement table, it simply means that the money is not yours. It is borrowed; it is other people's money. Through creative and imaginative financing, you can package your method of buying to provide maximum leverage using old money (assumptions) and new money (wrap financing, and commercial second trusts, and owner take backs).

It would be simple for me to state that *anyone* can do it, that all jobless individuals, factory workers, professionals, housewives, and others can use the program that I have described. However, it would be a disservice to those of you who have purchased this book if I stated that *anyone* can do it. The honest truth is that the majority of Americans will not invest in residential real estate. The problem is simply one of overcoming the psychological barriers. To those of you who choose to enter into the world of residential real estate investments, I welcome you to the Investment club, "where eagles soar."

Make a commitment to yourself to approach not only your investment program but all aspects of your life with a positive outlook—your job, your family, your vacation, everything. Learn to appreciate life, and believe that you can do anything you set your sights on. In the development of my own investment programs, I stopped counting the times that my friends, realtors, bankers, loan officers, and others would tell me, "Absolutely cannot be done!" I just simply did not believe it; I had a commitment to pursue my goals.

CONTINUE YOUR QUEST FOR KNOWLEDGE

Read all you can, have a thirst for knowledge. Attend seminars, discuss real estate with friends, realtors, brokers, builders, anyone. You will find that everyone from your six-year-old daughter, niece, or neighbor to your eighty-two-year-old grandmother are interested in real estate. Be sure to understand the tax laws that strongly favor the investor. Investing in real estate is complex only because the investment process as a whole involves psychological, financial, and physical forces. Each part of the process is simple and easily understood. Once you have overcome the psychological barrier, analyze each part as a separate issue and only proceed to the second stage once you understand the first. In the development of your investment program, you must assume a sizable debt. Being in debt is not a problem as long as you understand that the real issue at hand is simply one of managing your cash flow. With the new tax laws of the 1980s, which affect individuals, savings and loan institutions, mortgage houses, money market certificates, and all other parts of the investment process, it is absolutely necessary that the investor be knowledgeable in all areas.

Each phase of this book is simple and easily understood. If necessary, return to Phase 2, Critical Decision, and review how to determine your cash-flow position or, now that you better understand the benefits of investing in residential real estate, review the different methods of buying outlined in Phase 3, The Hunt. Daniel Webster once said that, "Failure is more frequently from the want of energy than from the want of capital." My hope is that you make every effort to gather your forces and have a safe, profitable journey in "investing in America."

Glossary of Terms Frequently Used in Real Estate Investment

Agreement of Sale Also referred to as *purchase agreement* and *contract of sale*. A written document in which the seller agrees to sell and the buyer agrees to purchase a specific property, with all conditions and terms of the transaction clearly stated. The agreement is signed by both the seller and buyer. It is not necessary to have a real estate agent involved in this transaction. Items normally included in the agreement are sales price, mortgage particulars (length of loan, period of loan, and so forth), date of closing, and any subject-to clauses. The agreement is usually secured by a deposit, referred to as *earnest money*.

All-Inclusive Deed of Trust (AIDT) A deed that wraps around all of the existing deeds on a specific property. The existing deeds continue to be paid by the seller, with the buyer paying the seller a schedule payment that is usually higher in interest than the existing loans. If the AIDT also includes some of the equity, its value is greater than the sum of the existing loans. The rate of return to the seller is the difference between the payments on the existing loans and the payment of the AIDT by the buyer.

Amortization The length of the loan period. During this period, the borrower repays the lender or the lending institution according to an agreed-to periodic schedule. The borrower gradually reduces his or her debt through these periodic payments.

Appreciation An increase in the value of property.

GLOSSARY OF TERMS

Assigned Mortgage A loan made to an individual wherein the collateral can be any designated property, that is, the mortgage is assigned to a specific property or properties. See *Moving the Mortgage.*

Assumption, Mortgage The buyer of the property assumes legal responsibility for the payment of the existing promissory note (mortgage). The buyer's name is substituted for the seller's name on the mortgage note. The seller is released from the responsibility of making any further payments. Certain mortgages, for example, VA and FHA, are assumable by any buyer who can continue the payment of the promissory note. With conventional notes, usually the lender must agree to an assumption. When dealing with notes held by individuals, it is best to stipulate that the notes are assumable by any future buyer of the property. This would increase the marketability of the investment property.

Balloon Mortgage A loan that is not paid back in equal installments over an agreed-to period. Payments made over the loan period are made on interest only, and the principal is due in a lump sum at some time in the future. For example, the principal of a five-year balloon loan, interest only, is due in full in five years. Payments made over the five years are made only on the interest.

Blanket Mortgage When more than one property acts as collateral for a loan.

Broker, Real Estate An individual who has a valid license to sell real estate on behalf of a second party. The broker may represent either the seller or buyer (in some cases both) and is paid a *negotiable* commission when the property is sold.

Cash Flow The net result of adding all one's incoming monies from salary, interest, dividends, investments, tax savings, and so forth, and subtracting all one's payments of debts and basic requirements to sustain life (food, energy, and clothes). Understanding one's cash flow and, more importantly, the ability to manage one's cash flow are critical to a successful investment program.

Certificate of Title A document prepared by an attorney or title company that the seller has a clear and marketable title to the property, one that can be insured.

Closing The process by which title is transferred from the seller to the buyer. All legal documents, such as deeds of trust, promissory notes, and so forth, are signed at the closing meeting. At the closing, or settlement, all parties are represented. Transfer of title must occur through either a licensed attorney or escrow company.

Cloud on the Title   A claim, encumbrance, or lien on the property that does not allow the transfer of title of the property from seller to buyer. For example, the city or county may have a lien on a property due to outstanding (unpaid) taxes. These taxes would require payment prior to transfer of title.

Collateral   Any item of value belonging to the borrower that acts as assurance that the loan or mortgage will be paid as promised. Failure on the part of the borrower to repay the loan as outlined at the closing meeting would result in the lender or the lending institution obtaining ownership of the item acting as collateral. The collateral for the loan is usually the property itself.

Commission, Realtor's   Money paid to a real estate agent(s) or broker(s) for completing a sale. Usually it is a percentage of the sales price and is stipulated in the sales contract. When both the seller and the buyer are represented by two different agents (brokers), the commission is usually split 50-50.

Contract of Sale   See *Purchase Agreement* and *Agreement of Sale*.

Conventional Loan   A mortgage loan that is not insured by FHA or guaranteed by VA.

Credit Rating   A rating made by the local credit bureau of the past performance of an individual to pay off debts. The credit history shows past and current financial obligations plus total indebtedness of the individual. Individuals do not usually have access to credit bureau information, thus, when purchasing a property, have the realtor assist you in obtaining a credit rating on prospective renters. Investment clubs or rental associations may also provide access to credit ratings.

Credit Report   A report requested by a lender from a credit bureau to assist in the determination of the borrower's credit rating.

Deed of Trust (Mortgage)   A loan made for the purpose of buying real estate. The deed of trust outlines all conditions of the loan, to include the rights of the lender should the borrower default on the loan.

Deed, Quitclaim   A deed that transfers title or right to a property from the seller to the buyer at the time of settlement. The quitclaim deed does not guarantee a clear title.

288 GLOSSARY OF TERMS

Deed, Warranty   A deed that guarantees that the title to a property is free from any title defects, liens, or encumbrances that may cause a cloud on the title.

Default   Failure of the buyer of the property (borrower) to repay the loan as agreed in the deed of trust, mortgage, or promissory note. Should the mortgage payment be in default after 30 days (the period varies in accordance with state laws), the lender may initiate foreclosure proceedings.

Delinquency   When the mortgage payment is past due.

Deposit   Money advanced with the purchase agreement to bind a sale of real estate. The deposit, or *earnest money,* declares the true intent of the seller to purchase the property. The deposit money (unless stipulated in the sales contract) will be advanced against the sell price at the closing meeting. Failure to purchase the property for reasons other than those listed in the purchase agreement could result in the forfeiture of the deposit money to the seller.

Depreciation   The loss of value of a particular investment due to wear and tear and the natural aging of components. The 1981 Economic Recovery Tax Act specifically gives income-producing real estate held for business purposes (rentals) a 15-year depreciation period. The investor may also select to use accelerated depreciation, since in theory the investment property depreciates faster at the beginning of the investment period.

Discounted Second   A deed of trust that occupies second position to the first deed of trust and that is discounted from its face value in order to secure its sale, usually for cash. The buyer of the discounted second continues to receive the agreed interest rate between the borrower and the original lender. However, because of the discount, the buyer receives a most favorable rate of return.

Don't Wanter   An individual who currently owns real estate who does not want his or her property. A don't wanter results from two conditions. Condition 1, problems with the property itself, for example, bad location or structural defects, see *Unloader.* Condition 2, problems resulting from issues other than the property, for example, the owner has financial problems or a job transfer has occurred, see *Must Seller.*

Earnest Money   See *Deposit.*

Effective Interest Rate   The rate of return on all money being loaned by the seller and/or the lending institution. For example, the buyer assumes a loan of $50,000 from the seller at 10% interest. The seller carries back $50,000 as a second trust at 14% interest, amortized over the same period as the assumable loan. Total amount borrowed is $100,000. The effective interest rate is the difference between 14% and 10%, or 12%.

Encumbrance   An item or issue that questions clear title to a property, for example, a mortgage, a lien, a deed restriction, unpaid taxes, an easement, or a cloud on the title.

Equity   The owner's value in the property. Equity occurs through the appreciation in the property value and the reduction in the principal of the mortgage loan. When the mortgage is fully paid, the owner has 100% equity in the property.

Equity Participation   An arrangement by which two or more individuals share in the equity buildup of a home of residence, an investment property, or a combination of the two. For example, one investor advances the down payment and the second individual lives in the property and pays the mortgage plus all expenses. The investor and homeowner share the equity that has accrued.

Escrow   Money or documents held by a neutral third party until all conditions of the contract of sale are met.

Escrow Agent   The neutral third party who is responsible to the seller, buyer, lender(s), and borrower(s) for holding the money and documents until all the terms of the contract of sale are satisfactorily met.

Exposure Factor   The maximum allowable monies that a lending institution will advance against the purchase of real estate. The limit is usually expressed in a percentage of the appraised value, for example, 80% of the appraised value in periods of tight money and 90% in periods of available money.

Federal Housing Administration (FHA)   A division of the U.S. Department of Housing and Urban Development (HUD). The FHA insures home mortgage loans made by private lenders.

Finance Charge   The charge directed against the borrower for the right to obtain a loan from a lending institution. The finance charge is often referred to as *loan origination points*.

Firm Commitment   An agreement from a lender to make a loan to a particular individual (borrower) on a specific property. This can also be an agreement made with the government (FHA) or with a private mortgage insurance company to insure a loan on a specific property to a specific borrower.

First Deed of Trust A loan made for the purpose of buying real estate. This loan has first position over any other loans that use the property as collateral. For example, in the case of a foreclosure, the first deed of trust will be paid off first from any monies resulting from selling the property. All other deeds of trust (mortgages) are subordinate to the first deed of trust, which is also called the *first mortgage.*

First Mortgage See *First Deed of Trust.*

Forbearance The act of delaying legal action to foreclose on a mortgage that is overdue. Usually it is granted only when a satisfactory arrangement has been made with the lender to pay all delinquent payments at a future date.

Foreclosure The legal process by which a lender takes possession of a property from the borrower due to nonpayment of the mortgage loan. The lender then has the right to sell the property to pay off the debt. Any lender, regardless of his or her position in the deeds of trust (first, second, or third) has this right.

Graduated Payment Mortgage The repayment installments of this type of loan will increase in graduated steps sometime in the future. For example, a buyer agrees to 10% interest the first three years and to an increase of 2% every three years thereafter, not to exceed 15% interest.

Grantee The party in the deed who is the buyer.

Grantor The party in the deed who is the seller.

Hard Money Seconds Loans made by commercial lenders that occupy a subordinate or junior position to existing loans on the property. These loans are usually at higher interest rates and carry shorter amortization schedules (payment periods) than the first mortgage. Obtaining this type of money is excellent as long as the amount borrowed is a small percentage (less than 20%) of the overall price of the property.

Homeowners Insurance Policy Insurance that covers the house and its contents in case of fire, wind damage, theft, and other natural disasters. The policy also provides protection against lawsuits by someone injured on the owner's property.

Income-Producing Real Estate   Real estate or property that can be rented.

Installment Contract   A contract of sale by which the buyer pays the seller in specified installments over a set period of time. For example, the buyer and seller agree to pay off the existing mortgage at the day of settlement, however, the owner's (seller's) equity is to be paid off in equal installments of $5,000 every two years for the next eight years. The seller would receive $20,000 over the next eight years. Actual transfer of title can occur at any time during the installment period. This formal transaction is agreed to at the settlement table and requires the services of a competent attorney or escrow company.

Junior Mortgage   A mortgage, also called a *subordinate note*, that occupies a position of less priority to existing mortgages on the property: A second deed of trust or second mortgage is junior to the first deed of trust; a third deed of trust or third mortgage is junior to a second deed of trust, and so on.

Land Contract   A form of a wraparound loan, however, the existing loans on the property remain in the name of the original owner or current seller. Equitable title to the property occurs at the time of settlement, with legal transfer of the title to occur at some time in the future. Land contracts can be complex and require expert handling to ensure that all parties are legally protected in case of defaults and/or clouds on the title. This type of contract should be written by a competent lawyer or escrow company that understands all the legalities of equitable and legal title transfers.

Lease Option   See *Option to Buy*.

Leverage   The increased means of purchasing an investment or anything of value by borrowing a percentage of the required funds. The more the buyer borrows, the higher the leverage. For example, a $100,000 home may be purchased with a down payment of $10,000. The ratio of down payment to total value is one to ten, thus you can purchase a property worth $100,000 with a $10,000 down payment. If the property is purchased using all borrowed monies, the leverage is infinite.

Lien   A claim by an individual or institution against the property of another, such as property that is security for a debt or charge. As long as a lien on a property exists, that property may not be legally sold until the lien is properly removed.

Listing   The listing of real estate properties with one or more real estate brokers or agents advertising the properties to be sold or rented. These listings are often referred to as *multiple listings,* since all real estate agents have the right to inspect and buy the properties for their customers. Often referred to as an open listing.

Loan Disclosure Note   Document spelling out all the terms involved in obtaining and paying off a loan.

Loan Origination Points   The amount of money charged the borrower by the lender to obtain a loan. A point is 1% of the amount borrowed. Also called *finance charge.*

Long-Term Capital Gain   A profit made from an investment that receives favorable tax treatment. Specifically with real estate held for a period of one year plus one day, any profits resulting from a sale will be taxed as follows: 60% is tax free and 40% plus any recaptured depreciation is added to the individual's ordinary income.

No Money Down   When all monies involved in the purchasing of real estate are borrowed. Sources for borrowed money are infinite—assumptions, seller financing, hard money seconds, discounted seconds, plus many more.

Mortgage   A special loan for buying real estate properties.

Mortgagee   The lender who provides the mortgage money.

Mortgagor   The person borrowing the money from the lender (mortgagee) to purchase real estate.

Moving the Mortgage   When the collateral used for the purchase of a property is a second property owned by the buyer, the movement of the mortgage occurs. This is an extremely powerful tool in buying properties with no money down to achieve excellent leverage. For example, the buyer asks the seller to carry back $10,000 of the equity of the property in question, and the mortgage on the property is moved to the buyer's home of residence. Moving the mortgage will now allow the buyer to obtain a commercial second with the property that is purchased acting as collateral.

Multiple Listing   See *Listing.*

Must Seller   A type of don't wanter. Must sellers, however, are selling their properties because of circumstances other than the property itself, for example, carrying two mortgages, job transfer, family problems, financial difficulties, and so forth.

Note A document that specifies the conditions of repayment of a loan. All deeds of trust (first, second, third, and so forth) are notes. For example, the seller and buyer create a note by the seller carrying back his or her equity in the form of a subordinate note. The terms of the note would be that the buyer agrees to pay back the seller according to a specified schedule.

Other People's Money (OPM) This term is used extensively in real estate investments to identify money that is borrowed to purchase real estate. Sources of OPM are savings and loans, mortgage bankers, commercial lenders, sellers, individuals who buy discounted subordinate notes, life insurance companies, investment clubs, plus many others.

Owner to Take Back (OTTB) Sellers who are willing to finance all or a portion of their equity through the use of deeds of trust, take back mortgages, or other notes are often identified as OTTB. This type of financing is also referred to as *Owner Willing to Carry (OWC)*.

Option to Buy An agreement between the owner and potential buyer for the right to buy real estate at a stated price within a stated period of time. Often used in a lease.

Ordinary Income Regular income earned from a job. Income earned from a source other than a long-term investment. All ordinary income is taxed using Form 1040 or 1040A tax tables.

(OWC) Owner Willing to Carry See *Owner to Take Back.*

Partnership A formal agreement between two individuals, institutions (for example, corporations), or a combination thereof to share in the profit and losses of an investment property. The partnership can be structured in any desired format depending on the initial investment and/or the management of the investment property. The IRS recognizes partnerships and allows partners to share in the depreciation and gain of an investment property.

PITI An abbreviation for principal, interest, taxes, and insurance, which is the sum total of all principal and interest paid on all mortgage loans plus taxes and insurance paid on a specific piece of real estate property.

Points An amount equal to 1% of the amount of a loan. Points are a one-time charge collected by the lender at closing to increase the return on the loan. On VA and FHA loans, the interest rates are set by the government.

In order to offset any losses by the lending institutions due to low interest rates on these federally backed mortgages, the seller charges points to further increase his or her profit margin. When obtaining either an FHA or VA loan, the borrower is not allowed to pay any points, the seller of the property must pay the additional points.

Prepayment Penalty A charge made by the lender if the mortgage loan is paid off before the specified due date or if there is any acceleration in payments. Prepayment usually occurs due to the refinancing of the loan.

Principal The amount of money borrowed from the lender that must be paid back by the borrower. The amount of interest paid is directly dependent on the value of the principal. In a normal amortization repayment schedule, the principal-to-interest ratio will be weighted heavily in favor of the interest at the beginning of the loan period. As the payments continue, the amount of monies that are advanced against the principal increases, thus increasing the owner's equity in the property.

Principal Partner The partner in a partnership who carries most of the responsibilities and shares in the majority of the gain (profits). In a regular partnership, the principal and junior partner(s) split the responsibilities, depreciation, and profits in specified percentages. In a principal-silent partnership, the principal would enjoy all depreciation; however, the silent would share in the equity buildup.

Promissory Note See *Note*.

Purchase Agreement A written document in which a seller agrees to sell and a buyer agrees to buy a specific piece of real estate property. All terms and conditions of the sale are stated in the agreement. It is not necessary to have a real estate agent involved between the seller and buyer; however, either an attorney or certified escrow company must act in the actual transfer of title at the settlement table (closing process). See also *Agreement of Sale*.

Pyramiding Using the equity in one investment as collateral for a loan and using the borrowed monies to purchase additional investment properties. Moving mortgages is a beautiful method to accomplish this task as the loan is most often held by a private individual at favorable interest rates.

Quitclaim Deed See *Deed, Quitclaim*.

Real Estate A piece of property composed of land and building structure. All items of a permanent nature, such as trees, water, rocks, and minerals, are considered to be an integral part of the property.

Real Estate Agent An individual who can show property on behalf of a seller or buyer. An agent can represent either the seller or buyer or both. However, the agent must be affiliated with a real estate broker to fully satisfy the legal requirements of the sales transaction.

Real Estate Broker The broker is an agent who has the legal qualifications (valid license) to sell real estate on behalf of his or her customers. Normally, one broker will have several agents working under his or her supervision.

Realtor Either a real estate agent or broker holding an active membership in a local real estate board affiliated with the National Association of Realtors.

Recaptured Depreciation The amount of depreciation that was claimed during the investment period over and above straight-line depreciation. For example, if straight-line depreciation for a given year was $5,000 and accelerated depreciation (175% declining balance) allowed $8,750, the difference between $8,750 and $5,000 is excess depreciation. This excess depreciation ($3,750) is referred to as recaptured depreciation. It is taxed as ordinary income upon selling the property.

Recording Fees The charge by an attorney or escrow company to legally record the transactions of the property sale. Such documents as the deed of trust or mortgage details are recorded at the city or county courthouse and are available for public inspection.

Refinancing The process of paying off the existing loan with new money resulting in a new loan.

Reverse Paper When the interest on a loan does not cover the principal, the value of the loan (note) will steadily increase. This type of loan is referred to as reverse paper. For example, a loan is made of $10,000 at 12% interest. In order to maintain an outstanding debt of $10,000, the borrower would pay $1,200 (12% of $10,000) per year of interest. If the amount paid is less than $1,200, the amount below $1,200 would be added to the loan value of $10,000, thus increasing the debt. This type of loan is referred to as reverse paper.

Rollover Mortgage A mortgage that is converted from a short-term construction loan to a long-term mortgage loan.

Sales Agreement See *Purchase Agreement.*

Sales Contract See *Purchase Agreement.*

GLOSSARY OF TERMS

Second Deed of Trust A deed of trust or mortgage that occupies second position behind the first deed of trust. The position of a deed of trust is usually related to the first deed on record unless formally agreed to by all parties in writing. The agreement would be through an accredited attorney or escrow company.

Short-Term Capital Gain Gains realized from the sale of a property that was held for less than one year are referred as short-term capital gains. These gains (profits) are taxed as ordinary income.

Silent Partner The partner who plays a silent, or junior, role in a partnership. The silent does not share in the management or depreciation of the property. His or her profit comes at the time of sale by splitting the equity gain.

Subordinate Note See *Junior Mortgage.*

Tax Bracket The percentage that any earned income is taxed. For example, if a taxpayer earns $10,000 more than his or her present taxable income and $4,000 of the $10,000 is paid as tax, the taxpayer is in the 40% tax bracket.

Tax Shelter An investment that allows for two major tax advantages: (1) the value of the investment may be depreciated over the useful life of the property and the amount depreciated may be deducted from an individual's taxable earnings; and (2) the gain (profit) of the investment is taxed at favorable tax rates, for example, 60% of the gain is tax free.

Title The right of ownership to a specific piece of real estate. The document that describes ownership is referred to as the *deed.*

Title Insurance Insurance that protects the lender or the buyer against loss of their interest in the property due to legal defects in the title.

Title Search An examination of the public records to determine if the property is free from any title defects or issues that may cause a cloud over the title.

Unloaders Individuals who are selling their properties due to a problem with the property itself, for example, bad location, structural problems, and so forth. Usually these problems cannot be corrected or the correction is cost prohibitive.

Veterans Administration (VA) The VA guarantees loans, sometimes referred to as GI loans, made to qualified veterans by private lenders for the purchase of real estate. These loans are assumable by any buyer in future years. Veterans are allowed up to a certain dollar value of guaranteed loans. Once a veteran allows his or her VA loan to be assumed, the value of the assumed loan is subtracted from the allowable limit to determine his or her new eligibility limit.

Warranty of Deed   See *Deed, Warranty*.

Wraparound Mortgage   A contract of sale in which the seller (owner) of the property continues to pay the existing mortgage. The buyer then pays the seller a payment on a second mortgage that includes the first mortgage plus any equity less any down payment. Since the second mortgage has a larger value and is usually at a higher interest rate than the first mortgage, the seller will always receive more from the buyer than he or she has to pay the holder of the existing first trust. The end result is that the seller realizes a positive cash flow. Wraparound mortgages can be complex in cases of default or clouds on the title, thus it is always best to seek the services of a competent attorney or an escrow company that specializes in wraparound mortgages.

Index

Abbreviated Vector Cash-Flow Analysis, 79–83, 85–87, 177
  See also Cash-flow analysis
Accelerated cost recovery, 84–85
  See also Depreciation
Accelerated depreciation, 6, 7, 25, 36, 84–85, 236, 237
  of improvements, 41
  See also Depreciation
Adjustable-rate mortgage, 170
Adjusted basis of property, 241–242
  defined, 248
Advanced Mortgage Corporation, 168
Advertising, 30, 31, 213–215
Agreement of sale, 197
Agreements with renter, 225
All cash financing, 97, 195
All-inclusive trust, 28, 32, 62, 113–115
  See also Wraparound mortgages
Amendment to application-Lender's Estimate of Settlement Charges, sample, 210–211
Application fees, 202
Appraisal fees, 201
Appreciation
  of land, computing, 252
  of property, 11–13, 77
Assumable first trust, 31
Assumptions, 91, 98, 178
  buying below market value and refinancing to maximum allowable, 124–125
  moving mortgages, 130–131
  owner to take back and discount second trust, 103–104

owner to take back discounted second trust, down payment, 105–107
owner to take back second trust, 100–102
owner to take back and small down payment, 102–103
partnership, 131–133
using rent as down payment, 129–130

Baby boom, 48, 164
Balloon mortgage, 91, 100–102, 179
Bank-to-bank transfers, rent payments by, 227–228
Bankruptcies, 160–161
Basis of property
  adjusted, 241–242, 248
  defined, 248
Bookkeeping system, 230–233
Bracketed decision-flow diagram, 41–43
Brainstorming, 63
Building Industry, 51
Buy phase, 175–211
  closing process, 200–202
  forces affecting negotiations, 186–195
  maintaining balance, 176–177
  negotiable items, 177–186
  negotiating for new money, 196–197
  objectives, 175
  sample contracts, 202–211
Buyer's market, 194, 282

Capital gains
  long-term, 32–34, 237, 248, 249–252
  short-term, 33
Cash buy, 97, 195

299

300 INDEX

Cash flow
  negative, 12
  positive, 12
  zero, 7
Cash-flow analysis, 23, 25, 72–88
  abbreviated, 72, 79–83, 85–87, 177
  calculating with $75,000 investment, 74–78
  give-year, 78
  interest rates and, 78–79
  reasons for, 73
  tax bracket family curves, 87–88
  taxes and, 73, 75, 76, 79, 82–85
Children, tenants with, 216, 218
Closing costs, 102, 201
  added to basis of property, 248
  estimates of, 210–211
  typical, 201–202
Closing process, 200–202
Cluster concept, 157–160
Contingent interest, deferred payoff of, 169
Contracts
  land installment, 91, 135–137
  of purchase, 197
  rental, 30, 212–213, 222–225
  sales, 197–200, 203–204
  samples, 202–211, 222–224
Contracts for deed, 91
Corporations, 174
Crash of real estate, 46–53
Creative financing, 91–95
Credit, 56, 102, 137, 202
Credit rating of prospective tenants, 220
Critical decision phase, 22–23, 72–88
  abbreviated cash-flow analysis, 79–83, 85–87
  objectives, 72
  tax bracket family curves, 87–88
  tax laws, 79, 84–85
  vector cash-flow analysis, 72, 73–79

Debt-asset data sheet, 18, 22
Decision-flow process, 14–16
Declining balance depreciation, 35–41, 84, 86, 234, 236–241, 243, 247
Deed, sample, 205–206
Deferred judgment, 64
Deficit spending, 164, 166
Demand in housing, 49–52, 92
Depreciation, 34–41, 234–252
  accelerated, 6, 7, 25, 36, 84–85, 236, 237
  declining balance, 35–41, 84, 86, 234, 236–241, 243, 247
  influence on taxable income, 38, 40, 41
  methods, 34–38, 39, 234, 238–241

  pre- and post-1981 laws compared, 84–85
  reason for, 235
  recaptured, 237, 242
  reporting to IRS, 242, 244–248
  straight line, 35–37, 39–41, 84–86, 234, 237–243
  sum of years' digits, 35–41, 234, 240–243
  taxable gain and, 237, 241–242
Depreciation Form 4562, 242
Development plans, 60, 61–62
Discounted second trusts, 91, 95–98, 103–107, 137
  See also Second trust financing
Divorce rate, 52
Down payment, 102, 105–107
  borrowing from seller, 112–113
  negotiating, 177–178
  using rent as, 129–130

Earnest money, 199
Economic Recovery Tax Act of 1981, 7, 25, 34, 36, 79, 84–85, 236, 237, 239
Energy costs, 186
Equity participation mortgage (EPM), 26–27, 97, 117, 121–122, 168, 169, 170
Estimates of closing costs, 210–211
Exchanges of investment properties, 241–242, 253–255
Expenses
  recording, 229–233
  reporting to IRS, 242, 244–246, 248

Federal budget, 3–6, 49, 164, 166
Federal Home Loan Bank Board (FHLBB), 168, 170, 171
Federal National Mortgage Association (Fannie Mae), 125
  purchase of owner-held trusts by, 173–174
Federal Reserve, 4, 8, 51, 168, 282
FHA mortgage, 161
Financing
  basic methods, 96–98
  cash, 97, 195
  creative, 91–95
  new, 109–112
  owner, 97, 98, 100–107, 178–180, 183–184
  second-trust, 32, 53–54, 62, 63, 91, 95–98, 100–110, 113, 137–142, 178–183
  See also Assumptions; Hunt phase
Finder's fee, 214
First trust, assumable, 31
Five-year development plans, 61

Flip mortgage, 172
Foreclosures, 17, 160–164
Form 4797, 249–252
Forward edge of building (FEBI), 145
Front-end analysis, 35

Goals
commitment to, 68–69
setting, 18–19, 66–68
Graduated-payment mortgage (GEM), 172
Group discussions, 20, 63–65

Highways, 146
Homeowners Associations, 156–157, 179
Hunt phase, 23–28, 89–174
  basic methods of finance, 96–98
  creative financing, 91–95
  foreclosures and bankruptcies, 160–164
  future trends, 164–170
  hunting for properties, 143–160
  maintaining presence of mind, 90
  objectives, 89
  other people's money (OPM), 95–96
  purchase methods, 98–137
  rental prices by area, 160
  shopping for second trust money, 137–142
Husband-wife teams, 19–20, 65–66

Inertia, overcoming, 16–22, 45–71
Infinite leverage, 96, 133
Inflation, 3–5, 49
  future trends, 164–166
  profit and, 9
Inspection fees, 201–202
Installment Sales Revision Act (1980), 135–137
Insurance
  life, 18, 22–23, 54–55
  property, 99
Intent to purchase, 197
Interest rates, 4–6, 8, 91
  on carry-back second trusts, 181–183
  of commercial lenders, 138
  future trends, 166–169
  negotiating on second trust loans and wraparounds, 181–183
  in 1980's, 282
  rental rates and, 98
  variable-rate mortgages and, 170–171
  vector cash-flow analysis and, 78–79
IRS, 235
  reporting rental income, depreciation, and expenses to, 242, 244–246, 248
IRS Form 1040, 32
IRS Form 1040, Schedule E, 242, 244–248

IRS Form 1040A, 32
IRS Form 4562, 242
IRS Form 4797, 249–252
IRS publication 527 (Rental Property), 134
Interstate highways, 146
Investment property ownership phase, 212–233
  agreements with renter, 225
  finding good renters, 213–215
  managing property, 226–233
  pricing rent, 215–216
  rent with option to buy, 225–226
  rental contract, 212–213, 222–224
  renting to specific group of people, 220–221
  selecting rentor, 216–220
Investments, comparison of, 10

Land
  appreciation of, computing, 252
  calculating value of, 35
Land installment contracts, 91, 135–137
Lawyers, shopping for, 29
Lease option, 30, 133–135, 200, 225–226
  sample contract, 206–210
Legal fees, 201
Lender's estimate of settlement charges, sample, 210–211
Lending institutions, money market analysis of, 20–21
Leverage, 6–8, 13, 49, 95, 96, 98, 133
  infinite, 96, 133
  telephone, 57
Libraries, 20, 59–63
Life insurance, 18, 22–23, 54–55
Locations, 8, 31, 49
  analyzing, 20
Long-term capital gains, 32–34
  defined, 248
  depreciation and, 237
  reporting to IRS, 249–252

Maintenance of property. *See* **Management of property**
Management firms, 227
Management of property, 29–30, 213, 226–233
  collecting rent, 227–228
  mortgage payments, 228–229
  records and expenses, keeping records of, 229–233
Market analysis, 60
  of lending institutions, 20–21
Market value, buying below, 124–125
Money market analysis, 20–21
Mortgage institutions for second trust financing, 137–138

302 INDEX

Mortgage payments, automatic, 228–229
Mortgage title insurance, 202
Mortgages, 17
  adjustable-rate, 170
  balloon, 91, 100–102, 179
  buying off at discounted prices, 119–120
  equity-participation (EPM), 26–27, 97, 117, 121–122, 168–170
  FHA, 161
  flip, 172
  future trends, 166–173
  graduated-payment (GEM), 172
  moving, 98, 115, 130–131, 179–181
  renegotiable rate, 26, 27, 109, 120–121, 170–171
  rollover, 122–124, 172–173
  shared-appreciation (SAM's), 27, 168–170
  VA, 161
  variable-rate, 26, 27, 49, 97, 120–121, 170–171
  wraparound, 24, 28, 32, 62, 91, 98, 109, 113–117, 183
Multiple listing, 214
Must sellers, 146–149, 189–190

Negative cash flow, 12
Negotiations
  for new money, 196–197
  for owner financing, 178–180
  for property items, 185
  through real estate agent, 192–193
  with seller, 28–29, 177–195
New promissory notes, 97
Newspapers, 24, 25, 153–154, 156
Notice of default, 162

Offer to purchase, 199–200
Oil, 3, 4, 164–165
Open listing, 214
Option to buy, 30, 133–135, 200, 225–226
  sample contract, 206–210
Ordinary income, taxation and, 32–34
Origination fees, 201
Other people's money (OPM), 95–96
Owner-financing, 97, 98, 100–107, 178–180, 183–184
  See also Assumptions; Second trust financing

Partnerships, 27, 117–119, 131–133, 169, 171–172, 174, 184
Pets, tenants with, 216, 218
Population, estimates by age groups, 50–51
Positive cash flow, 12

Positive reinforcement, group discussions and, 64
Price
  when buying, negotiating, 184–185
  rental, 160, 215–216
  when selling, 31–32
Principal-silent partner relationships, 27, 117–119, 169, 174
Profit
  computing, 248–249
  inflation and, 9
  reporting to IRS, 249–252
  tax-sheltered, 9
  See also Sell/profits phase
Promissory notes, 97–98
  existing, 97–98
  new, 97
Property items, negotiating, 185
Property taxes, 99, 186, 202
Proposal to purchase memorandum, sample, 204–205
Purchase agreement, 197
Purchasing. *See* Buy phase; Hunt phase
Pyramiding properties, 255–259

Real estate agent, 17, 57–58, 150–153
  advertising through, 214–215
  discounting commission by, 193
  finding, 21–22
  negotiating through, 192–193
  renting through, 220
  second trust financing by, 138–140
Real estate crash, 46–53
Real estate management firms, 227
Real estate taxes, 99, 186, 202
Real estate transactions, library records of, 59, 60
Recaptured depreciation, 237, 242
Record keeping, 29–30, 229–233
Refinancing, 98, 101, 102, 115–117, 124–125
  in equity-participation mortgages, 168
  See also Assumptions; Financing
Renegotiable rate mortgage, 26, 27, 109, 120–121, 170–171
  See also Variable rate mortgage
Rent
  collecting, 227–228
  interest rates and, 98
  payment of, 30
  pricing, 160, 215–216
  reporting to IRS, 242, 244–246, 248
  using as down payment, 129–130
Rent with option to buy, 30, 133–135, 200, 225–226
  sample contract, 206–210
Rental contract, 30, 212–213, 225
  sample, 222–224

Renters
  agreements with, 225
  bad, 55-56
  finding, 212-215
  selecting, 216-220
  specific group of people as, 220-221
REO (real estate owned property), 162-163
Reverse paper, 179
Risk, 8-9, 14
Rollover mortgage, 122-124, 172-173

Sales agreement, 197
Sales contract, 197-200
  sample, 203-204
Salvage value, 238, 239, 242
Schedule E, 242, 244-246
Schools, 186
Second trust exchange, 96, 108-109
Second trust financing, 32, 62, 63, 91, 95-98, 100-110, 113
  interest rates, negotiating, 181-183
  length of loan, 181
  owner to carry back, 178-180
  psychological barriers to, 53-54
  shopping for money, 137-142
Sell/profits phase, 30-41, 234-284
  case studies, 259-281
  depreciation, 236-243, 246, 247
  exchanging or trading property, 253-255
  1980's, 282-283
  objectives, 234
  positive thinking, 283
  pyramiding properties, 255-259
  reporting to IRS, 242, 244-246, 248
  selling, 248-253
  tax laws, 235-236
  See also Depreciation
Seller financing. *See* Owner financing
Sellers, types, 146-149, 189-190
Settlement, 200-202
  See also Closing costs
Shared-appreciation mortgage (SAM), 27, 168-170

Short-term capital gains, 33
Silent partners, 27, 117-119, 169, 171-172, 174, 184
Straight-line depreciation, 35-37, 39-41, 84-86, 234, 237-243
Sum of years' digits depreciation, 35-41, 234, 240-243
Supplemental Schedule of Gains and Losses (Form 4797), 249-252
Survey fees, 202

Tax, real estate, 99, 186, 202
Tax laws, 6, 7, 32, 79, 84-85, 234-237
  See also Economic Recovery Tax Act; Depreciation
Tax Reform Act (TRA), 1976, 7
Taxable gain, 237, 241-242
  defined, 241
Telephone leverage, 57
Tenants. *See* Renters
Terminology, negative, in real estate, 53-55
Terms of purchase, 23-24, 57
Trading investment properties, 253-255

Undervalued property, 125-126
Unloaders, 146-149

VA mortgage, 161
Variable-rate mortgage, 26, 27, 49, 97, 120-121, 170-171
Vector Bracketed Decision-Flow Diagram, 15-16, 19
Vector Cash-Flow Analysis, 23, 72, 73, 74-87
  abbreviated, 79-83, 85-87, 177

Worth, determining, 18, 22-23, 69-70
Wraparound mortgage, 24, 28, 32, 62, 91, 98, 109, 113-117
  negotiating interest rates, 183

Zero cash flow, 7

Now ... Announcing these other fine books from Prentice-Hall—

HOW YOU CAN BUILD A FORTUNE INVESTING IN LAND by Nat Sofer. Here is a basic source for those interested in the land investment market. Identifies the reasons and methods for acquiring land. Covers benefits of land vs. paper investments; the future of land investment and the protection it can provide; negotiating, buying, and selling land; tax advantages of land ownership; foreign investment, and more.

$7.95 paperback, $15.95 hardcover

A PRACTICAL GUIDE TO THE COMMODITIES MARKETS by Ronald C. Spurga. This is a complete orientation to commodities future trading—from how a futures contract works to the advantages and risks of investing in gold, copper, sugar, grain, and many others. Especially useful to first-time investors, it covers opening an account, trading techniques, perspectives on specific commodities, sources of market information, and more.

$9.95 paperback, $19.95 hardcover

To order these books, just complete the convenient order form below and mail to **Prentice-Hall, Inc., General Publishing Division, Attn. Addison Tredd, Englewood Cliffs, N.J. 07632**

Title	Author	Price

Subtotal _____

Sales Tax (where applicable) _____

Postage & Handling (75¢/book) _____

Total _____

Please send me the books listed above. Enclosed is my check ☐ Money order ☐ or, charge my VISA ☐ MasterCard ☐ Account # ___ _____ Credit card expiration date _____

Name_____

Address_____

City_____ State_____ Zip_____

*Prices subject to change without notice. Please allow 4 weeks for delivery.